utopie

Court essai réflexe sur les fragments d'un urbanisme

Ville-culture / Nature

La répression

Formes

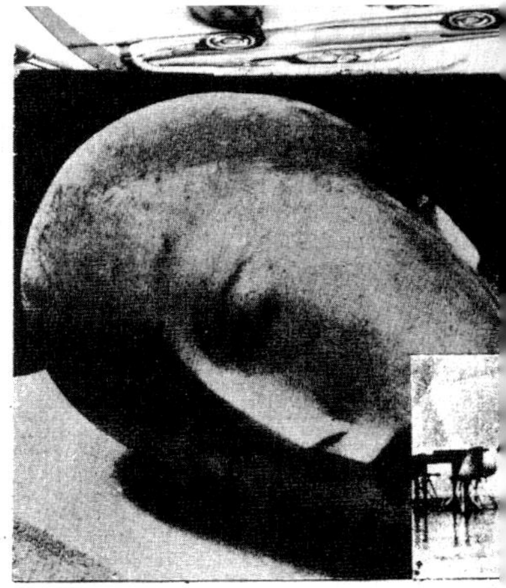

REVU

éditions anthro

15, rue Racine, PARIS 6'
Tél. 326 99-99

jean au

isabelle auric

jean baudril

catherine

jean-paul jungm

rené lo

antoine st

hubert to

L'art ?
SOCIOLOGIE DE L'URBAIN
NOUS NE SAVONS RIEN DE CE QUI NOUS ATTEND SI NOUS NOUS POSONS DANS CET... CET ENDROIT ET... CHERCHONS PLUTÔT UN ENDROIT ÉLEVÉ QUI NOUS SERVE DE POINT D'OBSERVATION...
NON, CRIQUET ! C'EST ENCORE PLUS FANTASTIQUE QUE JE CROYAIS ! REGARDE LA SPATIO-BOUSSOLE... NOUS SOMMES BIEN AU-DESSUS DE LA VILLE, MAIS ELLE A DISPARU !
Villes de papier

SEMIOTEXT(E) FOREIGN AGENTS SERIES

Published by Semiotext(e)
2007 Wilshire Blvd., Suite 427, Los Angeles, CA 90057
www.semiotexte.com

This project was made possible by a grant by the Graham Foundation for Advanced Studies in the Fine Arts.

Jean Baudrillard's *The Ephemeral*, *Technics as Social Practice*, *Requiem for the Media* and *The Mirror of Production* were previously published in *Utopia Deferred: Writings from Utopie (1967–1978)* and are translated by Stuart Kendall.

The editors thank Rey Akdogan, Jean-Louis Cohen, Jean-Marie Clarke, Marc Dessauce, John Ebert, Hedi El Kholti, Sylvère Lotringer, Marc Lowenthal, Kevin Repp, Meredith TenHoor, and Noura Wedell, whose motivation, support, and work contributed immensely to the project. Special thanks are due to Isabelle Auricoste, Hubert Tonka, Jean Aubert, Jean Baudrillard, Charles Goldblum, Jean-Paul Jungmann, and Antoine Stinco for generously sharing their time and insight with the editors during the research for this volume.

Design: Hedi El Kholti

ISBN: 978-1-58435-095-8
Distributed by The MIT Press, Cambridge, Mass. and London, England
Printed in the United States of America

Printed in China

TEXTS AND PROJECTS, 1967–1978

Edited by Craig Buckley and Jean-Louis Violeau

Translated by Jean-Marie Clarke

utopie

Contents

pacification
des
contradictions
France-Soir
PARIS-PRESSE
L'INTRANSIGEANT
Le Monde
télémagazine
spécial dernière
Changer la ville...
Herald Tribune
LE FIGARO
dernière heure
NOUVELLE CRITIQUE
LIFE
L'Humanité
L'EXPRESS
le nouvel OBSERVATEUR
ENTREPRISE
POLITIQUE ET SOCIAL
Le Parisien
L'AURORE
TEL QUEL
L'EXPANSION
LES CHOSES DE LA VIE
L'ÉQUIPE
PARIS ET RÉGION PARISIENNE
DU MONDE ENTIER

Introduction: The Echo of Utopia

The magazine *Utopie: Sociologie de l'urbain* surfaced in Paris in May of 1967, a moment in which a wave of economic and technological optimism met with a rising crosscurrent of intellectual ferment and political radicalization. When the magazine disappeared just over a decade later in 1978, the landscape had changed completely; the intervening years witnessed the worldwide student and worker protests of 1968, economic recession, oil crises, and the rise of international terrorism: an era of pervasive political uncertainty. During this decade *Utopie* was the name adopted by a changeable grouping of architects, urbanists, sociologists, and theorists—an experiment in collaborative thought carried out in the group's eponymous magazine, but also through exhibitions, pamphlets, posters, and articles. The group was bound together less through a shared approach to design, than by the desire to radically question the manner in which postwar modernization reorganized the urban fabric and large swaths of everyday life. *Utopie* was preoccupied with the new spaces and new media through which power was materialized, but equally with the ephemeral, fleeting, and mundane, elements that slipped through the grasp of architecture and urbanism. As the decade wore on, the group and its interests slowly shifted, coming to focus upon an inverse condition: one in which social space appeared to have imploded, leaving a vacuum completely enclosed by media and simulation.

While certain writings from the magazine have been translated and republished—notably those of key group member Jean Baudrillard—the vast majority have not, leaving the larger scope of *Utopie*'s intellectual production in the dark. And while the group's experiments with pneumatic architecture have garnered attention in recent years, they have not infrequently been taken to represent the production of the group as a whole, leaving the relationship of these experiments to the magazine's rich field of reference and debate largely unexamined.[1] By bringing together an extended selection of the group's

1. See: Marc Dessauce, ed. *The Inflatable Moment : Pneumatics and Protest in '68*, (New York: Princeton Architectural Press, 1999).

published work for the first time and making it available to an English-speaking public, the present volume seeks to shed light on the broader range of the group's activities and the contexts in which they appeared.

Utopie appeared amidst an international flourishing of small-scale, independent publications during the 1960s and 1970s, whose density and effect rivaled the little magazines of the historical avant-garde in the 1920s and 1930s. Fueled by a desire for alternative channels of communication as well as by the greater accessibility and economy of printing processes like offset lithography, such publications were a crucial vehicle for producing and disseminating thought on the margins of official institutions.[2] The arguments developed in *Utopie* were designed for reproduction; the physical manner in which they were laid out and shaped by the media used to disseminate them are a key part of their meaning. The present selection reproduces the graphic layout in which these statements originally appeared, both in the pages of *Utopie* and in the different pamphlets, and articles the group produced. *Utopie* was an intensely collective group project, yet it was not one that sought strict ideological uniformity, but rather deliberately placed ideological and iconographic differences in the foreground. The magazine's initial format was the result of a standard column width used for pamphlets to which an enlarged margin was added. Dubbed the *colonne critique* (critical column), the margin contained texts and images that contradicted, elaborated, commented, and parodied those in the central column. Such a layout produced a clash of egos and an exchange of voices, but also a collision of ideas from differing domains, from theories of obsolescence and technological transformation in contemporary architecture, to philosophy, critical urban sociology, semiology, and art history, together with a lineage of revisionist Marxism which had developed outside of the French Communist Party beginning in the late 1950s. In place of unified, outward denunciation, the group sought exchange and disagreement; rather than interdisciplinary collaboration, a more complete fusion and a shared process of autocritique.[3] Hence the magazine's inaugural editorial: not a programmatic statement of intent, but two blank rectangles outlining the column width, prefaced by a notably skeptical statement on the nature of the critical journal itself.[4]

Finding ways of working with rather than against ideological heterogeneity can be seen in the context of the era's struggles to reform education at the École

2. For a lucid analysis of *Utopie*'s place within the broader lineage of revisionist Marxism, see Jean-Louis Violeau, "Utopie: In Acts," in *The Inflatable Moment*, pp. 36–59; on the broad role of journals on the left during these years see Michel Trebitsch, "Les Circulations de la pensée critique de 1956 à 1968," *Les Années 68: le temps de confrontation* (Paris: Editions Complexe, 2000) pp. 69–87. On the phenomenon of little magazines in architecture see *Clip/Stamp/Fold: The Radical Architecture of Little Magazines 196X to 197X*, Beatriz Colomina and Craig Buckley eds, (Barcelona: ACTAR, 2010).

3. In certain respects, *Utopie*'s use of the margin reactivated a practice with roots in archaic textual commentary; but it can also be seen as part of a broader post-structuralist emphasis upon the materiality of writing and the conventions of the printed text. Similar strategies can be found in Charles Jencks and George Baird, *Meaning in Architecture* (New York: Braziller, 1969) and as well in Jacques Derrida's "Tympan," in *Marges de la Philosophie*, (Paris: Editions de minuit, 1972).

4. "Presentation," p. 25 (all page references are to the translations in the present volume, unless otherwise noted).

Nationale Supérieure des Beaux-Arts (ENSBA), a significant site in the group's formation. The iconic protests and occupations that erupted in May 1968, bringing an end to the Beaux-Arts system of education, were a flashpoint within a much longer struggle for reform, dating back to the early 1960s. A key demand amongst reformers was to make architectural teaching a part of the university system, enabling it to join related fields of inquiry such as urbanism, sociology, history, and philosophy.[5] A committee of students, assistants, and professors established to make proposals for the reform of education at the ENSBA in 1966–7 engaged this desire for rapprochement, bringing together figures from a range of backgrounds, including the philosopher-sociologist Henri Lefebvre.[6] Arriving with Lefebvre was Hubert Tonka—his assistant at the Institut d'Urbanisme de Paris—who had already begun to forge a link with the architects Jean Aubert, Jean-Paul Jungmann, and Antoine Stinco.[7] These four, together with landscape architect Isabelle Auricoste, the urbanist Catharine Cot, Jean Baudrillard and René Lourau—assistants to Lefevbre in the sociology department at the university of Nanterre-Paris X—made up the initial group in late 1966. If Lefebvre served as a key intellectual influence, he also played a material role in the creation of the magazine, connecting the young editors with his longtime colleague Serge Jonas, whose small publishing house, Éditions Anthropos, put out *Utopie*'s first three issues.[8]

Utopie's diverse disciplinary backgrounds and intellectual interests also drove the magazine's iconographic heterogeneity. Composed from newspaper and magazine clippings, advertisements, headlines, drawings, photographs, and transfer lettering, *Utopie* may have drawn on the intellectual legacy of journals like *Internationale Situationniste* and *Arguments*, but it did not look much like them. *Utopie*'s visual universe was closer to the short-lived ENSBA journal *Melp!*, which Hubert Tonka helped edit in 1966.[9] Composed of six large newsprint sheets folded in thirds and stapled, the layout flowed horizontally across several sheets, requiring the reader to perform a complex movement in order to follow a single text. A platform for a number of leftist factions within the school, *Melp!* assembled a broad range of critiques of the teaching and administration. While Marxist concepts of

5. The oversight of architectural education was the responsibility of the French Ministry of Cultural Affairs, headed at the time by André Malraux. The teaching of architecture is still not within the university system in France.

6. On the history of the reform movement see Jean-Louis Violeau, *Les architectes et mai 68* (Paris: Recherches, 2005). See also: Martin Pawley and Bernard Tschumi, "The Beaux-Arts since 1968," *Architectural Design* v. 41, (September 1971) pp. 533–566.

7. Aubert, Stinco, and Tonka first collaborated in the Seminaire Tony Garnier, an external seminar which served as the sole opportunity for the study of Urbanism at the ENSBA. Together they produced the small book *Propos sur le Logis*, (Paris: École nationale supérieure des beaux-arts, 1966).

8. The first three issues of the journal included advertising for Editions Anthropos and its related publications, including Anatole Kopp's landmark survey of Soviet architecture and urbanism from the 1920s, *Ville et Révolution*, Henri Lefebvre's *Le droit à la ville*, the complete works of Charles Fourier, as well as Marcel Poète's *Introduction à l'urbanisme*, for which Tonka wrote the introduction.

9. The two issues of *Melp!* in 1966 marked a more militant framing of the problem of educational reform which had begun to be developed in *Melpomène*, the longstanding journal of the student body at the ENSBA. *Melp!*'s editors included Nelly Barbieri, Jacques Barda, Roland Castro, Bernard Faye, Jean-Paul Gautron, Pierre Granveaud, Antoine Grumbach, Dominique Montassut, Hubert Tonka, and Bernard Trilles.

ideology, production, and alienation were central to such critiques, they were formulated via an iconography drawn from British and American Pop, from the Beatles *Help!*, to the painted comics of Roy Lichtenstein, and the technological expendability explored in *Archigram*.[10]

A similarly unstable, agonistic mixture of Pop and Marxism contributed to the tension animating the first issues of *Utopie*. While critical of the role images played within contemporary architecture and consumer culture, the magazine was itself literally assembled from a wide array of image material, albeit in a manner that resisted and undermined pictorial coherence. Hubert Tonka and René Lourau's "Repression" (*Utopie* 1) included advertisements and slogans clipped from *Elle*, *Playboy*, and *Le Nouvel Observateur*, photographs taken on the suburban fringes of Paris, and texts cut from *Liaisons*, an obscure bulletin published by the Parisian police. Everyday commodities such as plastic sunglasses, clip bras, and spray deodorants—objects whose novelty in 1967 was beginning to wear off—were placed adjacent to images of flexible, lightweight components, construction cranes, and the repeating façade patterns of buildings, creating a "magic chain" of connotative association, in which new promises of liberation were linked to new forms of repression.[11] Like many other contributions to the first three issues, "Repression" merged visual interest with a concern for the semiotic status of the combined elements. If the relationship between word and image was not that of text and illustration, neither was it collage, nor exactly Situationist *détournement*. Unlike letterpress, in which type and image were produced separately, with offset lithography the page was composed through a "paste-up" process, in a which a heterogenous array of material—which might include clippings, photographs, typewriter pages, patterns, and transfer lettering—were affixed to a support and captured photomechanically in order to create flexible printing plates. Drawing upon the expanded concept of "écriture" within the period's semiological discourses, *Utopie*'s blocks of image-text can be seen as a hybrid mode of writing, that was simultaneously an attempt to structure the printing medium used to produce the magazine.[12] From "Repression," to Jungmann's article "Paper Cities," or from Aubert's "Becoming Outdated," and Antoine Stinco's "Art?...!," the paste-up process involved not only taking apart and reassembling images, but also their "rhetoric," a practice calling for a different engagement with reading.

10. In *Melp!* 2, (April 1966) Archigram appears both in the form of a quote taken from a letter from Peter Cook, but also in the form of an image of a gasometer reproduced with the ironic caption "HLM Archigram," referring to the acronym for state-subsidized housing in France: *habitations à loyer modéré*.

11. Tonka and Lourau's mixture of new commodities with construction equipment can be seen to parallel the manner in which connotative terms such as "clip," applied to detachable, flexible, and lightweight, industrial components, were appropriated more broadly by architectural discourse at the time. See Reyner Banham's "A Clip-On Architecture," *Design Quarterly*, 63 (1965).

12. See for instance, the discussion of écriture in Hubert Tonka, "Court essai reflexe sur les fragments d'un urbanisme," *Utopie* 1 (1967) 64–90. The semiology of Roland Barthes was of particular importance. Barthes served on Baudrillard's dissertation committee and members of the group attended his seminars during these years. See: "Interview with Isabelle Auricoste," *Clip/Stamp/Fold: The Radical Architecture of Little Magazines 196X–197X*, pp. 197–200.

If the group's particular combination of image and text responded to the context of Paris, it also engaged an international architectural scene, including figures like Archigram, Cedric Price, Hans Hollein, Kisho Kurokawa, and Frei Otto. The group's international orientation was bolstered by early attention accorded to the group by the London-based magazine *Architectural Design*.[13] In contrast to a contemporary Parisian group like Claude Parent and Paul Virilio's Architecture Principe, Utopie refused to link their theoretical work with the design of architectural and urban projects. But neither did *Utopie* seek to leave the field of architecture and urbanism altogether. Rather, *Utopie* claimed an Althusserian notion of a "theoretical practice," whose central material was to be the contemporary discourses and representations of architecture and urbanism circulating both within their disciplines and in the popular press.[14] If one had to point to the keywords marking the group's theoretical practice, they would be urbanism, utopia, technology, and media: focal points that have served as the basis for the selection of texts within this volume.

The Urban

We are describing an institution whose doors are being closed, if they are not closed already. We are defining the strange ambiguity of "urbanism," a specialized and partial discipline and field that is struggling with its own contradictions and those of society as a whole.[15]

By 1967 the critique of urbanism was hardly new. No longer confined to Lefebvre's seminars in Nanterre or to the pages of critical journals, it had attained a wider currency, as could be seen in Jean-Luc Godard's *Two or Three Things I Know about Her*, which appeared in cinemas that spring. Urbanism appeared as the benign face of a new, more total form of alienation, the mask of a class strategy to monopolize and contain the contradictions of postwar social development. Yet unlike Lefebvre, the *IS*, or Godard, the critique of architecture and urbanism in *Utopie* was one carried out by architects and urbanists, a type of autocritique developed from individuals implicated in the practice. If the tone of the group's writings was frequently militant, it was also at times fragile, an attempt to hold open a closing door, and to interrogate a discipline whose contradictions were seen to be those of society more generally.

13. Jean Aubert, Jean-Paul Jungmann, Antoine Stinco, Hubert Tonka, "Architecture as a Theoretical Problem," *Architectural Design* (June 1968) p. 255.
14. The particularly strong presence in *Utopie* of the term *pratique* (practice) carried a specific theoretical meaning: practice was used to denote the particular manner by which raw materials are transformed into specific products in the realm of economics, but also in the domains of politics, ideology, and theory. Louis Althusser's theorization of practice served as the source for the group's use of the term, and more particularly, Althusser's concept of theoretical practice, a form of transformation whose raw material were "representations, concepts, and facts," and was proposed as a means by which ideological formations might be broken up and transformed into scientific knowledge. See Althusser, "On the Materialist Dialectic," *For Marx*, trans. Ben Brewster (New York: Vintage, 1969). See also: "Architecture as a Theoretical Problem," pp. 124–145, as well as "Architecture as a Theoretical Practice," and Tonka's "Critique of Urban Ideology," pp. 155–177.
15. Tonka, "Critique of Urban Ideology," p. 176.

If *Utopie* drew their material from the disposable realm of newspapers and magazines, advertisements and promotional brochures, their arguments ultimately took aim at the concrete history and development of urban legislation and practice. This took place in the magazine, but also in the form of pamphlets, such as *The Logic of Urbanism*, which served as punctual interventions distributed at professional conferences and meetings.[16]

The early 1960s had seen the rise of the discourse of "urbanisme spatial" in France, linked to the emerging concept of megastructure, and like it, to a broader wave of technological, speculative optimism.[17] Bold proposals at a massive urban scale were seen less as monuments, than as facilitating aspirations towards individual choice, flexibility, and change. In France, such speculative proposals were combined with a discourse of futurological forecasting dubbed "prospectivism," in which the impending, dynamic transformation of urban life was contrasted with the insufficiency of an older, modernist rubric of functional zoning and statistical planning.[18] For Utopie, such visionary proposals appeared politically ambivalent, not so much providing an alternative as mirroring and amplifying the futurological orientation latent in the technocratic urban planning developed by the state in wake of Charles de Gaulle's return to power in 1958.[19] "Spatial" or "visionary" urbanism were but another facet of more normative and bureaucratic forms of urbanism; in both cases urbanists were caught in a "vortex," consigned to the project of "[reducing] social complexity to simple, easily manipulable elements at the level of the 'urban' plan."[20]

The Logic of Urbanism, together with other analyses of urbanism in the first three issues of *Utopie*, sought by contrast to distinguish between "the urban," (l'urbain) and the city, or more particularly, from the urban and representations of the city deployed by contemporary urbanism. In close dialogue with the ideas of Lefebvre, the group identified "the urban" with the massive explosion and reorganization of the built fabric effected under industrial capitalism through the course of the nineteenth and twentieth centuries, a wave of development that destructured and exceeded the historical

16. *La Logique de l'urbanisme*, (1967), *L'Argent de l'urbanisme*, (1969), and the poster *Utopie ne s'écrit pas au futur*, (1969) were produced for and distributed at specific events. Other pamphlets, such as *Des raisons de l'architecture*, expanded existing texts that the group produced so as to address the debates surrounding the reformulation of architectural education in the wake of May 1968. Still others, such as *Urbaniser la lutte de classe*, gathered together and recirculated short texts that the group had produced in disparate contexts. See Chronological Bibliography, pp. 321–323.

17. The term "megastructure" was coined in 1964 by the Japanese architect Fumihiko Maki. Reyner Banham, the first historian to chronicle the movement, included a survey of "urbanisme spatial" in his *Megastructure: Urban Futures of the Recent Past* (New York: Harper and Row, 1976). See also: Fumihiko Maki, *Investigations in Collective Form* (St. Louis: Washington University School of Architecture, 1964). On "urbanisme spatiale" see Larry Busbea, *Topologies: The Urban Utopia in France, 1960–1970* (Cambridge: MIT Press, 2007).

18. The key critic to frame spatial urbanism in the terms of "prospectivisme" was Michel Ragon. See: Michel Ragon, *Où Vivrons-Nous Demain?* (Paris: Robert Laffont, 1963).

19. A key landmark of this planning was the *Schéma directeur d'aménagement et d'urbanisme de la région de Paris* (1965) developed under the direction of Paul Delouvrier. Delouvrier, who embraced the forecasting visions of prospectivist discourse, was appointed by De Gaulle to administer the replanning of Paris following his role in directing the so-called Constantine Plan from 1958–1960 during the Algerian war. Attempting to steer the course of Parisian development over the next forty years, the *Schéma* effectively doubled the metropolitan area and broke it up into seven suburban regions, foreseeing the creation of new satellite town centers, a new regional commuter train network (the RER) and an extensive highway system. See: Délégation générale au district de la région de Paris, *Schéma directeur d'aménagement et d'urbanisme de la région de Paris* (Paris: 1966), and Pierre Lavedan, *Histoire de l'urbanisme à Paris* (Paris: Hachette, 1975).

20. Utopie, *The Logic of Urbanism*, pp. 117.

city, ushering in a new condition in which former oppositions—city and country, center and periphery, nature and culture—collapsed. The urban was a more weakly distributed and unstable mixture than the city, but it also contained new typologies (dormitory suburbs, factories, university campuses, housing estates) as well as new "urban practices" that continually altered the urban fabric. The unstable nature of the "urban crisis," as it was frequently termed at the time, was to be seen, *Utopie* insisted, not solely as disorder but as the locus of unpredictable and revolutionary transformation.

Tonka's "Critique of Urban Ideology" (Utopie 2/3) thus proposed to define "city" as an ensemble of urban practices—the product of struggle between groups and classes—rather than as a particular type of "space."[21] Lefebvre, in "From Urban Science to Urban Strategy," (Utopie 2/3) raised the stakes further, arguing that urbanization was not a byproduct of industrialization, but rather that industrialization was a stage within a global process of urbanization.[22] Consequently, postwar urban planning could no longer be regarded, as a liberal, humanist "art" of city building, nor as the scientific planning claimed by a technocratic administration; but rather, as the ideological and practical apparatus developed to manage and direct the "mutation" of industrial society into urban society. Lefebvre called for the use of philosophical concepts to address practical political issues, to replace urbanism's pretention to scientificity with the active construction of urban strategies.[23]

The group highlighted the demand for "synthetic coherence," as a chief trait of the ideological apparatus of urbanism, a demand expressed in State planning documents but also in the prospectuses of private developments such as "Paris 2," the first shopping mall to be realized in France.[24] Behind the State's urbanistic ideology of "synthesis" and its private mirror, the project of restoring the city's coherence was the projection of particular and partial concepts of the city (whether formal studies, analyses of traffic, or growth forecasts) onto a larger urban reality. In contrast to a project of social segregation for the sake of consumption, they looked to the unintegrated and unstable diversity of existing "urban practice," the residual means of using, producing, and transforming the urban fabric, that urbanism threatened to liquidate. Rather than draw distinctions at the level of urban design or urban form, what needed analysis and critique, they argued, were the more fundamental political and economic goals underpinning the institutional framework of urbanism under de Gaulle, from the creation of documents like the "Code of Urbanism" to legal instruments such as the Zones à Urbaniser en Priorité (ZUP) (Priority Development Zones).[25]

21. Tonka, "Critique of Urban Ideology," pp. 155–177.
22. Lefebvre, "From Urban Science to Urban Strategy," pp. 180–208.
23. Ibid, pp. 180–208.
24. "Paris 2," whose name was changed following legal action to "Parly 2," was completed in 1969. Not only the first shopping mall in France, it included a private housing development envisioned for 20,000 inhabitants; promoting itself as a form of urbanism, capable of reproducing the lifestyle of the metropolis within an orderly, efficient private suburban enclave. The same example would serve as the conclusion to Lefebvre's *Le Droit à la ville*, published the following year. In both cases, the example took on particular importance as an example of the complementary relationship between the legal apparatuses mobilized by the Gaullist state and the role of private development in the realization of the urban fabric.
25. See *The Logic of Urbanism*, pp. 111–123.

Utopia

> *Utopia has become the emasculated expression of the tensions that reveal a conflictual reality.*[26]

Utopie starkly criticized the formalization of utopia as one of the central illusions masking conflicts within advanced industrial societies, yet the group nonetheless held onto the category. One of the group's most concerted statements on the subject took the form of a poster distributed at the conference *Utopie e/o Rivoluzione*, a meeting organized by students and assistants in the faculty of architecture at the University of Turin in the Spring of 1969.[27] There Utopie joined and entered into sharp conflict with a diverse cast, which included Archigram, Archizoom, Yona Friedman, and Paolo Soleri, among others. Where many utopian schemes of the period were projected into the near or distant future, Utopie's utopias were more frequently drawn from the past: the Paris Commune's attempt to suppress the Ecole des Beaux Arts in 1871, the speculative descriptions of Paris found in writings of the forbidden, prerevolutionary author Louis-Sébastien Mercier, or the utopian socialism of Charles Fourier. Utopias appeared equally in the guise of cautionary fables, as in Lourau's citation of Jose Luis Borges's brief fragment "On Rigor in Science" (*Utopie* 1), a parable in which the imperial cartographers' quest for ultimate rigor—a map the size of the territory—crumbles into absurd ruin. Utopia appeared not in what was just beyond the horizon, but rather in what was lacking in the present.[28] For Utopie, utopia was less the "good place" (*eu-topos*) than the "no place" (*ou-topos*), a place whose existence could not be located on any map.

If the group's negative definition of utopia could appear nostalgic, it was motivated by an attempt to comprehend the place of criticism within the historical process. In the fragmentary text "Dialectical Utopia" (Utopie 1), utopia was born from thoughts that found no possibility of realization within the existing order, and yet were ultimately appropriated, transformed, and integrated to that order.[29] As a dialectic, the negation and integration of utopia was not total and without remainder, but rather a process that dislodged revolutionary possibilities that were previously unforeseeable.[30]

Hence the description of the negative conception of utopia also as a "phase of theoretical construction."[31] The emphasis upon construction stresses the

26. "Utopia is not written in the future tense," p. 241.
27. See *Marcatrè: Rivista di Cultura Contemporanea*, no. 50–55, (1969).
28. "What constitutes the urban," Lourau noted, "is as much what is lacking in the city as what it offers." Lourau, "Outlines of Urbanism as a Critical System of Thought," pp. 29–46.
29. The "rehabilitation" of utopia had taken on increasing importance in Lefebvre's reflections on contemporary urbanism beginning of the early 1960s. See: "Utopie expérimentale: Pour un nouvel urbanisme," *Revue Française de Sociologie*, Vol. 2, No. 3. (Jul.–Sep. 1961) pp. 191–198; "Introduction," *L'Habitat Pavillionnaire*, ed. Raymond Haumont, et. al., (Paris: Centre de recherche d'urbanisme, 1966), and "Propositions" *L'Architecture d'aujourd'hui*, (June–July 1967), p. 16. Philosopher and historian Françoise Choay also placed particular emphasis upon the role of nineteenth-century utopian socialism in generating key urban concepts of the twentieth century in *L'urbanisme: utopies et réalités, une anthologie* (Paris: Édtions du Seuil, 1965).
30. "Dialectical Utopia," pp. 62–63.
31. "Dialectical Utopia," p. 63.

formation of theory rather than the application of doctrine, it mirrors Utopie's own desire to place themselves in a provisional, blank spot within the era's intensely factional Gauchiste politics; it evokes the disparate materiality of an intellectual project assembled from the contrasts between fashion advertisements and sociology, police bulletins and works of philosophy; but it also speaks to the recurrence of architecture, both metaphoric and literal, within the group's writings. The attempt to engage architecture was at its most explicit in "Architecture as a Theoretical Problem," a text which addressed the ex-ENSBA in the wake of the school's closure in 1968, a moment of intense debate regarding the future of architectural teaching and practice.[32] Published in *L'architecture d'aujourd'hui* in September 1968, and quickly expanded and republished in the pamphlet *Des raisons de l'architecture*, the text described the need to "disassemble/dismantle (démonter) the economic, political, social and cultural manifestations of architecture."[33] To emphasize dismantling was to model ideology not upon visual illusion, but rather upon a structure whose logic could be taken apart. Not by chance, the term was also central to a preoccupation with demountable construction within the group, a fascination with how processes of disassembly had been interpreted in the realm of architectural production. To disassemble the manifestations of architecture, they argued, ran contra to the Beaux-Arts understanding of architecture as an "oeuvre," "creation," or "synthesis," but also questioned the sufficiency of emerging ex-Beaux-Arts slogans, which sought to define architecture as "a service to the people" or simply as "a political act."[34] In the end, *Utopie*'s "rhetoric of disassembly" was an attempt to understand architecture as a particular type of product. Grasping architecture as a product demanded in turn a different conception of architecture as a technical and social production, one that could come to grips with architecture's place within a changing postwar consumer society.

Technics

In any era, technical knowledge and its use has divided the social body into distinct areas, categories, zones of privilege.[35]

If Utopie were unsparing in their critique of technocratic planning, their position was not anti-technological. The group collectively wrestled

32. The version published in this volume appeared in *L'architecture d'aujourd'hui* in September 1968, and was republished in March of 1969 as *Des raisons de l'architecture*. Both texts developed out of a much shorter text published in *Architectural Design* in June 1968. The ministry of culture officially dissolved the ENSBA in August 1968, and until the government-mandated creation of five schools known as *Unités Pedagogiques* (Pedagogical Units) to replace the ENSBA system in January 1969, the future shape of architectural education in France remained uncertain. In protest over the government-mandated UP, over 1200 students and teachers refused to join the system, and were turned into a supplementary school known as "UP6."
33. Utopie, *Des raisons de l'architecture*, pp. 124–145.
34. Utopie, *Des raisons de l'architecture*, pp. 127.
35. Baudrillard, "Technics as Social Practice," pp. 209.

with the Lefebvrian slogan "All technics in the service of everyday life," as can be seen from the exchanges between Auricoste, Aubert, Baudrillard, Goldblum, Jungmann, and Stinco that make up much of *Utopie* 2/3.[36] Not unlike the rhetoric of disassembly enunciated in "Architecture as a Theoretical Problem," the magazine's larger reflection centered on the relationship between technological forces and a collective social imaginary.[37] Such an emphasis sheds a different light on the group's interest in pneumatics, most famously, the panoply of objects and devices assembled for the exhibition "Structures Gonflables" in 1968.[38] Seen from such a perspective, the fascination with inflatable technology appears less about the poetics of air, than about the place of pneumatics within the longer technical and social history of demountable construction.[39] Jean Aubert's "Becoming Outdated," (*Utopie* 1) traces just such a lineage, from the Crystal Palace to Cedric Price's Fun Palace, as evidence of architecture's unsettled place within an expanding logic of obsolescence. Antoine Stinco's image-text "Art?...!" (*Utopie* 1) poached pages from journals of industrial aesthetics and furniture catalogues, the *Ford Guide to Styling*, and magazines like *Domus* and *Art International*, to outline its own "system of objects," reminiscent of the importance of furniture systems and design objects within Baudrillard's contemporaneous book of the same name.[40] If qualities of mobility and ephemerality were frequently aligned with claims to liberation within architecture and urbanism during these years, for *Utopie* they also testified to a more radical generalization of obsolescence as a norm. In such an evolution, the forces of industrial mass production appeared to transcend not only the physical deterioration of commodities, but the even more powerful and immaterial force of stylistic obsolescence. As the physical combination of objects into "systems" within the period's architecture and design discourse seemed driven not by logic, but by regimes of signification, they appeared no longer as simply the reification of social relationships by the magical agency of commodity fetishism, but rather as the manifestation of an emerging, and more radically superficial, yet encompassing, form of sign exchange value.[41]

36. See for instance, the passage on urban strategy in Lefebvre's "From Urban Science to Urban Strategy," pp. 180–208.
37. In French the term "technique" is capable of denoting technique (the particularity by which a task is executed), an individual technology, as well as technics, the larger combination of habits, ideas, and practices shaping technological development.
38. The exhibition provided an extensive industrial inventory, including everything from hovercraft, gazometers, and high-altitude weather balloons to medical equipment and beach toys, and ran from March 1–30, 1968, at the Musée d'art moderne de la ville de Paris. During the exhibition two conferences were held, bringing the group into contact with figures such as Cedric Price, who was involved in similar research into pneumatics. Also of note is the catalogue essay "Essai sur technique et société," which prefigures the reflection on technique within *Utopie* 2/3.
39. Demountable construction would have been a part of the pedagogy within the Atelier of Edouard Albert, where Aubert, Jungmann, and Stinco, met as students. Albert was a specialist in light metal construction and was friendly with Jean Prouvé, who was brought to the atelier as a guest critic. Aubert, Jungmann, and Stinco also sought out the instruction of David-Georges Emmerich, who had developed an extensive series of proposals for lightweight, demountable structures from the late 1950s onwards.
40. Jean Baudrillard, *Le Système des objets* (Paris: Gallimard, 1968), translated as *The System of Objects* (London: Verso Books, 1996).
41. See Baudrillard, *Pour une critique de l'économie politique du signe* (Paris: Gallimard, 1972) , translated as *For a Critique of the Political Economy of the Sign* (New York: Telos Press Publishing, 1981).

Death and the Media

Everything seems to depend on the treatment of death.[42]

If power had wavered in 1968, it had not fallen, and while unrest and labor disruptions continued into the early 1970s, the prospect of revolutionary transformation appeared increasingly distant. Amidst the violent radicalization of factions on the far left and the slow reconstitution of power, the tenor of *Utopie* itself shifted and hardened, turning towards themes of violence, pollution, and death. In 1970, Jean Aubert and Jean Baudrillard traveled as part of a French delegation to the Aspen Design Conference, where Baudrillard produced the short statement "The Mystique of Environment."[43] Aspen organizers placed the concept of environment at the center of the design agenda that year, a move which Baudrillard and Aubert saw as complicit with the rising political emphasis upon pollution and contamination, redirecting attention from internal social conflict and external foreign wars, in an attempt to reunify a fractured body politic against a common enemy.[44] Recalling that year's conference, the architectural historian and Aspen chronicler Reyner Banham noted it as particularly fractious, a turning point that exposed "a gulf across which only shouting, not dialogue, was possible."[45] 1970 would mark a turning point for Utopie as well. That year the magazine's publisher, Anthropos Editions, launched *Espaces et Sociétés*, a more academic journal of urban sociology, and the group, who had already quarreled with the publisher over the periodicity and price of the magazine, struck out on their own. The original group, increasingly scattered amongst a range of institutions created after May 1968, was also by this time beset by internal conflicts.[46] By early 1971, Aubert, Jungmann, and Stinco, feeling there was no longer room for the architectural problematic within *Utopie*, left the group.[47]

42. "Codicil," (U 4) p. 277.
43. In Reyner Banham's *The Aspen Papers: Twenty Years of Design Theory from the International Design Conference in Aspen,* the text, attributed simply to the "French group," was republished as "The Environmental Witch Hunt." While they were not involved in drafting the statement, the members of the delegation included François Barré, Gilles de Bure, Henri Ciriani, Claude and Francoise Braunstein, Alain Fischer, Odile Hanappe, Eric Le Comte, Roger and Nicole Tallon. The text also appeared as "Du scoutisme au napalme," in *Robho* 5/6 (1971), 53.
44. On the political redefinition of the term "environment" within architecture, from the general notion of surrounding to that of natural ecology, see Reinhold Martin, "Environment, c. 1973," *Grey Room* 14 (Winter, 2004), pp. 78–101, and Florian Charvolin, "1970: L'année clef pour la définition de l'environnement en France," *La revue pour l'histoire du CNRS*, no. 4 (2001), accessed January 15, 2011. URL : http://histoire-cnrs.revues.org/3022.
45. See: Reyner Banham, *The Aspen Papers; Twenty Years of Design Theory from the International Design Conference in Aspen* (New York: George Braziller, 1974).
46. Tonka taught at the Institut de l'urbanisme and helped to found the urban planning department at the experimental university of Vincennes, established in 1969 in response to demands for university reform. He also continued to engage with the ex-ENSBA through "cours sauvages," public classes organized in supermarkets, offices, and neighborhoods by striking architecture students, in the fall and winter of 1969–70. Jungmann taught at the short-lived Unité d'Enseignement et de Recherche sur l'Environnement in the partially demolished Les Halles market, before returning to the UP6 at the former Ecole des Beaux Arts, where he founded the "workshop for graphic expression" known as *ZZZ*. Aubert briefly taught courses on urbanism and communication at Vincennes, where he started the short-lived magazine *Rufus*, before returning to UP6 in the early 1970s. Baudrillard remained at the sociology faculty in Nanterre until the mid-1980s.
47. Aubert, Jungmann, and Stinco continued to practice together in the firm Aerolande until the mid 1970s. The three collaborated again with members of Utopie in the magazine *L'Ivre de Pierres,* four issues of which were edited by Jungmann and Aubert between 1977 and 1983.

Thus, when the fourth issue of *Utopie* appeared in late 1971, it was with a smaller editorial group and in a more modest, standard pamphlet format.[48] Published by the Imprimerie Quotidienne, a printing and publishing house founded by Tonka, the magazine retained its signature typography—designed by Auricoste in 1967—but lost the "critical column" so important to the early issues.[49] From then on, texts in *Utopie* were printed mostly unsigned, with individual authorship subsumed to the collective enterprise. The covers were printed in bright, artificial colors and the interior typography was set on tinted paper in contrasting ink, a relationship that changed with each issue. It is tempting to see *Utopie*'s late-Pop exterior as a cheerful, protective mask for the growing somberness of its themes, which proceeded in tandem with a redoubled theoretical ambition. The group's focus upon death and excess was in tune with the broader intellectual climate emerging in the 1970s, whether in the renewed interest in the writings of Georges Bataille, or in Michel Foucault's turn towards the biopolitical spaces of hospitals and prisons.[50] If death marked a theoretical horizon, it was one constantly refracted through the more immediate prism of contemporary events, from the shooting of activist Pierre Overney in 1971 ("Codicil," *Utopie* 4), to the terrorist attacks at the Munich Olympics in 1972, the protracted demise of Franco, and the controversy over the suicide of the leaders of the Red Army Faction in 1977 ("We Are all Stuffed, like Animals," *Utopie* 18). If death seems to displace utopia during this later phase of the magazine, the group remained devoted to a project of thinking about phenomena that were stubbornly inassimilable to the existing order of things.

The magazine also sought to intervene in other theoretical debates during these years, notably surrounding the status and use of mass media, and regarding concepts central to Marxist theory itself. In "Requiem for the Media," Baudrillard challenged both the "strategic illusion" that media could be liberated from capitalist monopoly, as well as the "technological idealism" of Marshall McLuhan's global village.[51] In place of mass media's simulated responses and feedback loops, Baudrillard defended a more fundamental, antagonistic reciprocity and response between subjects. If the lure of the increasingly relentless, sophisticated, and seductive enclosure described in Baudrillard's later writings on simulacra are already apparent, he retains at this point the possibility of responding to such powerful forces.

48. Altogether *Utopie* appeared in three different formats between 1967 and 1978. Issues 1–3 were 22.5 cm x 18 cm, issues 4–15, as well as the pamphlets, were 22.5 cm x 14 cm; and issues 16–18 were 28 cm x 19 cm.

49. In 1969 Tonka purchased a printing machine, which was housed with other machines belonging to an anarchist group in Montrouge for a short period before moving to the rue Clavel in Paris' nineteenth arrondissement. By 1972, Imprimerie Quotidienne, which by this time included Auricoste and Nicolis Politis, moved to Fontenay-sous-bois, where Tonka and Auricoste continued to operate it until 1991.

50. See for instance, Denis Hollier, *La prise de la concorde: essais sur Georges Bataille*, (Paris: Gallimard, 1974), translated as *Against Architecture*, (Cambridge: MIT Press, 1989); Michel Foucault, *Surveiller et punir: naissance de la prison*, (Paris: Gallimard, 1975), translated as *Discipline and Punish: The Birth of the Prison* (New York: Pantheon, 1977); and Jean Baudrillard, *L'échange symbolique et la mort* (Paris: Gallimard, 1976), translated as Symbolic Exchange and Death (Thousand Oaks: Sage Publications, 1993).

51. Baudrillard was responding specifically to Hans-Magnus Enzensberger's "Constituents for a Theory of the Media," which appeared in the *New Left Review* in December of 1970.

The limits of Marxist theory in adequately accounting for the nature and influence of mass media noted in "Requiem for the Media" prefigures the more radical critique of a Marxist conception of production in "The Mirror of Production" (*Utopie* 6). Here Baudrillard questions both Marx's idea of production, but also various post-'68 attempts to expand and redefine production, from the "textual productivity" outlined in *Tel Quel* to the desiring-machines theorized by Gilles Deleuze and Félix Guattari. Baudrillard proposed that the relationship between use value and exchange value in Marx be understood by analogy with Jacques Lacan's theory of the mirror-stage, as a formative, imaginary, outside of which man "can no longer think of himself other than as something to produce, to transform, to make visible as value."[52] While the centrality of production in Marx, Baudrillard argued, "persuaded men that they are alienated by the sale of their labor power," it simultaneously censured "the much more radical hypothesis that they could be alienated as labor power."[53]

Caught up in such a play of mirrors, in the later phase of *Utopie* almost every opposition comes to take on a highly uncertain status, including the very notion of "radicality." "Revolutionary Exoticism," (*Utopie* 9 "Radical Follies") sharply commented on the manner in which national liberation struggles in emerging nations served an increasingly compensatory function for radical groups within Europe. Alongside such extended reflections were shorter, punctual observations regarding the softening of once frozen Cold War oppositions, from the convergence of US and Soviet satellites ("Satellites and Ideograms," *Utopie* 13), to electoral indecision across Western Europe ("There's no more government," *Utopie* 9), to the seeming "nonevent" that marked the withdrawal of US troops from Vietnam ("War Scenario," *Utopie* 13).

In the course of its decade-long run, from the initial emphasis upon urbanism, architecture, and technology to its final concentration upon the mass media and political events, the reflection on both liberation and power within *Utopie* changed drastically. It passed from an exploded urban condition, understood as the new battleground of class struggles, to a domain of escalating symbolic contestation, in which more total forms of media simulation faced off with more extreme manifestations of political violence. If this shift brought with it an increasing skepticism about liberation, its complement was a deeper consideration of the interiorization and normalization of power's operation in both contemporary communication networks and in the body politic. The journal itself vividly reveals the particular objects and phenomena, drawn from architecture, urbanism, industrial design, art, mass media, and current events, which formed the concrete basis from which the group's theoretical "models" were extrapolated. If the perspective appeared increasingly bleak, the continued existence of *Utopie* can itself be seen as a commitment to claiming the possibility of a response.

— Craig Buckley

52. "The Mirror of Production," p. 282
53. "The Mirror of Production," p. 289

A Magazine of Urban Sociology

Presentation

Have you ever read two presentations of journals that differed? No matter their object, purpose, or will; whatever their ideological, political, philosophical stance, what better way to present one's intentions than to proclaim a willingness to critique, a willingness to change society? Invocations to the god Revolution will hardly change....

UTOPIE

Outlines of Urbanism as a Critical System of Thought

I. The Map and the Territory

"On the Rigor of Science"

"In this empire, the Art of Cartography was taken to such a peak of perfection that the map of a single province took up an entire city and the Map of the Empire, an entire Province. In time, these Oversize Maps outlived their usefulness and the College of Cartographers drew a map of the Empire equal in Format to the Empire itself, coinciding with it point by point. The Following Generations, less obsessed with the Study of Cartography, decided that this Overblown Map was useless and somewhat impiously abandoned it to the tender mercies of the Sun and Seasons. There are still some remains of this map in the Western Desert, though in very poor shape, the abode of beasts and beggars. No other traces of the Geographical Disciplines are to be seen throughout the land."

— J.L. Borges, *A Universal History of Infamy*

An ideal map, a reduction so perfect that it reduces reality to a pure symbol, an intellectual model that coincides with the spread of the real things that it is supposed to *represent*. Borges' nightmare is a disquieting one indeed for those who—pushing the division of intellectual labor to the extreme—struggle to hoist what they believe to be its reflection to the highest level: a line that is nothing more than the intersection between its greatest logic and its greatest hallucination. Where light, by dint of illumination, dazzles and blinds. Where seriousness turns into a game. Where no one else can hear or answer. A lonely place, devoid of references, roads or signs. A place where language talks to itself, by virtue of the internal forces of a discourse freed of the bothersome variables known as the subject of the statement and the subject of the enunciation.

That is where we dream—and are afraid of finding ourselves. Knowing what awaits us: the folly of the Emperor's cartographers.

Fortunately, the “rigor of science” is a rigorously uninhabitable place: in principle, of no interest to urbanism. That is our first *chance*.

The map imagined by Borges presupposes a rigorous, methodical and scientific destruction of the territory. A diabolical substitution of the sign for the thing signified. There is something remarkably refined in using, instead of the signifier of geographical representation—what? (as in one of Lovecraft’s stories): the ground of the Empire, with whatever could be found on it. If this map is the Empire that has sunk into the imagination of the cartographers, then science may well be the fantasy of scientists.

Of scientists and of those who make intellectual labor possible, or commission it. The cartographers certainly did not act without getting orders from the Emperor.

As for us—and this is our second *chance*—no one has given us the order to hallucinate on the topic of urbanism.

Still, we should realize that we have the permission and the leisure to do so. A permission and a leisure, I would like to understand, insofar as such an analysis is possible. It would keep me from having to provide too many imaginary justifications, or lapsing into the finalism of an official discourse. In doing so, I may be making explicit the situation of those who suffer from or adopt the great opposition between intellectual and manual labor. Now, this opposition has something to do with the problem of cities. If Marx is to be believed (and of course I believe him on this point, without question, but this does not preclude the beginnings of an explanation), the opposition between the intellectual and manual labor culminates and explodes in the opposition between city and country.

This statement has something excessive about it, something unexpected that might invite ridicule. Could it be one of these near-impossible, or at least intolerable, thoughts, the precarious existence of which I located on the crest that separates and joins the most systematic criticism (unbridled reason) and the imagination (folly)?

Fourier, a precursor of Alphonse Allais?

The program of CAPTAIN CAP, according to Alphonse Allais

- The seaport of Place Pigalle
- The reinstatement of license in the streets to stimulate repopulation
- The extension of Boulevard Trudaine all the way to the large boulevards

• The abolition of bureaucracy
• The creation of a Plaza for bullfights and a lake for water sports on the Butte Montmartre
• The abolition of the Ecole des Beaux-Arts, etc. etc.
(Legislative elections of August 20, 1893)

• *Considerations pertaining to the abolition of the budget of the Ecole des Beaux-Arts.*

"Since art is a free and original expression of the mind, it follows, from the pedagogical point of view:

That any official direction imprinted on the judgment of the student is dangerous and to be condemned;

That it cannot even be the property of an artistic majority,

Since:

Even if we assume the direction to be a good one, it still tends to destroy individuality. That is why:

We consider the rational teaching of art to be fulfilled when the aspiring candidate has acquired the sum of elementary and practical knowledge that permits him to translate his sensations with assurance.

In witness thereof we declare:

By virtue of the principle of equality, the Commune owes each of its members free instruction at all levels, with the highest level being given the following limit: the point at which the teaching goes beyond the realm of acquired fact and steps into that of authoritarian doctrine.

In other words: it owes the student the tools, while the artist owes the work.

The commission therefore concludes with the abolition of the budget: of the former Ecole des Beaux-Arts, of the schools of Rome and Athens, and of the Beaux-Arts Section of the Academy, and expresses the wish that the buildings of the School be given over to courses in science applied to art."

May 1871—*Journal officiel* of the Paris Commune.

Report of the federal commission of artists (painters, sculptors and medals engravers, architects, engravers and lithographers, industrial artists), to citizen Vaillant, delegate of Public Instruction, on the reforms to be made to the administration of the Beaux-Arts.

When the imagination reaches and oversteps the *boundaries authorized* by the institution of culture, we speak of poetry, of utopia.

When critical thinking reaches and oversteps its boundaries (much stricter than those of the imagination), we speak of deviance, madness, serious errors, overly theoretical systems, gratuitous vision, etc.

When the event reaches and oversteps the *boundaries authorized* by judicial law and by the anomic rules, we speak of revolution.

Or: a series of tall tales.

II. Tall Tales

If what urbanism produces and values today is private life—life deprived of everything—then utopia no longer appears as an exorcism, a waking dream, delight of the imagination, but as the very concrete affirmation of a lack. This lack does not reside solely in the object of desire called *the city*, any more than the lack of desire in general resides solely in the sexual object. Who knows where the site of desire is and what legitimizes desire?

Tall tales: such may be utopia. As long as we know that the ongoing dream of desire is heading toward something that resembles a habitable world.

Today's city is composed of a pile of rocks *and* a pile of dreams. What constitutes the urban is as much what is lacking in the city as what it offers. And what it offers is distributed according to a parsimonious rule, the counterpart of another rule: the one that distributes the various social categories. For whom is Paris *Paris*? For how many Parisians, *banlieusards*, provincials, foreigners? For how many adolescents, old people, vagabonds, deviants, traveling salesmen? For how many Algerians of the Goutte d'Or, or how many Spaniards of Rue Montorgeuil?

> "But if comparisons [between various social conditions, various ways of life] very often kill happiness—which I do not doubt—I would confess at the same time that it is almost impossible to be happy in Paris, for the haughty pleasures of the rich follow too hard upon the stares of the poor." (Mercier)

Like knowledge, the city of light no longer shines for anyone: no one can "make the most of it" anymore, for it infinitely overflows the horizon of the everyday. A nightmare bloated by fantasy: the wide open hand of the drowning man can no longer grasp the branch he seeks to latch onto. Like science, the city castrates. The desire of the city is slumbering at the heart of this thrilling anticipation of the Other, an Other in the pure state, anonymous, castrated. The city is there for no one.

It stands up not because it is built of solid stone, but because it is planted like a stake in desire. When Rabelais suggested that a rampart of female genitals be built around Paris, he gave a fairly exact definition of the city's enclosure: the call of desire of those who dream of "getting into Paris," or a shelter in the motherly womb for those who have managed to find lodgings there.

Utopia is not in the sick imagination of the failed architects or the doctrinaire sociologists: it is purely and simply in each city-dweller. Without it, without the projected image of *THE* city (I won't say of the city they live in), they would not be able to stand their daily crossing of the desert. Those who can no longer dream *THE* city, no longer have anything to do in their city: they dive into their holes, the prey of agoraphobia, they slip into schizophrenia. The old utopia extends and organizes the daily fantasy of the city-dweller: the ideal city stammers more than it articulates, liberated from time and space.

As for us, do we have an image of *THE* city? Just like everyone else. But it is not one that we are trying to project. Recognizing it, analyzing it, confronting it with other images, with reality—that much we can attempt. Most of all, we do not think that the imagination can settle its score with the so-called real by fixating on a particular object such as the city, for example. The last avatar of the old utopia is the theory of *unitary urbanism*. The Situationists suppose that the urban problematic covers and resolves the entire problematic of society. City becomes world, and world becomes city. Poetry into life, etc.

> "From my own particular observations, I have gathered that man is an animal subject to the most diverse and astounding alterations; that Parisian life is perhaps in the order of Nature like the wandering life of the Savages of Africa and America; that the great hunts and the ariettas of the Opéra Comique are equally simple and natural practices; that there are no contradictions in what man does because he stretches the power of his intelligence and of his whims to both ends of the chain that he covers; hence this

Haussmann's Nightmare

Cast of characters:
Napoleon III
Monsieur Thiers
The Earth Mover
The Prospector from 1985
Corbu
The Minister of Nature
The Integrated Sociologist
The Non-Integrated Sociologist

A round table.

Earth Mover: *We are gathered here and now to mind other people's business. Have I made myself clear so far?*

Prospector: *And to study the case of people who are elsewhere and later. I mean the consumers.*

Earth Mover: *You can interrupt your colleague if you deem it necessary. This is a democracy.*

Napoleon III: *Humph…*

Corbu: *My philosophy of urbanism being what it is, I can…*

Earth Mover: *Monsieur Thiers has the floor.*

Non-Integrated Sociologist: *Beware. I protest. We are threatened by a veritable American invasion. The great frontier of the U.S.A. is no longer in the West, but in the East. We do not want to be white Negroes, I mean the Indians of a system that…*

Earth Mover: *Monsieur Thiers has the floor.*

Thiers: *I have almost nothing to say. Just don't forget my armored cars.*

infinity of forms that effectively metamorphose the individual in keeping with the time, place and circumstances. One should be no more surprised by the search for luxury in the palaces of our rich than about the red and blue stripes that Savages cut into their limbs."

Sébastien Mercier, *Tableau de Paris*, 1781

How to speak of urbanism? By making the city speak in as many ways as possible. Perhaps this is the only way to get the grime out of the writing of the city. Reading of a palimpsest. The discourse on the city will be alternately poetic, clinical and critical. In fact, the object of our research is neither the art of the architect nor that of the regional planner and similar prospectivists. The utopia of the planners—a utopia cut into tiny segments of five years that never stop writhing—reveals the limits of what the liberal economy in its present phase can permit itself. Drawn between the necessity of liberating the greatest amount of possible forces and the necessity of controlling these forces as much as possible, industrial society grants itself time off for five years, all the while taking the precaution of ensuring the surveillance of an economy on furlough. Liberty under surveillance. It may be well and good to entrust oneself to the future, but legislating in the future is more prudent. If need be, precautions are taken to show off the technocratic utopia: one manages to offer Orly up for consumption just as one does the Louvre.

Neither the old utopia, nor a prospective one—*where* is our utopia?

Only in this twofold refusal? No. Also in a simple assertion, according to which the "world system" that we are subjected to has nothing "natural" or eternal about it; in the sense that the city/country opposition is one of the aspects of historical evolution, one of the signs (almost invisible by dint of being thrust in front of our eyes) by which society strives—fortunately in vain—to legitimize its continuity and the direction of its change.

How does the system of the city fit into the other systems that constitute society? Or: how to conceptualize the notions gravitating around urbanism without falling precisely into a sleepy systematization that signs the death warrant of critical thinking?

Marx and Engels's thinking about the end of the city/country opposition created a breach, a vast semantic blank in the map of the signifier. Until now, critical thought has indulged in

Very important. Capital. Build your cities in the air, in the water, underground, I don't care. But I need…

Napoleon III: *…wide open ring roads to enable the armored cars to move around, anti-slogan, counter-demonstrator armored trucks in case of trouble. But I am convinced that our Earth Mover and our Prospector from 1985, in a generous spirit of understanding, all the while reserving the future of technical progress… where was I?*

Corbu: *Whoever considers my philosophy of the city…*

Minister of Nature: *The city, the anti-city that we are in the process of building will meet all the conditions required by the Minister of the Interior.*

Thiers: *Conditions, conditions! Let's not exaggerate. I love nature!*

Napoleon III: *Will the Central Labyrinth be mobile or fixed? My Eugénie suggested last week…*

Earth Mover: *Sire, you have just brought up the thorn that lies at our feet. While I am not saying that there is a disagreement between us, there is nonetheless, within the committee for the U.T., nuances, opinions which, to be sure, but all the same…*

Integrated Sociologist: *The study conducted on the workers of the Massif Central produced excellent results. Sire, Total Urbanism corresponds to the deepest motivations of the working class, which is fully aware of how much Your Majesty is taking care of it.*

Non-Integrated Sociologist: *I would point out that the opinion polls constitute a weapon that, under the cloak of empiricism, hides an* some arrangements and derangements of an immovable material: a sort of eternal "social material" that legitimized once and for all the oppositions between directors and executors, intellectual laborers and manual laborers, philosophy and reality, politics and daily life, city and country. The de-structuring and re-structuring that the revolutionary and reformative visions permit themselves have this in common: they posit as self-evident and technically untouchable, the elements of reality that thought takes into consideration. A fine example of intellectual *bricolage*, whose combinations are surely quite numerous and quite ingenious—as in all *bricolage*—but limit themselves by impossibility, or by refusal, to call upon new *raw materials* and ways of thinking about matter.

The philosophical utopia, the old utopia, from More to science fiction, passes through the dream-like architecture and ideological projections of Ledoux (even if the latter attempted to surpass the limits of the genre), and defines itself by calling upon a *secondary material*, composed of the accumulated representation acceptable at a given time. The signifier is rarely disturbed. The new is made out of the old. With the ideological, aesthetic and technical residue deposited by technological development, one attempts to patch up some fragments of possibility. On its poetic fringe, the philosophical utopia becomes a heterotopia: the bricolage object becomes simply the negation of the objects really built by contemporary technological means. Utopias, generally speaking, never find much success during their author's lifetime; being easy to integrate into the official culture, they are shelved in the museum of the future. All societies leave to deviance the task of *representing* themselves for their own eyes, for the eyes of the rest of the world and for the eyes of the future. A very strange mission, which "scientific" and functionalist sociology cannot describe, being too preoccupied in analyzing what it believes to be the real functioning of society, while it is busy, unwittingly, justifying the functioning of its own ideology. The philosophical utopia is one form of this deviance, resulting in Le Corbusier's having obtained very few contracts in France, but of having *represented* for the sake of export—even in his own lifetime—the creative daring, the visionary generosity, and other gadgets "Made in Eternal France."

To disturb the signifier means to change the institution of language, to speak another language, and to take the risk of

underlying ideology that I denounce with the utmost vigor.

Minister of Nature: *Everything is clear. No more cities. Country. The French people, from Rousseau on, have been consumers of the country. No need for research to realize this. As for me, I consult the base: the shoulders of our national roads. Tons of litter constitute, in my opinion, messages that are much clearer than statistical research.*

Napoleon III: *What do you think of this, Thiers?*

Thiers: *Oh, you know me, if you don't forget...*

Corbu: ... *the armored cars. But one does not build a nation-city by neglecting the major needs of man. Housing, mobility, distraction, work, washing the car, watching TV, flirting, watering the peas, and so on. Look it up in the Tarte des Chaines*

Non-Integrated Sociologist: *The urban revolution takes place through a political revolution. The political revolution takes place through a coming to awareness of the proletariat. The coming to awareness of the proletariat takes place through non-alienated labor and leisure. Non-alienated labor and leisure take place through the overturning of the relationships of production. The overturning of the relationships of production take place through the* stroumkarderpapistrerage. *Gentlemen, I regret to have to tell you that you are trying, in vain, to jerry-rig the future, to patch up superstructures. Who drank my whiskey?*

Earth Mover: *Here is the present state of the Plan. The capital as a fixed place is abolished. The institutions that guarantee the security and proper functioning of the cities are nomadized. Ministries, public buildings, police stations, courtrooms, savings banks, tax bureaus, post offices, schools, prisons, churches, banks, veterans associations, hospitals, etc, etc., all of this goes into motion. The economic, cultural and entertainment centers, etc., move. We have finally discovered, I dare say, the means for controlling social mobility, unpredictable movement—yes, Mr. Prospector—in a word, History. All it took was a bit of thinking. And think we did. Thanks to the teams of sociologists, psychologists and sociopsychologists directed by the admirable devotion of a scholar—here present—whose authentic integration into the system I am glad to salute, we have been able to do what no one else had done before. To ride the wave, instead of fighting it with ludicrous means. From now on, we are afraid of nothing.*

Napoleon III: *Excuse me, but where are the people going to live?*

Thiers: *Wait a minute, what about my armored cars?*

Corbu: *No philosophy. A pure utopia, your U.T.*

Prospector: *We are not entirely sure, Sire. But if our forecasts are exact, the population should be able to adapt easily—although it is pursuing directions that are divergent and impossible to outline in advance—to this new structuring of its relationships to power.*

Integrated Sociologist: *Society is a system. The "people" exist only in the brains of nostalgic doctrinaires, leftovers from the humanism of '48.*

never again being heard. Just as urbanists are more often than not entrusted with patching together our exploded cities than with building cities—so too, does the urbanist's practice fit into the system (a system thought out by others) of regional planning: His real projects never leave the drawing board. And so it is difficult to judge how much he accepts or refuses the social order in which he tries to work. All that is asked of him is to confirm, arrange, and make the meanings already embedded in society a little less unlivable. Above all, nothing is to be disturbed—except maybe the sterile surroundings of some isolated constructions, churches, or cultural centers. In this way he is condemned to seek shelter in architecture.

No more and no less than the physician or the teacher, the urbanist-architect is a good civil servant of the established order of things; established within a movement so unbridled, that the ultimate social service amounts to controlling, channeling and even repressing its motion, all the while appearing to follow and encourage it.

And so urbanism, as a form of unemployed thinking, helps to prop up a profession devoid of thought. The City becomes the residue of unemployed reflection. It keeps one from having too many sleepless nights. It constitutes the *transitional object* of a critical reflection on the city deprived of all theory about society. The child needs a rattle, its doll or a lullaby in order to go to sleep; the real or symbolic presence of its mother. The urbanist's transitional object is the City—imagination at work on the City—and is at the same time the impossibility or the refusal to struggle against this way of thinking, in order to attain reality.

The urbanist's greatest illusion resembles that of the Enlightenment philosophers and the utopian socialists. While aware of the fact that the accomplishment of their views and their visions, depend upon events still unprecedented, they believe instead that it will be brought about by legal decree, through the great magnanimity of established power. Each day at noon, Fourier granted an appointment to the improbable sponsor who would give him the money needed to conduct his phalansteric experiments. Proudhon, incarcerated by Napoleon III after the coup d'état of the 2nd of December, dedicated the work that contained his most subversive projects to the Emperor from the depths of his cell. Victor Hugo was fond of saying that aviation and mandatory schooling would restore world peace and the rule of democracy. As for the Christian socialists, ranging from Pierre Leroux to his many successors, they believed that the reign of justice would not fail to come, since it was the will of God.

Sébastien Mercier, who with de Sade and a few others, represented the last generation of 18th-century philosophers, published in 1771 a visionary novel titled *L'An 2240*, in which he imagined a "peaceful revolution" had taken place. Naturally, it was brought about by "the work of Philosophy." This philosophy seems to have spread like an epidemic between 1771 and 2240, like a veritable possession. This happy plague did not spare power, and it is delightful to note that the Bastille no longer exists in 2240. Did Mercier anticipate the 14th of July 1789? Not at all. The Bastille was "overturned from top to bottom by a Prince who did not believe that he was the God of men…"

This illusion would not be so bad if it were not generally accompanied by a strategic withdrawal of critical thinking. Resignation, pessimism, disenchantment and disengagement are part of the complex called ideology or false consciousness. Unusually enough for him, in the dedication of his visionary novel, Mercier gave voice to "good sense;" as usual it was this voice that proclaimed the absence of history, the end of time, the refusal to envision and prepare for change. "Already, Philosophy, weary and disheartened, has lost its strength; it cries out in the midst of men as in the midst of a vast desert."

The collapse of historical consciousness, as the condition for the appearance of false utopian consciousness (this holds true for the old utopia, but also maybe for "our own") is only, generally speaking, but one aspect of the loss of temporality that characterizes schizophrenia. In the case of this collective schizophrenia known as false historical consciousness, we notice that exaggerated spatialization, a major pathological sign, is what best defines the imaginary *elsewheres* and *laters*, and especially utopian urbanism (regarding false consciousness, see Joseph Gabel's book of the same name, éditions de Minuit).

Tall tales, negating time, are means of settling into an illusory space, of living on the territory as if it were only a map. It means killing thought, and killing oneself by means of thought. This temptation is only too visible in the undertaking which presently consists of dealing with questions of knowledge in terms of space. The "pedestals," "landscapes" and other "spaces" of knowledge that haunt Michel Foucault's style have the disquieting charm of a transcendent and autonomous "world of ideas" in which it would be "foolish" to want to intervene. A no man's land.

Napoleon III: *Excuse me, excuse me. You are not taking me for a…?*

Earth Mover: *Our sociologist only wanted to suggest that doctrinaires who believe in their doctrines are dangerous.*

Napoleon III: *Oh! That's more like it.*

Non-Integrated Sociologist: *A whole population of nomads, as controllable as gypsies. Signs everywhere: No Parking! I wonder what I'm doing here. Who took my whiskey?*

Prospector: *Good heavens, pneumatic architecture answers all the questions, including the least opportune ones. The future is inflatable. Sire, just think that a house—a house!—will occupy no more room than your workers's camping gear as they leave for their paid vacations.*

Thiers: *Inflatable! And my armored cars, are you going to inflate and deflate them, too? And my machine guns? And my billy clubs? And my men? Are you going to inflate and deflate them?*

Corbu: *Ambulatory architecture! Architecture for screwballs! Utopia!*

Napoleon III: *In short, we are in perfect agreement.*

Non-Integrated Sociologist: *Pfrem piaffick piaffock mouraaaaaa stckf!*

Earth Mover: *Of course. Believe me, your suggestions have been integrated into the Plan.*

Integrated Sociologist: *As an outside project. To pad the introduction, the general considerations, so to speak.*

Non-Integrated Sociologist: *And the geronilavisers, are you going to integrate them, too, my geronilavisers in direct and polyphased self-management for the education of adults?*

Earth Mover: *That goes without saying. We have even considered the noll plustics.*

Prospector: *All it took was getting the idea. A nation without cities, that is a land without history. The rurals vote well, that's a fact, isn't it?*

Integrated Sociologist: *Let's say, from a more scientific point of view, that they vote in function of…*

Non-Integrated Sociologist: *And what do you do with the dictatorship of the toleparia, and the efficiency of the overdeterminist-praxis?*

Earth Mover: *You have been appointed High Commissioner for overdetermined-practice energy.*

Napoleon III: *Well, yes, from now on the overdetermined-praxis, that's you. You aren't going to refuse, are you?*

Non-Integrated Sociologist: *I'd love to have another shot of whiskey.*

Thiers: *When you get down to it, what good are my armored cars?*

Corbu: *My philosophy of urbanism had no need for armored cars. I am afraid that you'll miss my splendid barrack's style. I mean that of my disciples.*

Napoleon III: *Gentlemen, I am immediately going to inflate the first U.T. house. I hope it doesn't take a lot of blowing?*

Minister of Nature: *Sire, a sigh will suffice.*

(They leave the round table)

Non–Integrated Sociologist: *Boulou boulou, piranave?*

Integrated Sociologist: *You'll get used to it.*

III. The Man in the Street

The object of a certain sociology, whose implicit value system coincides with the state of affairs that it studies, is less social relations than the *man* of Humanism: *the man in the street*. By way of this "scientific" approach the entire sociology of the means of mass communication dissects this Martian, this transient being, this impersonal, anonymous passerby whose function is to appear at random and disappear at a street crossing, whether into a mathematical table, a ticket line or a public opinion poll.

The man of urbanism has supplanted the man of humanism. The other race, the race of the "domesticated animal of the country," as Marx put it, exists perhaps in the elsewhere, the past (and the later) of paid vacations. He must be assigned an existence of some kind, however embryonic, in order to understand (but is this absolutely necessary?) the piles of fruits and vegetables, the displays of fresh meat and the smell of moist earth that assault one in the Rue Mouffetard, the Carrefour de Buci, or the Halles.

Rather than the man of urbanism, urban man. Indeed, the man in the street does not appear against a backdrop: that would be the rationality of a milieu called the "city," a milieu made for human encounters. That would be good enough for villages, small towns and some privileged places, oases of luxury, or cheap mirages amidst the "desert of cities." If urbanism were something other than a myth, its rationality would be based not on an identikit or on a totalitarian ideal of the city, but on an analysis of the institutions and the social relationships that they imply. By *institution* I mean not only the official or informal organization of everyday life by various systems of power (the division of labor and leisure, education, the police, justice, etc.), but what keeps man *upright*, in the primary sense of the word: everything that signifies his desire, his plans, his reasons for bearing one more day, one more year, one more life. A common ground that does not include humanist Reason, that gave and still gives bourgeois universalism its justification, but upon which the Freudian structures of the unconscious allow us to imagine language, sexuality and money.

A critique of urbanism by people who are *not even* urbanists cannot be taken seriously—it is literature. Fortunately, literature is the only serious thing there is; I am tempted to say beauty or love—if you know what I mean.

The city is conceived (which is to say, not thought) in such a way that man and man, man and woman, woman and woman cannot meet anywhere else but in the no man's land, the no man's land reserved by institutions. One should not confuse sexual saturation with mad love, the institution of the failed encounter with the institution of encounters, the gospel of the carnival with the gospel of the lightning bolt. In any case, Balzac expresses this better than I can at the beginning of *The Girl with Golden Eyes*. The first fifty pages provide one of the best psycho-sociologies of Paris circa 1830—perhaps even of today's Paris. If you read the entire novel, you will have a better understanding of the unwholesome games that desire and its object play in the city.

> "One of those sights in which most horror is to be encountered is, surely, the general aspect of the Parisian populace—a people fearful to behold, gaunt, yellow, tawny. Is not Paris a vast field in perpetual turmoil from a storm of interests beneath which are whirled along a crop of human beings, who are, more often than not, reaped by death, only to be born again as pinched as ever, men whose twisted and contorted faces give out at every pore the instinct, the desire, the poisons with which their brains are pregnant; not faces so much as masks; masks of weakness, masks of strength, masks of misery, masks of joy, masks of hypocrisy; all alike worn and stamped with the indelible signs of a panting cupidity? What is it they want? Gold or Pleasure?
>
> "By dint of taking interest in everything, the Parisian ends up being interested in nothing. No emotion dominating his face, which friction has rubbed away, it turns gray like the faces of those houses upon which dust and smoke have blown. In effect, the Parisian, with his indifference on the day for what the morrow brings forth, lives like a child, whatever may be his age. He grumbles at everything, consoles himself about everything, jests at everything, forgets, desires, and tastes everything, seizes all with passion, quits all with indifference—his kings, his conquests, his glory, his idols of bronze or glass—as he throws away his stockings, his hats, his fortune. In Paris no sentiment can withstand the drift of things, and their current compels a struggle in which the passions are relaxed: there love is a desire, and hatred a whim; there's no true kinsman but the thousand-franc note, no better friend than the pawnbroker. This

> universal toleration bears its fruits, and in the salon, as in the street, there is no one *de trop*, there is no one absolutely useful, or absolutely harmful—knaves or fools, men of wit or integrity. There everything is tolerated: the government and the guillotine, religion and cholera. You are always acceptable to this world, you will never be missed by it. What, then, is the dominating impulse in this country without morals, without faith, without any sentiment, wherein, however, every sentiment, belief, and moral has its origin and end? It is gold and pleasure. Take those two words for a lantern, and explore that great plaster cage, that hive with its black gutters, and follow the windings of that thought which agitates, sustains, and occupies it!"

A sociology of the encounter would show in what way the urban increasingly models itself according to bureaucratic relationships: impersonality, "rationality," hierarchy. The man who passes by is a combination of ID card, driver's license and social security number. He has an age, probably a profession, perhaps a family. And an address. A radio or TV reporter, a "hack" journalist working in some bureau or advertising agency, could stop him and ask him his opinion about a brand of soap, long hair, happiness or truth. The answers of the man in the street have been known forever by those who pretend to ask him questions.

The uniformity of passersby is composed of a series of variables which urban habituation transforms into shades of gray. This one is dressed like a senior executive. This guy does not seem to be wallowing in wealth. The couple emerging bleary-eyed, overwhelmed and exhausted from the orgies of consumption held every Saturday afternoon at the B.H.V and the Galeries Lafayette hurry home to keep from missing the serial before the evening news. The clothing, the appearance, the gadgets (car, handbag, *Le Monde* or the *Parisien libéré* in hand) of the passerby constitute a system of distinctive signs which the passerby deciphers *in passing*. An ambulatory sociology permits the nonstop decoding of words and silences, of faces and bodies, of wallets and bank accounts.

Must streets be eliminated so as to end the reign of the man who passes by, the man without qualities? A wonderful subject for an architectural utopia. We are waiting for the program, the sketches, the models. Hurry!

The man in the street, the passerby, is deprived of what used to be called a vocation. The problems he raises are traffic problems. His pedestrian existence is regulated. If he wants to frolic, all he has to do is go into one of these fragments of the petrified forest dubbed "green spaces."

Provided, of course, that one doesn't forget just how strictly regulated urban "nature" is. Even in winter, when we look in vain for greenery or bright colors, the "keep off the grass" signs still bloom on the lawns and where the lanes begin. In the daytime, the Bois de Boulogne is made for idle women or nannies taking their desires for a stroll in a baby carriage. The men with decorations in their lapels prefer to walk the dog. At night, the parks are closed or kept under surveillance. Patrol cars lurk like eunuchs around the harem. Flirting and fleeting ecstasies in a Peugeot 404 are no longer tolerated after dark. It is simply that the city not only invented nature and the feeling for nature: decency and correctness are also part of what one calls urbanity.

The city I speak of with such bitterness does not exist, of course. The drifting I describe is not even my own, but a projection of calm desires, desires wisely *taken back* home. Dead city, city of light, slum city. If I allow myself to say what is happening inside me when I talk about the city, instead of discussing the current problems of urbanism, it is out of rancor, and because it never occurred to me that the current concept of urbanism, the one we are subjected to, involved a necessary fate. All around us, within us, the city ceaselessly changes its transient being, and the passersby themselves end up stopping, too; seeing themselves, watching themselves, talking to themselves, touching themselves, meeting. I cannot say if the subversion of the urban will come from the cultural revolution, from the suburbs, from the towns on the urban periphery, from the summer houses, from the weekends, or from the "civilization of leisure." I read with curiosity but also with skepticism, the latest news from China: it is said that the people are fighting for the eradication of the contradictions between manual and intellectual labor, agriculture and industry, city and country.

> "The path to the resolution [of the city-country contradiction] has been blazed by the pioneers of the oil field of *Ta'king*, which is cited everywhere in China as a model… *Ta'king* is neither a city, nor the country. It is at once a vast factory and a vast commune, as well as a vast school in which the residential centers are dispersed, in which collective services are generalized and very often free of charge. This new physiognomy of the city-country, as opposed to

our concentrations of skyscrapers, constitutes a completely novel experiment" (*Study Group on the Thought of Mao Tse-Tung*, no. 1, January 1967).

The greatest division of material and mental labor is the separation between town and country. The opposition between city and country begins with the transition from barbarism to civilization, from tribal regimes to the State, from the locality to the nation, and can be found throughout the history of civilization down to our day… The city entails at the same time the necessity for administration, for police, taxation, and so on; in a word, the communal system and, consequently, politics in general. This is where the division of the population into two great classes appears for the first time, and it rests directly on the division of labor and the material means of production. The city already exists due to the concentration of the population, of the material means of production, of capital, of pleasures, of needs, while the country displays exactly the opposite: isolation and separation. The opposition between city and country can only exist within the framework of private property. It is the crudest expression of the subordination of the individual to the division of labor and to a specific activity that is forced upon him, a subordination that makes of the one a dumb animal of the city, and of the other a dumb animal of the country, and reproduces every day the opposition between their interests. Here again, labor is the main thing, the power that is superior to individuals, and as long as this power exists, private property must exist. The eradication of the opposition between city and country is one of the first conditions of Communism, a condition that depends in turn on a mass of material presuppositions, which mere will cannot achieve alone, as anyone can see at first glance (we will have occasion to develop these conditions further). The separation between city and country can be considered as the separation between capital and landed property, like the beginnings of an existence that would be independent of landed property, as a development of capital, a property that has its basis only in labor and exchange.

— Marx, *The German Ideology*, 1845–1846

We admit therefore that the bourgeois solution for the housing question has failed: it ran into the *opposition*

France depends upon workers from abroad to do the work that its nationals consider unworthy of themselves. No one cares about their living conditions. The word "decency" often occurs in this context. This time, it is ours that is in question.

The greatness of a country is inversely proportional to the annual number of slum fires.

[About forty thousand people live in the 89 *bidonvilles* (slums) of the region around Paris, including 20,000 Portuguese and 15,000 Algerians. Last year, the government drew up a plan to absorb these miserable settlements within five years. It requires building 2,500 units for families and providing 25,000 rooms in homes for the unmarried. Even if this program is implemented, experts fear that the slums will be refilled as soon as they are emptied, unless the authorities also take measures to control immigration, especially coming from Portugal.

The government plan must be finished by 1970. Until then, is it worth planning and organizing the slums?

There are two conflicting schools of thought on this matter: the one believes that improving the conditions of life will only consolidate the slums; the other says, on the contrary, that there is no reason not to undertake a minimum of safety and hygiene measures

between city and country. And now we have come to the very heart of the question: it will be resolved only if society is transformed deeply enough for it to be able to tackle the eradication of this opposition, which is pushed to the extreme in today's capitalist society. Far from being able to eradicate this opposition, it renders it more and more acute each day. Owen and Fourier, the first modern utopian socialists, perfectly recognized this. In their model constructions, the opposition between city and country no longer existed… It is not by resolving the housing problem that the social question will be resolved in the process, it is rather the resolution of the social question, that is, the abolition of the capitalist mode of production, that will make the resolution of the housing problem possible. To want to resolve the latter all while maintaining the great modern cities is absurd. These great modern cities will be eliminated only by the abolition of the capitalist mode of production, and when this process is underway it will be another matter altogether than providing each worker with a house of his own."

— Engels, *The Housing Question*, 1872

(water supply, telephone, electricity), since the slums are condemned anyway… Considering the present state of affairs, it would seem that the first school has gotten the upper hand: we still refrain from improving the lot of the slum-dwellers, while waiting to be able to provide them with decent housing. Last year, as you may recall, three children died in a fire in the *bidonville* of Nanterre.]

Le Monde, January 1967

IV. Inky Darkness

We do not often ask ourselves questions like this: who was the man writing the passage in *The German Ideology* which speaks of the end of the city-country opposition? How could a young man of twenty-six or twenty-seven, a philosopher living in a Germany that had yet to be born as a state amidst the upheavals of 1848, have pressed his dialectics into the service of such a strange idea? A study of the genesis of Marx's thought conducted from this angle might perhaps tell us which silent, unformulated—unformulatable—questions his ideas responded to. I am thinking of the poignant questions that are never raised, or only in friendship or love, when one can *let go* and be oneself because one is finally recognized by another. You know, I don't give a damn about my job… If only we could always be like this… No, I don't believe in what I do every day, I believe in you, and that's all there is to it…

Since my "projection" on the young Marx is obvious, I would like to be able to formulate in his tone, but to myself—and assuming that the answers implicit in the questions we almost never ask ourselves openly are largely the same for everyone—the idea of a world in which the regime of separation no longer holds absolute sway. A world in which, while persisting more or less in fact, the separation between manual and intellectual labor, between city and country, is not valued like a natural and eternal self-evidence. Without denying that every calling into question of separation involves the "immaturity" of an "ego" unable to accept the institution of separation *on the level of the unconscious* (as it is said); in recognizing therefore (to whatever degree possible!) that anthropology situates the origins of social life in the institution of separation known as the incest taboo, I would suggest that the GREAT SEPARATIONS, however legitimate they may seem, are not archetypes, or transcendent objects, but belong to human history. As such, it is not possible to confuse or lump the original institution of the incest taboo—which permits social life, language, and more generally the institution (in the sense of education) of this unfinished being called the child—together with other instituted separations, apparently just as "natural," and the legitimacy of which Marx contests.

Indeed, while the division of labor is often considered as a counterpart of the natural division between the sexes, it is not an ineluctable result of it. To convince oneself of this, it is enough to notice the extent to which human history—for example, the recent history of technics and the relationships of production—never stops altering them, to the point of calling them radically into question in certain advanced sectors of industrial society. As for the separation which—in the context of the division of labor—brings these two "worlds" of intellectual labor and manual labor into being, there are too many exceptions from the past and the present that illustrate its contingent and historical character.

If the city draws its reason for being (and not just its functions) from the establishment of institutions, with the first being political power, if its appearance is linked to the progress of the division of labor, it may seem futile to entertain a utopian reflection on the Marxist utopia. But if the city, as Marx points out, is also synonymous with private property, capital, and labor reduced by capital to the state of merchandise, then thought may be brought to bear on the scant reality of the so-called evidence by which the social system justifies the unacceptable, and legitimates the limits of what it will "sacrifice" for the sake of the greater happiness. Engels's point takes on its full meaning here: the "good will" with which society—today and in his own time—strives to solve the "housing question" without ever managing to, in spite of its immense means, can only be taken as a joke.

Reducing the city to one of its "functions," such as repression, is likely too tautological and not very interesting. It is better to recognize the institution of repression as inseparable from what society preserves, defends, transmits and exalts in the name of "culture." The city refracts a society's culture of the society, with all the contradictions that ceaselessly define the relationships between nature and culture. It is in this sense that in one of the few ludic sites that Napoleon III built in Paris—the labyrinth at the Jardin des Plantes—there is a sign that reads: "No Games."

The soft revolution: Schick Band Razor

The separation between city and country is no more inscribed in space than it is in the unconscious or a system that transcends man. That the Judeo-Christian tradition locates the beginnings of time in a Garden of Delights and its end in the World-City (the Celestial Jerusalem), that science fiction projects a fully urban world into the most remote futures (cf. Trantor, city-planet, capital of the galaxy, in Asimov's novel *Foundation*)—this tells us something about the myth of the *urban*. Certainly, our "destiny" is in the city. The important thing is to understand that the model of the total city, of the urban as the only way of life, is only a weak likeness of what we recognize or imagine in the term "city." The city, once again, is the urban minus the city's lack of being. Minus the contradictions and pathologies of the city. A unified, *non-separated* world. A world in which the forces that created the city as thing and idea, the country as thing and as an idea of a rural or natural society, have finally been defeated…

In the dark night in which the writer struggles amiably or grudgingly with his own fantasies, in the writer's *inky darkness*, the greatest confusion crops up as soon as it is a matter of concluding an interminable sentence at all costs, of answering a question too silent and too impassioned to really be beyond the limits of aphasia. Beware of the complacency that lurks like a cat one believed was asleep. At night, all cats are gray—except for the great white cat that displays its invulnerable wisdom, whose eyelids half closed or half-open, transmit a self-evidence as old *as stone*.

For a way of thinking that is not ashamed of calling itself utopian (without this signifiying any claim to designing a city), for a utopia that does not take itself so seriously that it confuses the history made by men and its own fantasies, for a critique that attempts to analyze its own *representations* so as not to substitute the Map for the Territory—in spite of it all, *the night is as bright as day and just as sleepless.*

R.L. 2.13.67

Les Arts li
éraux - Les
Beaux arts -
Les Arts d'a
réments - Les
Arts ménagers -
Le Grand art -
L'Op art - Le
Pop art - Le
Mec art - Arts
t Loisirs L'E
tic art - L'art
Vedje - L'art
Urbain - L'art
es Jardins -
L'art de la
Publicité - Ki
etic art - Les
rts décoratifs -
Lesartsmineurs
tc. - L'art et
a technique -
L'art et la na
ure - L'art
t l'industrie -
L'art et l'hom
e - L'art et
a ville - L'art
t la vie - L'art

Avant-garde art is not only at the center of today's aesthetic debates but also the impetus behind the most legitimate efforts by new societies to cater to the economic and technological demands of Western science.

Pierre Francastel

Indeed, even Michelangelo's solution is only an escape.

What Medieval artist would have been led by a religious experience to quit his artistic activity? In the Middle Ages, the greater the faith, the greater was the artist's source of inspiration: and not just because he really was a Christian, but because he was really a creator. By giving up his artistic productivity, he would have lost his reason for being.

On the contrary, after having dropped art, Michelangelo kept his prestige and importance, not only in the eyes of the world but in his own eyes as well.

Arnold Hauser

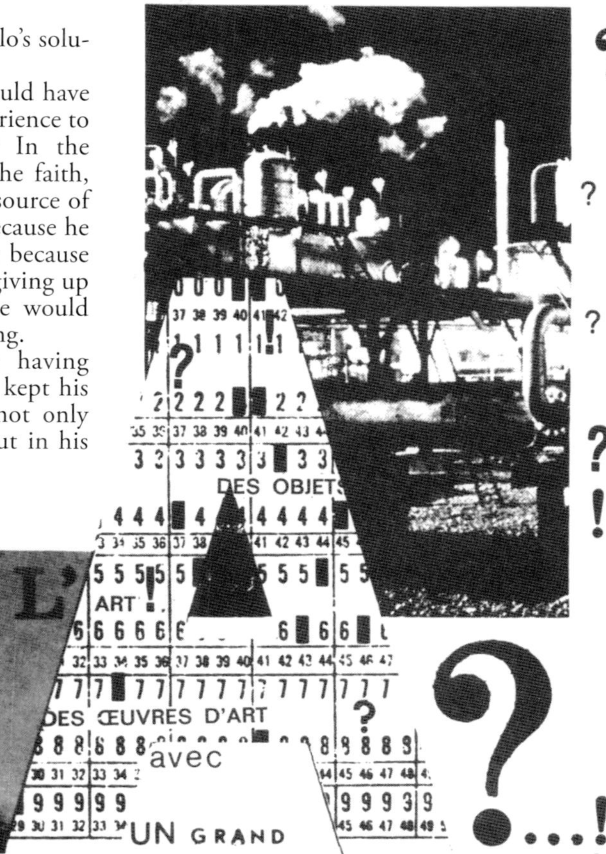

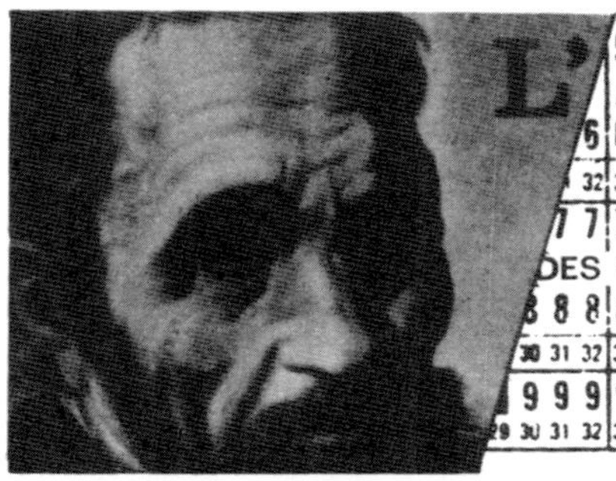

M. Duchamp

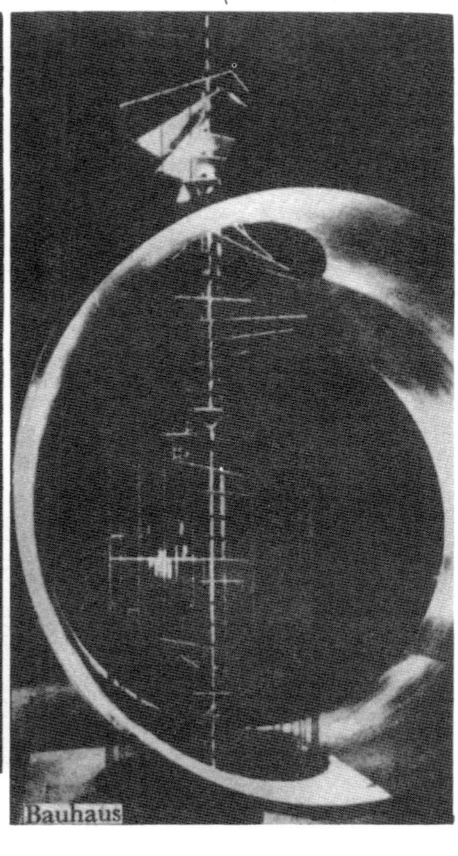

WORKS OF ART

OBJECTS

Cascella

Brancus

SCULPTURES

In the last analysis, the extreme, polemical and exacerbated forms of contemporary artistic production remain attached to the sites, salons, galleries and museums, where a privileged class, remote from the world, from practical life and from religion, indulges in spiritual pleasures of a very special kind.

These sites are the counterparts of the ivory tower in which the artist since the Renaissance has found himself a prisoner of the inspired, individual and non-transmissible nature of his genius.

WITH TRADITIONAL TECHNIQUES,
WITH MODERN TECHNIQUES,

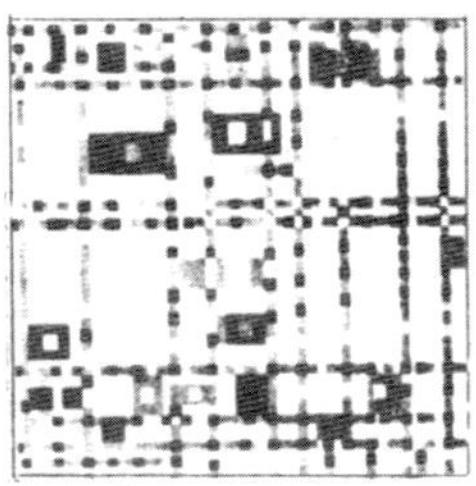

Mondrian

Whitney Museum, New Yor

À TRAVERS LES GALERIES

En quête des clefs de notre époque

ALWAYS PRESENTED TRADITIONALLY

PAINTINGS

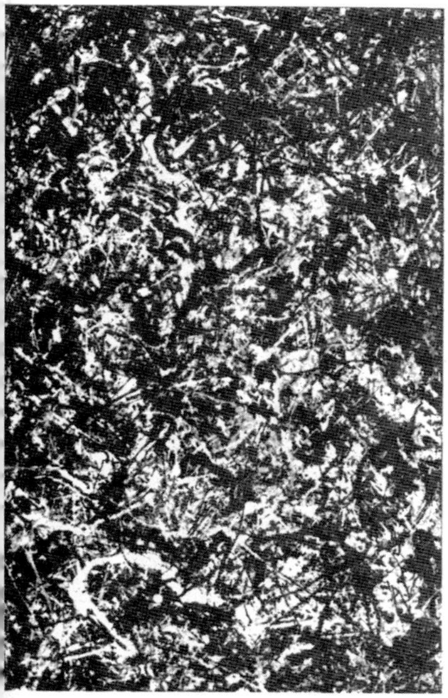

Pollock

ON A WALL OR IN A ROOM,

May Ray

Takis

ALWAYS ON THE SITES TRADITIONALLY RESERVED FOR ART.

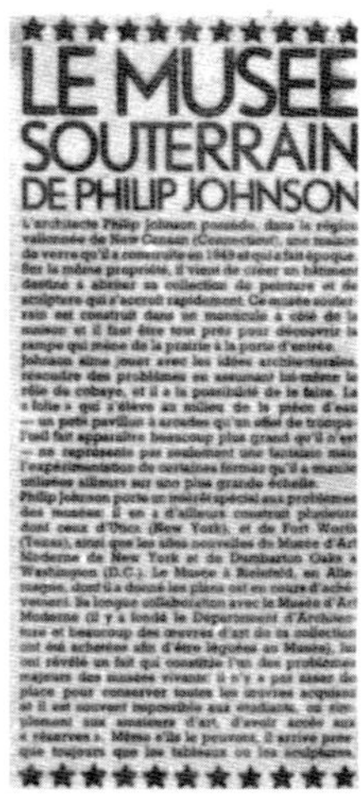

LE MUSEE SOUTERRAIN DE PHILIP JOHNSON

Notes on Marxism and Aesthetics

With the exception of Paul Lafargue (Marx's brother-in-law) and Trotsky, the thinkers in Marx's lineage were not very interested in aesthetics and generally analyzed the phenomenon of modern art *only in terms of "bourgeois art and literature." Lukacs and his school dealt only with novels and essays of the nineteenth century, leaving poetry and art aside, as well as, generally speaking, the aesthetic revolution.*

This lack can probably be "explained" by the inadequacy of the Marxian and Marxist sociology on this point (art). The artist was lumped together with the bourgeoisie, and Marx himself did not see the ambiguity of the artist's function in capitalist society: an expression both of the aristocratic culture and of the contradictions of this culture.

To the extent that he works on the linguistic structures and sign systems entrusted to a society at a given time, the artist is directly connected with what Marx called "the social material," that is, language. Are the institutions of language and culture superstructures or infrastructures? This may be the question to be asked in relation to the artist. Believing that his work does not act in, with *and* on *the signifier of social relationships leads to thinking that his work is secondary. Yet, at the same time, Marxism wants to regulate art and press it into the service of the revolution, and so proves—unwittingly—its social function.*

Marxist aesthetics, insofar as it exists, has not extracted itself from this contradiction. Nor has it done so in China.

We need a serious analysis of the relations between the political revolution and the aesthetic revolution.

R.L.

To speak of a "disinterested pleasure" or "additional" aesthetic value in connection with art shows less incomprehension of the aesthetic object than a misrecognition of the relations we maintain with desire. *Francastel was right in reproaching sociologists—especially Mauss—for the idea of a "supplemental artistic value"; there would thus be objects created by the artist for the sake of aesthetic pleasure on the one hand, and, on the other, unpreconditioned aesthetic effects, or at least effects without aesthetic intention. Thus the Venus of Milo and a sunset would be in the first category (assuming the belief that nature has a Creator). The shape of an automobile or a piece of furniture would be supplemental values.*

In the first case, aesthetic pleasure would be our response, addressed to the creator's manifested desire to please.

In the second, our pleasure would come, not from shared desire (between creator and consumer), but from a fortuitous, almost clandestine, encounter between the form and the function—useful and pleasant.

On the one hand, mutual good will, and on the other, a secondary attribute of matter; these would be the two manners of apprehending the Beautiful.

The oppositions between mind and matter, legitimate pleasure and physical pleasure, etc., are projected from bourgeois morality into bourgeois aesthetics. The legitimate spouse need not be desirable, since marriage automatically confers this status upon her. The streetwalker does not have the right to be desirable, since she is beautiful.

To clear things up, it might be better to drop the idea of a social category responsible for producing beauty. We are beginning to see that artistic practice has little to do with the endless commentary that drones on at openings or in art criticism. It would be better to ask oneself how it *happens when, in the presence of what we call the external world, representations take shape within us, some of which are recognized as being aesthetic. Studying the "aesthetic object as a*

R. Lichtenstein

Today, more than ever, as the artist finds himself outside of this social reality which obsesses him, he is more than ever fascinated by the technique to which he is bound and in particular by the industry that creates forms which, for the first time, are made without him.

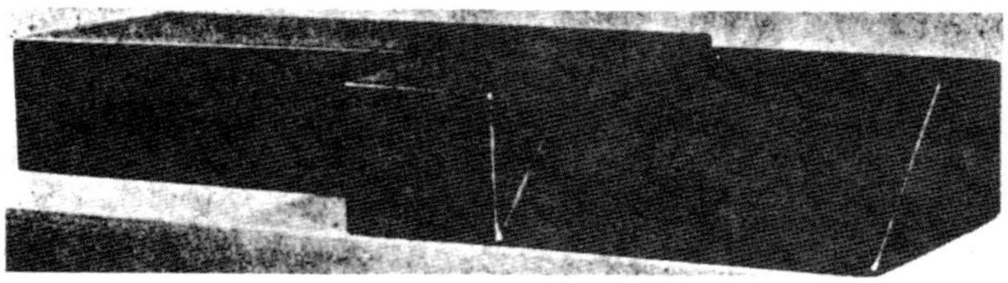

Steiner

ON THE ONE HAND A PROJECT THAT MAKES NO OBJECTS
ORDER WITHOUT REALITY

Judd

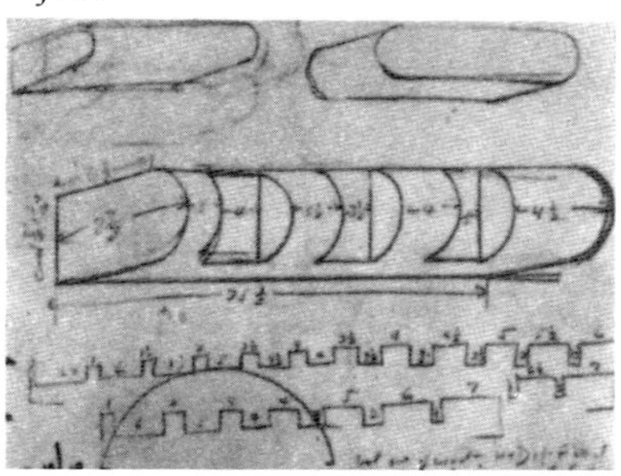

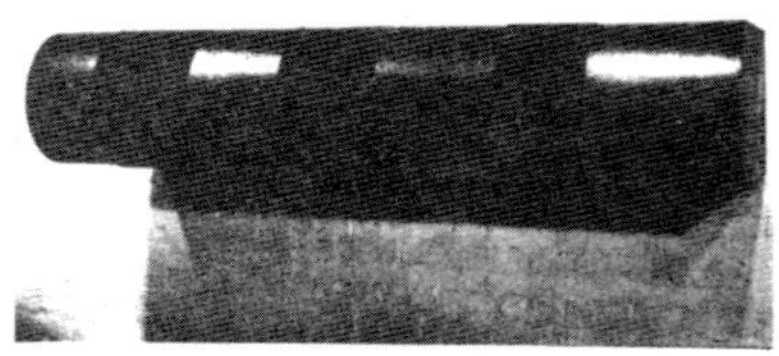

Lewitt

Snelson

A. Jacquet

To present his works, Alain Jacquet has made a triple exhibition: the first at the Galerie Lawrence, the second at the Galerie Rémy Audouoin, and the third at the Galerie "J." Each of these galleries presented a single series, for Alain Jacquet works only in series comprising from twenty to one hundred pictures. He claims to be an industrialist instead of an artist.
Otto Hahn, *Lettre de Paris in Arts International*, p. 43

The Object

The exhibition organized by the Galerie Breteau on the subject of he Object has raised a polemic of sorts. There is much to smile about. The fact that, after having taken its main *reason d'être* from humor, the rt of Dada objects, reviewed and corrected by Pop artists and the New Realists, cannot stand a joke—demands reflection.

The exhibition of the real-fakes at the Galerie Breteau, however, is nerely a question mark. It does not anticipate a particular response or burden itself with a preface. It only raises the question: "Are we going to ome to the point where we consider everything that comes out of a facory or a store to be the manifestation of the genius of an artist who has not laid a hand on it? Are we going to be able to look at a box of camembert, a beer bottle, or a bottle rack with the eyes of a mere consumer?

Of the selected objects (with the exception of the posters), we note hey have two authors: the one who designed it for its industrial use and the one who chose it in the name of wit.

We will also note that these objects have two prices: a discount or hardware store price and a collector's price. The collector's price is drawn from the sophism that brings it into being in the world of art: by choosing a trade object, the artist restores art to a more popular and ocial life. At a distance of forty years we can measure the difference of quality marked by the baptism of Pop. Dada did not base itself on any values in order to give itself weight, it was itself a new standard of nihilism in art. We may blush at having given the name "popular" to a regular means of cashing in on the foolishness of art lovers and the ndustrialization of contempt for the common. Here we are not fighting against the stupidity of the world, we are exploiting it.

One must recognize that if Duchamp's giving the green light to Rauschenberg and his friends may have ruined his reputation, it nonetheless let him pull off the best coup of his career: to open wide the doors of stupidity and destroy in a few years all the good that America may have contributed in the realm of painting. Otto Hahn, who finds the exhibition loathsome, gets himself off the hook by claiming that one could just as well have singled out Malevitch's white square, Tobey's Sumi works, or Pollock's drippings. However, this would mean forgetting the fact that, this time around, industry is at the forefront, that it has made a great many copies of these objects, that it was an industrial draughtsman who designed them and that we are better off naming the author and leaving the things at their price, as long as one does nothing more than take them out of a department store and put them into an art gallery.

It remains to be seen who will pick up the tab for this silly adventure.

Julien Alvard

ON THE OTHER OBJECTS MADE WITHOUT A PROJECT

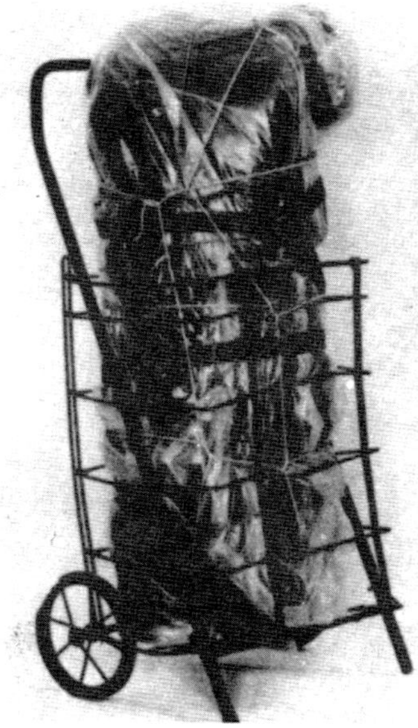

Christo

REALITY WITHOUT ORDER G.C. Argan

Rehabilitation of the Object. Galerie Breteau Photo A. Morain

kienholz

Christo

Oldenburg

Raysse

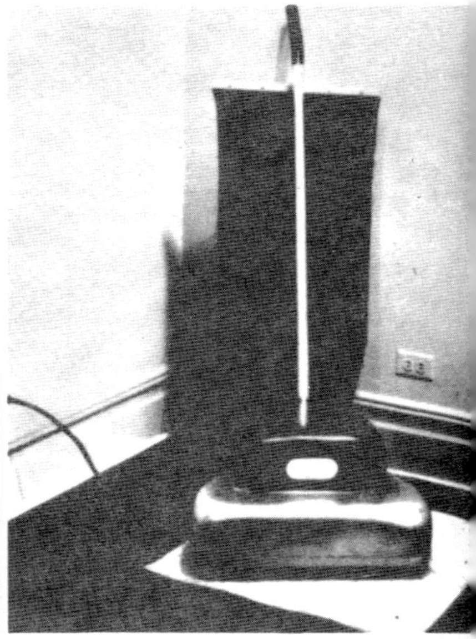

One of the main consequences of the notion of genius is the idea of intellectual property. It di not exist in the Middle Ages, nor did the aspiration to originality, to which it is closely linked. A long as art is oriented solely to representing divinity and the artist is only a means through whicl the eternal and supernatural order of things manifests itself, we can speak neither of the autonom of art, nor of artistic property. It is not difficult to establish relationships between intellectual prop erty and the beginnings of capitalism, but such a connection would be based on an ambiguity. Th idea of intellectual property is a consequence of the decay of Christian civilization. As soon as reli gion no longer dominates and unifies spiritual life, the autonomy of the various forms of spirit arises and therefore also that of art as a form with its own meaning and finality.

Despite all of the later attempts to restore the whole of culture—and thus also art—to the unit of religion, it will no longer be possible to reconstitute the cultural unity of the Middle Ages and t deny completely art's autonomy.

Arnold Hauser, *Social History of Ar*

Warhol

totality and as the site of transaction," Umberto Eco (The Open Work) *was able to introduce psychological, linguistic, and cybernetic findings to the analysis of aesthetic phenomena that aestheticians, until now, had barely used or used badly.*

As for finding out whether architecture—and on top of everything, urbanism—has an aesthetic purpose or only a supplemental aesthetic value, see the Michelin Guide.

R.L.

César

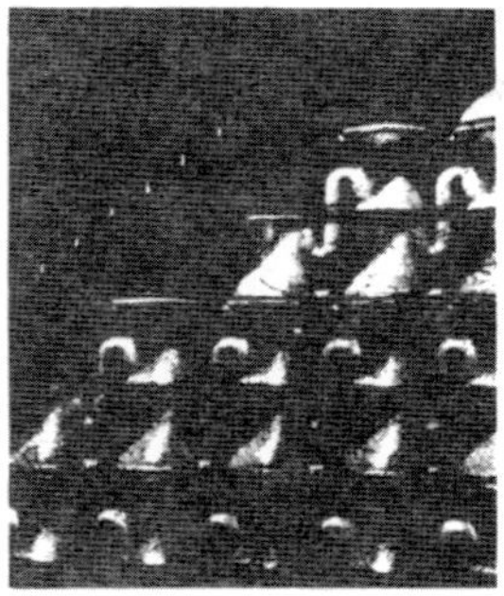

Arman

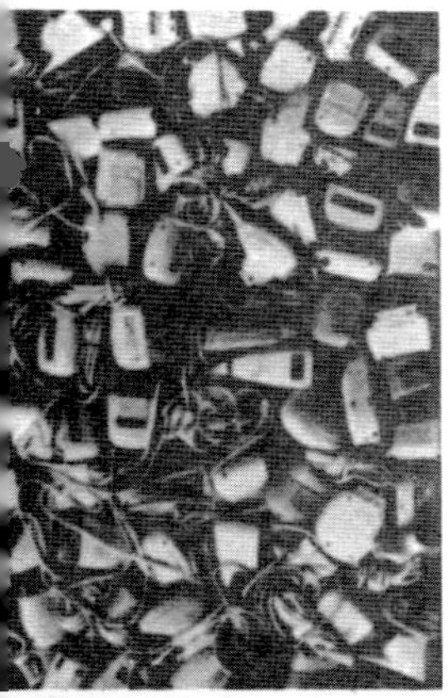

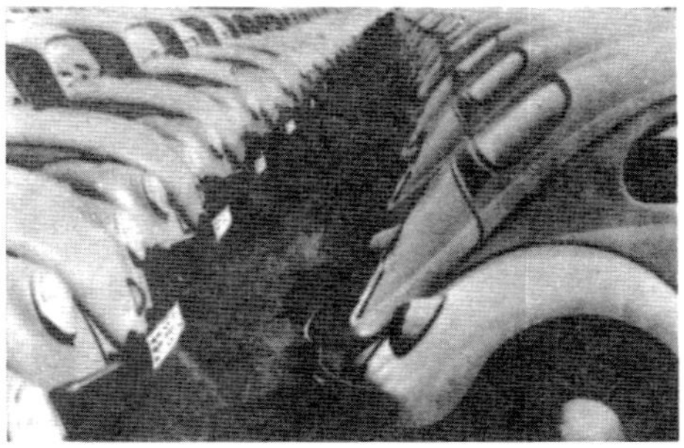

Segal

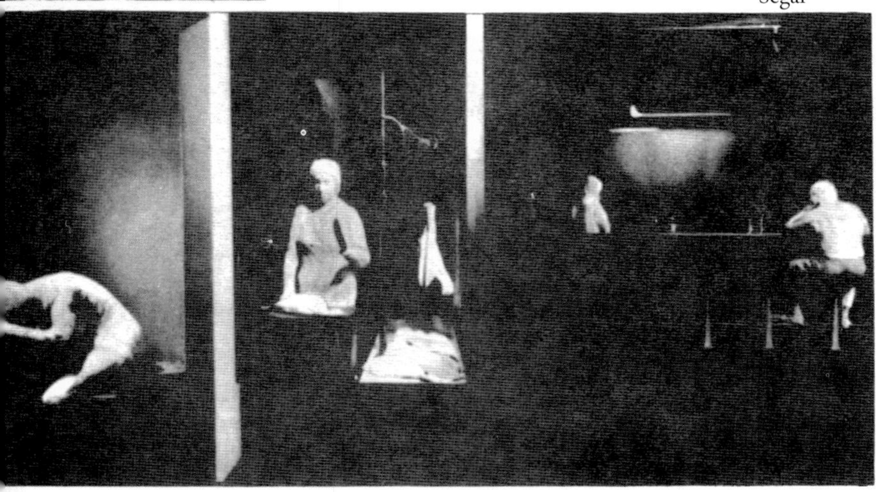

To participate in this social life by supplying the "art market" and the general race to consumption which generalizes itself by an "artistic" production of shock effects as ephemeral as industrial production—is this any solution?

Often, these ephemeral ideas, displaced to where they are presented to us—by mistake, weakness or calculation—are cruelly lacking in all those creations whose context is urban, the site of their birth, where their ephemeral aspect would find the ideal context for its unfolding.

The art of the Quattrocento could still, even if it was misunderstood, interest broader groups: the poor and the uneducated could be attracted to it even if not especially for aesthetic reasons. The masses no longer have a relationship to the new art. What meaning would Raphael's School of Athens or Michelangelo's Sybils have had for them even if they had happened to see them?

Arnold Hauser, *Social History of Art*

WHY ARE THEY INDIFFERENT?

The Dutch Peter Stuyvesant Foundation, which had presented the exhibition "The Museum in the Factory" at the Musée des Arts Décoratifs, has just opened this same exhibition at the Palace of Fine-Arts in Brussels. On the day of the inauguration, the Minister of Culture, Mr. Wigny, personally recommended industrial patronage and invited the major Belgian companies to follow the example of the Foundation. As it was, 70% of the visitors were directors of companies and the Federation of Belgian Industry asked that guided tours be [...]

This worker, formerly intimidated by galleries and museums, by the lack of resemblance between modern works and ordinary reality, today looks at these works with curiosity and sympathy.

He even buys the works of the artists that he has learned to like (lithographs, works on paper, reproductions). To permit these purchases, the administration of Peter Stuyvesant *has established a loan system that permits the worker to buy a work acquired by the factory and pay for it gradually through their monthly salary.*

La Galerie des arts

The expansion

Full employment

The pulverization of the social practices and the persistence of the myths of the nineteenth century maintain a confusion regarding the function of art in its traditional forms. Not only that, but the aesthetic quality of industrial forms and the complexity taken by industrial production in general since the institution of an ideology of consumption, force us to undertake a systematic study of art, of its relationships with technics and industry, in view of finding a possible methodological approach. Apart from the work of Etienne Souriau and Pierre Francastel, these theoretical problems do not seem to have interested many people in France. As for the public, it is poorly informed and still disturbed by the existence of institutions like the Ecole des Beaux-Arts, the Ecoles des Arts Décoratifs and the Ecoles des Ponts et Chaussées—the cumbersome materialization of these myths around which discussions about art are still bogged down.

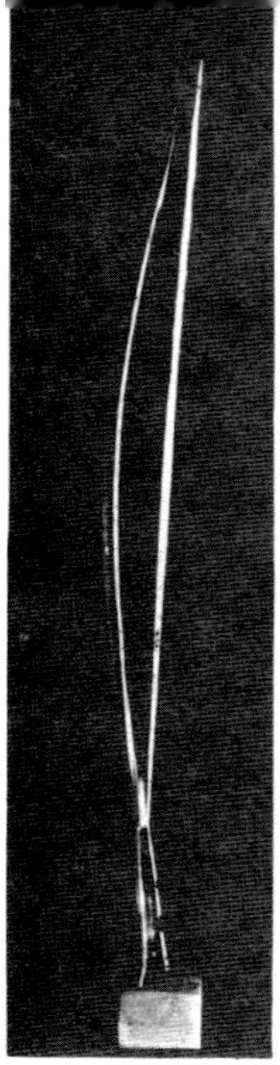

At its heyday, craftsmanship placed the unique and non-reproducible piece (the work of art) at the top of its scale of values, letting the highest quality coincide with the least quantity. Industry, on the contrary, puts the series at the top of its value scale: the object can be repeated in thousands of copies without losing its quality; far from it, its value consists precisely in its ability to be reproducible and infinitely reproduced.

The change of values in the order of production corresponds to a change in the values of the social order: value passes from industry to the series of individuals and, not from society as a system of differentiated human activities, but to the mass that eclipses the individual, or considers him only as a unit in a series. Quantity takes the place of quality in the hierarchy of values.

G.C. Argan, *Progetto e Destino*

A ce jour, plus de 100 millions d'appareils à manivelle sont sortis des usines d'Alençon.

Colombo

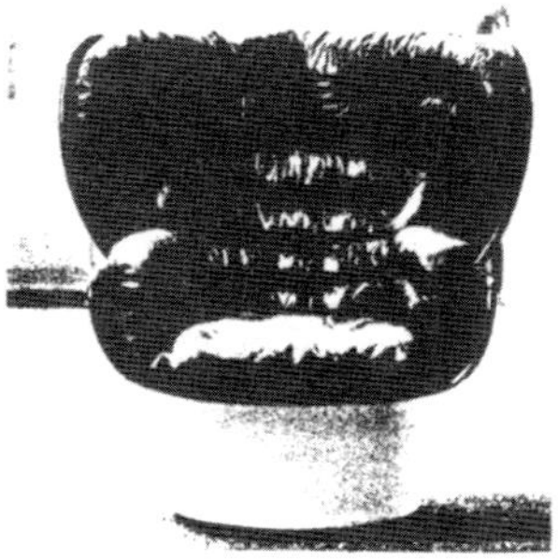

Loevy

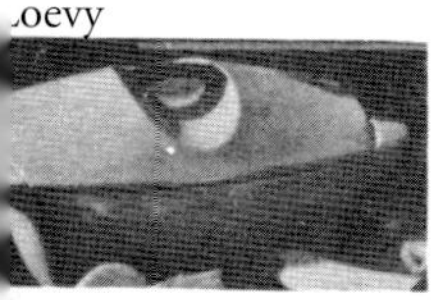

FORGETTING THE FINALITY OF THE OBJECT?
VOLUNTARY ADVERTISING THEME

NEW FORMULATION OF THE EPHEMERAL?

Oldenburg

Caravaggio painting

Composition

Color

Michelangelo sketch

Drawing

wheel turning

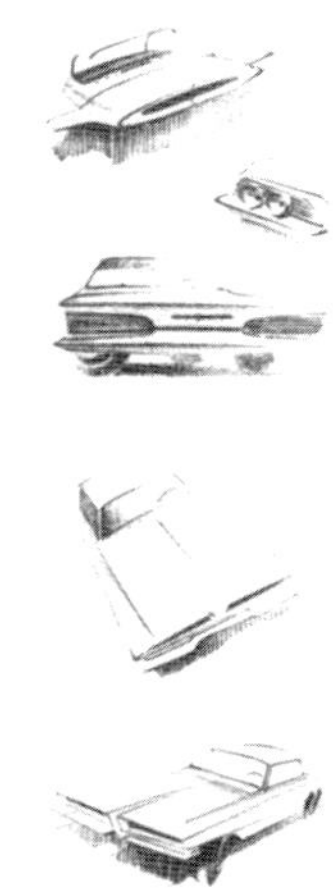

metal in pencil

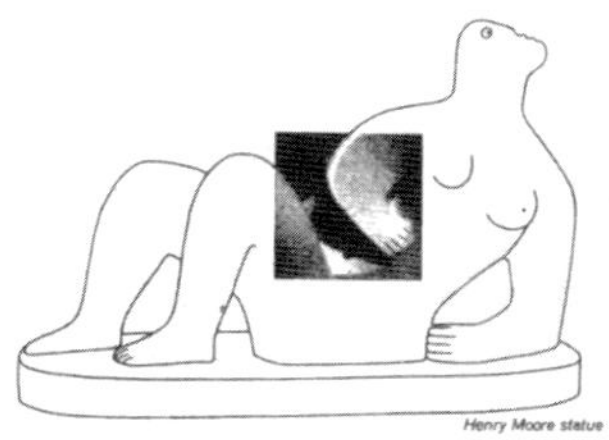

Henry Moore statue

Sculpture... and motion

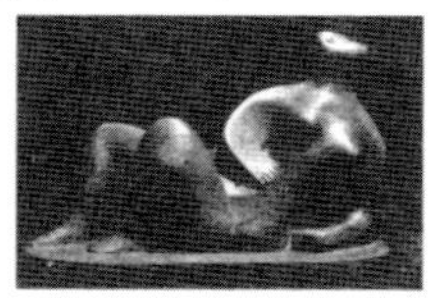

In sculpture, composition and drawing are expanded into three dimensions. The student found it to be the art form most closely related to industrial design. Modeling in clay helps determine mass, balance and proportion in a design to be viewed from many angles. Like the sculptor, the stylist uses light and shadow. Unlike the sculptor, he must visualize a "fourth dimension"—movement. The statue expresses strength in repose, the car power in motion.

1964 Thunderbird

Not only can we not imagine ourselves returning to a craft type of production as Ruskin and Morris would have wanted, but we cannot even imagine that, faced with the complexity of the economic world—a complexity that responds in fact to the complexity of our needs—each of the thousands of choices that we have to make each day is a rational choice; that is, a choice based on an analytic procedure that would require such a mass of scientific knowledge that it would paralyze all other kinds of activity.

The problem becomes concrete in the question: what kind of message, what kind of communication is transmitted, entrusted by each object.

G.C. Argan, *Progetto e Destino*

As long as art is considered a reflection of a real but eternal world or as a generator of illusions, it will be impossible to reconcile practical activities with contemporary art. The world's industrial aesthetics will merely attempt to superimpose borrowed elements onto forms derived from technological rationalism.

Pierre Francastel, *Art and Technology*

Mourque

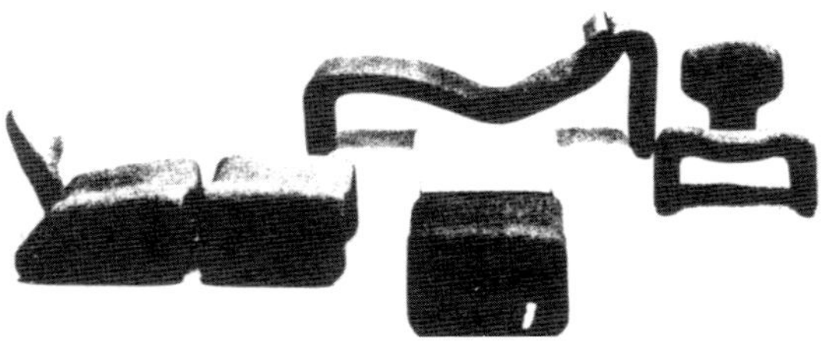

ANOTHER KIND OF IMMEDIATE IMPACT

Rietveld

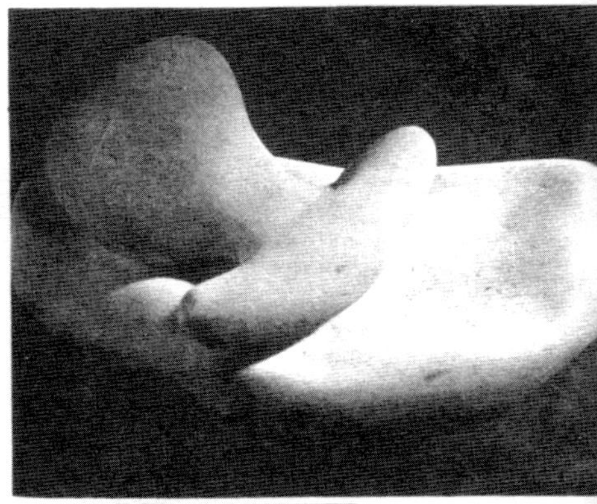

Arp

Mangiarotti

A UNITY THAT IS ONLY FORMAL

Mondrian

Boile

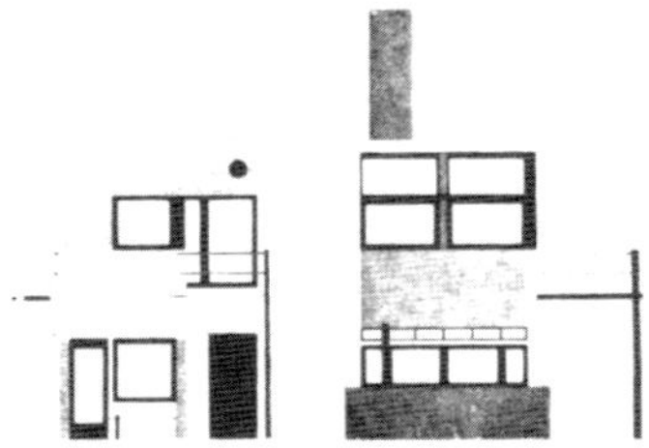

UNAVOIDABLE EXPERIENCES

Couelle

POSSIBILITIES? OR TECHNICAL OPPORTUNITIES?

Mathieu

Mies van der Rohe

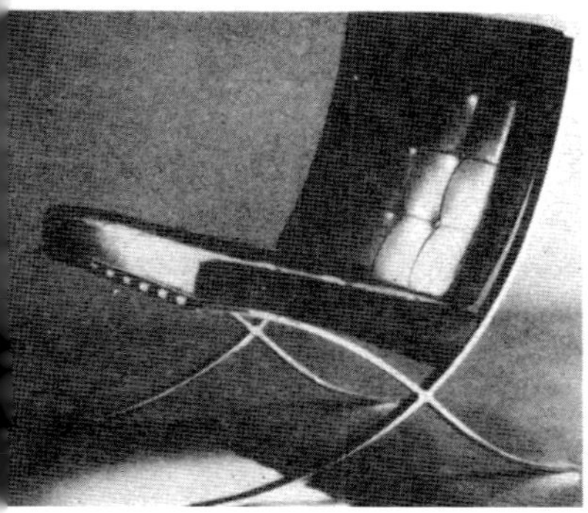

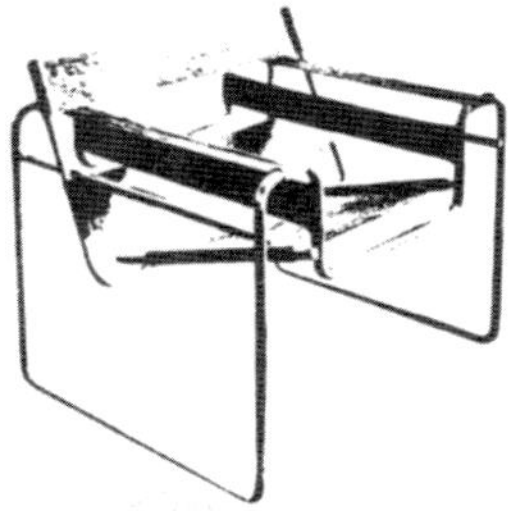

Le Corbusier

Breuer

OBJECTS

WITH LESS IMMEDIATE EFFECTS

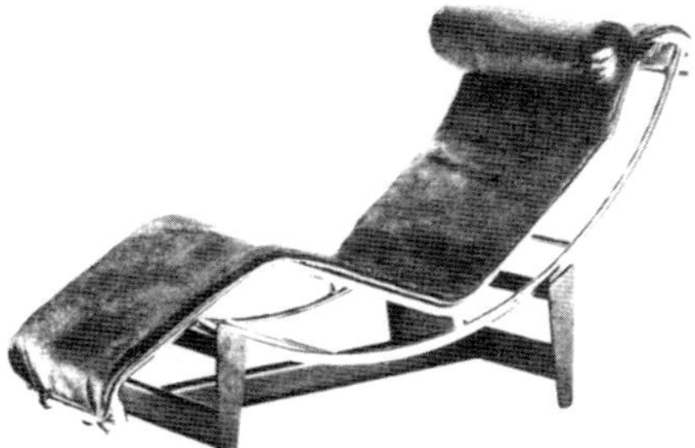

SYNTHESIS PRODUCED BY A MORE COMPLEX RESEARCH

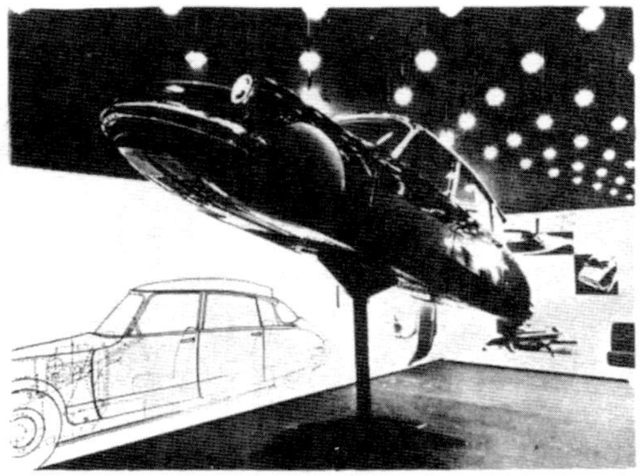

THONET 1859

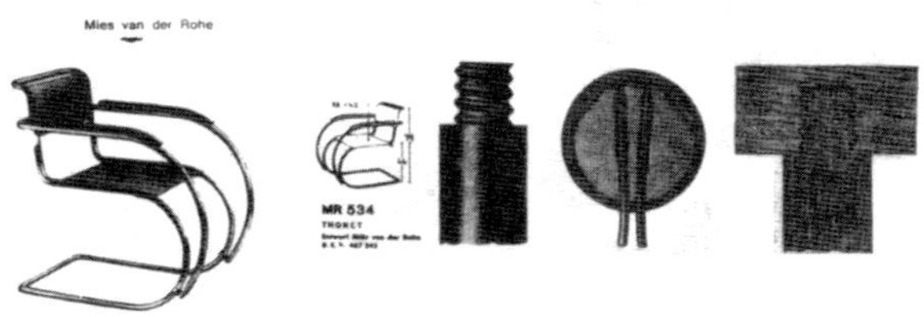

20, 000, 000 UNITS SOLD IN 20 YEARS

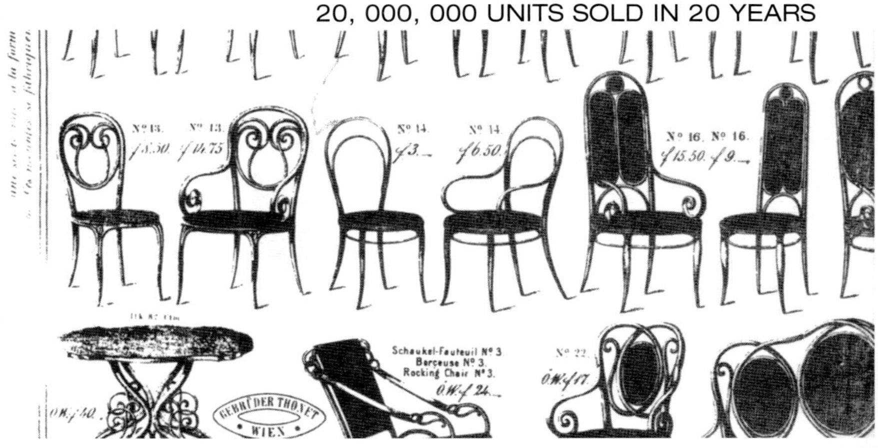

If, during the Middle Ages, the Renaissance and the seventeenth century, there was a remarkable unity between the most modest and humble works, it was because the models were created by men who belonged to art and not to industry. Not all great artists are capable of translating the formulas of their imagination into utilitarian objects; a solution has to be found. But the style of a period can exist only via the encounter between the technicians of material tasks and the technicians of style, who are not popularizers, but artists. Neither the engineers, nor the psychologists will reestablish the connection between art and the world of manufactured objects. The various movements of industrial aesthetics will soon exhaust themselves if they do not strive to initiate real artists with a modern spirit—instead of industrialists—into the problems raised by the production of the objects of today's world.

Pierre Francastel, *Art and Technology*

"...of this present industrial style, the rejection of supplemental ornamentation, the indefinite repetition of a rigorously rational and standardized type, are less inherent in the basic canons of industrial aesthetics than one might believe and than is often said today.

"The reproduction of the standard model... this is certainly a fact of our times against which the future will react."

"It is even probable that industrial progress itself will soon take a new leap, reintroducing into the concrete possibilities of ongoing production some of the aesthetic advantages that often belonged to craftsmanship, a much greater factor of variety, perhaps even an individualization of the products: probably by using the almost infinite resources of combination.

And we may boldly predict that, soon, a large number of production machines will be equipped with this type of variation control, which will give the unit the idea of a serial production in which the model may nevertheless be subject to any number of variations, even to the point of industrialization.

And this of course implies the idea of quasi-artistic manufacturers, great specialists in productive inventiveness, having at their disposal, thanks to this new industrial progress, the means for a sort of personal improvisation during the process of execution itself."

Written in 1951 by Etienne Souriau,
excerpt from the special issue of *Edilizia* on Design.

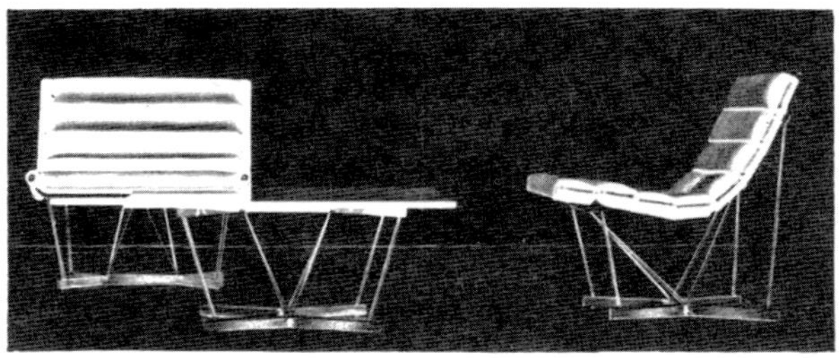

Nelson

Thon

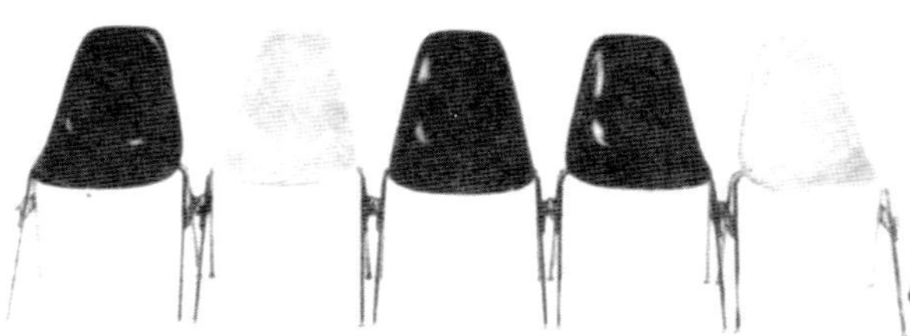

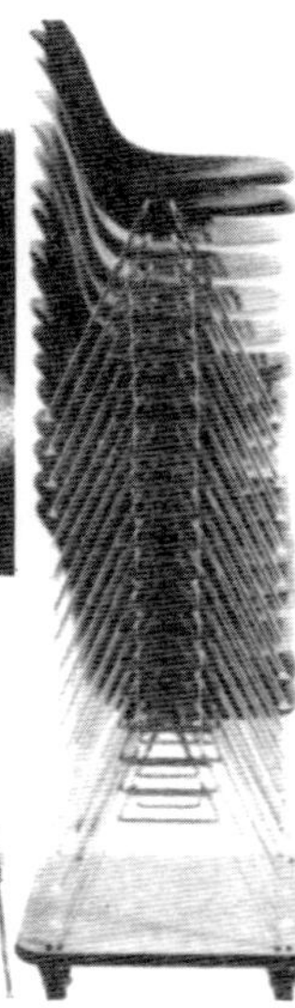

C. Eames

It is difficult to speak of the problem raised by technics and industrialization in architecture or urbanism. The problem, abstracted from the object and its mobile, ephemeral aspect, presents itself completely upside down. How can it be that, despite the techniques at our disposal and our very fine architectural successes, in this domain we remain at the stage of coarse constructions and distant prospects.

It is difficult to speak of the city, of housing projects, of new towns. The problem is another, much vaster one, linked to the streets of the old metropolises and to all of the felt, moving and ephemeral elements that furnish them.

Dialectical Utopia

We want to situate ourselves in the uncrossed interval between theory and praxis. Praxis (conservative) situates itself in the existing order. Grasping the urban totality and all of its contradictions; apprehending every possibility. The social possibilities are presented and remain to be created—in the sense of made to appear; the urban contains and confines them; it is essentially a question of freeing them and putting their revolutionary potentiality into play.

The existing order is a topos. *Criticism and analysis of this topos permits the elaboration of* utopia; *the definition and situation of utopia, the criticism of* utopia *and the updating of its means of realization (philosophical, political, economic…).*

UTOPIA *has two fields of possible realization. 1. Existing power, whatever it is, assimilates the means, the criticisms, and*

the project of utopia, *therefore, in a certain measure, its goals, by rejecting them. But, if there had not been a fundamental modification of the existing order, a share of utopia nevertheless passed into reactionary praxis. 2. The revolution that destroyed the topos theoretically permitted a total realization of* utopia, *which becomes a (revolutionary)* topos. *In advance, one cannot determine what will constitute the revolutionary praxis of this topos and what will remain theoretical and reintegrated in theory.*

The realized utopia *is a new* topos, *which will provoke a new critique, then a new utopia. The installation of utopia passes through a (total) urbanism.*

And that is the complete process.

Topos (conservative)—critique/utopia/revolution—urbanism/ topos (revolutionary and conservative)/new utopia… etc.

We call that DIALECTICAL UTOPIA.

Utopia *is the phase of theoretical construction, but it is absolutely indissociable from the other phases and can only exist as part of* dialectical utopia. *It is only through dialectical utopia that we can elaborate, outside and within the present system, an urban thought.*

(To be continued)

Repression

For Cleaner Streets: The "Anti-Beatnik" Operation

Once again this year, the center of Paris has had to play host to the *Beatniks*. This term refers to individuals whose hairstyle gives no indication as to their gender, whose common trait is a filth upon which they confer a philosophical meaning, who live from more or less obvious begging, *and who, in any event, crowd certain streets which they consider to be their territory.*

garde.
erde.
trav
votre
aide d'un crayon
ABC
votre
crayon
texte
votre
convenablement.
Placez
de
Retirez
feuille
feuille
feuille
lettre
papier
(préférence)
Symboles & Lettres
noir
2
un noir
REALITE
EN NOIR & EN BL

Some of them strum guitars, some make chalk drawings on the sidewalk, others spend most of their time just hanging around. This year this fauna was concentrated in the Rue de la Huchette, probably because the nearby quais along the Seine provided shelter for the night.

The Municipal Police dealt with this problem in two ways.

Starting July 17, a constant police presence was maintained in the Saint-Séverin quarter, and especially in the Rue de la Huchette. The peace officers prevented *loiterers from settling down in the street*. The police presence was usually enough to preserve this very touristic area's *normal appearance*.

In addition to this, the police conducted daily *sweeps*, in the morning and often in the evening.

Between the 17th and 31st of July, 377 loiterers (French citizens and foreigners) were taken to police headquarters for questioning, of which 139 were taken into the custody: 88 foreigners (including 12 minors) and 51 French citizens (including 3 minors) on various grounds, mostly because of "*vagrancy*" and "illegal immigration."

From the 1st to the 25th of August, 582 loiterers were taken to police headquarters, 84 of which were taken into the custody: 49 foreigners (including 3 minors) and 35 French citizens (including 2 minors).

In all, 959 neo-clochards were taken to police headquarters for questioning, of which 223 were taken into custody, for the greater improvement of the neighborhood.

After routine checks were conducted, and *if they could not be charged with any further infraction*, the police officers made them understand the *unacceptability of their behavior*: Most of the foreigners confronted in this manner took the advice to heart and were not seen in the area again. Others, unfortunately, took no account of this warning whatsoever and persisted in living in their filth…

In *Liaisons: bulletin d'information de la Préfecture de Police*, no. 97, 6 September 1966, 7–8.

The increase in population and urban congestion, both aggravated by long-standing neglect on the part of the public authorities, have made urban planning a necessity. Is it any wonder that, in the name of philosophical principles, certain voices express concern, while others deplore the architectural style of the "*grands ensembles*" (housing projects) and regret that man no longer has any choice between collective and individual housing? It is not astonishing, as such controversies are completely normal in the context of our civilization of dialogue, to cite a phrase coined by Gabriel Marcel.

Yet both those who deplore architectural trends and those who approve of this planning agree in their desire to see the creation, enforcement, and affirmation of "humanism in urbanism." Phonetically, the formulation is not very good, but it does express a need; perhaps that of trying to foresee the "man of the year 2000." What will this man be like? What will he do? What will he eat? What will his work rhythm be like? How will he move around? etc... The new housing conditions call for that "supplement of the soul" that Bergson wanted to see in technics. Can urbanism bring it to urbanization?

This problem concerns us directly. The police cannot afford *not* to be interested in any of the factors that contribute to the creation of the "self" and the elaboration of behavior. The placing of man in his lodgings, the placement of the lodgings in a housing development, of this development in the city, of the city into a territory and into a civilization... these problems have a human side for us, for it is on them to a large extent that the degree of asocial disturbances that the police must prevent or repress depends.

ibid., no. 112, February 1966, p. 2

For the protection of youth: the beach experiment

Minors advised by the Police Department are perfectly integrated into the group and nothing is heard of them anymore—at least as long as they are kept busy.

The idle are tempted by the activities and games proposed, and adolescents lacking in financial resources may benefit free of charge from pleasures that they otherwise would not have been able to enjoy.

In 1963, 3,000 adolescents, of which 163 were "disturbed," were able to fill their free time in summer.

It may be asked whether a police initiative of this kind will solve all the remaining problems.

But there will always be a deficit. However successful it may be and however many participants it attracts, the project will always be shunned by some whom we would like to win over.

Participation can only be made on a voluntary basis, a decision made of one's own free will. The minors presented by the

Police Department are not forcefully detained: only those who want to will stay.

Nevertheless, the severity of the admonition, the intimidation and, to a certain extent, the fear of police intervention, lead some to play along and participate in the activities of groups into which they have been forced in a way.

Others, having benefited from the help of the police, for example having found a job for the season, are less afraid and more easily persuaded.

Finally, we can only hope that the efforts will not have been in vain; the youth taking the lead, bring in those who are recalcitrant.

All demonstrations of good will are welcome but, here, more than elsewhere, they are desirable. The ideal would be if these

DE BIJENKORF
Catalogue
la feuille de garde.
le plaisir
Frottez
PARIS
sans fatigue,
des vitres claires !
Placez
un format
production

COMMENT
TRANSFORMER
LA MODE
65 ▶
EN
◀ 66
facile
ABC
CHAINE MAGIQUE
A la fin de cette manifes
tion, les personnalités ont qu
la cour sous les huées.
issez
PURE LAINE VIERGE
ces combinés sont en vente
LA PEUR DU SILENCE
Nouveau !
JEUNESSE. bombe
a raconté la semaine dernière que la
police avait mis son nez dans le spec-
tacle de Marc'O, sous prétexte qu'on
y voit, bénissant les yéyés, un
archevêque et une religieuse. En
notant que ces personnages font du
tort au spectacle de Marc'O, ce journal
rance a présen
es gosses et u
e et plus qu'
homme et u
DECOUVREZ COMM
VIVENT LES VILLE
INVENTEES
ville
REALITE
oui
non
UNE FEUILLE DE PAIE DE CHEZ W.
Salaire brut total : 601,51.
Retenues mensuelles totales : 547,82.
Ancien arriéré : 364,55.
Net à payer : rien.
Nouvel arriéré : 310,86.
La lutte des classes?
A Cannes,
facile
a
MANIPULER
politique
Briser la parole

projects were to multiply, to the point that no young people would be left to themselves: all would be occupied and accompanied.

But the vastness and complexity of this task shows that nothing should be undertaken lightly.

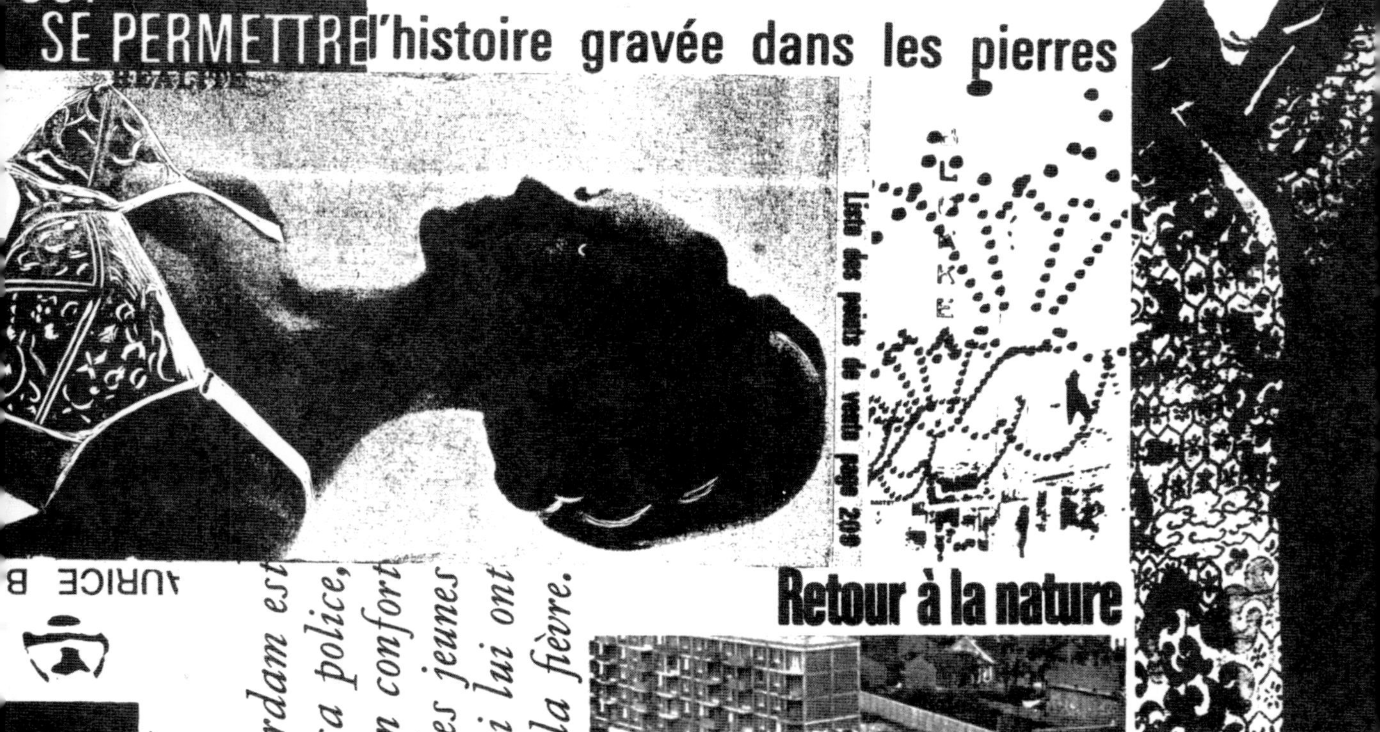

It is essential that there be as much participation as possible and that this participation also involve teachers and educators.

It is also important that the active members be especially competent.

All the municipal police officers involved during the summer, previously informed and equipped by their professional experience, were prepared for their task by a training program stressing the basics of psychology, sociology and education suitable for the child.

ibid., May 10, 1966, p. 4

obsolescence

The ephemeral **The durable**

becoming outdated

considerations on the obsolescence of the "built" within the city

essay in eight tableaux, an explanation and a finale

Materiality is composed of objects, of things; objects as material beings have an existence, a life span. They are born at the moment of their manufacture, they live, are worn down through service, allow themselves to be used, and then expire when they become useless. We may speak of the life of an object and call it *obsolescence*. The obsolescence of an automobile today is 4 to 5 years, the obsolescence of a paper dress is only a few hours.

tableau 1

1967

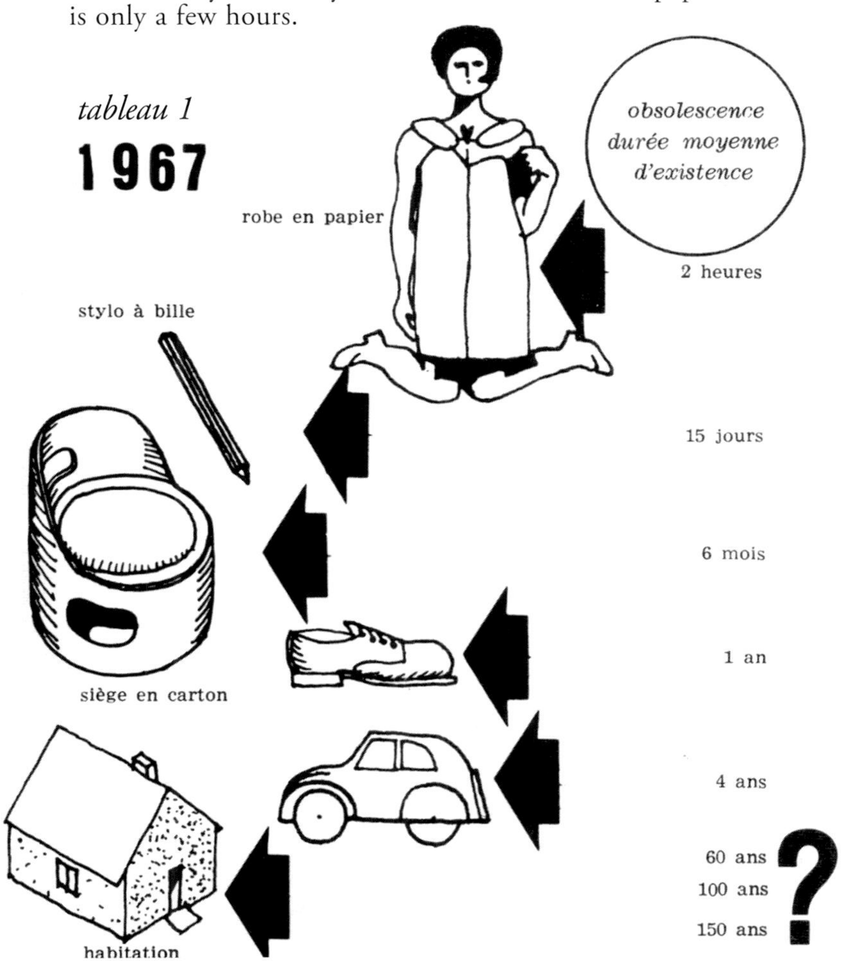

Latin
obsolesco, es, er, etum, vb.:
go out of use

English
obsolescence:
1. tendency to become out of date
2. Biol.: tendency to atrophy, vanish

French
obsolète adj. (Latin obsoletus, from solere, being accustomed):
hors d'usage, mot obsolète

The proprietary nature of a dwelling—other than in the case of boatsmen and nomads—is not the only specific character of this good, next to its high cost. Housing is a possession that traditionally is built and consumed slowly... But the traditional house, so slow to build, will shelter four or five generations, and be used by three or four more. The period of inhabitation for houses is such that the standard of housing of a population is always behind what it could be. The airplanes and electric razors of a country should not be older than five years. In Europe, however, an average age of 45 years is considered quite normal for its buildings. The time needed for the construction and use of housing is surprising in our time. It probably puzzles our contemporaries and dissuades them from making such a long-term investment, in comparison with other investments made in our industrial civilization.

J.E. Havel
Habitat et logement
Que sais-je, P.U.F.

tableau 2

années

1900

1930

1960

while the obsolescence of many objects that we use daily tends to diminish, the duration of existence of the "built" remains practically indefinite.

Obsolescence

?

Architects grant that we build for at least 50 years.

inside view

aerial view

installation setting up a piece of a cylindrical structure

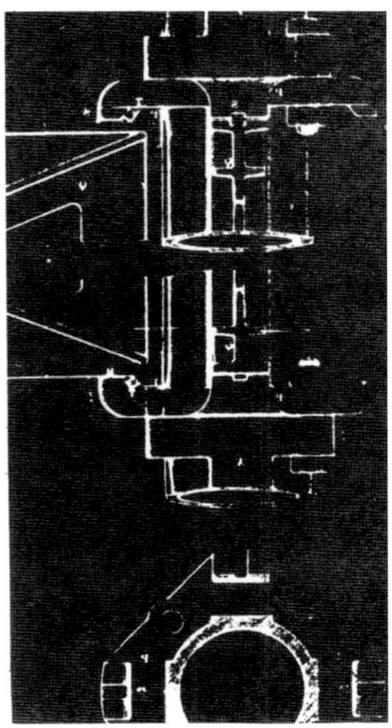

construction: detail of the butt-end of a joist

tableau 3

A construction that can be disassembled, and that is consequently ephemeral. Its obsolescence can be defined.

history of the Crystal Palace

On the occasion of the Great Exhibition of London (1851), an international contest for architects and builders was launched for an exhibition hall.

Joseph Paxton's project was accepted, although he had not participated in the competition: a hall built entirely of prefabricated elements that can be reused after being disassembled. In fact, the Crystal Palace was disassembled after the International Fair in London and reassembled at Sydenham, where it stood until its accidental destruction by fire in 1937.

objects, objects, objects,

objects, objects, objects,

Explanation: becoming outdated

1. *Obsolescence of the "built"*

It is not our purpose to speculate on the future of urban space in general. We are looking at urban space from the particular angle of the duration of existence of the material objects that compose it.

Traditionally, the value of duration is attached to building. This quality is linked to *durability* at least as much as to the service rendered or to the aesthetic value, although this notion of durability is not quantitatively defined. Good construction is solid and durable. On the other hand, the "*ephemeral*" is imposing itself in our everyday lives in the form of objects whose existence is of limited duration (ballpoint pens, paper clothes, cars, etc.). The use of these ephemeral objects does not raise any particular problem; we throw them away when they are no longer useful.

From there to thinking that the objects that constitute the space in which we live, the containers of our everyday activities, the elements of our environment, could also become ephemeral takes but a step, although a considerable one. It might be worth taking if we intend to awaken the "built" and its techniques from their torpor and their ambiguous status in the industrial economy.

Let us try to define this question more clearly. We will consider the following simplified scheme: on the one hand, a social practice, and on the other, the materiality in which this social practice is inscribed.

Social practice, a Brownian motion, constantly changing, subject to fluctuations, cycles, fashions, perpetual modifications, from the most common actions of everyday life to the most abstract philosophical reflections: this social practice develops, inscribes itself, and exists in a materiality that also varies, although generally less rapidly. Materiality is discontinuous, it is composed of objects, of things; objects as material beings have an existence, a life span. They are born at the moment of their manufacture, they live, are worn down in yielding a service, allow themselves to be used, then expire when they become useless. We may speak of the life of an object and call it *obsolescence*. The obsolescence of an automobile today is 4 to 5 years, the obsolescence of a paper dress is only a few hours.

The objects that interest us here are those that constitute urban space, in particular constructed space in the strict sense of the word. Their obsolescence, their life expectancy is indeterminate in most cases. The architect does not know how long what he builds is to last. The number of 60 years is put forth, two generations. Yet while the dwellings built of timber frame or rubble fill masonry in the last century or at the end of the eighteenth century still stand quite well today, those built more lightly but more durably today (fire-resistance, safety through the calculation of statics) are in no danger of collapsing within the next 100 years or so. The manufacturing techniques in general use in Europe today (especially for masonry and concrete construction) are much too imprecise to permit a dosage of the necessary and sufficient qualities that each element of the "built" would need, to allow for a planned obsolescence. The precision applied to the analysis and execution of metal constructions should permit the life expectancy of the various parts of the architectural object to be better defined.

Synthetic materials, a characteristics of which is precisely to keep the mechanical, physical and chemical properties intact for a given length of time and then rapidly deteriorate, respond exactly to the possible determination of the obsolescence in question. We said that the obsolescence of the objects constituting urban space was generally undetermined; yet exceptions exist, one of the most interesting being the sporadic appearance of great exhibitions.

Let's now turn to these ephemeral, constructed complexes.

2. *The manifestations of the "ephemeral" in construction between* 1850 *and* 1900.

We will devote a more in-depth study to this subject in a future article; let us briefly note that, between 1850 and 1900, a series of large metal constructions were realized. These were often exhibition halls intended for the various international exhibitions held during the second half of the nineteenth century. These constructions, practically none of which have survived, appear as quite remarkable manifestations of ephemeral architecture. They are situated historically at a moment when the technique of metal construction had attained a degree of perfection it seems subsequently to have lost; and which has

The ephemeral is undoubtedly the truth of our future habitat. Mobile, variable, retractable structures inscribe themselves in the formal demands of architects and in the social and economic demands of modernity. But this is only true in an ideal dimension. One must not lose sight of the fact that:

1. Neither the ephemeral nor the durable are absolute and exclusive values. Only their constant relation, and the multiple play of oppositions between them, founds a logic of cultural significations. One can soften their relationship, loosen it as a function of social rhythms: in this sense everything pushes us strongly toward the accelerated mortality of objects and structures. Meanwhile, these two terms have meaning only relative to one another.

More precisely, if clothes, objects, appliances, and automobiles increasingly obey (but there is a limit threshold) the norms of the ephemeral, nothing says that they do not, taken together, oppose "inhabiting"—which itself constitutes a specific function which could be brutally or ideally assimilated to other aspects of consumption or fashion. Their symbolic schema is that of ventilation and expenditure, the symbolic schema of inhabiting is that of provision and investment. To reduce the two to the same ephemeral synchrony is undoubtedly to liquidate an entire field of very rich contrasts. Lived culture (and thus the logic of sense) only exists through the tension between two such poles.

2. It is true that the social deficit that modular or prefabricated construction, in permanent or durable materials, represents today is colossal. It contradicts economic rationality and social

exchange with the irreversible tendency toward greater social mobility, the loosening of infrastructures, etc. Meanwhile one must account for the latent psychological, familial, and collective functions, of the "durable" and the solid, very powerful functions of integration that also return in the social "budget."

3. The ephemeral will perhaps one day be the collective solution, but for the moment it is the monopoly of a privileged fraction whom its economic and cultural position permits to question the myth of durability.

It is because generations of bourgeois were able to enjoy the permanent and traditional décor of property that certain among them can today grant themselves the luxury of refusing to cut stone and delighting in the ephemeral: the fashion belongs to them. On the other hand, every generation of the lower classes, who had no chance in the past of acceding to the cultural models at the same time as to durable property,—to what does one wish that they aspire if not to live the bourgeois model, and to found in their turn, for themselves and their children, a derisory dynasty in the stone buildings and bungalows of the suburbs—how can one demand of these classes, now "promotable," that they not regard their buildings as sacred and accept outright the ideality of mobile structures? They have vowed to desire that which lasts and only this aspiration can translate the cultural destiny of their class.

Reciprocally, the cult of the ephemeral ideologically connotes the privilege of the avant-garde: according to the eternal logic of cultural distinction, a privileged fraction savors the instantaneousness and the mobility of architectural structures

perhaps not been recovered today, at least in those realizations bogged down in a search for stylistic effects and with unconscious attachments to certain mythologies (such as reinforced concrete).

List of noteworthy constructions

1851 London, Crystal Palace by Joseph Paxton; disassembled and then reassembled at Sydenham Hill, where it was destroyed by fire in 1936.
1855 Paris, Palace of Industry, disassembled in 1900.
1867 Paris, oval exhibition hall (provisional), 1st Gallery of Machines.
1878 Paris, 2nd Gallery of Machines.
1889 Paris, 3rd Gallery of Machines, disassembled in 1910.
Eiffel Tower; ephemeral construction made durable through high maintenance costs.

These are but a few examples, as international exhibitions multiplied throughout the world after 1878: in Sydney in 1879, in Melbourne in 1880, in Amsterdam in 1883, in Antwerp and New Orleans in 1885, in Barcelona, Copenhagen and Brussels in 1888, etc. Each of these exhibitions created a world of temporary constructions, tangible manifestations of ephemeral architecture.

3. *Factoring time into the urban "construct."*

- Since the "built" is not determined in the temporal dimension, it has an ambiguous status in the economy, and thus an unfavorable position relative to investment—whatever political ideology or economic system this investment happens to be associated with.
- The obsolescence of an object does not only depend on simple criteria such as the durability of a material, it is also a function of the general state of the economy and is closely integrated with social practice: a concrete wall may be more ephemeral in New York than a cardboard wall in Paris.
- Now, at a time when the study of cities is making its first steps, it would be highly advantageous to build ephemerally, to allow for mistakes that do not involve too long a future.

- Attached to the notion of *durability* are notions of fixity, finiteness, immobility, invariability, unchangeability, *dependence on a site.*
- Attached to the notion of the *ephemeral* are notions of mobility, adaptability, variability, growth, retraction, independence from a site

at the moment when others accede barely to the quadrature of their walls. Only the privileged classes have the right to the actuality of the models. Others have the right once these models have already changed.

If, therefore, the "ephemeral" represents the truth of modernity in the logic of forms, if even it represents the future formula for a rational and harmonious society, it still takes on an entirely different sense in the present cultural system. In its logical foundation, culture continually plays on the two distinct *terms: the ephemeral and the durable, neither of which can be made autonomous. Whereas in the socio-cultural class system, this relation breaks into two* distinctive *poles, one of which—the ephemeral—becomes autonomous in a culturally superior model, returning the other to its "obsolescence."*

This is not at all to disqualify the formal research of the architect: but there is a bitter derision in the fact that the search for social rationality manages to precisely to reinforce the irrational logic and the strategy of the cultural class system.

J.B.

tableau 4 *ephemeral objects: furniture*

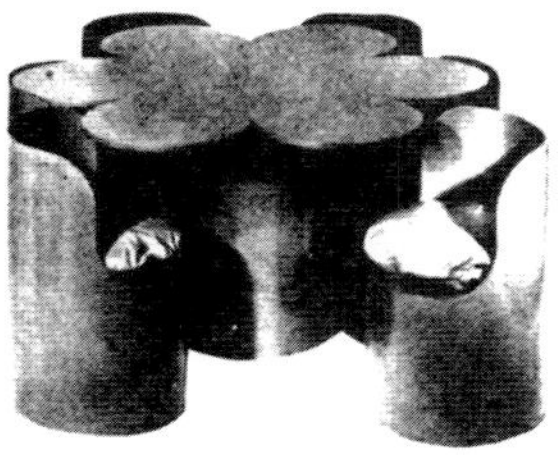

Painted cardboard seats made in London

… the present event is the personality of objects, they come more and more to the fore…

paper dress

La Mode

… *we must invent at all costs.*
The adaptation to fashion is inferior and far from the problem to be solved. I adapt, you adapt, he adapts, this is the elegant formula, the least effort, the seated position. Today's life never adapts, it ceaselessly creates every morning, for better or worse, but it invents.
Fernand Léger

plastic pool with durable wall

éphémère

tableau 5 *ephemeral building objects: shops*

éphémère

…The idea of polychrome cities came to me during WWI, during one of my furloughs. I met Trotsky at Montparnasse. He was very enthusiastic about the idea. He envisioned the possibility of a polychrome Moscow.

If we consider the city as a whole, or a street, or a building in relation to a colored action on the outside, we immediately have many possibilities. For example, the coldness of the floor of a building is offset if color is brought into play; even the volume of the building can be affected …

During the World's Fair of 1937, I thought of using 300,000 unemployed workers to scrape down all the buildings in Paris. The idea was to create an "astonishing event" for the visitors; Paris all white, and at night airplanes and projectors flooding the city with bright, moving colors. Why not? My project was not adopted, although it was the only way to create a new event on the scale of a world's fair.

Fernand Léger
Fonctions de la peinture
éd. Gonthier, Médiations 1965

ephemeral objects: shops getting remodeled, Paris, February 1967

shop in Paris

shop in Paris

ephemeral building objects: emergency housing

emergency housing prototype (sectioning, assembly, and installation of panels) by Buckminster Fuller 1950 U.S.A.

emergency housing by Buckminster Fuller 1958 U.S.A.

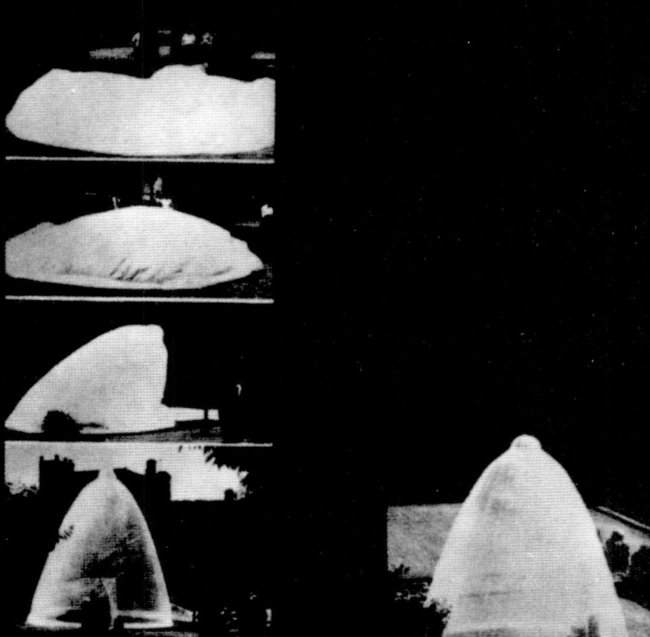

inflatable experimental structure: parabolic dome, height: 7.5 m.; weight: 34 kg. Materials: transparent polythene. Inflation time: 2 minutes. A. Quarmby architect (Great Britain)

… Any space that is really lived in contains the essential idea of a house. We will see in the course of this book how the imagination works in this direction when a being has found the slightest form of shelter: we will see the imagination build "walls" out of impalpable shadows, comfort itself with illusions of protection, or, inversely, tremble behind thick walls, doubting the most solid ramparts. In short, in the most endless of dialectics, the sheltered being sensitizes the limits of his shelter. He experiences the house in its reality and in its virtuality, through his thoughts and dreams.

Gaston Bachelard
The poetics of space
P.U.F. 1964 (pp. 24–25)

ēphēmère

tableau 6 *ephemeral building objects: exhibition halls*

Gallery of Machines. Built for the Universal Exhibition of 1889 in Paris and demolished in 1910.

The Great Wheel: built for the 1900 Universal Exhibition in Paris. Height: 106 m (348 ft.), with 40 cabins that could hold a total of 1,500 passengers.

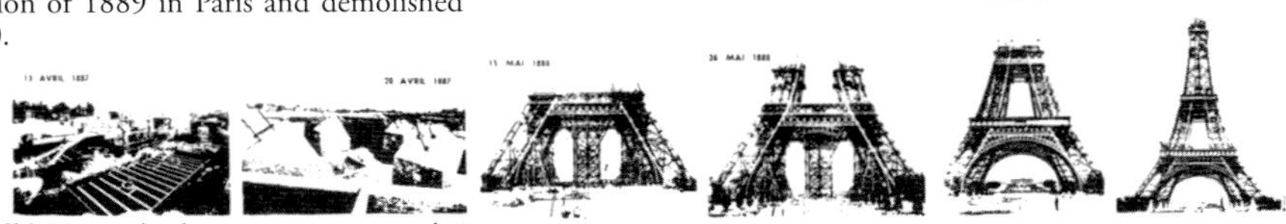

The Eiffel Tower, built in two years and 2 months, turned into a durable monument through high maintenance costs.

Gallery of Machines. Built for the Universal Exhibition of 1889 in Paris.

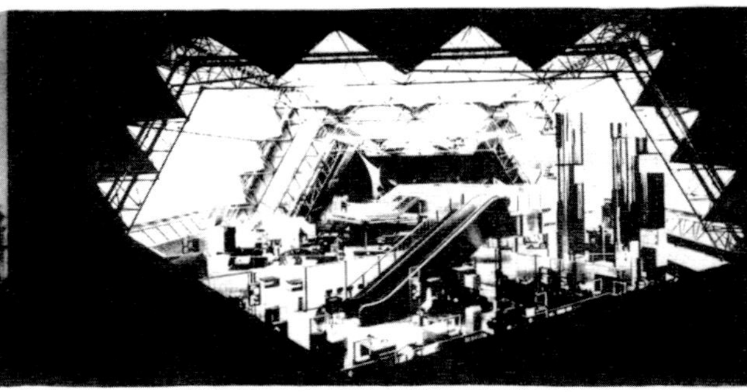

Industry and Crafts Pavilion, Swiss National Exhibition, Lausanne, 1964.

Exhibition structure made of fib reinforced polyester.

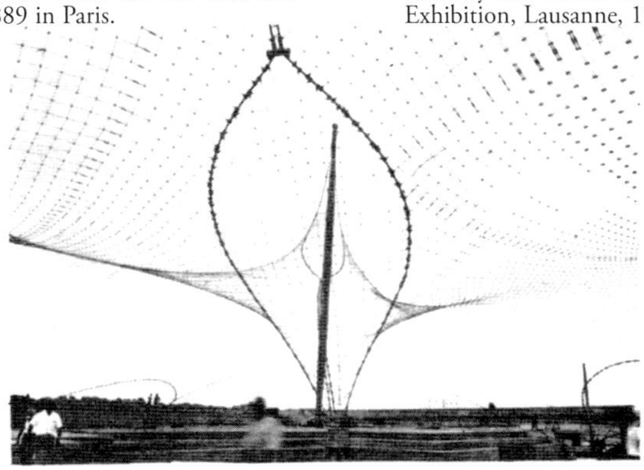

Construction of the pavilion of the German Federal Republic at the Montreal World's Fair in 1967. A suspended net of steel cables (diam. 12 mm., ½ in.) held by 8 steel masts, covering a surface of 8,000 m2 (9,568 sq. yards).

The Port. Swiss National Exhibition, Lausanne, 1964

Universal Exhibition, New York, 1964

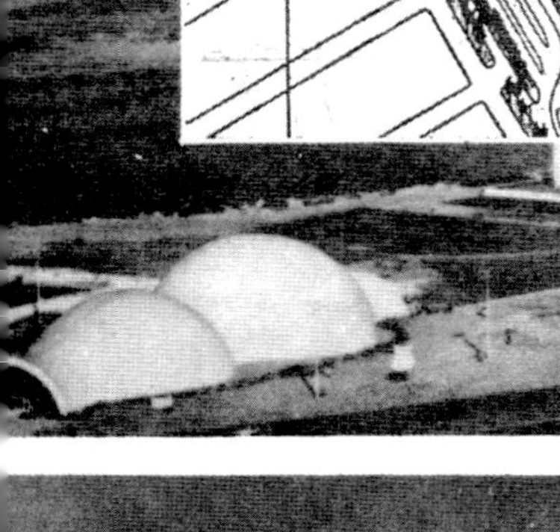

éphémère
demountable, mobile

ibition hall of the U.S. Atomic Energy mmission, Rio de Janeiro, 1962. Architect, tor Lundy.

éphémère

… The structurally controlled life of an "air house" stands in opposition to the life aimed at eternity of the Great Pyramid.

In addition to being architecturally aware of a calculable life, there must be a constructive use of the mobility of ideas, energy, men and matter.

Everyone (except most architects) calls the sociological meaning of the permanent character of the constructions and cities of the past into question …

Cedric Price
Aujourd'hui, no. 50

building-towers with interchangeable housing units, A. Quarmby architect (Great Britain)

Plug-in City

The formation of the plug-in City is based on the use of a large-scale structural network that encloses all the access roads and essential services, and can be built on any kind of terrain, whether already constructed or not. Within this network are units that meet all the needs of the city. These units are planned in relation to their obsolescence (as is the overall structure). They are put into service and replaced by means of cranes that move on rails at the top of the network.

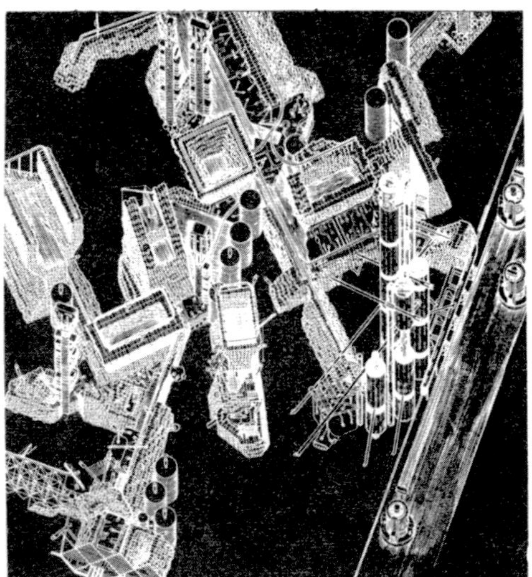

Aerial view of *Plug-in City*, (1964).

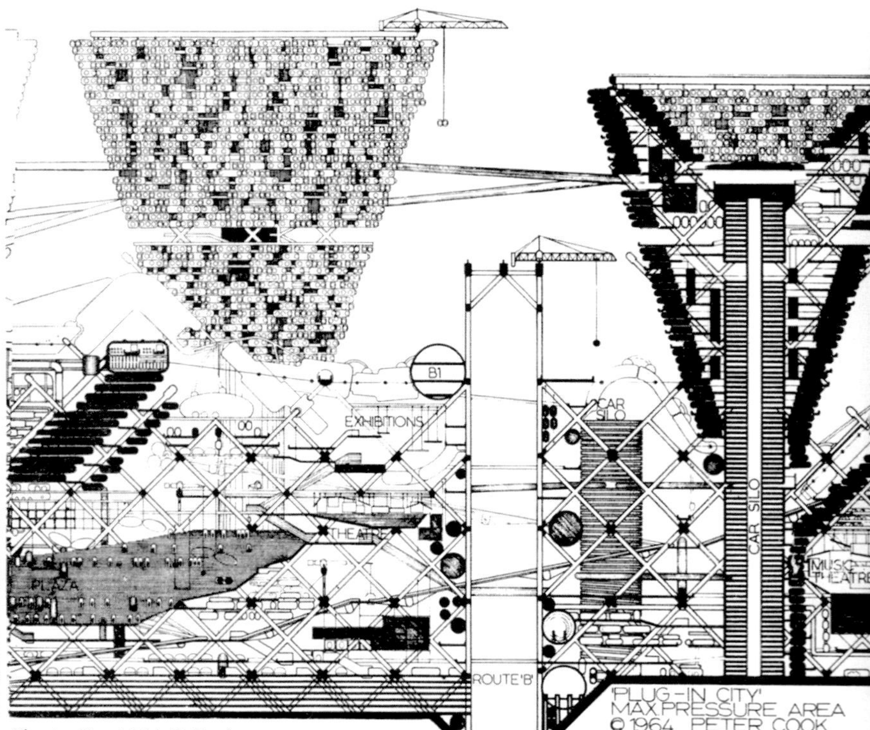

Plug-in City, 1964. P. Cook

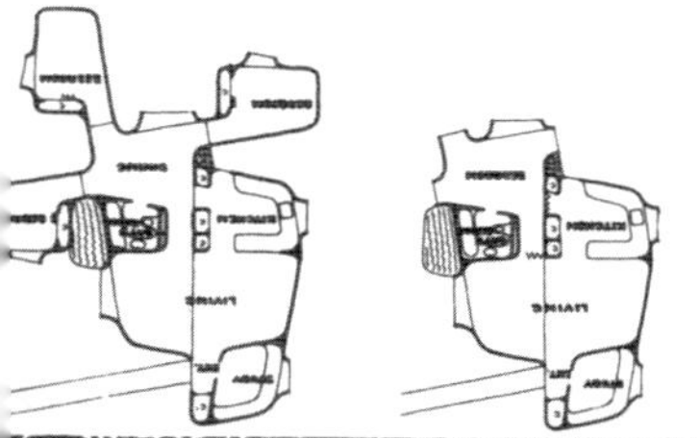

e d'habitation extensible. Unite
: 1 et 3 chambres à coucher

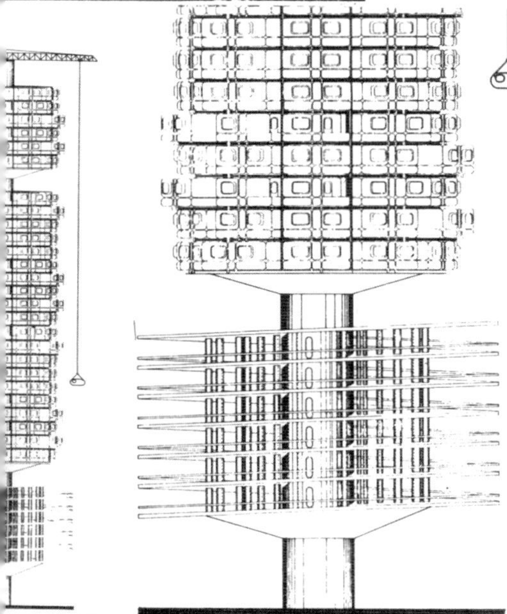

g-in city : tour d'habitations, ou
organisation possible de capsule-
itable Warren Chalk — 1964

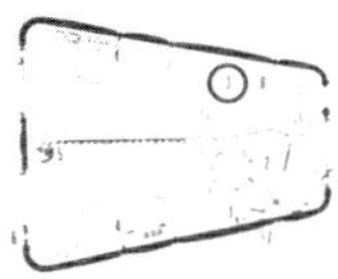

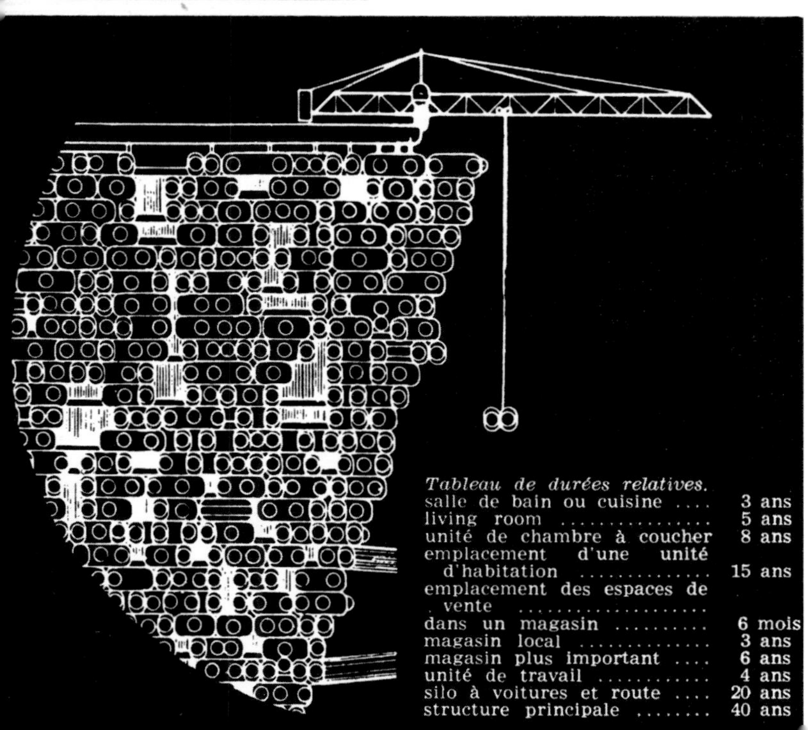

Tableau de durées relatives.

salle de bain ou cuisine	3 ans
living room	5 ans
unité de chambre à coucher	8 ans
emplacement d'une unité d'habitation	15 ans
emplacement des espaces de vente	
dans un magasin	6 mois
magasin local	3 ans
magasin plus important	6 ans
unité de travail	4 ans
silo à voitures et route	20 ans
structure principale	40 ans

...First of all the phenomenon of *formation* in its dual relation to the initial start and the conditions of life, of formation as the implementation of the mysterious impulse to realize an intention.

The phenomenon was already perceptible in the effective activity at its crudest beginnings, when the form began to constitute itself on a small scale (structure). Once observed at the structural level ("cellular," "tissue-like"), this fundamental relationship between formation and form retains its full meaning in later stages precisely because a principle has been recognized in them.

This meaning can be stated as follows: the road to form, whose itinerary must be dictated by some internal or external necessity, takes priority over the ultimate goal, the end of the journey. The slow progression determines the nature of the work accomplished. Formation determines the form and therefore prevails over the latter.

Nowhere and at no time is form the result achieved by finishing, or concluding. It must be seen as a genesis, as movement. Its being is in becoming and the form as appearance is only a malicious apparition, a dangerous phantom.

Form is good as movement, as doing, as form in action. Form is bad as inertia, enclosed in a final stop. Form is the end, death. Formation is life.

This is revealed in the growth of a work that is still in its earliest stages. The later development of this organism would have permitted us to make a second observation:

durable

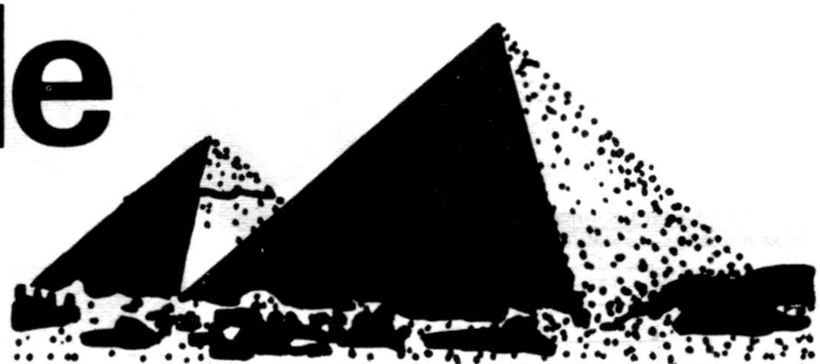

The pyramids of Chefren and Mykerinos, Kings of Dynasty IV.

When the creative journey moved on to wider paths, we realized the drawbacks of a uniform itinerary: how to tolerate a tedious process when the way is the essence of the work?

The way necessarily had to increase in complexity, ramify in exciting ways, climbing and falling, straying off, becoming more precise or unclear, wider or narrower, heavier or lighter …

Paul Klee
Pedagogical Sketchbooks

L'IMMOBILIER
N° 49 ■ DU 5 AU 19 JANVIER 1967

INVENDUS INVENDABLES

Si, comme on le pense, la crise du marché immobilier dure toujours vers 1970, qu'adviendra-t-il d'un certain nombre d'appartements construits en 1965 et 1966 ou actuellement en voie d'être terminés ? En effet, les promoteurs vont sans doute, pour affronter la concurrence, offrir des services meilleurs, des équipements supplémentaires. En ce cas les appartements dont nous parlons risqueraient de se trouver très « démodés » dans quelques années et voir leur valeur baisser considérablement. C'est du moins ce que pensent certains spécialistes.

Yet there is no other way out than to let the ephemeral develop freely, without too many norms or rules other than those of abundance in the immediate. And so the main problem will be: what to do with the buildings built under the regime of durability, these bunkers and vaults that stand like so many unmovable obstacles in the midst of a generous and continuous creation?

We will surely create a Scientific Center for the Demolition of Buildings that will devote itself to the task of rendering them ephemeral …

D.G. Emmerich
Obstacles immuables, Melp 2

Essay for a Total City, J.-C. Bernard, architect.

The *Maison de la Radio,* Paris, H. Bernard Architect.

Endo Laboratories, Garden City, Long Island, Paul Rudolph architect, U.S.A.

Harvard School of Education, 1965.

Demolition of the Montparnasse station, Paris, 1967.

The long and difficult demolition of edifices built for eternity.

Yale School of Architecture, New Haven, U.S.A. Paul Rudolph architect.

Chichester Theological College, U.K., 1965

Endo Laboratories, Garden City, Long Island, Paul Rudolph architect, U.S.A.

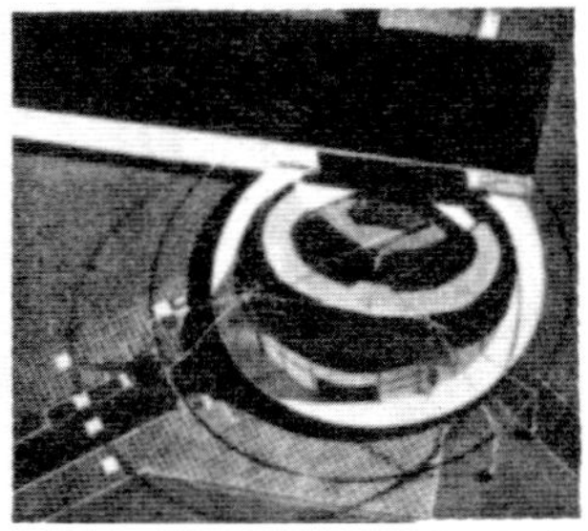

Universal Theater, F.J. Kiesler, Architect.

becoming outdated

this theater planned for Woodstock in 1927, but never built, was supposed to be a light and inexpensive construction that could be used for a variety of purposes. Kiesler renounced stone construction in this project. The structure was to be made of steel tubes and intertwined steel cables, prefabricated so as to be quickly put into place. The tarpaulin walls were fire resistant and waterproof. The entire construction of the frame rests on a concrete block. The only decorative elements were to be light and color, which could be changed according to the outfitting of the building.

●

Arrive and leave by train, bus, monorail, hovercraft, car, or on foot, at whatever time you wish—or merely cast a glance in passing. The posters keep you informed about what is happening. No need to look for the entrance, you can enter anywhere. There are no doors, no halls, no waiting rooms or receptionists—you can help yourself as you please—look around—use the elevator, the ramp, or the escalator to go to the activities that appeal to you.

Choose what you want to do—or watch someone else doing it. Learn how to use tools, machines, paint, take care of children, or stay by yourself just to listen to your favorite music. Dance, discuss or go up to the terrace to see how the machines work. Sit in a chair with a drink and listen to the hum of all that is happening in the city. Try to start a riot, begin a painting or relax while gazing at the Milky Way.

What time is it? Any time of the day or night, winter or summer—it does not matter. If it is raining, the roof will keep out the downpour, but not the light. The artificial cloud will provide coolness or a rainbow. Your feet will be kept warm while you look at the stars. Why not enjoy your favorite dish while the storm blows over?

Why all this? "If any nation is to be lost or saved by the character of its large cities, that nation is ours" (Robert Vaughn, 1843). We will build an Attraction Center where we will be able to see the possibilities and pleasures that a 20th-century environment is supposed to offer. This center will disappear as soon as the needs are satisfied.

Fun Palace: project by Cedric Price.
London, 1965
archigram

... the forms of the constructions are infinitely varied, neutral, unfinished, mechanical, floral, non-existent, soft, mobile, exasperating, present, deliquescent, superb, turgescent. The search for taste, harmony, correspondence between the landscape and building still subsist in remote corners of the city and are considered archaisms with a certain old-fashioned charm by the Esthetes responsible for the organization of the daily-visual-spectacle of the streets of the city. Color is everywhere; light, too. Day and night, color and light recreate the forms in never-ending variations, created by chance or sometimes by a specific will, that of the Esthetes who are past masters in the composition of the most amazing urban landscapes, and at the service of industrial firms using their talent to commercial ends. Curtains of steam, curtains of insulating air, translucent paper, synthetic materials are deployed under the control of the light to create a continuous spectacle. The places change, but maintain their character by the sweet fragrances and colorful shades that preside over their sensorial definition. Fluorescence, Luna Park, advertising, nighttime. Quality is synonymous with perpetual invention: a dynamic that can be stopped for the desired length of time, boredom settling in just long enough for the space to become slightly uncomfortable for the population, and just then it changes and a new cycle begins.

Some parts of the city remain as they are, like remnants and witnesses of the past, elements of comparison with life-in-motion. They are the reserves of urban memory, veritable museums enabling the inhabitants to plunge again at will into a particular period of the past ... In Phoebis, the residential areas are located on the border between the worlds of the durable and of the ephemeral, which interact. The inhabitants can choose to live in old houses of little comfort, built of durable materials as they used to be, or they can live in new ones: shells built of translucent molded synthetic materials, the internal organs of which can be replaced as one pleases. These dwellings preserve little of the memory of the past, the beauty of eternal renewal is their privilege …

… The city is a great gallery, its vertical surfaces decorated with ephemeral works printed on paper. They vanish in a few days and are replaced just as quickly. Each inhabitant can participate in these works, change them, remove them, repaint them. These kinds of paintings are very often figurative, in opposition to the perfect abstract and mechanical world of ephemeral constructions, the rigorous geometry of which would soon become intolerable if it were not corrected by some decoration, real or kinetically projected.

Jean BARUTE
—*Phoebis, the city without a past*—
Collection fiction Z

Tower of Light, Universal Exhibition, New York, 1964.

J. A.

Fun Palace: a project by Cedric Price, London, 1965.

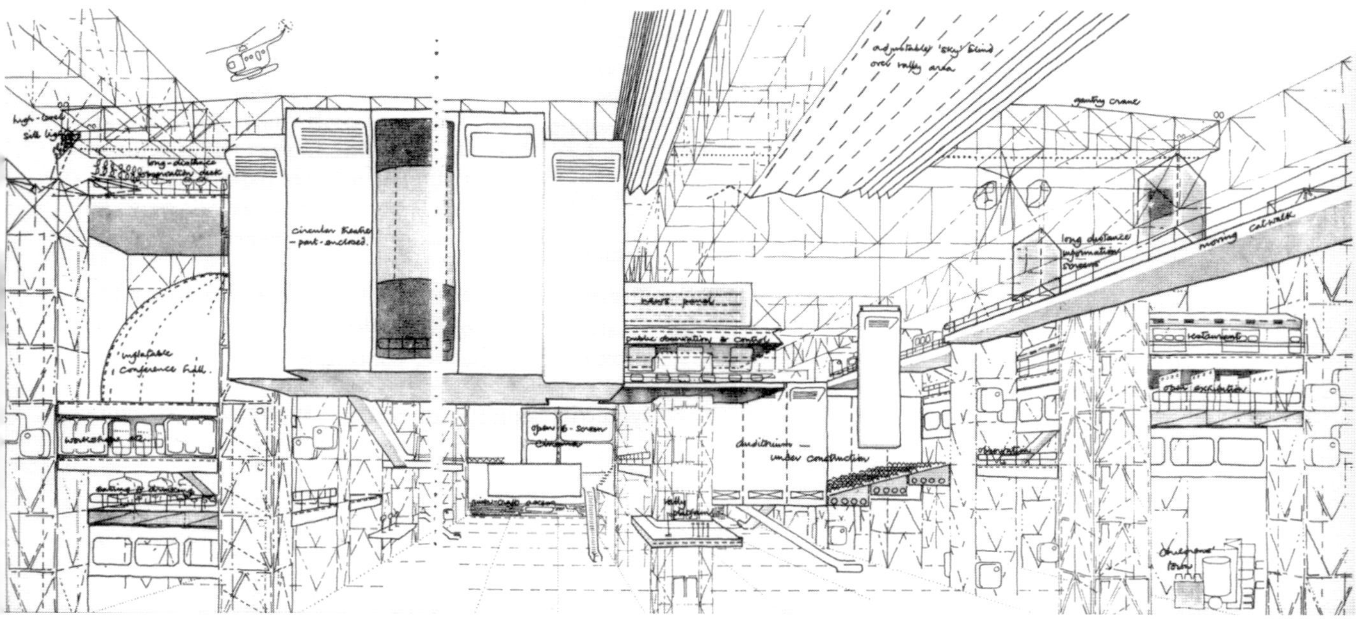

Luc Bradefer, *Les pirates de l'espace*

Paper Cities

"City design"

conception, shaping of urban spaces to come, representations by means of words and lines.

The determinants of a choice, like the political and economic ideology, the measurable data (geographic, climatological, demographic...), as well as the preliminary information and studies are not the only limits to the conception and design of the city. These determinants only offer possible spaces.

The demand spatialized by "city design"; essentially a graphic writing, the specificity of which itself seems determinant.

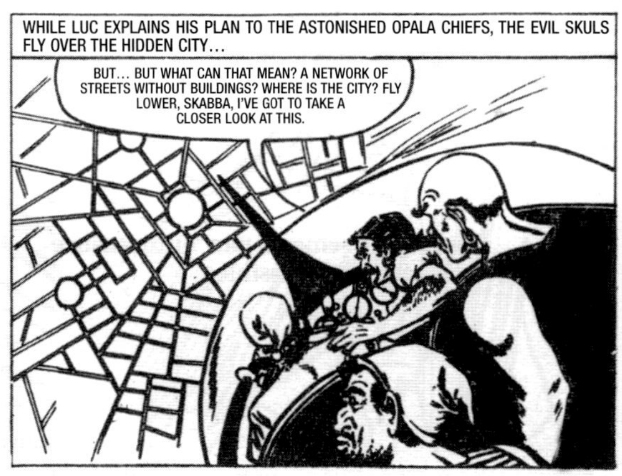

The passage from the word to the line
urbanography
urbanistic calligraphy
the design of cities
the formal conception
city design

the image of the future is being drawn

technical images
circulation diagrams, zoning, networks
accumulation and expression of information
manifestos
images for competitions
plans for implementation
administrative drawings

Through these expressions, the most complicated of which are intended to produce pieces, we can "see," know, the spaces to come, know if the demand has been satisfied.

Reading a model, a drawing, a report; imagine how these spaces could be experienced, or would they exist only when experience has established itself in the architecture?

Are these spaces seen before being built?

Is a true critique possible in the course of the elaboration, or do urgency and operational efficiency preclude any dialogue and contribution at the stage of formal synthesis?

"to see," image, ideology

is there a vision of the future town, at any level of the study?

is there a mental creation, image before the graphic transcription?

vision, faculty of inventing, of conceiving a totality of the spaces to come?

If there is a vision, if it is expressed or uncommunicated, it will remain the privilege of the imagination of a few specialists whose intuition, culture and the trust which they are given are the only guarantees of the realization; in that case, is urban art possible?

impoverishment of spatial possibilities via self-censorship

It is probable that there is vision (in the best of cases), but only of spaces easy to communicate in words and drawings; the possibilities of the demand therefore seem to have little influence on the formal conception; it is an urbanistic conception dominated by the imaginary, but a very fragmented imaginary permitted by the limits of the graphic writing and formal references of the period.

entropy

collective images,
models
The memory of other spaces,
experienced, unknown,
drawn spaces,
fantasies
The Three Penny Opera
first images
total spectacle
the Spartakists

Der Tannenbaum
In the jungle of the cities
memory
the imaginary
AMERICA
dregs

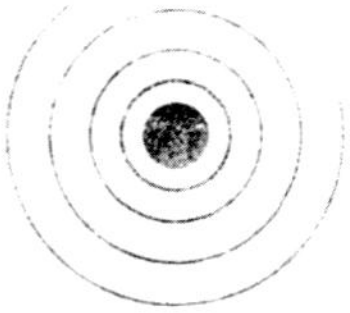

fig. 32—The city is not a target…

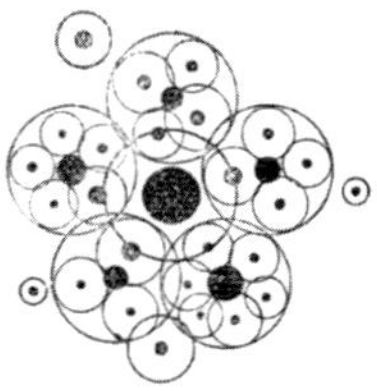

… but a cluster of interpenetrating communities (author's diagram).

G. Bardet, *Mission de l'urbanisme*

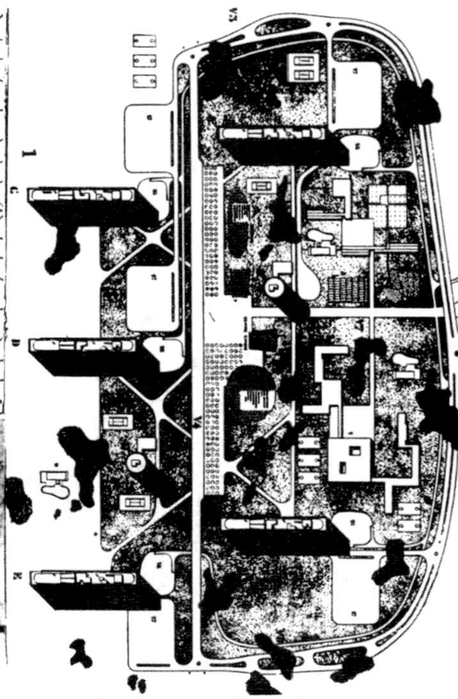

Le Corbusier, *Meaux (France).*

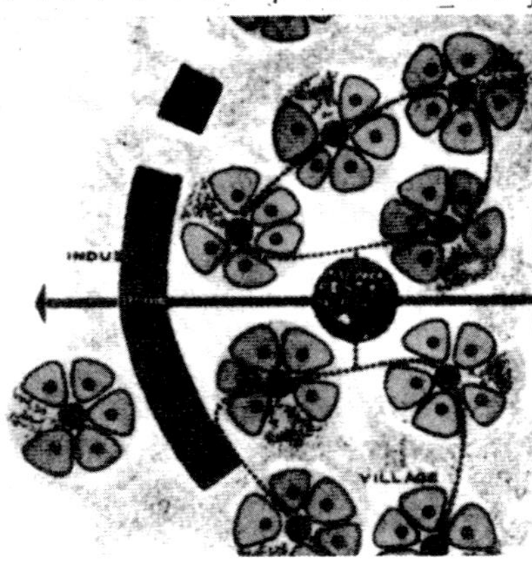

C. Alexander, *a city is not a tree*

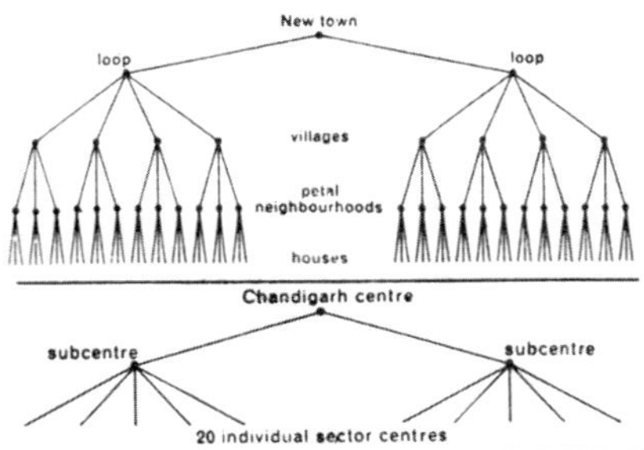

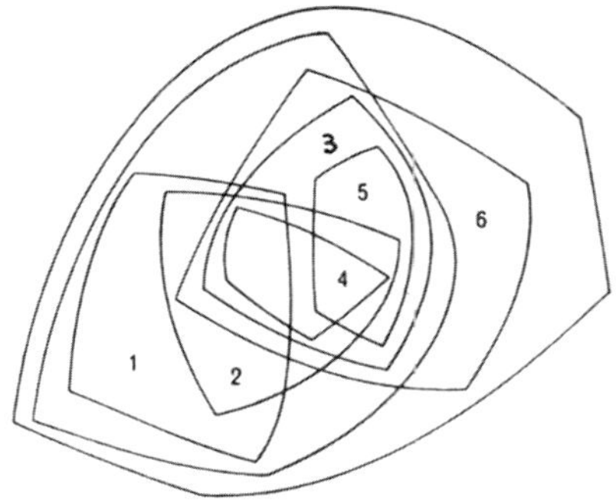

to express the intuitive criteria, the unconscious habits, the inertia and entropy in the shaping

The passage via the two-dimensional expression of a multi-dimensional totality, recognized as necessary, underscores the importance and pregnancy of drawn models;

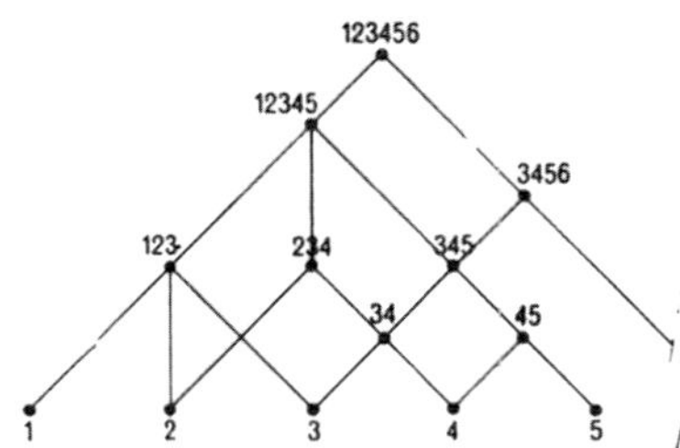

the spatial imagination in urbanism

arborescence

visual memory monocentrism typology

housing unit

The models, rarely collective ideologies, are born in the very process of urbanistic creation through the graphic writing, which is dominated itself by other drawn spaces that rarely intend to be representations of real or experienced spaces;

Is there a spatial ideology of society?

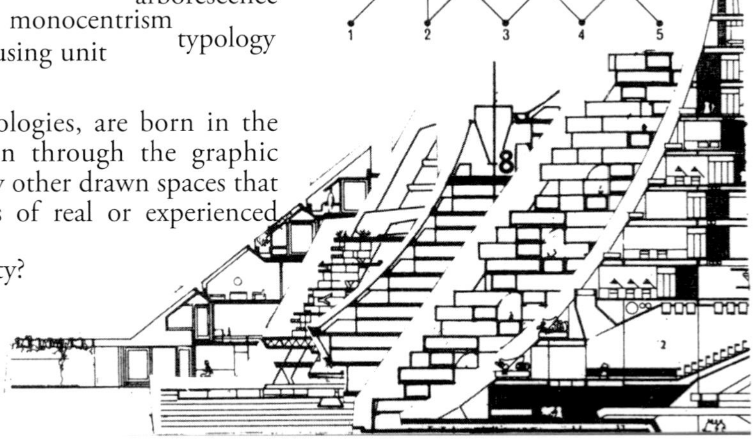

graphic models

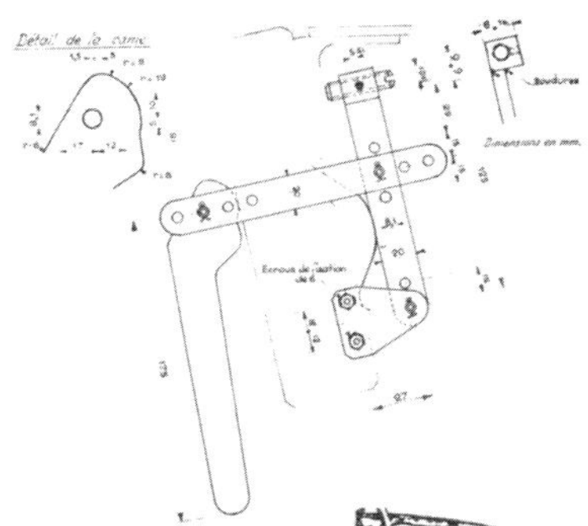

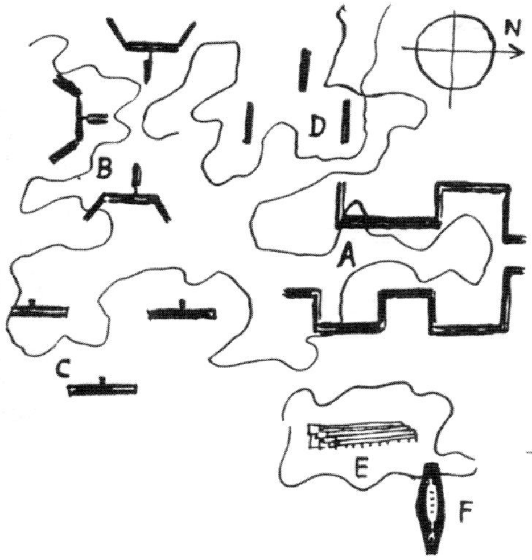

Volumes built for habitation
A the saw tooth type
B the "Y" type
C the frontal type
D the splinter type
E the tiered type
Volumes built for business
E the "Y" type
F the lens type

Le Corbusier

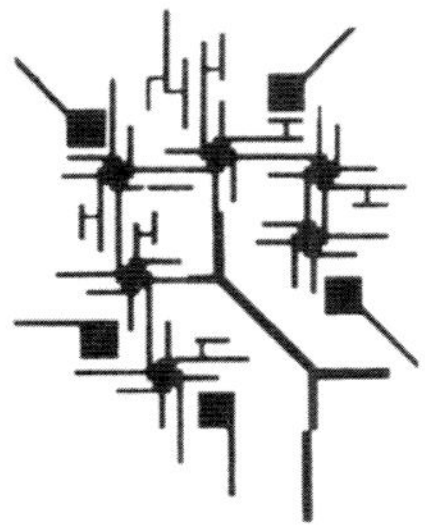

G. Candilis, A. Josic,
S. Woods,
Fort-Lamy (Chad)

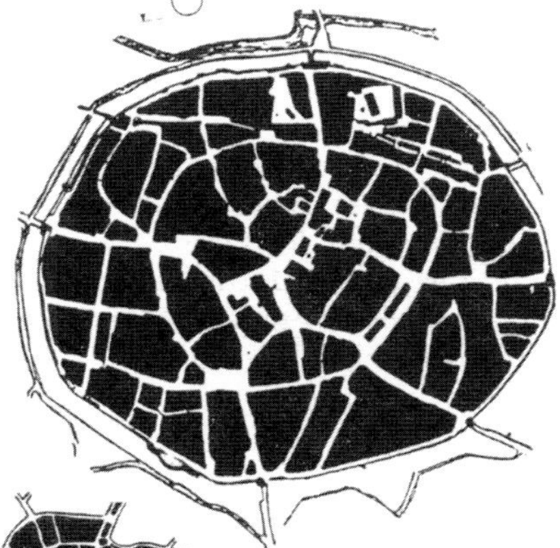

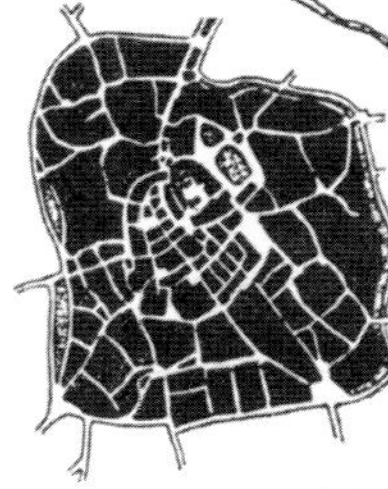

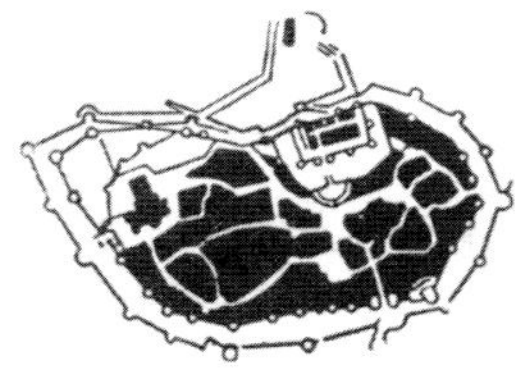

Towns of the organic type
(after Eliel Saarinen):

Nordlingen (Germany)
City of Carcassonne (France)
Udine (Italy)

visual images of utopia, fomal urbanistic world

Life establishes itself in the constructed, takes possession of it and transforms it; nevertheless, this maturation through history has a hold only on one space and an *initial* spectacle of the constructed. Urbanistic creation seems to have suspended time during its gestation and it can be said that at this moment only what has been projected will be built, *what is initially constructed is what has been drawn.* Less drawings were probably made in Perrault's time, the contribution of the various building trades, or particular programs and tradition considerably enriched the initial structures. Nowadays, programming and construction techniques probably require a greater density of information and previsions.

The building machine realizes any drawing, whether its content is rich or a simple sketch; a ground plan may be enough to build from.

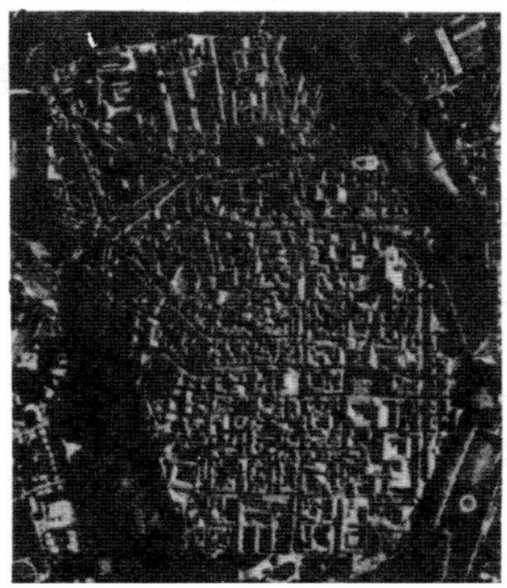

Lucca (Italy)
a renaissance town

J.Cl. Bernard, *Essay for a Total City*

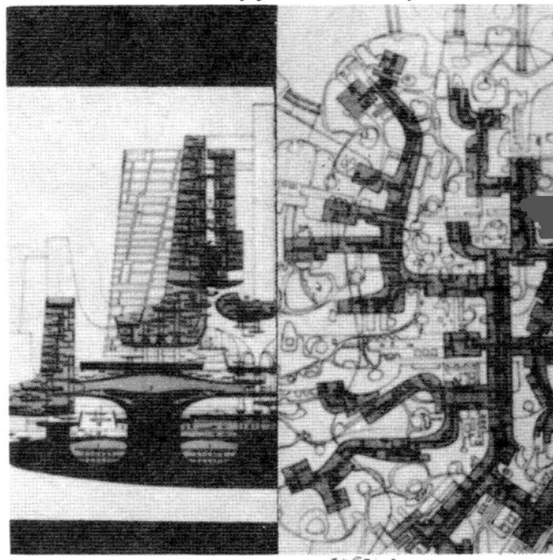

in descriptive geometry a point or a volume is defined by its horizontal projection and frontal projection

"We are used to Cartesian systems of representation in which each point of a form is projected onto a plane. Subsequently, all forms that were difficult to project were considered bizarre. The difficulty of treating them within a system of Cartesian coordinates led to their elimination. However, we were naturally drawn to using forms that were practical to plot, like the cube, whose sides are parallel to the planes of plotting. Yet if a form is complicated to define in the Cartesian system, that does not mean that it is complicated to build."

D.G. Emmerich
in *Livre d'or de l'architecture et de l'urbanisme*

simple, prismatic and vertical, cubic, linear spaces
spaces determined by the use of planar projection systems
Repetitive systems facilitating construction and the study of models

M. Andrault, P. Parat,
Z.U.P. center in Epernay.

topography reduced entirely t[o] the carving of the vertical edg[e] of contour lines

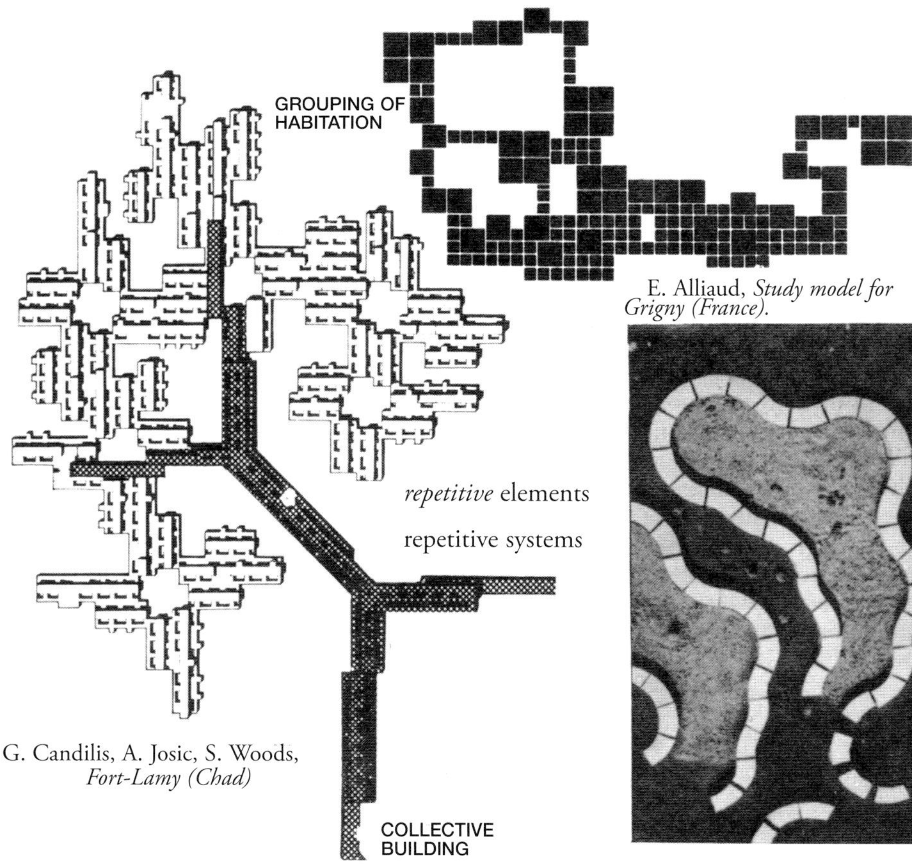

repetitive elements

repetitive systems

G. Candilis, A. Josic, S. Woods,
Fort-Lamy (Chad)

E. Alliaud, *Study model for Grigny (France).*

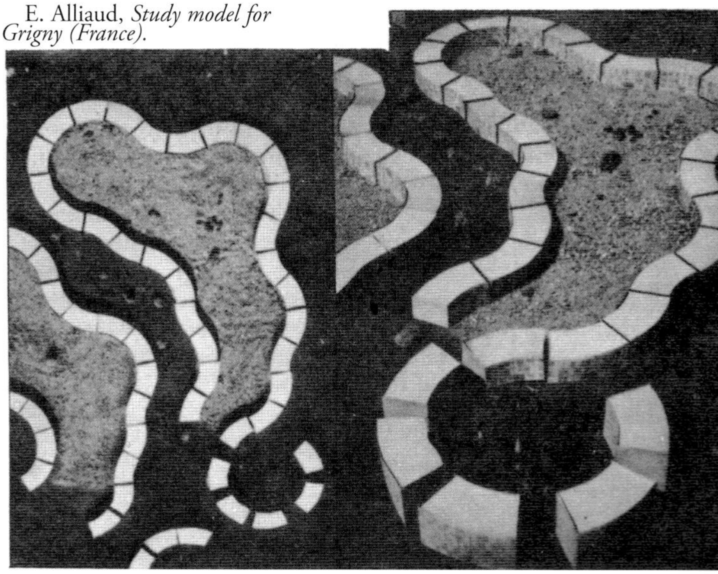

cartesian world without mystery or surprise

A. Studer

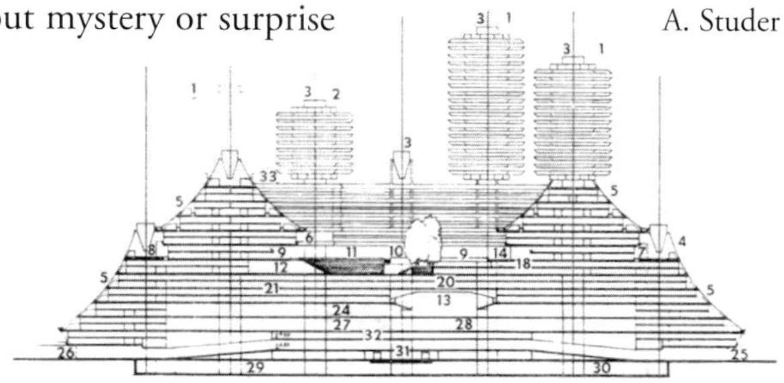

Sketch for an agglomeration of 5,000 inhabitants

P. Hodgkinson, *Urban center, London*

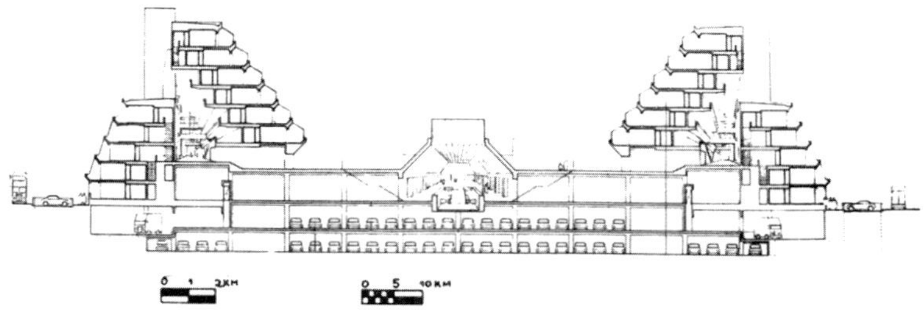

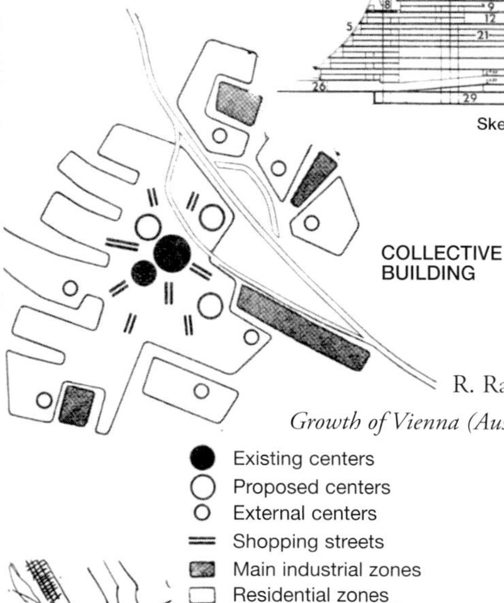

R. Rainer,
Growth of Vienna (Austria).

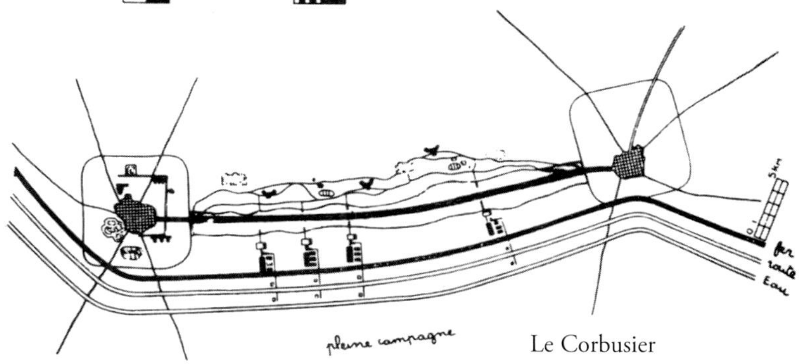

Le Corbusier

The linear industrial city
For the sake of synthesis in the drawing, above, we used three different scales to draw the industrial center, the radioconcentric city, and the network of three roads.

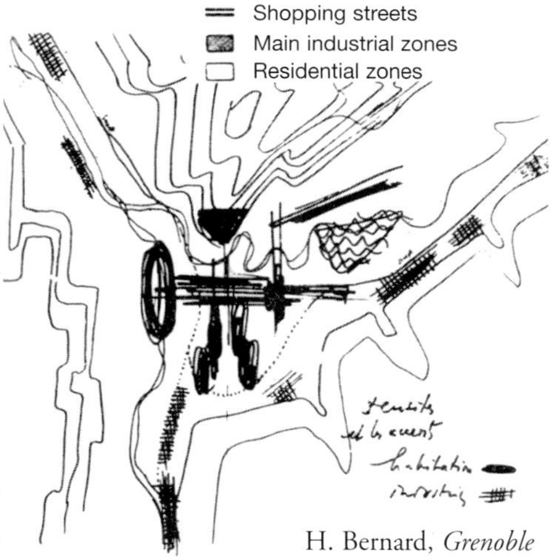

H. Bernard, *Grenoble*

Accents of the composition

empty spaces and planes described with a *minimum of drawings*, speed of conception and reading

distribution of zones of activity in terms of their legibility in a horizontal or frontal projection

overlapping and superposition are taboo

a social distribution in space has been treated only in a few essays, especially literary ones (Cedric Price's Fun Palace) or graphically combined by a very simple spatial grid (Y. Friedmann, Plug-in City)

"This harmful routine is the by-product of the development of intermediary mechanisms between thought and the work, such as graphic expressions and graphic calculations, which finally produced the cell-plan, project types, at the same time as the universal abacus."

D.G. Emmerich
Architecture aujourd'hui, no. 115

"The small streets became of rather ordinary size; I mean, one could, for example, break all the windows of a building opposite from the sidewalk on which I was standing."

L.F. Céline
Journey to the End of the Night

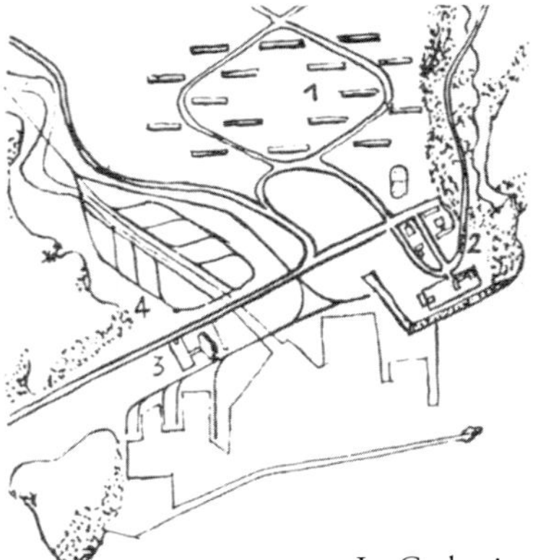

Le Corbusier, *Nemours (North Africa)*

L. Costa, O. Niemeyer, *Plaza of the Three Powers in Brasilia*

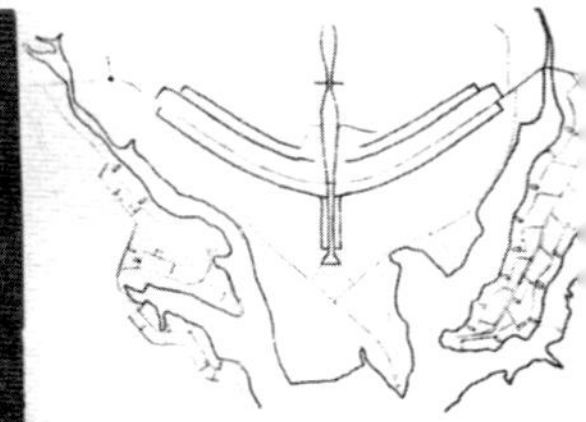

L. Costa, *Ground-plan of Br*

An urbanism entirely conceived by *spaces that are easy to draw* with chalk on a blackboard at a meeting and immediately graspable by the public, *easy to formulate, describe*;

P. Maymont, *The Vertical City*

Floating city (Monaco)

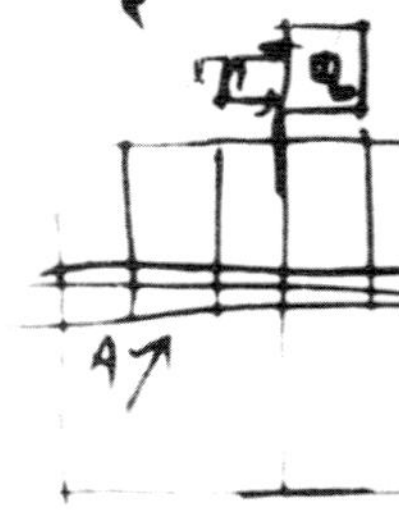

Le Corbusier,
first drawing at Chandigarh.

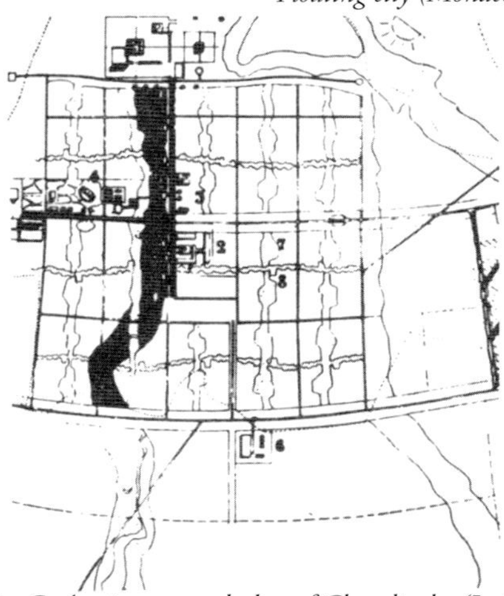

Le Corbusier, *ground-plan of Chandigahr (India)*

a straight line

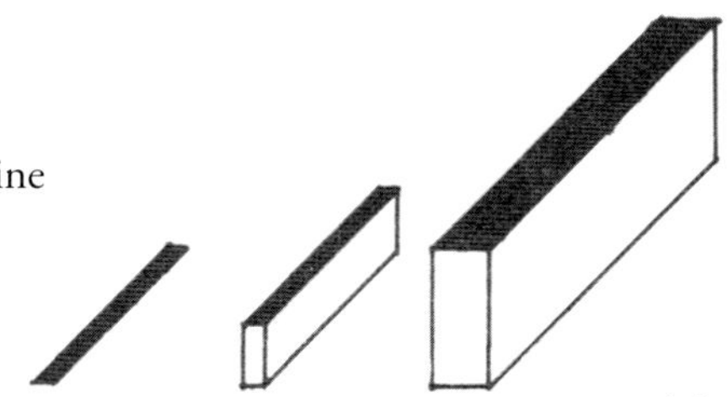

its graphic transcription, its construction as a model and its final form;

O. Niemeyer, *model and building of the presidential palace in Brasilia.*

exploded view of the Mirage IV jet fighter.

A. Mutnjakovic, A. Srnec, *competition for Tel-Aviv*

functionalism

education brief (N.A.S.)

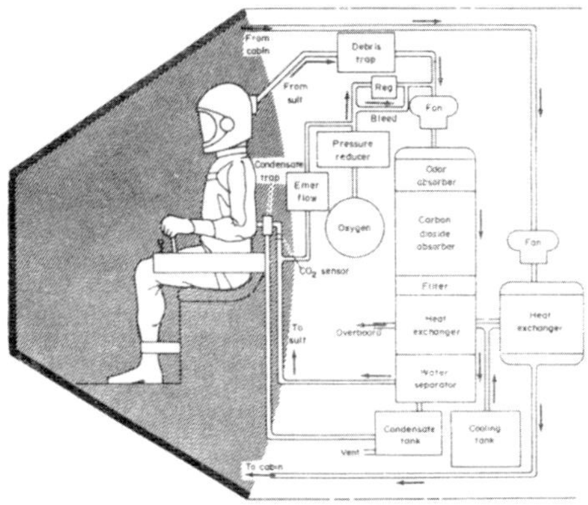

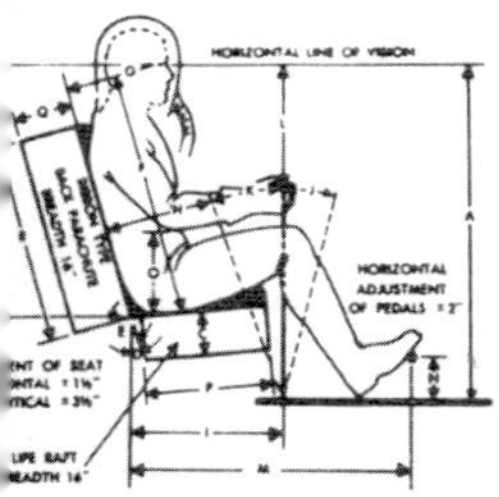

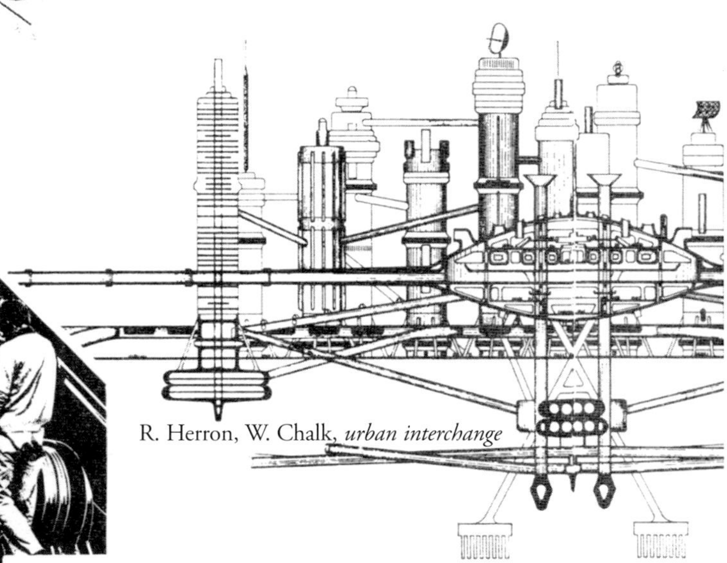

R. Herron, W. Chalk, *urban interchange*

adscape, railway landscape,
ilitary landscape

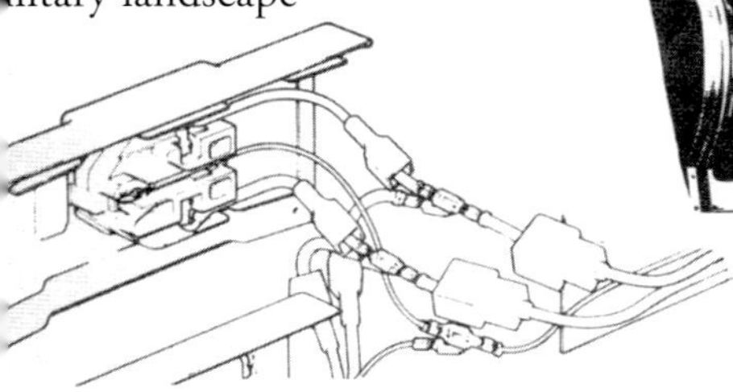

these plates are neither studies, nor representations of cities, but simplifications (often for a competition) for didactic purposes and intended as information or education.

N. Kurokawa, *Tokyo*

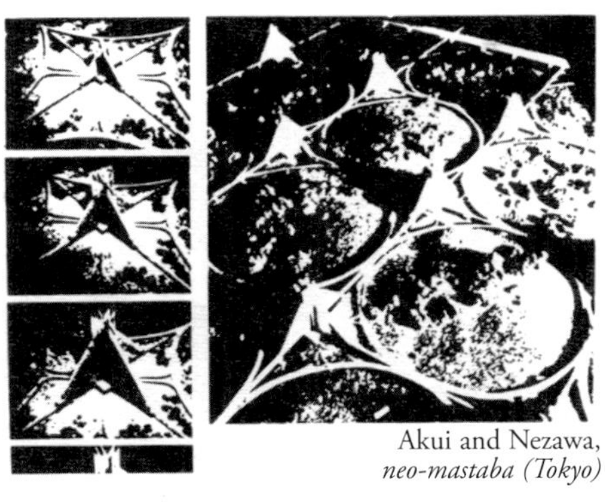

Akui and Nezawa, *neo-mastaba (Tokyo)*

K. Tanga, *Tokyo*

R. Herron,

These simple, hypertrophied, evident images, these diagrammatic expressions on which the spatial imaginary of contemporary urbanism feeds, and the purpose of which resides in the communication of several master ideas at a very journalistic level, and by virtue of their pregnancy, being the sole representations of a future, are identified with reductions of spaces which, incidentally, are destined to be built.

competition:

all the commercial and pictorial techniques to express the project: doesn't the notion of a contest of ideas exclude study, experimentation, a more elaborate approach?

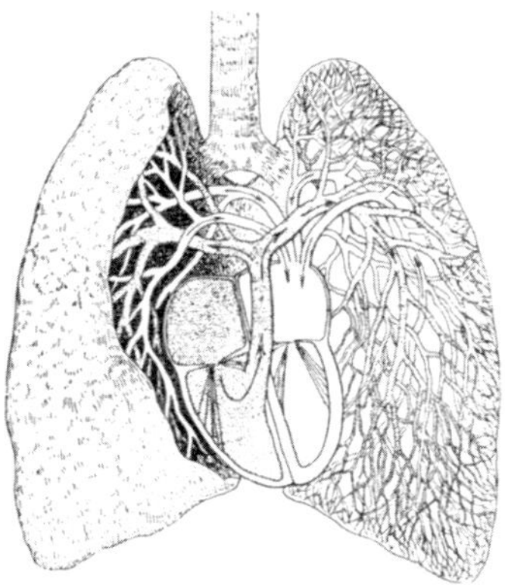

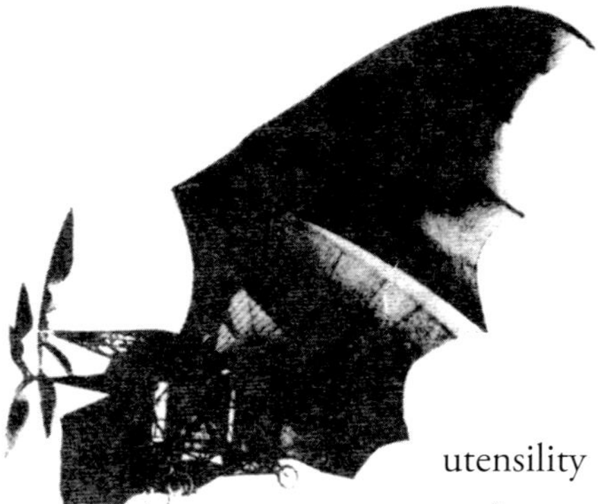

airplane No. 3 by Clément Ader

A. Isosaki, *Cluster in the air (Tokyo)*

utensility

anthropomorphism

monocentrism

perception

photo

B. Baschet's costume in "Who Are You, Polly Magoo?"

dresses by Yves Saint-Laurent

K. Kikutake

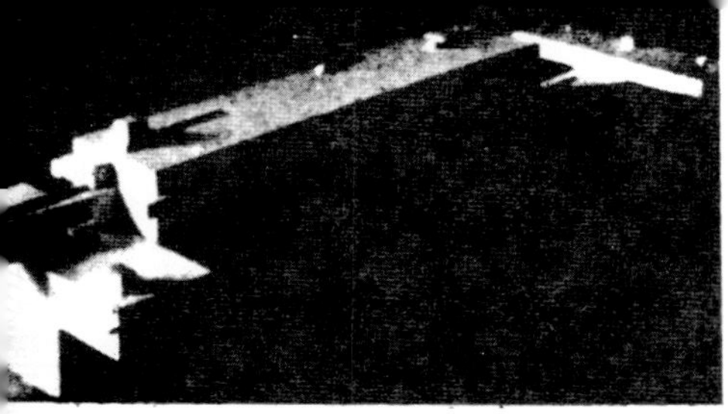

Malevitch. 1922

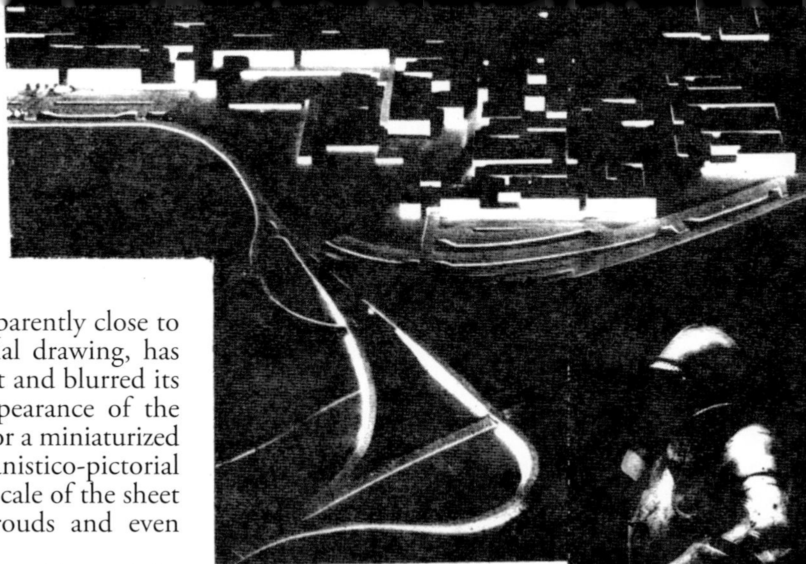

The confusion of means of expression, apparently close to painting, sculpture, commercial or industrial drawing, has modified the purpose of the urbanistic script and blurred its reading. The refinement of the formal appearance of the drawings or models, the quest for harmony, for a miniaturized organization, smooth and closed, an urbanistico-pictorial order, an apparently balanced whole, at the scale of the sheet of paper or object, impedes "seeing," shrouds and even destroys legibility and the imaginable.

"Art does not produce the visible, it makes visible. And, by its very nature, the realm of the graphic legitimately fosters abstraction. The wonder and the sketchiness that are proper to the imaginary are given there in advance, and at the same time are expressed with great precision. The greater the purity of the graphic work—that is, the more importance is given to the formal basis of a graphic representation—the more the apparatus proper to the realistic representation of appearances is reduced."

Paul Klee
Theory of Modern Art

L. Arretche, J. and P. Génard, P. and P. Glénat,
Competition, Toulouse Le Mirail

J. Lubicz-Nyez, *competition for Tel-Aviv*

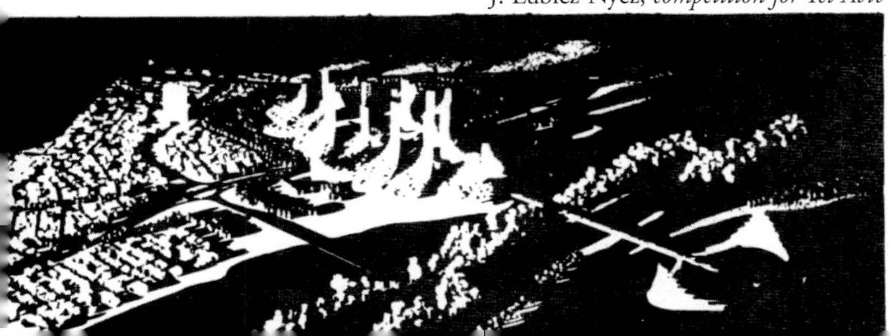

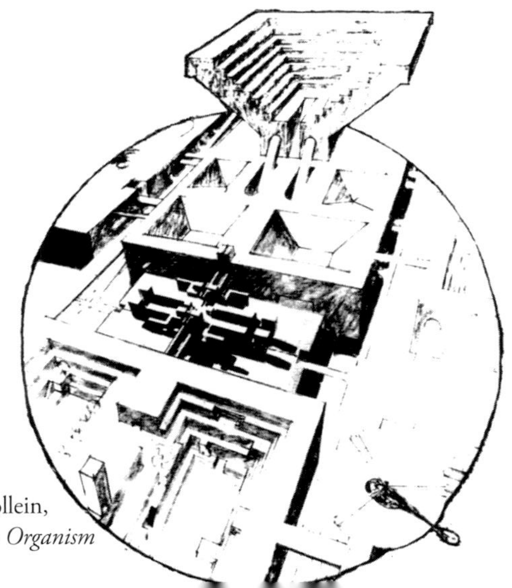

H. Hollein,
Urban Organism

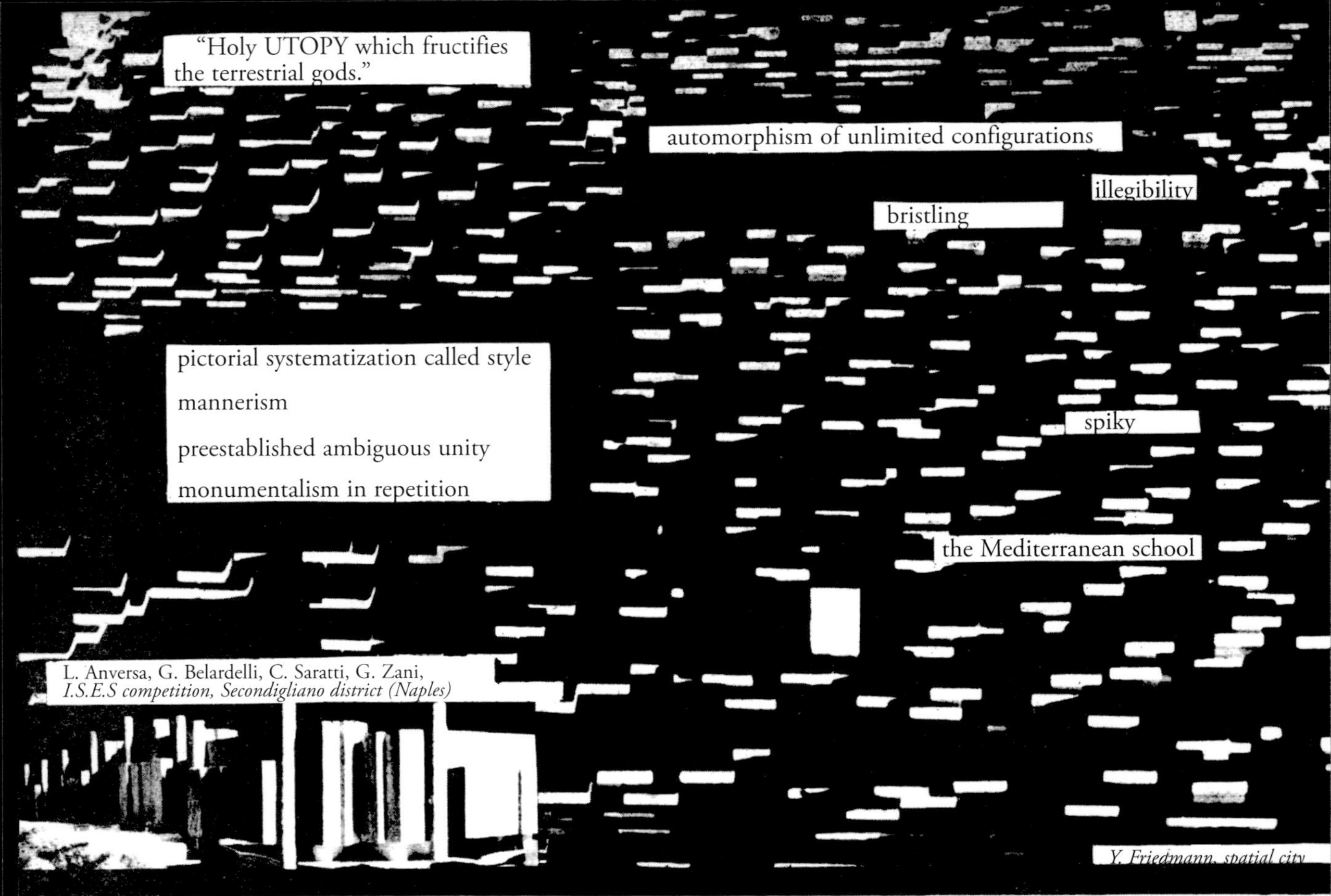

L. Anversa, G. Belardelli, C. Saratti, G. Zani, *I.S.E.S competition, Secondigliano district (Naples)*

Y. Friedmann, spatial city

"Man has the notion of a world better than this one. But better does not mean different, then; better means unified."
A. Camus, *The Rebel*

"a rather superficial art, as M. Bartmann used to say, a purely decorative art, an art of space, but not of dreams. Even if it enriches our world of appearance by some new suggestions, such bagatelles would make art more and more superficial. There were hurtful words on both sides and M. Bartmann's position became difficult, the artists made him clearly understand that separating art from the world of appearances would mean taking away its very foundation."
The Emperor of Utopia, a novel, Paul Scheerbart, the artists' feast

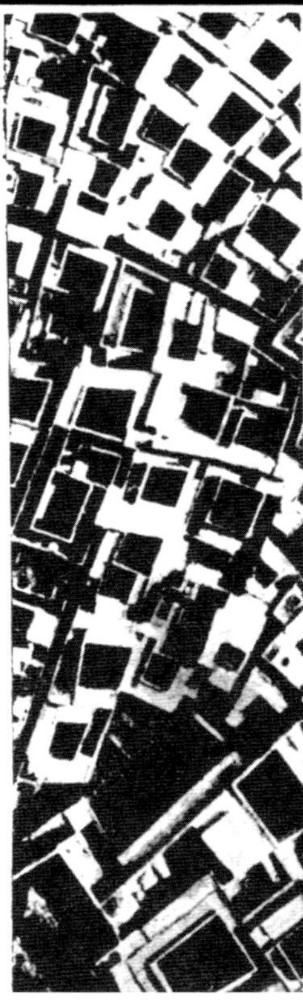

urban structures (Department of Architecture, Florence).

C. T. Stifter, *Urban center*

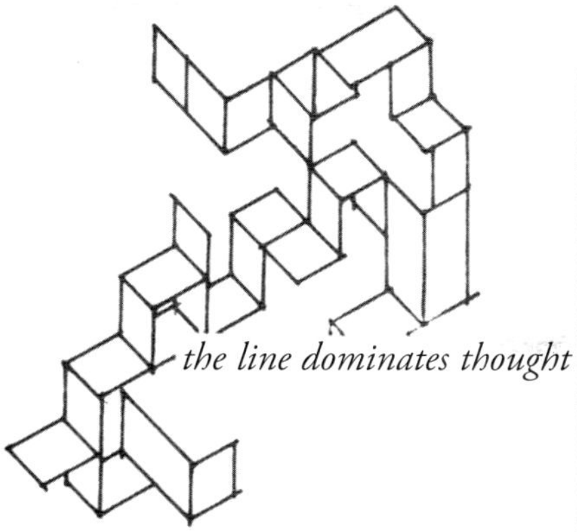

the line dominates thought

G. Candilis, A. Josic, S. Woods, Free *University of Berlin*

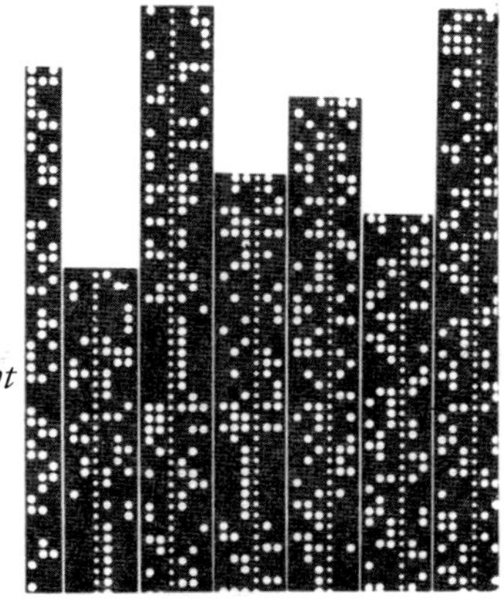

Key to the city

Who will look beyond the strict limits of the page

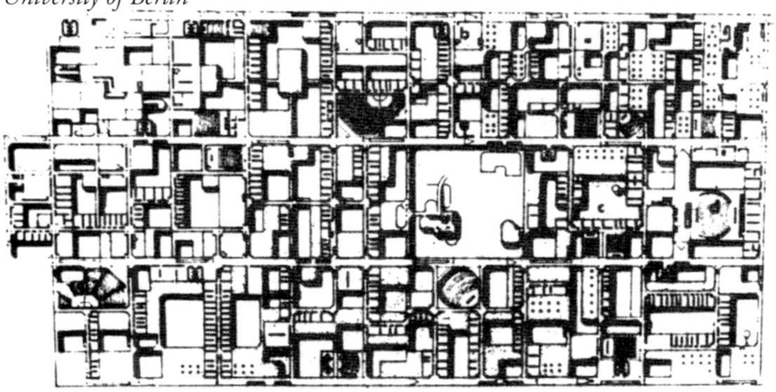

L. Arretche, J. Renaudie, P. Riboulet, G. Thurnauer and J.L. Veret, *urban center, Rouen Saint-Sever.*

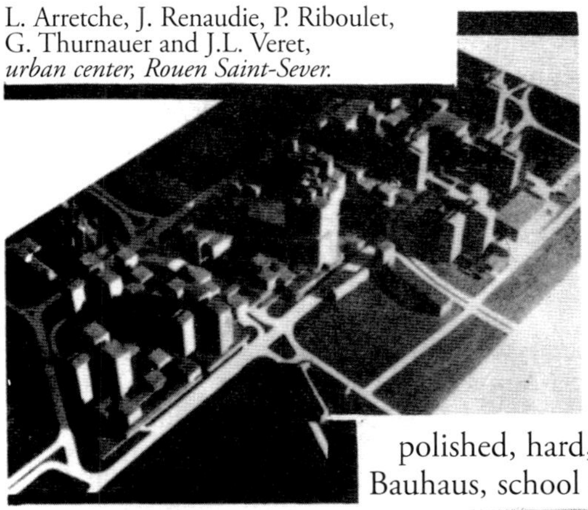

polished, hard, impermeable images
Bauhaus, school of industrial aesthetics

E. Schulze-Fielitz, *University of Berlin*

Many questions should be posed, it seems to me, questions that might shift our considerations beyond the strict limits of the page. Such questions shall doubtlessly remain unanswered, yet I insist, they foreground the existence of a problematics of urbanistic creation. They do not pertain to the ways in which urbanists express themselves or elaborate their "tools," but concern, rather, the usage of the sites thus created. Such means of expression or elaboration cannot be assessed, that much is clear, they compose the matter of a code, only decipherable by initiates, one that, proliferating upon its own domain, ends up no longer finding justification in its object, but in itself. Although it claims no literariness, such writing *paradoxically finds its own finality in itself, leading in this way to simplifications as well as to excessive stylistic proliferations. Before pursuing the issue farther, however, I would like to ask three questions:*

1. "Urbanistic language," although it issues from stylistic variations rather than from a rigorous functionalism, seems to me largely dependent upon the society in which it develops. It is completely implanted there, the models it uses, whether consciously or not, are those conferred by that society. I would even add that it is one of the

continued on page 107

Guy Leclair, *The Terrible Forest.*

W.A. Hablik

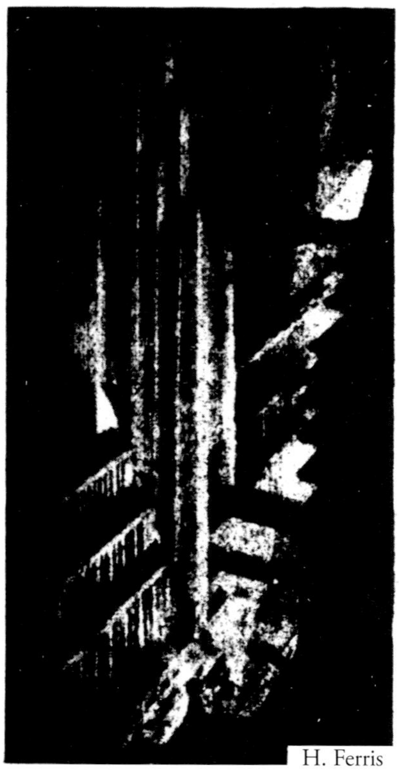

H. Ferris

Critique of the imagined

Vision of the city on the basis of drawing; the difficulty of imagining a possible lived experience. Reading and critique are based on tightly closed formal images, on fragmentary expressions, comic or promotional, or on technical expressions accessible only to specialists.

To show, *seeing before building.*

"How would these drawn geometries be lived?" is a subject rarely insisted upon during development; we build, doubtless, without any spatial vision forming.

Do these paper cities exist?

urban morphology, spaces of chance?

an urban art form, social art form?

Dreams that come alive, poetic essays on the future city, experimentation, critique by means of other sensibilities representative of society, simply demanding expression.

"…But these buildings, conceived as monuments to mankind, were dreamed without man. Sant'Elia's city is dynamic but unorganized and unpopulated; the 'Planites' of Malevich, the maze of Tatlin, the apocalyptic forms of Mendelsohn are independent of any scale of reference: they could become giants or paperweights. Concentrating their interest on the emotional value of form, these utopists avoided the exploration of urban problems and, above all, the definition of any design method. They tied architecture to a full response only to occasional passions. In contrast with Le Corbusier's social dream, they produced a merely formalistic Utopia detached from the social dialectic of their time. The destiny of such Utopias was clear, in its lack of understanding that technology had the possibility of transforming the

Sant'Elia

A. Raymond, *Flash Gordon.*

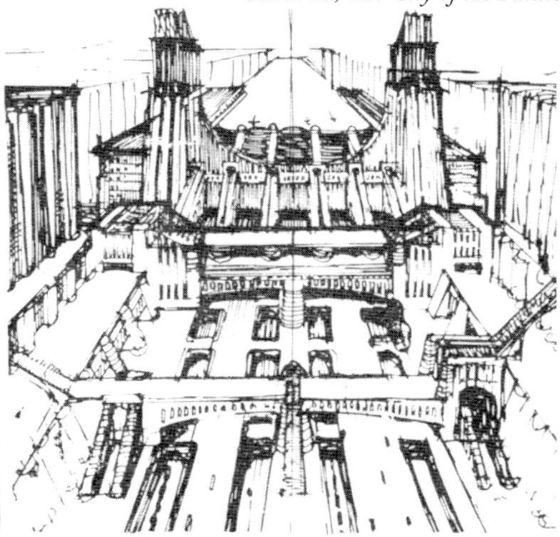

Sant'Elia, *The City of the Future*

H. Poelzig, sets of UFA film *The Golem.*

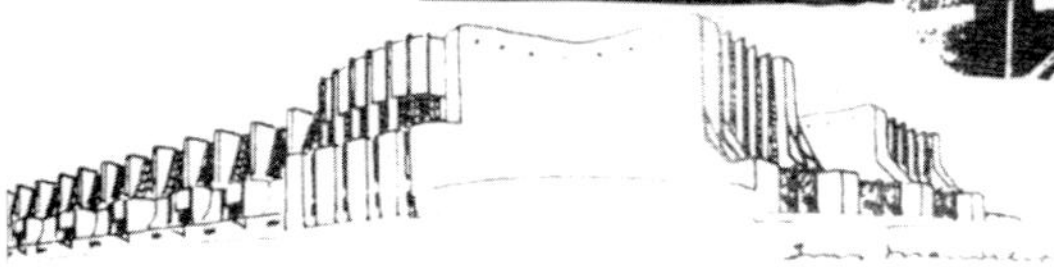

E. Mendelsohn

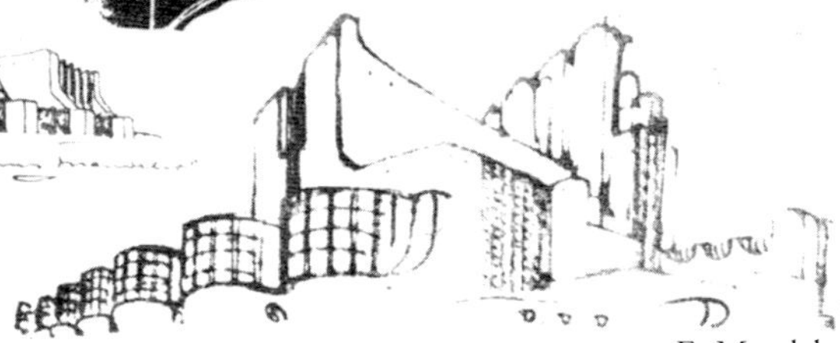

E. Mendelsohn

structure of society by its own power and in its own way, if not otherwise directed. Therefore, when technology and industrial production decided that it was more convenient to become servant to a dictator, the end of all the metaphysical dreams had come.

In 1932 Stalin abolished the free architectural groups in Russia, the Bauhaus was closed in 1933 and at the same time Mussolini imposed in Italy the 'Imperial Style.' Strangely enough, Flash Gordon's extraterrestrial Utopia was born of the forms invented by the formalistic Utopias of the 'twenties. We recognize the 'twirliness' of Tatlin, of Hermann Finsterlin, of Virgilio Marchi, the dynamic power of Mendelsohn and Sant'Elia, the magniloquence which was peculiar to this formalistic Utopia.

In the cartoons of Alex Raymond, the Futurist, the Constructivist and the Expressionist dreams find a new life or, rather, they gain life for the very first time. These buildings, conceived as hallucinating architectural deserts, are finally populated by Raymond. The inhabitants are the incredible extraterrestrial races of Mongo's planet: the Falcon Men, the Frog Men, the Lion Men, all of them people who are men plus something else—in other words, caricatures of human beings. No one could have found a sharper architectural criticism."

Manfred Nicoletti
"Flash Gordon and the Twentieth-Century Utopia"
(Architectural Rreview)

the curious story of the bubbles from space.

Critique by reference to other, more or less similar realizations does not create anything.

M. L'Herbier, *L'Inhumaine*,
sets by Mallet Stevens

Godard in the numerous basements of the installation of la defense or among the slabs of Sevran, Aulnay-sous-Bois.

"I've attached a little map to the volume to allow the reader to get his bearings more easily, which I think will be helpful if he is to understand subsequent events."

Alfred Kubin, *The Other Side*

D. W. Griffith, Babylon in *Intolerance.*

the construction of an entire city for the UFA film *The Golem* by Paul Wegener (1920): a medieval ghetto based on Hans Poelzig's drawings of imaginary architecture.

A. Kubin, *The Other Side.*

H. Poelzig, sets of UFA film *The Golem.*

J. Huston, *The Bible.*

F. Lang, *Metropolis.*

Are there techniques for describing activities in and around the future construct?

F. Lang, *Metropolis.*

B. Taut

the cinema, the journalist
the photographer, the writer
the painter

reconstructions of urban atmospheres based almost exactly on existing ruins, Korsabad.

subtle factors, and not the least, of the establishment of an immobility, a permanence towards which society gravitates. Even in its most chimeric reveries, "urbanistic language" claims to be realistic, possible to build, and perfectly concrete. It thus implicitly confirms the immutability of the contemporary social order, and, far from disturbing it, functions as a consolidating force.

2. On the other hand, setting aside all considerations of "value," if we consider "urbanistic calligraphy" under a strictly technical angle, we realize that it is not a homogeneous language to be used by specialists and that it can certainly not be assimilated to a scientific language. Its own expression, just like scientific language, does not determine any functional simplification, but pertains to an aesthetic domain whose relations with the object of urbanistic language are difficult to decipher. It would be desirable that a more rigorous formalization constitute in this sense a true code.

3. It remains to be seen whether this language must be accessible to the people who inhabit or will inhabit the site. What is at issue here is determining levels of use, and for each level, elaborating an appropriate means of expression.

For example, on the level of

— research
— technical implementation
— public information

Each of these constituting different means, and not necessarily possessing any formal similarities. Incidentally, it is difficult to decipher on which

continued on page 109

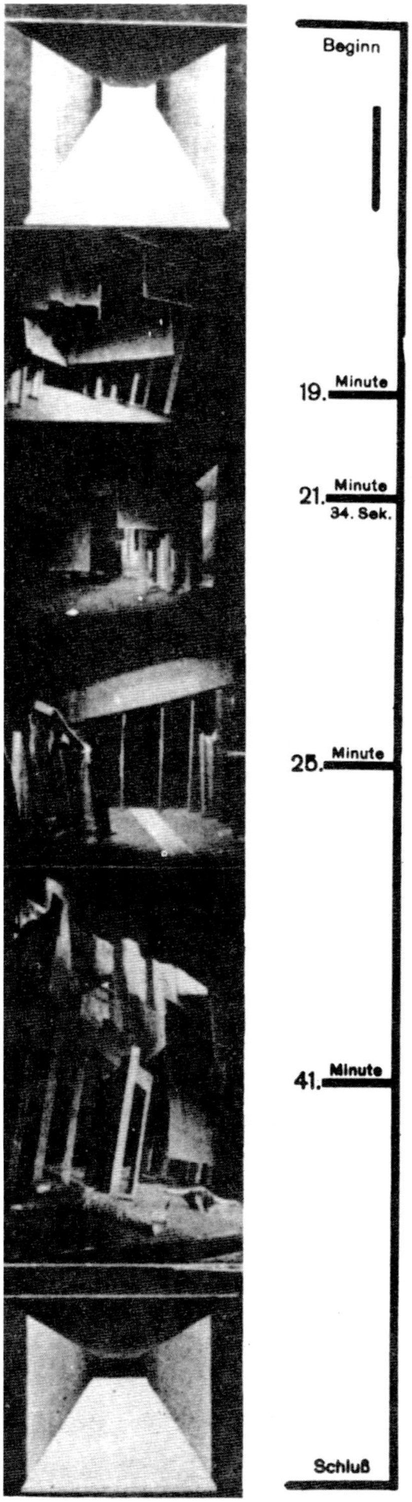

F. Kiesler,
6 moments of spatial mechanical scenography

L. Martin-Colin, *Whitehall*.

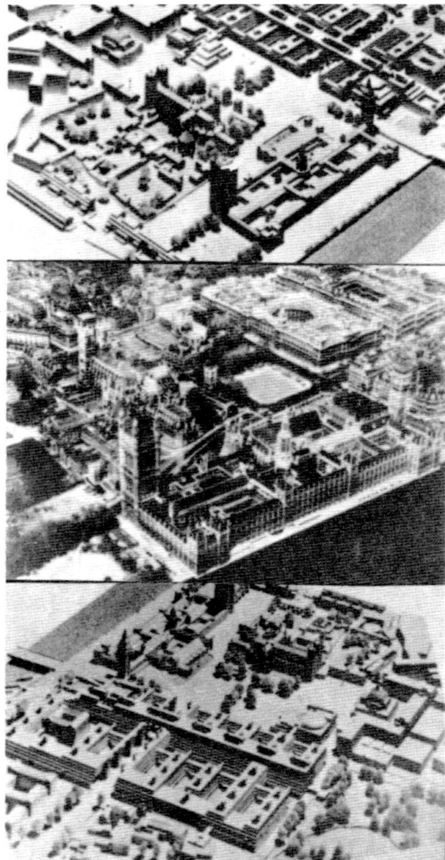

Model and aerial photo of *Downtown*.

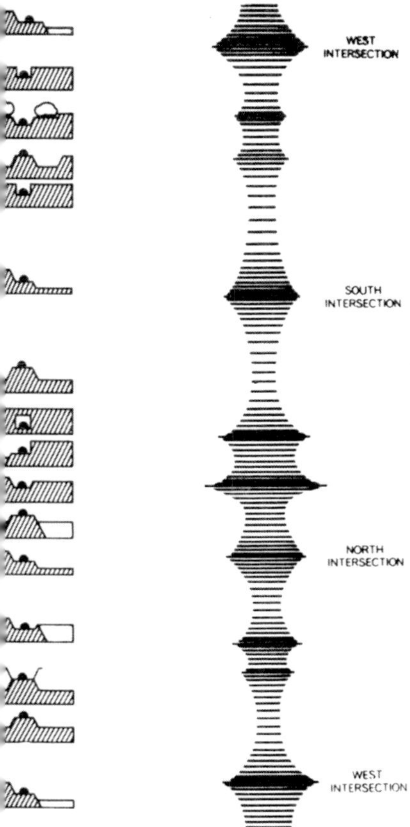

“Poetry: the art of playing for time.” B. Cendrars

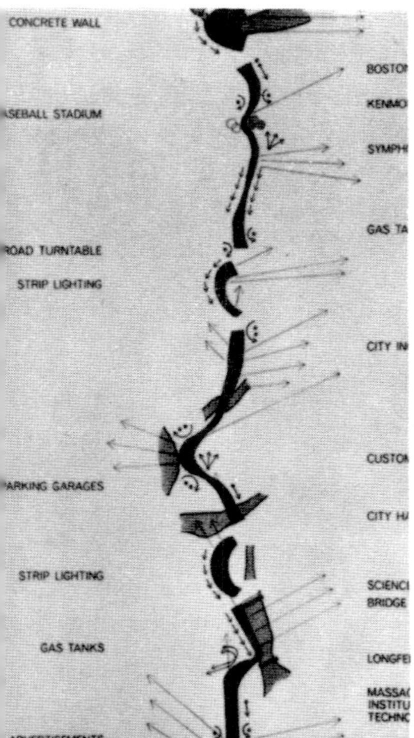

K. Lynch, *The City as Environment.*

T. Garnier, *An Industrial City.*

level the planning occurs and even if its author felt it desirable to differentiate between levels. It seems to me that this is necessary preliminary planning and research, to which subsequent details can be added. I regret, however, that the problem has not at least been posed.

The relation I have assumed above between the social realm and “urbanistic language” brings me to a new series of questions:

1. To what extent does language express the social realm, or lived experience, due to its existence within that social realm? This is a question inherent to all language.

2. Is the attempt to express lived experience justified?

The latter ambition reveals, in a somewhat naïve way, a profoundly paternalistic aspect of urbanistic creation; it is also impossible to realize. And indeed, what lived experience do we wish to set up? What lived experience can we imagine if not the projection of a subjective one. At best, or worst, such a subjective experience can be elaborated into a general theory of the way in which the inhabitants of the future site shall have to live, in a slightly coercive ethics. Moreover, the very attempt at establishing sites that shall determine conducts seems vain to me, for lived experience will anyway be perfectly ignorant of what is built. Such experience shall be constructed according to functional, perceptive and motor schemes. Forms, of course, are constraining in that they canalize and necessarily frame experience; but we should more clearly determine what qualities the word “form” encodes: “exterior configuration of bodies" (Larousse Dictionary); "the specific constitution, or mode, of certain things—the appearance a body assumes before our eyes" (Littré Dictionary); local stimulus in Gestalt theory; or the process of organization of sensory data. In the latter case, what shall the polarities, the pivotal points of this organization be? How shall they emerge? Probably not how demiurge constructors will have foreseen them in plans, *models, "reports," in short,* on the page. *"What we would like to know is how, precisely, do processes get distributed and regulate themselves in all specific cases."*

Lived experience is predicated upon individual and social experience that cannot be dissociated from the autonomous combination of perceivable data. Such data, in our case, can be assimilated to what is built. What is built is not, and cannot, be foreseen in as much as what is constructed is the result of plans*: what is built is the three-dimensional materialization of a system of lines conceived according to flat, and thus global and immediate, vision, whereas in three-dimensional perception, at least time and space intervene. The lived experience of the person who inhabits the space is certainly not the same as the intentional experience of the constructor; such an experience of inhabitation is probably even quite indifferent to the frame in which it unfolds, for it is already saturated by its own "motivations." The inhabitant, just like the constructor, indefinitely pursue in parallel their own egocentric fantasy.*

I.A.

animation,
crowds,
trajectories,
traffic,
movement,
crossing point,
swarming,
shadows,
concentrations,
color,
flags,
open spaces,
empty spaces,
random spaces,
seasons,
party,
gastronomy,
shadows,
echoes,
noises,
children,
peace,
shadows,
rain,
sound,
winds,
entertainment,
echoes,
snow,
the show,
what is illegal, *fear,*
memory,
night,
the unknown, leisure,
slums,
lighting,
the unknown,
clandestine,

H. Dreyfuss,
Measure of Man

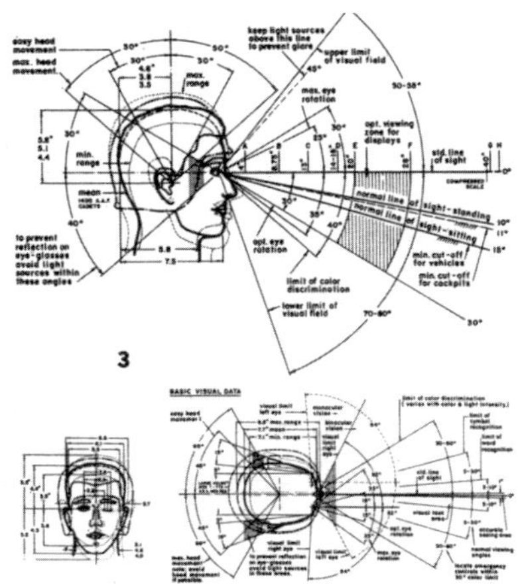

J. P. J.

THE LOGIC OF URBANISM

The direction in which the "science of cities" is developing in our society is an often misinterpreted phenomenon.

Historical analysis has brought to light the intermeshing of the city—as a material entity and a practice—and the structures of industrial society. In *The Housing Question*, Friedrich Engels raised this problematic in connection with the life of workers, and, in 1845, Karl Marx set the city within the general process of history. In their descriptive analyses, turn-of-the-century historians like Marcel Poëte, along with certain geographers like Maximilien Sorre and Vidal de la Blache, pointed to the articulation between the city and social groupings. They all demonstrated its political impact and the possibility for understanding the city in terms of the historical process of the social appropriation of space.

History shows how, from the eleventh century onwards, the city is taken over by the reality of finance and how the class in power integrates this reality into the city as a whole, for the process of capitalism infiltrates all social relationships to alienate them according to its own rationale: appropriation becomes exclusive and comes to be called private property. The city has had a hold upon financial and cultural power, and has controlled their circulation as early as the eighteenth century. The city is the seat of capitalism. Issued for the most part from the financial system, the capitalist city devises repressive structures to sustain itself. It becomes the seat of the oppositions between wealth and poverty, the oppressors and the oppressed: the space of social contrasts. The urban practice contained in the city becomes inseparable from social practices overall.

However, by demonstrating the specificity of urban practice, this analysis may have led some to think that the city formed the sufficient object of an autonomous body of knowledge called "urbanism."

Within the science of history, "urbanism" is the specific concept applicable to a particular social practice: namely, urban practice, to which society as a whole is accountable. Promoted to the status of systematic knowledge, "urbanism" undergoes an alteration by virtue of this very extrapolation. Despite its ambition, the discipline of "urbanism" cannot encompass the totality of the urban phenomenon (in terms of materiality and practice) because it already partakes in the process of the division of labor. Urbanists allow that, in the past, the city had been integrated into society and constituted by specific practices within a space organized according to social needs. This cohesion between society in general and the city is supposed to have been replaced by the modern city's incoherence and disorder, as urbanists failed to discover any traits specific to the contemporary city.

Coherence seems, for that matter, to be the central concept of "urbanism": "Urbanism means the opposite of the disorganized or haphazard intervention of the group; urbanism means the opposite of incoherence, but rather, the necessity of a constant attempt at synthesis."[1] This incoherence of social and urban space is in fact just the expression of the coherence of capitalistic society governed by the laws of supply and demand. Proceeding, as it does, from the same political-economic model as the space of the contemporary city, "urbanism," is nothing but the search for this same "incoherent" coherence (internal rationality of the capitalist system). The absence of a radical critique of society by the "urbanistic" approach makes of "urbanism" a direct accomplice of this social order.

1. PARTIAL "URBANISM,"

OR THE SHAMEFUL DIVISION OF LABOR

Knowledge of the world is wholly subject to the division of labor, that is, to hierarchy and particularization. Division of labor came about through the transformation of the natural capital found in cities into mobile capital circulating between cities from the moment the guild economy turned into an industrial economy—the first consequence of which was the formation of classes, class conditions and class oppositions. The process of the division of labor helps us to understand approaches within "urbanism" that result from the essential role played by the city in this socially vital process. "Urbanism" calls itself a science of synthesis, but a synthesis would be possible today only by means of a radical critique of the division of labor. Urbanism, however, shrinks from this critique, because it itself participates in the hierarchization of knowledge: not only has it not become aware of this epistemological situation, but, in keeping with the process of the division of labor, it makes no effort to elucidate its relationships with the other areas of knowledge. Moreover, the "urbanism" that claims to ensure the "betterment of society" has no intention of undertaking a critique of this process, which remains the main obstacle nonetheless.

By synthesizing, the urbanist believes that he makes the unity of the city legible in order to read it. In fact, he does nothing but project his own concept of the city—heir to the cultural and commercial ideology of contemporary society—onto urban reality. The discipline of "urbanism," which is particularized by the rationality of its creations (development plans, structural diagrams, regulations, etc.), attempts to take possession of urban space with the help of the "urbanistic" ideology of the class in power. The country becomes a map dotted with symbols and references in which is set a unitive practice, itself a parody of unitary urban practice.

Since it does not formulate any radical critique, "urbanism" can only accelerate the organized logic of society; namely, through a super-organization of space and time, a grid that conforms to the models provided by the existing order—models which are ratified into the bargain. If the ruling class and its "urbanism" are part of the historical process, the legitimacy sought by this "urbanism" through its conspicuous respect for the vestiges of history is an attempt to fossilize the social space and put it outside of time: an attempt to adjust it once and for all to the existing order. This amounts to a denial of history. While claiming to change the city in order to change society, it tries to conceal (from itself) the fact that it participates in this existing order. Even if it has adapted, perfected, and equipped itself with more or less explicit ideologies, society remains based on the system of finance, private property, and class power. No one, not even the representatives of the opposing parties, looks for solutions for going beyond this, or for a way to call the principles of the Z.U.P. (*Zone à urbaniser en priorité*, Priority Construction Zone), the limitation of agglomeration, or *servitude non aedificandi* into question. By accepting the very idea of "urbanism" and its present structure, urbanists and politicians of all stripes give their approval to the principle of the "soft revolution."

To change the space in which man interacts, to create harmonious surroundings for man, to free man from the machine, to disalienate him and prepare his future: these are some of the vague formulations that haunt the urbanists whose philosophical ambitions have been frustrated—and who are the first to fall under their spell.

Why and for whom does urbanism work today?

2. THE LIQUIDATION OF URBAN PRACTICE

1.

Urbanism conceived in this way remains a *partial "urbanism,"* one that reduces reality to a science or a specialized art. Far from opening the vistas it proclaims, this growing activity in our society entraps (integrates) urban existence within the imperatives of a cultural ideology. The class power from which the present cultural and commercial ideology emanates strives to appropriate urban space and its practices and to rationalize them in terms of "urbanism."

The science known as "urbanism" found its place within this ideology through the absolute necessity of circumscribing a social practice dangerous to power, for it creates the conditions for calling society into question. The experiences of the nineteenth century, with the uprisings of 1830 and 1848 and the Commune of 1871, highlighted the importance of the city in the coming to consciousness of the classes subjected to power. Because of its contradictions, urban practice eluded the rationality of the State. The science of the city came into its own, submitting this practice according to its rationale and disintegrating it by establishing segregations between the various sectors of activity. Zoning is a characteristic example of this process: residential areas, commercial areas, industrial zones, priority construction zones, zones of future development, sensitive areas, etc.

"Urbanism" has produced an "urbanistic" ideology whose intentions are more global, but are nonetheless of the same substance as the reigning cultural and commercial ideology sanctioned by the actions of the urbanists. By a historical irony, the "urbanistic" ideology in our society has a stronger impact than the professional institution that carries out the "urbanism." "With lines of stone, metal or cement, urbanism plots the order of human settlement across the land... At stake is the drawing upon the ground of tomorrow's France. This mission devolves upon urbanism at a time when the expansion of technology profoundly denies the structure of human settlements, overturning traditional ways of life. Our cities in particular must be developed in such a manner as to reconcile the ever deeper subjection of the group to labor with the personal need for well-being and freedom. The infrastructures of production and the contradictions related to economic progress have to be deployed together with the surroundings in which people settle for the purpose of leading more worthy and complete lives... For it takes harmonious surroundings to mold men who are happy to be alive."[2] Such is "*urbanism*," and such is the task of the *urbanists*. This kind of thinking is a pure mystification: it conceals a class strategy that conceives of Planning as nothing more than an organization of practices until they perish or vanish—the final goal of a super-rational organization. Thus partial "urbanism" is just one of the many repressive structures of society. The liquidation of urban practice effected by the ruling class parallels the recrudescence of urban *activity*—a mere simulacrum of *practice*—part of the general process of the bureaucratization and technocratization of thought and the control of everyday life required for the reconstitution of neo-bourgeois thinking along new lines.

"Urbanism" is protected—as imaginary and dream—finding its most spectacular development in "urbanistic" ideology. It represents the escape from a programmed society that constantly launches new reports from the future, representations in which the "slightest detail" of the future "is supposed to be exact" (*Paris-Match*, no. 95, p. 45). The unknown is silhouetted against the horizon of the contemporary city, whose reality is already blurred as if in a memory: the Spectacle is before our eyes. But the accomplishments of "urbanism" are constantly under attack by a criticism accepted and even encouraged by the organs of power, for the reality and the construction that materialize this imagination *must* be criticized. The avowed imperfection of these accomplishments makes it possible to avoid the basic question of their origin and the intentions that created them. Here, this type of critique reveals its limits: it permits the class in power to enact measures—necessarily incomplete and deficient—demanded by the urgency of social needs, to present models and to spread an "urbanistic" ideology that consolidates its hold on society, all under the pretext of socialization.

2.

We say "urbanism," meaning in fact two kinds of "urban planning": projective "*urbanism*" and *reality "urbanism."* The former would be the science fiction of the bourgeoisie as well as the prospective of the "supreme urbanists," or what we call the *planners' utopia*: a utopia chopped up into five-year segments that twist and turn in search of each other. Stretched between the necessity of freeing as many forces as possible and the necessity of controlling these forces as much as possible, this ludicrous utopia allows the expert who practices urbanism to keep dreaming; the urbanist is the first to be conditioned. The second "urbanism" would be that of repression; the "urbanism" of the police, of law and order. Its action is restricted to the definition of zones (zoning), perimeters, limits, areas of conservation and protection: "urbanism," such as it is practiced by the urbanists, is an effort to carve up social space, to maintain an immobile existing order whose creations are but systems enabling integration into more general systems.

To be sure, it is easy enough at the institutional level to ascertain the hold the Government has on daily life through all the guidelines, decrees, codes and regulations secreted by the bureaucracy. One example: whenever a major urbanistic decision is at stake, the decisions taken by municipal councils that appear to be the result of discussions between the various political factions elected by the people are in fact strongly influenced by the guidelines of the Bureaucracy. The agency of the Bureaucracy makes itself felt not only in the inclusion of the program into a master plan, but also in the content of the program itself. One example of this process is provided currently by the elaboration of a major *urban program* in Paris. The struggle between the representatives of the Administration and the municipal council is a struggle between a body of technocrats subject to the central power and a democratic—albeit hypothetical—representation of the people. In a conflict of this kind, the State always has the last word, for the State is an emanation of the class that owns the means of production (in a capitalist country). The State's grip on daily life is indeed the government of daily life by the class that holds power. The great humanist dream of "urbanism" bursts upon contact with reality "urbanism." As Henri Lefebvre has asked: "Could it be that what we call 'urbanism' today is nothing but an ideology (of the technocratic groups) whose intention is—like all ideologies—to hide the real problems, to offer false solutions, to cover up the 'real,' all the while revealing it unwittingly?"[3]

The real masters of "urbanism" today are, on the one hand, the State and its repressive organs monitoring the adherence to the "program," and, on the other hand, "the artificer who is both composer and conductor and who, in possession of all the facts[!], completes them with his own investigation, enhances them with his intuition and finally presides over the composition of the plan and the formulation of the regulations."[4] Put more clearly, "urbanism" is also done at the end of a pencil, the supreme symbol of creation: the urbanist-architect has the essential task of making the hazardous leap from the word (the language of society) to the line (forms that will render mankind harmonious!). Make no mistake about it, urbanism is also that, and at times essentially so: well placed color on good drawing paper. But no one—not even those who practice it every day—will admit as much. "Urbanism" as a "social" mission is so overestimated that it becomes a mystique, and from that point on veils itself with an aura of mystification.

The urbanist is trapped in this vortex. The reduction of social complexity to simple, easily manipulable elements at the level of the "urban" plan (or *structural diagram*) implies amazing pretensions if we consider the fact that the product fabricated by urbanists is nothing other than an "*art de vivre*"; that is, the conditioning of space and the population for the purposes of profit and consumption. Although a social being, man is a commodity presented in the packaging best suited to and most in line with the models foisted upon us by regulations, techniques, and advertising. It is alluring to think that "urbanism" could step beyond its present social determination and work for a future that contradicts the period in which it evolves. "Urbanism" is trapped in the present moment and the socioeconomic constraints of capitalism. Thus a humanist urbanism working for Society is pure illusion.

3.

A semiological "urbanism" based upon a rigorous systematization would be the most elaborate attempt at reducing urban practice. It researches the systems of signs that constitute the most complete representation of urban practice; that is, it tries to establish a pertinent classification of the characteristic types of this practice. At the analytical level, this represents one of the non-exhaustive approaches to urban materiality and practice. But to apply it to operational "urbanism" would be to understand the city as a system, which would turn it into an activity that consumes signs. This would, again, be extrapolating an analytical approach into a total intervention. If the sign and its consumption are indeed a reality of our society, and currently one of its main *productions*, and if these systems of signs are ideological processes that invert reality, that is, if society expends itself tirelessly in an attempt to infuse the real with meanings, and to constitute strongly and subtly organized semiological systems for converting things into signs, the perceptible into signifiers, all the while rationalizing these meanings by reifying all of the social (tragedy, creation, happiness, games), this does not mean that we need to establish urban semiological systems by means of a discipline, unless one wants to over-rationalize urban practice, or clarify it to such a degree that every particle of the practice is summarized in a sign and in a combination of signs. Far from paving the way to a more total "urbanism," the analysis of urban semiology *reveals the systems* that integrate the city in the process of consumption; that is, it points out what is in need of a radical critique. Any other use of semiology in connection with "urbanism" only reinforces our thesis of "urbanism" that is integrated into the existing order.

4.

"Urbanism" is obsessed with grasping totality in order to find its own reason for being; for in wanting to grasp everything, too much eludes it. Be it the supreme urbanist in the halls of power or the operational urbanist, the obsessive fear of not apprehending what they deem to be *the whole city* makes them build the most ludicrous methodological edifices. Of course, they do not integrate the real mechanisms that transform practice, but prefer the appearance of the reconstitution of a social pseudo-totality *in the laboratory* by adding specialists. Even if this were the "urbanism" elaborated by the doctrine of the interdisciplinary approach, it would be no less of an illusion. The interdisciplinary approach was an upshot of the overwhelming demand for a complete reconsideration of the concept of "urbanism." It seemed to be an easy-to-use instrument that called none of the ongoing practices into question. The spread of legislative constraints attests to the overwhelming nature of this demand: the *Cornudet legislation* (1919–24) called for the stimulation, orientation, expansion and beautification of cities; the *Prothin legislation* (June 15, 1943) established the legal framework of "urbanism" and was the first attempt at establishing an overall organization of the social urban space; 1950 gave birth to the first report on land management (*aménagement du territoire*); the 1958 *Code de l'Urbanisme* took total control of the entire organization of space; and as early as April 8, 1960, [Pierre] Sudreau set up the interdisciplinary team in order to apprehend the as yet intangible total-city, thus fitting the urbanistic action to the political context. In its current phase, interdisciplinarity pursues a frantic course to be equal to and in the image of the totality it strives to apprehend. In its practice, urban life swings between aesthetics—hence "urbanism" the *art*—and sociology, economics, demography and geography—hence urbanism the *science*. This is why "urbanism" is torn and in search of its raison d'être: art or science? The interdisciplinary approach tries to overcome this contradiction, a mystification that masks the breaking down of social practice. This interdisciplinarity represents an effort of methodological research: it tries to step beyond the framework of the division of labor. By tackling the problem through its various aspects—geographical, economic, sociological, and aesthetic—and by striving to articulate the contributions of the various disciplines loosely enough, it tries to move beyond their limited horizons. Yet this ambition conceals a lack inherent in the renewal of methods that only reinforces its ideological bias. The interdisciplinary team is concerned only with providing the ideal technical solution for the imposed programs. Thus it cannot refuse and will not call them into question, and contributes in this way to consolidating the existing order. The (very elaborate) technical solution that it proposes hides the urgent need for questioning, criticizing and progressing beyond the existing order. The interdisciplinary approach, more finely structured than its predecessor (which relied on architectural agencies) has the same purpose: to normalize the anomic space of the city within the global structure of capitalist society. Interdisciplinarity naively passes itself off as a micro-model of participation, something that the interdisciplinary team could only really be by integrating the "public."

5.

Participation is based on a nostalgic model and an integration of Marxist ideas, but is nothing more than a parody of self-management. It concerns management *per se* less than performance, for it sidesteps not only the issue of production but also that of the distribution of profits. It tries to reconquer urban democracy, the cradle of "true" participation. Participatory approaches to planning are a sort of socialism based on the socioeconomic progress made by our society in the nineteenth century. The ideologues of participation acknowledge and accept the thesis of the alienation of man in a world that unfolds beyond his control. In participating, man becomes aware of his alienation in consumption. The first system that calls man's attention to his alienation is advertising, which binds him at the same time to the servitude of choosing, of brands, of distinguishing between *good* and *better* products. Participation rests on the manner of acquiring the "regal thing," implying that, in the absence of participation, consumption is unintelligent, and that if it is intelligent, it is thanks to participation. Participation turns the consuming "animal" into a "Homo consumens." Man's partial awareness—still alienated in consumption—of existing for more than just the sake of labor is diverted from self-knowledge and knowledge of his social position. The man who steps beyond his subordination to work is immediately caught up within a whole set of activities that appear to be disalienating, but are nothing more than products of the system from which he thought he had escaped. Each participant in the act of participation believes himself to be a socialist who eludes the constraints of society: this is only the provisional freedom of leisure. In a way, this accentuates man's exteriority to the world (city) by filling the time freed by the reduction of work with objects other than himself; this maintains him at a certain level of lucidity and orients him toward an imagination presented in the form of images or signs to which he thinks he aspires—or really does aspire! Participation is presented as a civic obligation, which is then taken up by the objectivity of the news media ("*Tell France-Soir what is not going well in your neighborhood and France-Soir will tell...*"). Yet morality and consumption are one and the same: to participate means to respond to the ethical imperative to consume, to consume oneself, in the world of commercial goods whose place of deployment is the city.

6.

The extravagant privilege of "urbanism" is to facilitate the implantation of an atemporal and neutral society's living environments. "Urbanism" is only one of the facets of *modernism*, which can be defined as a twofold project. On the one hand, the *acceleration* by all and every means (compatible with the system) of the necessary mutations of the economy. On the other hand, the monitoring and concealment of the inadequacies and contradictions of this acceleration through a participatory ideology. Thus it is more and more difficult to harmonize the evolution of the relationships of production ("growth") and the evolution of social relationships ("prosperity"). The solution to this problem is a third term: none other than the ideology of consumption. Thus "urbanism" is modernist and one of the necessary factors in establishing modernism.

Society determines its plans on the basis of this particular representation, creating thereby the *ideology of necessity* that essentially governs the act of "urbanism."

Every necessity is presented as a historical obligation—under whichever regime happens to be in power. This means forgetting one's history. It means omitting the historical situation of capitalism based on private property and class struggle, forgetting that the city that gradually "engorges" itself is a city of the accumulation of capital. Necessity is secreted by the industrial society. It is an obligation only for maintaining the current economic structures and can be justified only from the point of view of reconquering society through neocapitalist thought—two interdependent reasons, incidentally. According to the ideology of "modernism" that we have just mentioned, this reconquest can be achieved only by a reconsideration of the means and reasons for production (workers having shares in their company) and of the system of distribution and consumption.

This new takeover of society cannot be achieved without a colonization of the city, and this necessarily requires an "urbanism."

The radical critique of the city and of "urbanism" is part of an overall critique of society. This critique will entail the reconstruction of the one and the ultimate impossibility of the other.

"Urbanism," a science of synthesis: therein lies the "social" mystification of the official texts, which are reinforced by the pseudo-scientificity of the theoretical writings of specialists.

This mystification expresses its deeper reality, which is actually a practical powerlessness in urbanism's productions. A case in point is the "urban environment" (formerly urban art) of the "*nouveaux ensembles*" (new housing projects). The monotony they instill does not come from the repetitive forms, nor from the identical volumes, for neither the form nor the volume are devoid of a social content. What is reiterated *by* the form is an identical social message: the monotony here can only be the residue of the rationality of the State, and so to attribute it to a formal reason is only an alibi. By highlighting its formal aspects (whether architectural or sociological), one dissociates "urbanism" from its integrative function within the socio-economic order and its articulation in the structure of society.

This would show how deeply this specialty is bogged down in the deluded consciousness of its action and the extent to which it destroys itself through its internal incoherence and its conceptual divisions. This dilution fosters the illusion of an overarching knowledge, a new urbanism that would be stabilized by a "prospective imagination."

Partial "urbanism" thinks that it is responding to a general social need, while in fact it only builds segregationary housing that is blurred by the homogeneity of the systems of consumption. The goal of society is to consume merchandise. To this end, complex mechanisms take possession of urban space and shape urban practice; the city becomes one of the major outlets for the distribution of packaged merchandise. When "urbanism" conceives or materializes an urban structure, it claims to liberate man from industrial society, while this liberation in fact enslaves man to the rational organization of free time and to the contemplation of "nature." The city and its environment are the space and time of organized forgetting, and they are all the more rational as they become subject to the general organization of society. The forgetting of a present—

less enslaved by its form, than by its structure—and the imagination of a harmonious situation are the two sides that articulate life and consumption: projective "urbanism" combines with reality "urbanism," and neither more real than the other. The real is blurred in favor of an imagination replete with the models of mass consumption.

Until recently, "urbanism" was the property of the State, which presented it as a necessary "socialization" of society. This up until *Paris 2*, the first instance of private urbanism in France; "urbanism" at least in terms of number (pop. 20,000), if not of ideology. It marketed the most "in" thing that the "avant-garde" of official "urbanism" had in the works: *a singular art de vivre*. The prospectus of *Paris 2* was the first treatise on class "urbanism" to contain both the urbanistic ideology of the powers that be and the urbanistic theory of the planners. This may have been the first time that "urbanism" was ever sold. It is the dream "city," with roots reaching down to the Sun King, and dedicated to the leisure of the king hidden in each city-dweller; it is pastime, fancy and capital all rolled into one. After all, is the city not his dream fulfilled? Will it be realized at last? Shrouded in the mists of oblivion: it is a city that existed for only two months. It remains the symbol of something or other. It served the same purpose as the packaging in which merchandise is wrapped.

"Throughout *Paris 2*… one can experience profound joys…" To this end, the streets of the city that is creating a new *art de vivre* are lined with a "Paris of the superlative class"[5]: a Place de la Concorde twice the size of the Orly airport, the area of the Champs-Elysées—apropos of what? Apropos of nothing and everything, since the "drugstore never closes."

"Throw your coat off at the cloakroom, leave your children at the nursery and do your shopping free of burden; meet with friends, have a drink together at the drugstore, it's a new lifestyle."[6] "It is an enhanced and simplified life" (*Paris-Match*), one that could be built only in a city of consumption "in which the only people who work are those who serve you." On the condition that you consume (yourself), "everyday life is like a modern fairytale." The consumer citizen takes appearance for reality and revels in pure appearance. Conditioning (from the packaging of the product to the alienation of man…) means the shaping of the desire to partake of the good fortune of consumption; the happy citizen attains the essence of the *art de vivre*…

With these claims, we reach the rock bottom of present-day "urbanism." We are confronted with an "urbanism" that unveils its global project. Social segregation; existence based on the protection of a collectivized private consciousness, to the exclusion of all socialization; a mythification of private property by the transformation of paper money into passes for free movement... Unlike Paris 1, *Paris 2* is a perfect conditioning machine, the product of which is Man. Could it be that true happiness lies in the over-organization of life and the city?

The urbanists laugh at this manifestation, but do we not find in it the exact application of the theories and the projection of the intentions that they put into their own creations—which the State never realizes? That is the question.

The dream shared by the "urbanistic" ideology and reality-"urbanism" display the exact conditions of the process of "urbanism" that excludes the city from the dialectics of history. The city becomes foreign to man not because it is "*incoherent and disorganized*, gigantic and loud, vicious and dirty," but because partial "urbanism" deprives it of its oeuvre: the city itself.

Versailles, November 8, 1967
World Day of URBANISM

UTOPIE

1. R. Auzelle, "Conditions et impératifs de l'urbanisme," in *La vie urbaine*, no. 11, April–June 1961.
2. ("General Instructions for urbanistic projects, April 8, 1960") *Code pratique de l'urbanisme*, Ministère de la construction, 1961.
3. Henri Lefebvre, *Métaphilosophie*, éd. de Minuit (*Arguments* series), 1965, p. 118.
4. *Ibid.*, note 2, p. 40.
5. Prospectus brochure for "Paris 2 au Chesnay," p. 9.
6. *Ibid.*

utopie

HUBERT TONKA
JEAN-PAUL JUNGMANN
JEAN AUBERT

ARCHITECTURE AS A THEORETICAL PROBLEM*

"Any step forward in a real movement is better than a dozen programs."
K. Marx

THE CAPITALIST MODE OF THE PRODUCTION OF ARCHITECTURE

Our intention is not to deal with architecture as a thing in itself, but to show its *being-in-society*, or rather in a society governed by a given mode of production that induces both a technical and an aesthetic practice. To remain at the level of a very general interpretation of the relationships between architecture and society would leave out some of the very articulations that constitute and maintain architecture in and by a given society.

The only way to comprehend *being* (*essence*) is through *appearance*, which is a coherent multiplicity or contradictions placed on identical or different levels. At first sight, architecture means quite different things to common sense than it does to professional institutions, to political power or to financial power. Are these apparently divergent and contradictory meanings juxtaposed, impermeable to one another, or will analysis show that there are connections between them, an internal coherence not unrelated to the coherence of society as a whole? To analyze what really takes place means first questioning the manifestations and appearances that present themselves to sensible perception, then trying to sort out the levels perceived; those that appear at the concrete surface of the things and events of everyday life. This primary level, of findings and appearances, is often the froth of reality, or, if you prefer, the ideological crust. Why give it any consideration? Why not go straight to the true facts, to the truth of facts? Why call the ideological crust a "concrete surface"? To take ideology, illusion, to be pure ideology or pure illusion, is one of the first mistakes of analysis. To consider ideology as pure falsification is to falsify the reality imprisoned in ideology. Finally, doesn't understanding ideology as inevitably negative leave aside the dialectic? Hegel shows us that the negative is never purely negative, that it already contains its opposite. To accept that the facts, that the events resulting directly from the production process of bourgeois society are invariably rotten and must be rejected as such, places analysis within the theoretical lens of those who strive to prove the impossibility of protest or of criticism in an industrially advanced society. Agreeing with this means agreeing with nihilism. All too often we forget Hegel's teachings. Regarding the practice of (critical) theory is unacceptable: criticism is neither rotten in itself nor pure in the abstract. History slips in where it can, it is up to us to look for it. The common omission that takes the negation of the capitalist world to mean the negation of life, or of pleasure, has brought international opposition to a positivism that negates political struggle, has lured class struggle away from the terrain of violence and led it to that of peaceful coexistence, whose stigmas and errors our "generation" lives. The brilliance of the true structure, of enduring things, of systems organized with their own blind coherence, homogenizes the manifestations, makes it impossible to understand objectively how base and superstructure interpenetrate. The radical leveling of the superstructure ("everything is integrated and integrating, alienated and alienating, etc.") sweeps away the latent elements of dissent. It took May 1968, for example, for a majority of conscious architects to define themselves no longer in grudging silence but in active criticism; that is, no longer in union demands stuck in the perspectives of bourgeois liberalism, but in a socialist perspective. The search

* An outline of this text was published in the May 1968 issue of *Architectural Design* with the title "Architecture as a theoretical problem," Paris, London, March 1968.

Owing to the circumstances in May–June 1968 in Paris, at the time that we were writing this text, we received few of the theses defended in the work commissions of the former École des Beaux-Arts. Since we could not follow these commissions at the time due to other commitments, we unfortunately could not take into account the theses discussed there. We have noted only the verbatim content of certain tracts and slogans, and one particular fact: the uprising of architects and their just struggle.

for the fragments of democracy in capitalist society and the residence of "latent socialism" (Marx) are part of theoretical practice. The advocates of the structure and, more exactly in architecture, the advocates of redeeming technology, delude themselves when they think that they can attain the reality of facts with their critical apparatus, and even more so—this is where they fool themselves completely—when they place their "positive" solutions on the crumbling ground of a capitalist society unable to listen to them. They go from failure to failure without analyzing their causes. Far from transforming the failures experienced on the technical level into an awareness of the political implications that necessarily follow any change in the bourgeois industrial code, they strive to integrate them into the capitalist mode of production. They leave out the following postulate, which explodes the thesis of the nihilism of critique: that the truly democratic elements appearing in the bourgeois order will take on their true meaning, and will be fulfilled, only after the establishment of a socialist society. To think that it is possible to get straight to the facts is not wrong in itself, but lets the main thing slip away. Implementing scientific analysis when one only claims to reach structures is absurd, for it permits the postulate that everything pertaining to ideology and alienation be referred back to ideology.

For us, it will at first only be a matter of dismantling the manifestations of architecture without making a manifesto. And then of attempting to penetrate—through and beneath subjective appearances (the manifest) and ideological illusions—the role and status of architecture, in order to apprehend our object as the result or the product of a society. Architecture and its product do not refer directly or immediately to the mode of production. Architecture is mediated by value systems, by culture and by the aesthetic economy, which are direct results of the mode of production; with the exception of the technical portion of architecture, which is linked to industrial development and to the power of the industrial monopolies. When we say that architecture does not immediately flow from the mode of production, we do not mean that it is excluded from the production process—it is in any case part of value systems and culture. We simply want to draw attention to the results of certain simplistic theses that purport to show the existing correlation between architecture and capitalism in a relation of immediacy. Here we face the dogmatic thesis of an entire socialist movement that denies the existence of an aesthetic practice unrelated to preestablished canons of beauty and to their importance in praxis. A Socialist Realism that neglects the existing mediations between the mode of production and the architectural product neglects to understand architectural reality as an accumulator of the figurative signs of history, for—and this is a characteristic of this particular realm—architecture (no matter for whom it is made: Princes, Lords, the Bourgeoisie...) is always *seen* (except for hidden architecture), it enters the field of the visible and sayable, it imposes *culture* in a tactile manner, and therefore designates—and even determines those who, in their filth—lack it.

This sectorial analysis conceals an ambition. Within our project, architecture in a bourgeois society is typical of certain social relationships between the object (aesthetic, technical, inhabited and inhabitable) and the subject (the individual determined by his social situation, his status in the labor system, his salary, his socio-professional category, etc.). In order to do this, architecture must be understood as the *product* of a society, which means understanding it as inherent in the productive forces and modes of production of the society in question. We will show the forces and actions at each moment of this product's transformation and take into account the relationships and articulations with other productions. For the question remains: either architecture transcends society's other productions—the "work of architecture" descending to society from a firmament accessible only to "creators"—or architecture is produced by a total society, and the ties of interdependence are closely interwoven, as with all other productions and moments of transformation of this society, called *social practice.*[1] On the one hand, it is the so-called "work" of pure art or technology, drawn from the intelligence and talent of "orchestra conductors," "men of synthesis," artists or "super-technicians." On the other, it is the expression of the coherence and logic of a total society.

To avoid the ambiguity raised by the already noted concept of *architecture as a product of society* let us be more precise. We can distinguish the idealist vision that sees architecture as a product of culture, an aesthetic vision, derived from the intelligentsia, without there being any organic and ideological ties between the economy, politics and the production of works. In that case, architecture would be the ideal product of an imaginary not subjected to the trivial reality of bourgeois commerce. In this sense we understand architecture as a product of the mode of production, a product that has its place in the process of production, this process that induces a certain social order, a certain society: in other words, architecture-as-"commodity," whose use value and exchange value

1. Cf. Louis Althusser, *Pour Marx*, p. 167.

are included in the logic of the products of alienated labor. Only this dialectical materialist concept of architecture as product (commodity) and production permits an objective understanding of architecture implied within, and programmed according to, the desiderata of the mode of production. And so there is nothing arbitrary, or more exactly, nothing normative, in declaring that there is a fundamental difference between architecture elaborated under a feudal mode of production and architecture conceived under a capitalist mode of production (bourgeois).

To grasp this difference, it is less a matter of studying architecture than the culture and the subcultures of a given society in relation to its formalizations, its spatiality. For example, the "redistribution" of products taken away in serfdom for the purpose of great festivals results in a certain architecture, and the aesthetic pleasure we may get from it today appears not in relation to the social situation that prevailed in the Renaissance, but reflects the imaginary that we construct around the idea we have about this period; a difference instituted, for example, by the fact that labor and the social relationship to labor are radically different. The *salary* establishes the possibility of evaluating the object that presents itself to perception and to life, not in relation to an absolute measure based on the abstract value of money, but in relation to the labor-time necessary to acquire this thing. The architectural object (the Work) is accountable and accounted for, representing a certain capital (tied to the laws of private property) and, in order to preserve it, the ruling class sublimates it into a supreme art object: the protection, which is created by the accumulation of an (actually and ideologically) inscribed wealth, represents this class. The "esthetic" value is proportional to the exchange value of the architectural object and, confounded, the two are transformed into the sacralization of the architectural object (the Work). It is cherished and protected by all kinds of laws, while, at the institutional level, commissions of all kinds hasten to safeguard it. At the same time, on the practical level, propaganda claiming a great respect for modern architecture is disseminated; a sacralization that is only a form of false consciousness incited by Wealth and not, as some seem to think, part of a new system of symbols. Instead of making life more livable, the sacredness of architecture is wedged between the individual who lives it and the one who capitalizes it. The work of *privation*—the bourgeoisie's model of the accumulative life established as a "lifestyle" for society as a whole—is carried out concretely. The gap between the haves and the have-nots widens. No aesthetic criterion intervenes in understanding a phenomenon of this kind. The divergence between the architecture for the people and architecture for the bourgeoisie is the very same that we find between those who cash in on surplus value and those who have only their salary; between those who have the capital to make architecture and those who pay to live in architecture. To speak of an architecture of class is not an illusion.

The novel idea that appeared around the 1920s, and to which many architectural modernists still subscribe (Le Corbusier, among others)—*the duty of architecture applied to housing*—allows us to show the part played by the architecture of housing in the growth of production. The postulates established here make it easy to understand this new architecture in the alienation of labor, as well as the set of relays and the softening of awareness enabled by such architecture. Power's unceasing efforts on behalf of housing does not eliminate the recuperative function necessary after a hard day's work, and the same goes for leisure and the architecture of leisure. But the fraud did not stay hidden for long, for legislation, caught in the collusion between power and capitalism, uses the language of repression: granting a little pleasure paves the way towards the demand for total pleasure. This simple contradiction of power becomes the basis for the protest against power. The proposition, "architecture as a political act," takes on its full meaning in extracting itself from its revolutionary euphoria and its aestheticism. This proposition has often been understood to mean a political power intrinsic to architecture, but this makes sense only if we consider architecture independently in its social practice: here again, as so often, we find the old idea that architecture has the power to transform social practice. This is what the functionalists believed and what the defenders of technology believe today. That architecture has an integrating power does not mean that it can be posited as a power of dissent. Isn't it rather that architecture is a consequence both of politics and of policy (*le politique*)? In that case, should we not understand the basic proposition mentioned above to mean: architecture as a political act can only be that of the dominant politics? By displacing criticism toward an architectural social practice instead, we place architectural production on the level of class struggle and not on that of aestheticism or the worldly success of the architectural act.

If we raise this question, it is because appearances make us hesitate, because the facts perceived do not permit immediate distinctions. Where is appearance and where reality? How to distinguish between the two? Might the reality of appearance not hide a deeper reality? Is this reality so shameful that it must be kept hidden? We will see that the connections between a particular product—architecture—and the means and reasons for its production could easily be defined and explained, if they were not modified, reflected, echoed, amplified or diminished, reinforced or weakened, by an active, effective, and complex game of ideas and concepts called *ideology*. And it is in the midst of a labyrinthine world of real and imaginary facts, of ideas more concrete than matter, of matter impregnated with ideas, in which distorting mirrors and ideology transform and reflect the unrecognizable images of beings and events, that we will have to grasp the *coherence* which, in our object, architecture, absorbs the insuperable contradictions hidden by the dazzle of the great Luna Park of the society of Capital.

On the side of the superstructures where ideologies are in play, we can discover the modes of production and the productive forces that include social structure as an organization of property, social functions and social classes. This is the level on which we find the city, or the "urban," from which architecture cannot be separated in an industrial capitalist society whose overall tendency is to become an urban society (the very fundament of capitalism, as Marx showed). Architecture is part of the urban problematic, which we have already dealt with elsewhere,[2] showing that it was not innocent in the overall strategy of class power, and that "urbanism" is not a problem in itself, external to class struggle. We do not care much for the old dichotomy between architecture and urbanism, the after-effects of which may be found in the recent fusion of these two categories into a single one called the "organization of space": the rationalizing simplicity of its solely spatial and formal vision is known, and we have shown that it liquidates social practice. Architecture as the production of society is one of the problematics articulated with objective urban reality.

In the city, where capital is accumulated and merchandise distributed, is all sociality erased? How does the base express itself? Can it still find a level of expression? In a word, is there a social demand? And if so, how does it make itself heard? Can it avoid the economism and growth that characterize our society? Demand can hardly be rationalized; it does not fit easily into the registers of management and bureaucracy. In the end, there is apparently only a social command normalized according to the categories of registers and punch-cards exactly transcribing the value systems and governing social relationships within the narrow confines of the probable. Is the possible a dream, a mythology for neurotics? Does it seem that the State and certain pressure groups have a decisive (and alienating) role in the expression and satisfaction of the commanded demand? Is architecture at the service of society as a whole or does it serve only one class in society? In May 1968 our class society unmasked itself once again to the less perceptive, when, for a brief moment, the ideological edifice tottered, a protest movement appeared, brutally denouncing the "hypocrisy of the State," the "myth of urbanism for all," "the repressive function and the camouflage function of present urban politics," and slogans also appeared: "architecture in the service of the people," "architecture is a political act." What do these expressions of sudden realization reveal or cover in the production of architecture in France?

The interpretation of architecture as a production of society is not self-evident, it requires a conceptual apparatus which—in a theoretical practice that does not yet exist—will attempt to grasp, beneath evident appearances and through ideological discourses, the moments of transformation of a commodity called architecture in the course of its production at the heart of French society. In order to realize this project, we will first have to discover certain levels of architectural reality not explicit in the received knowledge of architecture.

LEVELS OF ARCHITECTURAL REALITY

Do not expect us to speak of public architecture or private architecture, the architecture of cultural edifices, of labor, of housing, or of leisure. Considered in its relationship to social practice, the entirety of architecture that structures space and delivers it over to "dwelling"[3] cannot be analyzed in its typological form, as the answer to rationally differentiated "functions," such as *dwelling, working, cultivating body and mind,* etc. Similarly, to successively analyze architecture in relation to the economy or the "social" would totally ignore the tenuous links linking these various aspects together, and this analysis—once again typological—would not elucidate our social enquiry in any way.

The news media provide abundant material for analysis, whose content, whether precise or redundant, immediate or recurrent, apprehends and restores all the appearances of the phenomena of our lives, though not without ideological deformations, which we can then understand as such—at the risk of ourselves slipping into ideology. Newspapers, general

2. Cf. "La logique de l'urbanisme," *UTOPIE*, Nov. 1967.

3. "Inhabitation" [Fr. *l'habiter*, noun form of the verb "to inhabit"]: "Inhabitatio, the foundation of being, the fullness of the being of habitation: these two propositions transcend the mere uses of everyday life proposed by progressive architecture." Cf. "Notes sur Habiter," Hubert Tonka, Tony Garnier Seminar, in *Cahier* 65/66, *Propos sur le logis*.

interest magazines, trade journals, official and institutional texts, are the most usable of the media indicative of social phenomena. Knowing them can lead us to unveil the non-apparent links describing the internal logic of the superficial incoherence with which our sensible experience confronts us.

The complexity and multiplicity of participants involved in the architectural problematic will then appear to us. Some facts taken from real estate publications: after the "events" of May–June 1968, and with the ensuing risk of devaluation, the real estate ratings—a sure thing—are again rising. Investment in construction is going to increase, but it is assumed that it will be restrained by some "barriers" institutionally and in the economic framework: difficulties in financing due to the archaic credit system, real estate speculation, the cost of construction (too high because the means of production are not adapted to the needs), the sluggishness of commercial and legal transactions, bureaucratic hurdles (regulations for construction and urbanism), the misunderstandings and lack of information that isolates designers, builders and users, or consumers. These objective facts, which anyone can read in the press, are the ones that, with a few others, determine the number of cubic meters of architecture built in France in a given year and also determine the possibility that various segments of French society will be concerned, in some way, by architectural production. The facts are not appearances, but true realities.

It seems that the production process of the commodity called architecture no longer fits the schema that still governs the "Architect's Code of Professional Duties" : the equilibrium of the production relationships—traditionally based on the entities of architect, client and business, as defined by the Code established in 1941—is the expression of an eighteenth-century reality, no doubt already obsolete at the beginnings of industrial capitalist society. This reality cannot be extrapolated to account for present conditions. State intervention at many levels of architectural production, especially urban architectural production, along with the actions of various noninstitutionalized pressure groups, and finally the replacement of the reality of the *client* with that of the *user*—or more exactly of the *consumer*—have rendered the structures of architectural production obsolete, especially given that they are still experienced by most architects. The latter owe their survival only to the maintenance of powerful cultural ideologies, as we will see below.

After much analysis, we have come to distinguish three partially overlapping levels in the process of architectural production, which permit an interpretation that more closely follows the reality of this production's moments of transformation. The production of architecture presupposes concerted and willful action within the framework of professional institutions and structures, these actions being accomplished by specific persons acting on specific means of production. They are inseparable from the governmental instructions that guide and support them, ranging from professional training to the special directives applied to specific problems of professional activity. We call *architectonic activity* the level that accounts for these actions. It includes all the legal and technical authorities that participate in architectural production at all levels: from theoretical practice to construction in space, from education to the professional activity of the builders, from the establishment of an association or union to the existence of nonintegrated professional activities. Architectonic activity contains the *order* and the *doing*, and is directed by a state and professional will subject to bureaucracy. It *is* or *is not* the emanation of *social* practice. At this level it is interesting to analyze the relationships between the State and the ensemble of professional institutions. These relationships are very close, in law and in fact. The strictly apolitical stance that characterizes the exercise of the profession is not unrelated to this state of affairs. Until now, professional activity, from schools to universities to the highest social responsibilities, had completely abstained from criticism of governmental politics, which in the meantime became more and more prevalent in urbanistic and architectural decision-making, culminating in the present situation, which has made "urbanism" into the chief organ of the State's spatial planning.[4] Existing relationships between the State and professional institutions allow us to understand how advocates of avant-garde architecture and urbanism—for a time appearing as "cursed" modernists, rejected by society and culture—would be coherently integrated and soon provide the basis for the ruling class's ideology, the one that constitutes the State.

Architectonic activity does not account for all of architectural production, nor for each and every moment of the architectural act's production. It appears that very specific actions give rise to the moments of transformation, or production, and that do not belong to architectonic activity: these are actions which, because they are situated outside of the institutional framework, have a direct influence on production. Without *dirigiste* economic planning, or with only the echo of planning, conduct is guided by the values proper to the overall economy. This

4. Op. cit., note 2.

all of Science
all of Technology
in the service of order
devoted to
the refined perfectioning
of an industry that
produces objects
devoid of refinement
for everyday life

level encompasses the groups or micro-groups instigating capitalist or socialist economic structures. We will call this level *architectonic practice*. The financing and credit systems, real-estate speculation (in capitalist societies) and the role of certain forms of commercial organization refer to the level of architectonic practice. It is a practice with its own rationality, and not an activity whose rationality inheres in the material transformed, existing only by virtue of it.[5]

Architectonic practice is characterized by its unusual relations with architectonic activity. The actions or conducts that architectonic practice refers to are usually considered "immoral" or "shameful," and always acultural. They are fought at the level of the rationality of architectonic activity, and are indeed fought with at least apparent harshness by the State and institutions of architecture and urbanism. The State deploys an apparatus of directives and regulations and establishes new institutions to minimize the effects of these "immoral" actions in the architectural production; actions that are otherwise fully consistent with the general capitalist system. For example: it was in some sense to avoid real estate speculation that the Z.U.P. and Z.A.D. were created in 1961. Experience has proved this measure to be ineffective. Yet it gave the population the impression that there was a will on the part of the government to curtail the "horrible" speculation in real estate, the target of urbanists—unanimously convinced that it was the prime and principal cause of all urbanism's misdeeds—while no one can ignore that it is absolutely inevitable in a capitalist society. Otherwise, "dispensations" from State directives very often give a free hand to pressure groups whose effectiveness even in actions that are otherwise officially condemned make them decision masters when they deem it necessary.[6] An example

5. Activity: understood as the rationalization of a material's mode of transformation. Also as the "set of coordinated actions and labor(s) of human beings, a special fraction of this totality" (trans. from *Le Robert*).

Practice: "the set of activities effecting, in a given system of production, the transformation of a given material by a certain number of suitable instruments" (L. Althusser, *Pour Marx*). "Voluntary activities aiming at concrete results. Concrete manner of exercising an activity (opp. of *rule*, *principle*). Habitual manner of acting." This definition from *Le Robert* omits the dynamic principle inherent in every moment of a material's transformation by a suitable technique, which comes through in its definition of the adjective: "concerns action, the transformation of reality by human will (phil.). Which determines conduct; normative. Which concerns the sense of reality, the ability to adapt oneself to concrete situations and defend one's material interests" (*Le Robert*).

As far as the word *architectonic* is concerned, we will restrict ourselves to the accepted meaning: "Related to the art of the architect; suited to the technique of architecture" (*Le Robert*). Needless to say, the reference suspected in "related to" and "suited to" is the one that has currency in our mode of production: to *be related to* and *to be suited to* means to be integrated in the value systems, in the codes of the bourgeois order, its ethics, or its morals. In this connection we would refer to Norbert. Guterman and Henri Lefbvre's *La conscience mystifiée*, Gallimard, coll. Les essais, 1936, and to the introduction to *Critique de la vie quotidienne*, 1958, éd. Arche, coll. Le sens de la marche; in particular, "Brèves notes sur des lieux communs." These two publications outline what so-called bourgeois *life* is, what bourgeois ethics and morals are, and the ties that exist between production, the relationships of production, and *everyday life*.

concretely illustrates the level of architectonic practice: nearly all the newspaper stands in France are operated by a single company that builds, installs, and runs them. All the decisions involving the installation or removal of a stand obey purely commercial imperatives, imperatives that are either favored or hindered by municipalities, urbanists, and architects, who until now have always tried to reject this uncontrollable commercial element disfiguring their urban plans. In this way an important piece of urban equipment partially eludes the control of both the State and urbanists, asserting itself by virtue of its commercial necessity, which is linked to urban consumption, and so to everyday life.

The most remarkable particularity of the actions of architectonic practice upon analysis, is that, while ostensibly rejected by institutions, it constitutes the essential dynamic principle of architectural production. Resuming the example above, we would note that the research of the architect Antoine Grumbach on the possibilities for minimal urban interventions through elements of urban equipment, such as bus stops, newspaper stands, traffic lights, vistas, monuments commemorating the dead of the last two wars, abandoned squares, etc., often provide a rationalization for spontaneous acts of architectonic practice (within the framework of free trade). In the intervention there is a passage from "vulgar" architectonic practice to institutional architectonic activity that involves the "art" and know-how of the architect-urbanist. This is a perfect example of bureaucratization, followed by a conscious and rational organization of everyday life by power, or its fine structures of intervention, which only appear to be disconnected from the apparatus of the State. The same remarks could be applied to the theories and research of the American architect Christopher Alexander.

Architectonic activity and architectonic practice constitute two levels referring to actions which, although seemingly opposite, contribute to architectural production; the dynamic principle belongs to the architectonic practice which, in capitalist society, accounts most directly for the economic-political structures, particularly of free trade.

We put forth here two levels of reality inherent in the strategy of bourgeois society, not two levels of social reality that could be found in all structured functions of a society. This is what "seemingly opposite" meant above: the dynamics of architectural production in our social system are indeed architectonic *practice*, referring directly and without false consciousness to free trade and competition, and not architectonic *activity*, which all too easily becomes the target of criticism by the theoreticians of the "opposition." The clarity offered by state institutions is only a mirage. To correctly grasp the interplay of the dichotomy we have brought to light, we must take a closer look at the apparent distance imposed by the State, which has been in the process of reshaping itself for some time. To realize its liberalist and "ultra-socialist" plans, different agencies at different levels of power implement a strategy and a tactic which they refine as they go. The division of labor is one of the main foundations of so-called bourgeois society instilling an inevitable struggle between the separated, the rejected, and the torn apart. An obvious separation is that of the classes and, thanks to Marxist analysis, the ruling class tries by every means to effectively eradicate the symptoms that would authorize, in perfect objectivity, a dissenting action on the part of the have-nots, or rather the exploited—an expression we prefer, because for us it is not just a matter of an overturning of power—in a word, of the proletariat (in the form that remains of it). This State does not want to be bourgeois anymore, nor capitalistic. The theoreticians of the State say that class struggle no longer exists, and nor does the proletariat. They claim that to look for anything but individual freedom is illusory and utopian: at the present developed stage of the freedom of existence, promising a "better" future would be to fool those who have toiled honestly to acquire what they have in life—incommensurably more than what they had not so long ago. In the end, the socialist critics would all be subject to Engel's criticism, according to which their critique of today's society—a critique that would reject objectivity and deny the real achievement of progress—would be no more and no less than *utopian socialism*. Most of all, such critics would undermine the forces of liberation developed at the heart of society in the course of so-called renewal. According to progressive liberal theoreticians, this critique would be corroborated by the analyses of certain marxologists such as Herbert Marcuse, who also reach the conclusion that liberation would ultimately end with the achievement of human harmony in an advanced industrial society. Beyond a relative nihilism that Marcuse is said to develop regarding the future of advanced industrial society (which already means acknowledging that Marcuse has a revolutionary aim, but that he, and he alone, has not *yet* found the way to escape containment, although he points out that the power to *initiate*

6. This thesis was already advanced by us in the first version of this text published in *A.D.*: it was corroborated by the texts published by the striking personnel of the S.T.A.C.U. (*Service Technique Central d'Amenagement et Urbanisme*). However, they must be taken with caution, for they contain a certain revolutionary voluntarism, and while this does not detract from the intrinsic value of a movement that they initiate through the coming to consciousness of the political implications of the Administration, it deserves the full critical attention of theoretical analysis.

action has found shelter among those who are not subject to the process of labor and production in advanced industrial society), this ultimate human harmony would mark the end of the contradictions resulting from the end of history. It is true that in his last book, *One-Dimensional Man*, Marcuse wrote that "the traditional elements of disturbance have been *eliminated* or *isolated*, the dangerous elements have been *taken in hand*."[7] Speaking of contemporary society, he points out further that "its main features are well known: the interests of capital concentrate the national economy, the government plays the role of a *stimulant*, supporter and *sometimes* of controlling force; this economy is enmeshed in a global system of military alliances, monetary agreements, technical assistance plans and development plans; the "blue collars" are assimilated to the "white collars," the union leaders assimilate with factory directors; the leisures and aspirations of the different classes become uniform: there is a preestablished harmony between scientific research and national objectives. Lastly, the home is invaded by public opinion, and the bedroom is open to mass communications."[8] Marcuse presents the results of fifty years of efforts on the part of the advocates of capitalism. It may not be as pure as his language would make it seem, but that is the plan, the trend. The contradictions of capitalism, which, according to Marx, were supposed to cause it to collapse cannot be annihilated, and so they are integrated into the solidification of the society of capital. But is it true that what has been integrated cannot be disintegrated? Or, that what has been structured cannot be de-structured? In light of the history of May 1968—more precisely of the 13th of May and the 9 million strikers—we negate the ineluctability of integration. Will it not be by closure, by containment, that everything will begin again?

This is where the strategy must be dismantled. If we read objectively the institutional discourse delivered by the State and the powers that call themselves official, there is no doubt that it contains an effort at socialization and a certain measure of democracy. The State presents itself as the guarantor of honesty. It considers all the interests—and sometimes even this is true! It is the bearer of style and aesthetics (there is not a single text issued by the Ministry of Equipment that does not bear the stamp of aestheticism. It maintains the Honor of the homeland and refuses to compromise with the capitalist mire. It avoids mediocrity and repels the triviality of everyday life—all these laws and decrees intended to endow everyday life with a measure of grandeur, nobility, dignity… The State even goes so far as to dictate rules contrary to the tenets of free trade, but only in the wording[9]; it criticizes actions that are unworthy of a State worthy of this name. But it is merely the facade of the bourgeois edifice. It is a form that passes itself off as the structure of society. The State takes itself for history, takes on its appearances, but it is really nothing. The architectonic activity that comes from the State apparatus is the architectural guarantee in the eyes of the society of good taste and artistic treasures, of which the architect is the technical and aesthetic symbol; hence his apolitical stance at the institutional level. Architectonic activity in no way possesses the creative dynamics of the architectural act, hence the impossibility of "pure" architectural creations, of "works" protesting against the existing order. At all levels, the architectural act and its product are always imbued with ideology, due to the very fact that architectonic activity draws its substance from bourgeois social practice.

The game and mission of the pseudo-separation between state institutions and free "commerce," the exploitation of the proletariat, the systems for recuperating surplus value (through consumption), the employment of exhaustion, sexual repression, or in any case all the prohibitions against full enjoyment—in a word, the alienation of consciousness and of the body—camouflage the formation of a totality closing in on itself. The false dichotomy we present is a falsification that would make capitalism appear as a superior stage of democracy, and which tries to demonstrate its indestructibility, making us take effect for cause. If we show the causality between the State (power) and bourgeois social organization, we are not at all postulating the absorption of all the forces of liberation. They are contained at a third level: that of *social practice*. The first two levels that we have extracted (architectonic activity and architectonic practice) present themselves as detached so as the better to conceal their underlying coherence. The moments of transformation proper to the two levels we detected lead to the architectural act only through and on this third level, which permits architectural production to complete itself, and, above all, to be realized. Here, we could speak of "*architectural practice*," which should be understood as a specific part of overall social practice. It would unfold itself and find its sense in binding inhabitation and aesthetics; it is through it that architecture—which would be a zombie if it only existed at the level of architectonic activity and practice—would be filled out by everyday life.

7. Our emphasis.
8. Op. cit., p. 45, our emphasis.

9. Reread attentively the first texts published on real estate law *which remain unable to come out*; as well as the texts of M.Capitant on profit-sharing by workers.

Let us not give in to conceptualization or to a rigorous-clarity-at-any-price; the only guide is reality, by virtue of its very complexity. Rigor is uninhabitable; our goal is only to reinhabit life. Social practice (as a whole), a complex unity of practices, is determined by the mode of production and culture of a given society. This level (the most general one) is dialectically related to the two others. It contains and excludes them at the same time, depends on them and refers to them without being completely subject to them. It is the historical and ideological guide of the two other levels, since it partakes both of the economic-political system and of history. In our society, as in any industrial capitalist society, social practice tends to melt into *urban practice*. It contains architectonic activity and architectonic practice, as well as the "everyday, philosophy, non-philosophy, the dramas, joys, in a word, the praxis, the power of liberation, and above all a sum of have-nots of class society, who until now have been more or less subject to alienation, to integration, to cultural norms, and to the satisfaction of the System, but who make history in a class society."[10]

How are the actions of these three levels composed into an architectural production in French society—a class society—and to what does this production correspond, whom does it serve? How to take part in this production and what political position is implied in this participation? For this participation cannot be innocent of an overall strategy, which is that of the ruling class, unless one acknowledges that, somewhere, in a privileged place within these three levels implacably implicated in all the economic-political resources of society, architectural production refers to an activity-in-itself: architecture, as an art or technique free of all ideology. In that ethereal place inhabited by creators or "scientific" researchers, Knowledge, Technology, and Aesthetics would be unfolded, with no other problem than the consolidation of their own logic. It is there that the harmonious syntheses destined to save "man" from chaos, from the incoherence and stupidity into which he is plunged by his being unaware of the dazzling potentials of Art and Science, will be prepared, to soon triumph over political and economic ideologies and change the world. This kind of thinking is not unrelated to the attitude of many architects and engineers, especially those considered to be the avant-garde of architectural production. We will see that the idealist explanation of the world and the old humanist idea that considers "man" as a thing-in-itself—as revealed by an attitude that scorns trivial socio-political-economic

10. H. Tonka, "Pratique urbaine de l'urbanisme," *Urbanisme*, no. 136, Sept. 1968.

It accomplishes
the impossible
it brings technology, aesthetics
and finances together
WITH THE LAND BANK
VERSAILLES WITHIN YOUR REACH
FOR THE 1ST TIME IN FRANCE
A FURNISHED, DECORATED,
COMPLETELY INSTALLED, AND "KEY IN
HAND," "SQUARE METER,"
FOR THE USUAL PRICE OF AN EMPTY
"SQUARE METER"

Objects, is their purpose to absorb the social problematic or to maintain it?

Objects, whose use really liberates everyday life, or to be consumed in larger numbers and at lower prices, through ideological and promotional distractions?

Another class has chosen for you, perpetuating the social obligation to consume according to levels of culture, the order of things.

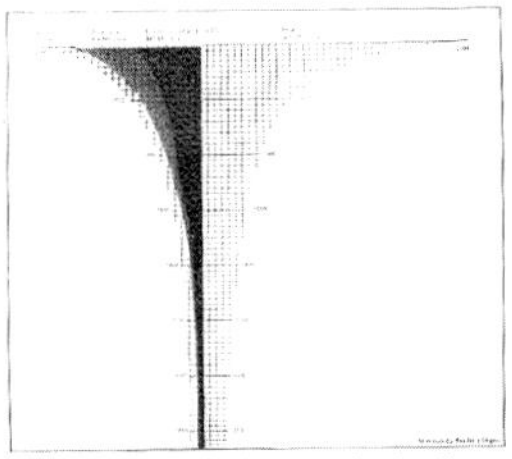

"The population explosion"
This graph can be seen in many of our research laboratories

It reminds us constantly of our work's purpose: to see to it today that the men of tomorrow will be sure to have what they need (and more, if possible!). This is why we spend over 200 million DM per year on research and improvement; we invest billions in new production plants. This is also why we constantly search for new chemical materials, fibers and dyes, phyto-sanitary products and medication. Indeed, we will have reached our goal only when we have put all the resources of modern chemistry at the service of progress, ready to face the population explosion.

National interest and the dispossession of life

Behind this anonymous facade

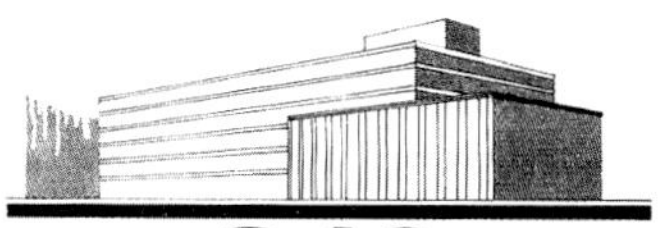

The happiness of the consumer

*Knowing how to buy, knowing how to choose between the brands, is something that needs to be learned; providing this education is the purpose of the National Consumer Institute

349

products which you use every day

You strike a match. You read a novel. You listen to Bach. You film your family. You drive a car. You go home. ...Without your being aware of it, Rousselot is involved in all your daily actions. Rousselot chemical products are there wherever man builds, works and lives, wherever man encounters progress and comfort.

Your shopping: it's so easy!

Numerous storekeepers are waiting for you in Villejuif, which has no less than 88 grocery stores, 16 fruit and produce stores, 5 supermarkets, 31 butchers, including 7 for horse meat, 17 pork butchers, 19 bakeries, 8 pastry shops, 15 general stores, 5 hardware stores, 19 dry cleaners, 8 laundries, 14 drugstores, 35 hairdressers, 8 tobacco stores, 12 electrical appliances stores, 85 cafés and restaurants.

"... Presently, if this postulate is accepted, the reality of an **object of consumption** comes to the fore: it is innumerable: an object of abundant consumption—housing. Consequently, at the moment, if the reality of this countless consumption is acknowledged, we have an (almost unlimited) **object of fabrication**. A program of vast activity. The program is such that its reality (city and countryside) greatly surpasses the capacities of the so-called "building" industry. It lends itself to the initiatives of major industry. More than that, if the event is interpreted with some clairvoyance, it is the very program of this industry: "**Major industry takes building in hand**" and builds housing.
Major industry takes building in hand. What do the triumphant fanfares mean? A victory has been made by modern technologies..."

Le Corbusier
The Destiny of Paris

ONLY MASS-PRODUCTION WILL SOLVE THE HOUSING CRISIS.

The industry architect is the builder of tomorrow

reality—automatically throws their advocates back into the cultural and commercial ideology of the society of capital, which invariably integrates them and obliterates the slightest hint of a demand. In any case, it is doomed to be without effect, for it does not take dissent to the critical junctures of society. This society, or rather a part of this society, uses to its advantage trivial socio-political-economic reality very well, and uses no less skillfully its pure geniuses and scientists as accomplices of the cultural ideology indispensable to the perpetuation of its own values and survival.

ARCHITECTURE IN CLASS STRUGGLE

The totality of social practice contains many particular practices (political, ideological, theoretical, technical, aesthetic) that could never exhaust the totality of social reality. The elusive *remainder* of analysis (the residue) is constantly employed in reality, in moments of transformation. We don't intend to grasp it. When the residue is no longer irreducible, it is immediately known. Understanding architectural production solely in its relationship to each of these isolated practices would lose sight of the richness and complexity of the interconnections between these practices. We must approach reality in its totality and not cut it up—even with the dialectical method—into fragments, with the idea of putting it back together someday. To be sure, we will not grasp all the articulations, all the sutures, at all the levels, in all the dimensions: prospectivist forecasting is not our theoretical project. The latter stands out against a vaster field, rendering the possible; not the possibility of a strange and alien philosophy, but a possibility within reach, just on the other side of utopia. "We" thought that only philosophers, stewing in their rhetoric, were capable of elaborating a vision of liberation from servitude, of understanding other social relationships, other social structures, but these great guides of history were being guided by it instead. The antelanguage of society and history was only their metalanguage. Social practice eluded them as they talked about it, as they refined its extent and scope, as they wrapped it in rigor.

Two fields of deployment regroup the particular practices that philosophy has bequeathed us—though derived more from pragmatic analysis than from philosophic reflection—: praxis (as reviewed and corrected by K. Marx) and poiesis. Two fields, and at the same time two moments in the overall process of production in society, whose relations and relationships are rooted in the dialectic while also founding it. The dialectic, ungraspable in itself, is deployed essentially in the praxis-poiesis duality, whose constant interplay of coherences and cohesions, of contradictions and dissension it can grasp. Here resides one of the keys to the comprehension of the criticism of the capitalist mode of production. The battle is waged along the front of the reappropriation of praxis by those who objectively possess the labor force capable of realizing poiesis, not in order to realize a distant and sacred ideal, but to realize their everyday lives. It is no use fighting to overturn the base, if at the same time we forget to wage another battle—theoretically the same one—on the level of the superstructure. The typical example was advanced by Wilhelm Reich. He demonstrated that no economic revolution could ever succeed without a preliminary and parallel sexual revolution. This thesis commands our attention. Without lapsing into any untoward psychologism, the problematic of sexual repression (and consequently all the repressions directly affecting the free expression of the individual in a given consensus) translates concretely into the realms of architecture and urbanism. This is not the place to go more deeply into this analysis, which we mention only as an example; but let us keep in mind the fact that, if Freud concluded that it was due to the sublimation of inhibition by certain individuals that the work (works) of Art came into being in a society and that aesthetics is nothing but the result of social repression imposed upon some, he forgot to stipulate in which mode of production he was situating himself. As far as we know, Freud (and this takes nothing away from his theory, which we only need to readjust) did not address any criticism at the bourgeois society in which he developed his theory, but only at its morality and ethics. On the level of observation, he was absolutely right, but he took only the superstructure into consideration, without noticing the repercussions of the base, especially in the economy and politics. Taking up this point in light of a Marxist reading of Freud, Marcuse will say that the refuge of aesthetics[11]—belonging to the pleasure principle—used by "some individuals" whose situation in the mode of production is "anomic," is the result of the burden of alienated labor; the positive side of a society completely given over to the principle of productivity. Reich, for his part, pointed out that bioelectrical energy (or the sexual energy that permits pleasure) is channeled and catalyzed not for the sake of self-realization and a truly democratic society, but for the sake of producing commodities torn away from oneself at the very moment of the act of transformation of material in the course of everyday labor. This practice, like all practices, produces a product: alienation (the transformation of consciousness, which creates mystified consciousness). Subject to the principle of profitability, the individual or productive social group, not to say society as a whole, loses sight of the fact that we are not here on Earth to unconsciously disgorge a production of unconscious objects, nor to absorb said objects, but to create. Create what? Works? No. Our lives. And, as the pure philosophers thought, our lives do not take place in Space and Time—purely abstract notions—but in concrete time and concrete space, the formal and aesthetic structure of which results from and is the result of social practice, of praxis. In its somewhat ordinary way, our language gives names to these various actions, one of which presently retains our attention; namely that of *architecture*. Architecture, indubitably part of the poiesis, will remain purely abstract if it is not the product of praxis, and the product of praxis (of social practice) will slip away from everyday life if it is artificially transcended by what we modestly call *Artists*. We are not denying a certain technical division of labor, but fighting against the social division of labor which is now reaching its peak in the split between aesthetics and everyday life, which in turn is nothing but the transcription of class opposition.

The word aesthetics frightens the architectural modernists, and so they replace it with the more immediate and noncommittal term "technique." They refuse to face their true problems. They stupidly reject what bores them so as to avoid dealing with, not the canons of beauty (about which we don't give a damn) but with social and political reality. Aesthetics as it is understood today is mere deliquescence, aestheticism, lack of freedom. Aestheticism transcends, through the works of the Great Masters, the lack of pleasure in everyday life. Organization (structural and formal) and bureaucratization offer themselves up as the most refined pleasures, the acme of our society. Imperceptibly, we oscillate between an objective aesthetic—offered by technical feats—and an aesthetics of obscurity—that of the pure creators unwilling to reveal their code, their meaning: Lettrism, the "new novel," and to some extent, Pop Art—the immediacy and realism of which is mere mystification, a real illusion of reality, and so on—we admire the firmness of a breast by Titian, revel in the everydayness hidden in the objects of a Duchamp, rejoice at Agam's absence of the object... And in the

11. *Aesthetics* is to be understood not in the academic or philosophical sense that refers to notions of Beauty, Harmony, etc., but as a way of life, of being, of guiding one's existence on Earth, of apprehending and approaching, understanding and sublimating labor, of understanding it as a reappropriation of labor not as alienated but as full of life (cf. Marx, *Grundrisse*). This is also what Henri Lefebvre understands in the term *style*. In short, it is a manner (habitus) of being (behaving and living/dwelling) according to one's self-determination in a given social consensus.

meantime we live stingily: "there's no other way," "we have to wait," etc. We all know the discourses that end with, "that's the way it is, we can't do otherwise…" "People" set up a parallel life for themselves that is supposed to be better than the other life of waiting. We suffer the outside without a word, and just when we want to appropriate the inside for ourselves (a little bit of utopia), we realize that the organized outside of our lives has already set up shop there. Isn't this what Reich had in mind when he said, "in the sexual act, the whole of society places itself between the two bodies"? The utopia of desire, of love, evaporates because it is irrational, and makes room for the bureaucratization of desire transformed into a satisfiable need, organizing love into mandatory fornication.

The dialectic maintained by the accord and the opposition between praxis and poiesis is not without a correlation between base and superstructure. To ignore these dialectics is to fall either into the "dogmatism of the advocates of the base," or into the "idealism of the advocates of the superstructure." Forgetting this dialectic means omitting just about everything. This is the theoretical explanation permitting us to reject the partial analyses in which so many architects like to indulge. The critique of architecture must not begin with architecture alone, nor with its technique, nor with its aesthetics. This version cannot be called completely false if it is conducted rigorously, but it leaves out the central point: the social structure and its impact. From this analysis came the idea according to which architecture was a language, and even more, a social expression, a projection of social structures onto the terrain. Although vague, it is not wrong. This critique of architecture has no means, no recurrence to attain the real play (at the base level) of social structures, which are always and only the province of sociability; it cannot grasp the political and economic power that acts on the architectural act, and above all nothing informs them about the intervention of architecture in the opposition between the social classes.

So many reasons to establish the absolute necessity of ending the theoretical falsification of many so-called theoretical analyses concerning architecture. We must answer the following question, which is not ontological in the least: *what are all these "spaces" that we continually leave to look for others, in order to leave in search of still others?* What are our instants, our time that moves from "space" to "space," ever since the theory of relativity showed that time defines itself by the displacement of one point in space to another point in space.

It is impossible not to mention this domain. It is useless to treat it, as used to be done, through philosophical reflection that tells us nothing about social reality. Before moving on to the concrete analysis of architectural reality, as it were, let us recall the main thrust of the analysis:

Activities referring to material production itself, as well as to the practice of transforming nature as given (raw material) into a product of usage by and for the activity of men, existing and working, through the use of specific means of production within the framework of specific relations of production (praxis), *maintain operative relationships of coherence and contradiction (dialectic) with activities referring to ideological and theoretical practice (religious, political, moral, judicial, artistic, aesthetic or philosophical)* (poiesis). In order to understand what really happens, practical activities (as understood by spoken language) are not dissociable from activities, ideas, ideologies, and concepts (all "nonmaterial" facts); the moments of a product's transformation are apprehensible only within the dialectical relationship between the two fields of human activity: praxis-poiesis. We will not add to these two fields the result of their interaction, which philosophers call mimesis, for that would take us too far. For our analysis, it should suffice to know that mimesis covers the activities of "mimeses" and "mimetism," of reproduction and identity, that take the form and function of either pure mystifications (copies, plagiarism, appearances), or as the renewal or distribution of products for the purposes of consuming the results of the transformation brought about by praxis or poiesis.

SOCIAL DEMAND OR COMMAND?

Is there a "disengagement" today between what "people" expect of architecture and the manufactured architectural product sold to them? What is this architectural product exactly in practice and for the social imaginary? In our preliminary observations we will consider the news media, then turn to the sanctuaries of architectural "creation" to understand the mode of production, and, finally, analyze the everyday practice of architecture.

In the press, the exercise of architectonic activity is the target of criticism, or rather *nit-picking*: the criticism indicts the credit problem, the incoherence of the regulations, the archaism of commercial formalities in construction, the (unbridled) real estate speculation, the overly high cost of construction, the insufficient production of "assisted" housing. The competence of the designers is often called into question, and they are harshly taken to task for their lack of "concepts" for architecture and for the "environment." In the wake of the crisis in May–June

1968, for example, the "housing" forecasts are pessimistic as the increase in demand (due to the increase in the minimum wage and to salaries permitting new segments of the population to acquire property) was offset by a trend towards reduced production due to an increase in the cost price of construction, as the means of credit had not been changed. These critiques of contingent reality are part of the humdrum of protests voiced over the last fifty years by malcontents who grumble and complain about the housing crisis; not unlike the protest the Left-Wing political parties in France direct towards the urban problematic which has been reduced to demanding a few more thousand housing units per year. These critiques do not put the expression of a real social demand in doubt.

Upon closer observation, however, new symptoms appear, leading us to suppose contradictions of another order. For example, the growing success of architectural solutions signifying leisure in everyday housing[12] shows that the content of habitation is being called into question. To live, or rather to survive, it is necessary to recuperate for tomorrow's workday in the rural leisure afforded by a house "just like in the country," while at the same time being near the city. This underscores the mythology of the suburban house, which refers either to "the American way of life, which is twenty years ahead of ours," or to the nostalgia for a more "natural" *art de vivre*, where the image of the Grand Trianon is never far behind. Is that what the social demand is about? No. For who cares about demand? *Paris-Match* shows what Paris *will be* in the year 2000; the advertising for *Parly 2* expounds on a "new *art de vivre*" stemming from the spatial arrangement of its housing, green areas, swimming pools, horseback riding facilities, drugstores—who could ask for more? They've thought of everything. The spectacle of your future life as predicted by advertising resembles "a modern fairytale."

And what about culture, that refined nourishment? You will take it in in the splendor of the Maison de la Culture in Grenoble. This monument, built at a cost of two and a half billion French francs, houses the most "modern" theater facilities in Europe. Yet amid the concert of applause and promotional praise for this "cathedral" of culture, this choice piece of modernism exhibited by the city of Grenoble, dissonant tones and dissenting voices are being heard in the press and elsewhere. Some of them take issue with the program of Grenoble's Maison de la Culture. The content that lies beneath the hype is being called into question. According to the latest critics, it would seem that the prestige of the theater linked to the

12. Cf. the exhibition, *Village de France*, Foire de Paris, 1968.

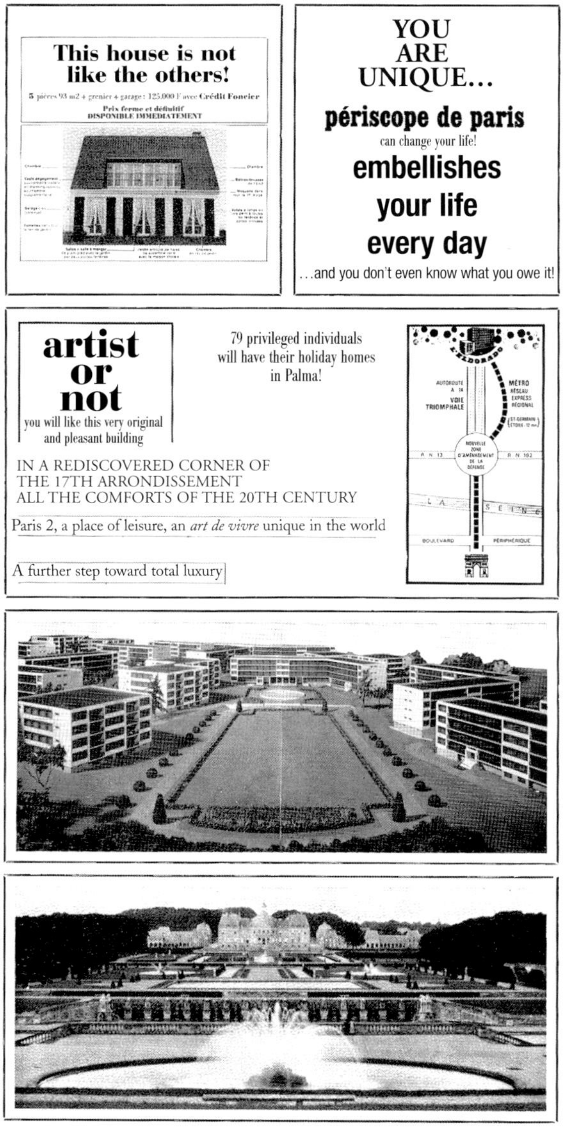

The majority lives with mass-produced objects that refer formally and psychologically to models with which only a minority lives.

"This system is upheld by a democratic ideology; it sees itself as the dimension of social progress: the possibility for all to have access to the models, little by little." The mass-produced series is experienced "as a world of luxury and prestige from which it is inexorably separated by wealth, but from which it is no longer separated by any legal class status, any de jure social transcendence. This is psychologically of the essence, for, in spite of the frustration, in spite of the material impossibility of ever reaching it, the use of mass-produced objects never comes without the implicit postulation of a model... This current running throughout the whole of society, carrying the series toward the model and continuously transmitting the model through the series, this unbroken dynamic is the very ideology of our society."

Jean Baudrillard, *The System of Objects*

bourgeois concept of culture, to the consumption of "great works" performed by "great artists," in fact camouflages the poverty of the other possible practices (exhibitions, workshops, visual arts, etc.), thus estranging from this place all those who are unfit to consume this culture, cheating those who are supposed to "participate" in it. One critic demands another content for the Maisons de la Culture, one in which the experience of art would be possible; authentic experience, and not the imperative of a political-cultural group, whose slogans are no less mendacious than those that urge us to buy a brand of detergent or preserves. The architectonics of the Maison de la Culture in Grenoble signify culture as a thing-in-itself; particularly culture as spectacle, part of the poiesis elevated to a pseudo-style in line with bourgeois ethics and morality. Its program was not the expression of a social demand, but a demand ordered for the sake of perpetuating the values of a bourgeois cultural ideology. We will call this the *social command*. But is demand not contained in the psycho-sociological surveys that attempt to reconstitute it rationally? The problematic that unfolds in our everyday reality and that passes itself off as coherent, universal and enduring, isn't that precisely the object of the solicitude of architects, of urbanists and of the State? Doesn't the commercial ruthlessness of architectonic practice anticipate demand in order to satisfy it at all cost?

How and by whom are the programs proposed to the architects made? In the case of vast architectural operations the programs are elaborated by a pluridisciplinary team that seeks to grasp the possibilities of future ways of life and offer spatial solutions. This programming entity has to take a large number of variables into account, as determined by geographic, economic, psycho-sociological and technological surveys. These surveys are a means of describing reality without elucidating it: not allowing criticism of the economic-political substrate that governs this reality, they project it inexorably into the future by means of expansionist forecasting. As Herbert Marcuse writes in *One-Dimensional Man*: "A new ideology is being developed that aims to *describe* what is happening (and the meaning to be given to it) by eliminating the concepts that would make it possible to *understand* what is happening (and the meaning to be given to it)."[13] Pluridisciplinarity is an attempt at methodological research, it tries to go beyond the framework of the division of labor. By tackling the various aspects of this problem—geographic, economic sociological, aesthetic—and, by doing its best to articulate the

13. H. Marcuse, *One-Dimensional Man*, 1964.

contributions of these various disciplines in a flexible way, it tries to transcend their partial horizons. But this ambition conceals a lack inherent in the novelty of the method, which only reinforces the ideological bias. The main concern of the pluridisciplinary team is to rationalize the complex programs it must submit and then to provide the optimal technical response for these programs. The very elaborate technical solution that it proposes masks the urgent need for a calling into question, a critique, and a transcendence of the existing order.

The illusion that this questioning and critique will become possible now through the "public's" intervention in the architectural and urbanistic act is contained in the "participation" promised at all levels of social practice. This recent invention is only a consolidating piece of the ideology, without being a real step toward democracy.[14]

One can ask whether the sanctuaries of architectural production are innocent of this mystification, and whether architectonic activity is the victim of machinations in which architects, pretending to look the other way, do not take the "people" for whom they are producing into account and deliver a merchandise the people have not asked for. Architectural products are not pure, materially tangible objects generated by an economy, technique or art, but pieces of everyday life. Articulated with other moments of a given social practice, it is a possible condition of: making love or being inhibited, loving or hating, knowing or doing, consuming or not consuming, criticizing, destroying or playing, living or dying. In the overall production process of society, the product of architects, idea men and designers, is objectively, with a supplemental something, which, if it is a way of life, of being, of guiding one's existence, that which is called *aesthetics*. Technical know-how in the service of architectural production, and therefore of everyday life, starts being problematic only if, by and through ideological representations (for instance, technology as a thing-in-itself) it becomes imperialistic.

The objects of architecture respond to the social command given by the State and its bureaucracy or by the logic of free competition; the divorce of architectural production from social practice is achieved by the rationalization of the lived experience of architecture in the "bureaucratic society of directed consumption." To refine our analysis, the lived dialectic of praxis/poiesis takes us from facts to ideas, from objects to concepts, from the lived experience to the ideology of the experience and its philosophy, forcing us to ask: what is the ideological significance of the architectural act for common sense, for the professional institution, for State authority, or for the holders of financial power? Are the contradictions revealed by the violation of social demand—turned into social command—hidden at the level of ideology? And by what means?

IDEOLOGICAL DISCOURSE OR MISAPPROPRIATION

Common sense nurtures its ideas of architectural production in the mass media—newspapers, magazines, some exhibitions about architecture and urbanism (always a great success) and some publications—that constitute the references of the social imaginary for architectural production (apart from its direct perception).

Architectural production is presented in a particular way in the media: the content (program) is generally "dropped" in favor of the formal values of a container pertaining to art or technology: drawings, pictures, photomontages or scale models show the shape of the future city, district or planned construction. Architectural science fiction is marshaled as a wealth of formal descriptions that obscure the representation of the possible lived experience. The visual impact of the signifier makes us forget the signified. Written (or spoken) commentaries avoid the problematic of content, while pointing to the cultural echoes of the art/technology duality.[15] The same predominance of form (undeniable publicity value) over content is to be found in the magazines for the general public that deal with habitation and what is connected with it. The illustrations in certain exhibition catalogues or journals of "design" (utilitarian objects) do not detail the objects objectively, but are turned into a media event through a search for aesthetics (the "beautiful shot," "lay-outs" reminiscent of "abstract paintings," etc.). The shape of these objects in fact refers to meanings that often mask their practical function. Our point in citing this example taken from design is the cultural and promotional value invested in the object of the signifier relative to the signified.

No one amongst the Parisian public who visited the exhibition of projects for the Quartier des Halles (winter 1967) could tell if the projects were schematic

14. "Participation" is a subject of too great an importance for us to be able to develop in a few words. Cf. "La logique de l'urbanisme," art. 5, p. 12, *Utopie*, Nov. 1967; *Utopie*, no. 2, "Direction de recherche sur la notion de participation," René Lourau (forthcoming).

15. A few examples: *Paris-Match*, no. 951, July 1, 1967; exhibition of the scale models for the renovation of the area around Les Halles, Hôtel de Ville, Salle Saint-Jean, Paris, winter 1967.

proposals or designs to be realized; no one was really informed about the potential contents of this area and about the different possible programs: public forum or business district, a place for culture and leisure, a residential and administrative center, or all of these at once—may the most influential authority take all. However, each could mentally choose between a vast French garden in which the buildings disappeared in the "greenery," a futuristic neighborhood with forms borrowed from science fiction, or an architecture respecting the traditional rooflines of Paris. The choice given to the base exists only at this cultural level. The content is deviated toward the container, and the main purpose of architectural production—to contain social practice—is forgotten. Public opinion and its elected representatives are trapped in discussions about form that are fueled by ideas such as the ideology of modernism—which induces the ideology of democracy—as opposed to the reassuring illusion of classicism, the mythic representation of the values of history, which leads us back to the values of bourgeois morality.

If social command establishes itself via cultural ideology, we must apprehend this cultural ideology and its surroundings must be grasped in order to understand what is really happening and be able to react in keeping with our analysis.

FROM COMMON SENSE TO THE INSTITUTION

For common sense, the formal representation of the architectural product refers to two opposite, but not contradictory, imaginaries: *modernism* and *classicism*. Superimposed onto this dichotomy, which appears in the media of everyday life, is the idea of *nature*, which is opposed neither to modernism, nor to classicism, and merges them into the same natural condition: at the formal level in the case of modernism (a system of signs referring to "natural" connotations), and at the symbolic level in the case of classicism (a holdover of traditional order).[16] Real estate advertising and all the actions of architectonic practice refer to the two clichés *modern* and *classical*, onto which the idea of "nature" is superimposed. Modernism corresponds to revolutionary forms, futuristic environments, science fiction, expectation, functionality, cutting edge technique, mass-produced objects. Classicism refers to tradition, antiquity, style, authenticity, craft, unique objects. Since these two registers of value are not mutually exclusive, the trick is to be both revolutionary and classical, or ultra-modern, but "with style." For example: "The form of the plastic house is not necessarily revolutionary, as you can see by the one shown here, which has a classical line." Another example: the houses of the architect Jacques Couelle at Castellaras are modern, yet unique objects referring to contemporary sculpture; they induce an authentic craft value that ties them to the cultural tradition of the bourgeois order. Jean Baudrillard, in *The System of Objects*, shows how two categories of the signified are brought into play for objects—not unrelated to our dichotomy, though not coextensive with it—and which he calls the functional system, or objective discourse, and the nonfunctional system, or subjective discourse. Objective discourse refers to modernism and subjective discourse to classicism; modernism and classicism being taken in their common, or even trivial, acceptations. It is here, parallel to the representations of common sense, that Art (subjective) and Technology (objective) appear, and we will question them now within the field of their connotations, that is, of their ideological significance.[17]

What Art and Technology mean to architects, engineers, idea men, designers and representatives of the institutions at the State level—in other words, everything that refers to architectonic activity—can be read in the trade journals. Open any architectural magazine published in France. The image of architectural production presented in such journals is rather surprising. The pages are filled with miracles of form and feats of technique enhanced by photography and graphic design that keep the gaze occupied while inspiring criticism solely by the reader (or rather, voyeur), as he is alone! Works by masters from all over the world are shown, signed, isolated from the conditions of their production; there is never any mention of money, prices, social classes, or technological potential related to the financial potential. Aesthetics are deployed without difficulty—and without critique. The commentaries, authored by the Masters, are about Art and Technology: the style, the parti, the spirit of an edifice, and now and then bits and pieces of programs disconnected from any particular social practice. New technical-aesthetic trends are given special attention, they provide the perfect opportunity for unusual images and give free rein to representations of an architectural imaginary

16. Jean Baudrillard, *Le système des objets*, col. les essais, CXXXVII, éd. Gallimard, Paris, 1967.

17. Which does not mean that, for common sense, *Art* is unrelated to the *classical*, and *Technology* only to the *modern*, but that the subjective values usually subsumed in Art by bourgeois cultural understanding *are taken up rather by "classical" in the common parlance about architecture* and that the values of objectivity habitually associated with Technology (and the exact sciences) *are taken up rather by "modern" in the same parlance about architecture*. We only want to show that the force of the Art/Technology opposition on the level of bourgeois cultural language is parallel (but not equivalent) to the opposition of classical and modern in common parlance.

The "true" *art de vivre*
Did you build for a particular class, "Mister Wright"?

whose causes change only slowly over time. New myths come to light, the latest avatars of threadbare intellectual trends whose last gasps inspire present production: the ephemeral, the inflatable, the mobile. Each one of these minor myths has its talented visionaries, its exegetes, its theoreticians. Nowhere in all of this does the socio-economic-political reality inherent in architectural production ever come into the picture. The problematic raised empirically and at the lowest level by the real estate journals does not appear here. There are no explanations whatsoever of real actions (property, pressure groups, decisions of the State). The question as to the validity of all these edifices, structured spaces, "pieces of architecture" within and through a specific social practice; where is it? The message is clear: spatialization and the structural shaping of space, the specific object of architectonic activity (professional institutions) and signified ideologically as a thing-in-itself, referring to two groups of activities devoid of any political and social implications: Art and Technology. But, as we have seen, architectonic activity is also the State, the guarantor of the institutions and honesty, as well as the keeper of the established order. We will see how this established order appropriates Art and Technology, which are ideologically signified as being pure, transcendent of everyday life, liberators of "Man" (that "humanistic" representation, also conveniently abstracted from social reality).

ORDER, TECHNIQUE, ART

The divorce of architecture from social practice can be consummated. The strictly sociological portion of the architectural act can be dropped for the sake of parodic programs, since by virtue of the double mediation of Art and Technology, this architectural act is signified as liberating, both subjectively (as art and aesthetic contemplation) and objectively (as the unlimited potential of technology). The repression of everyday life is sublimated by the liberation contained in the ideology of Art and Technology. In it, objective and subjective discourses refer to each other mutually; the one gaining ground over the other, or the two combining according to the fluctuations of the cultural order. Architectonic activity clearly shows its frames of reference. In the current phase, Art seems to be losing ground. The objective discourse of Technology, more pertinent, stimulates all activity, since it is the symbol of modernity and seduces the avant-garde of architectural production. Its rationality is recuperated by the State, which elevates it to the bureaucratic organization of space. This recuperation is made possible by the lack of political criticism of this avant-garde's own technical activity. A historical example of the integration of the architectonic avant-garde: the urbanistic thinking of Le Corbusier, rejected in 1925 because it did not comply with the cultural models of academic art, has become the very basis of the urbanistic thinking now supported by the State. Indeed, a study of the writings of Le Corbusier shows that theories still considered revolutionary fifteen years ago were nothing more than the vanguard of the technocratic

Forms that change, and also change the unchanging forms of alienation.

urbanism of the rationalization of space practiced today (cf. *On demande un Colbert*).[18] Le Corbusier himself justified his theories as leading in the direction of a greater production/consumption of the industrial object; that is, the survival of the industrial class society. Ideologically, progressive theories are always considered liberatory of "man" through technology dominated and placed at his service, and as it is liberating, "modernism" is supposed to lead to the political freedom contained in the democratic ideal.

To this ideology of a pure and liberating Technology[19] inducing democracy, we can attach the belief that the formal evolution of organized space produces a structural transformation of social practice. This belief, implicitly contained in the theories of the functionalist architects starting in the 1920s, has today become so successful that it ranks as an ideology. It is one of the architectural theories (based on an interpretation of Behaviorism) according to which individual behavior can be influenced, not to say rationalized, by the organization of space. Today these theories have gained a certain currency in Anglo-Saxon countries; in France, they are perpetuated more or less consciously in the teaching of an "architecture" and an "urbanism" that accounts only for the necessity of spatializing things social without searching for the essence of this necessity, which is nowhere else than in social practice.

The present advocates of the technicist avant-garde share the same ideology when they think that new structural solutions leading to an era of abundance derived from an "intelligent" and low-cost industrial production are by themselves able to solve the architectural problematic. To believe that an architecture can be "subversive" means taking this ideology to its culmination. In May 1968, the Sorbonne was subversive only through the signified that was deployed there; how can a spatio-temporal organization in a reactionary social milieu be revolutionary and affect the social relationships specific to this milieu? And if at a certain moment it can modify *the behavior of individuals or groups of individuals*, this does not imply that it is able to change social relationships. Here there is an obvious confusion between social relationships and physical behaviors.

Guided by the ideological significance of Technology, the technicians and super-technicians go to work as faithful servants of progress and industrial

18. Le Corbusier, *On demande un Colbert*. "Vers un Paris nouveau?," *Cahiers de la république des lettres, des sciences et des arts, XII Les Beaux-Arts*, éditions d'étude et de documents, rue de la Boétie, no. 9, Paris.

19. Cf. *Utopie*, no. (forthcoming), éd. Anthropos, "Modernité de la technique": Jean Baudrillard, "Pratique sociale de la technique," Hubert Tonka, "Le jeu de la technique," Isabelle Auricoste, "L'imaginaire social de la technique."

growth, since their professional practice is pure and ignores no political critique. They rationalize architectural production, for it is especially important to be efficient when dealing with the problems of demographic, economic and industrial expansion. This expansion motivates the principle of necessity and urgency in the name of which the centralizing State organizes activities and structures social space. In this way urbanism and regional planning control urbanity, liquidating social practice into parts that are irreducible to the logic of the commodity and the morality that flows from it, replacing it with activities that are duly classified and segregational, in perfect accord with the division of labor in business. The same process exists in architectural production: the method of organizing space is logically derived from the analysis of the needs of "man" (taken to be universal and abstract, but no less the bearer of the mystified consciousness of the bourgeois world) and the necessities of industrial production.

Method becomes primordial, as it has to make an ever increasing industrial production fit needs assumed to be more and more individual, rather than social or cultural. The techniques of the method are refined and they obscure, with the mirage of their own brilliance, the social and political questioning contained in everyday life.[20] Life as lived, grasped in bits and pieces, is restored into separate activities controllable by the programming machine and the State's forces of control. In the elimination of the contradictions and the search for coherence (whose corollary is repression) there is a liquidation of social practice for the ruled class, which is presently incapable of self-determination at any level of everyday life.

Nearly all current architectural theories are based on the hypothesis according to which, technological development that allows for greater industrial production at low cost heralds an era of abundance, that is, the end of shortage throughout the world. This hypothesis has no sound basis, for nothing indicates that the end of shortages (objectively possible) necessarily leads to a change in the social relationships that regulate the distribution of goods and that are at the root of class struggle. The alibi of Technology liberating "man" in the end rests on the skillfully maintained belief that class struggle will be dissolved in the opulence of industrial society.[21]

Faced with the objective discourse of Technology and the disquieting efforts made to rationalize architectural production, there is still a way out: Art. At

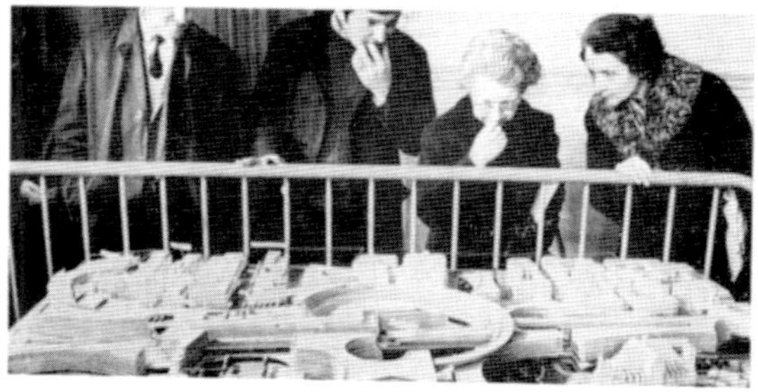

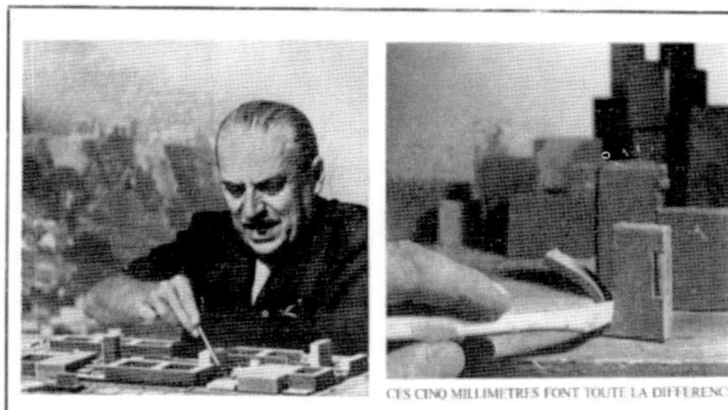

Hymn of the spectator-participants of the bureaucratic society of directed consumption.

Oh, Object work-of-art, we believe in your power to redeem the human race! You who are part of the Universal Harmony of Art, we believe in your great power to transform society which, by the very participation of all of its members, now opens itself to the effects of beauty.

Oh, Object work-of-technology, you by whom man has been able to dominate nature, be also the attentive master of the society that no longer knows where it is going! We believe in your almightiness to control the natural order of phenomena

20. Cf. Research at the Rue d'Ulm, British research on methodology (e.g., *Design Method in Architecture*, symposium at the Portsmouth School of Architecture, Dec. 1967).
21. Cf. Archigram.

and social development united in a same cosmogony. We ask that the society which, in its ignorance, still eludes you and fails to enjoy your benefits, be subjected to you for its own good and survival.

So that, through the saving tutelage of Art and Technology and through the intercession of your priests, the artists and scientists, we may be led to the Gentle Bourgeois Revolution and miraculously saved from the penury of the old world!

THE COMFORT CURVE IS THE PROFIT CURVE.

SPECIAL FUTURE

A single university for all of humanity, in the year 2000, micro-computers on a satellite will be able to store all of human knowledge. Every student, anywhere on the face of the Earth, will be able to communicate with it thanks to a laser-pen.

least, that is what appears in the official instructions concerning architecture: there are precise aesthetic guidelines on the rules of composition to be observed, on problems of "site integration," on the "character and spirit" of constructions. Exemption from the regulations is desirable "only to permit the creation of 'grandes ensembles' with a deliberate eye to composition and on the condition that the composer be talented… Between an architecture that is indifferent to the specificity of sites and climates, and a 'regional' architecture imitating models of the past, there is room for an architecture youthful in its techniques and traditional through its harmony with the environment."[22] In this way Art is always produced by the "talent" of "artists," "creators," or "composers." In these lines, the myth of the great "artist-creator" shines through; Art transcends social practice: it is not creativity in and by social practice. A study of the contribution of works of art to industrial production would reveal the considerable importance of artists' unconscious participation in this production through their belief in a world of pure Art, open only to the most talented, the object of a cult recognizing only the laws it gives itself. In schools and universities the training of the country's intellectual elite—the only initiates to this cult—determines the *de facto* exclusion of the greater part of society; the reference will also define the relationship of the *excluded* to works of art.

Architects respond with technical and visual solutions to the programs determined by the most subtly used reflex in our consumer society: the need to achieve a lifestyle that the members of the ruling class alone enjoy—for whom the model projects elaborated by architects, a part of the bourgeois class, are intended. In the professional exercise of their architectonic activity, architects will imperceptibly apply or project the models of the ruling class into their various realizations. The only possible cultural references common to the architect and the future inhabitants are grafted onto an economic reality. From the advertising brochures, to the moldings on closets or the chrome of the modernists, these references are based *de facto* upon the inequality that, from school all the way to the practice of the "love of art," divides society into two parts: those who have the privilege of a *cultural heritage* and those who, for all their education, do not.

We have shown the ideological significations taken by Technology and Art in architectural production. Technology appeared as being pure of all political implications and emancipatory of humanity, while Art appeared as a thing-in-itself transcending

22. General instructions by the Minister of Construction on April 8, 1960.

social practice and accessible only to a privileged elite. For architectural producers, this ideological practice rests on the idea they have of their mission in society. For consumers of architecture, it rests on the cultural level from which they formulate their needs and desires. The ruling class is in a position culturally to formulate a demand; the ruled class (the proletariat) is culturally constrained to suffer their command.

Both have a high idea of the mission of the architect and of the potential of the "brilliant man," a belief in the omnipotence of Technology and of the "humanizing" power of Art to solve the countless problems of our urban "civilization."

RADICAL CRITIQUE AND THEORETICAL PRACTICE

Our elucidation of the capitalist mode of the production of architecture has shown the *de facto* exclusion from this architecture of a part of French society, the proletariat; namely at the level of the base. At the superstructural level, the existence of two parallel cultures aligned along the same preferential axes appeared: a bourgeois culture and a proletarian subculture. By establishing the unchanging models for proletarian subculture, bourgeois culture manages to ward off the questioning and the dissent contained in social practice. It marshals powerful excuses to this end: Technology delivering abundance, the salvation of humanity, and Art, transcending society, and created by virtue of genius. Obsessed by these representations, the social imaginary withdraws, and sublimates aesthetics into aestheticism, and particular technologies into Technology-in-itself. These ideological sublimations obscure and confuse the realities of the capitalist mode of production and weaken the latent dissent that arises from difficult conditions and the awareness of alienation that everyday life in this mode of production inflicts on the ruled class.

A theoretical practice of architecture that avoids spreading agitation and unrest in demystifying an architectural production quietly erected into an illusory system of signs legible only by the bourgeoisie would only serve the latter. The positivity of a theoretical practice is measured by the action that it can initiate and not by the recipes or methods that it can propose. Its dynamism is inherent to the radical critique it brings to bear on society, and through it, on architecture, which is its product. This does not mean that the product should be neglected, but it must be grasped as implicated in its mythic aura and in its ideological envelope.

On the one hand,[23] architectonic activity can be considered only within social practice, that is, confronted with architectonic practice that results from economic-political structures, and not within a "humanism" to which it has desperately clung for the last hundred years and which, having only a mythic existence, has no longer an impact on the real, but rather plays into the hands of the institutions and capital, confining the present social practice. On the other hand, all the analyses of the so-called social sciences do not exhaust the "architectural object." What is the specificity of architectural discourse inasmuch as it articulates practices? This question is contained within the one raised more generally by Pierre Francastel, on the possibility of elaborating visual elements as specific instruments of communication. It remains to this day unanswered.

Considering the specificity of its object, the social practice of architecture exists only in relationship to the economic, ideological and theoretical practice of a society. The sum of these relationships remain to be established in the *theoretical foundations of the interpretation of architecture in an urban society*. The materials allowing for the elaboration of these theoretical foundations will come from the observation of the urban, industrial, and architectural, reality, caught up within a social practice, at once historical and present, especially since the advent of industrial capitalism.

That the search for a theory of the interpretation of "architecture" in urban society remains nonexistent shows how little it appears in the concerns of the social factions wielding political power. This would imply that architectonic activity does not function as a reflection on the space-time problematic, but simply as a decoration hypostasized into a code of illusory formal significations. If we consider the urban as a site of the deployment of conflicts in industrial society, the purpose of the search for theoretical foundations undertaken by *Utopie* must be to provide ammunition for social groups kept in a state of alienation and to act upon those structures tending to liberate their revolutionary potential.

Jean Aubert, Jean-Paul Jungmann, Hubert Tonka
Utopie, Paris-London, March–August 1968

23. From here on, we take up the same terms as the article of March 1968 published in *Architectural Design*. A more profound and detailed knowledge of the events of May 1968 at the ex-École des Beaux-Arts will help us to nuance our position, but this, for the time being, remains our statement.

On the participation of the whores Nature and Culture in the ploys of the pimp Capitalism to perpetuate women's servitude

I MET A HAPPY WOMAN...

WHO BELIEVED SIMPLY IN BEING HAPPY!

Together we will discover, or rather recognize, you and I, the serene and radiant joy of a family living in the old French tradition of the magazines that were the delight of my childhood. There, the senseless hustle and bustle was forgotten and, thanks to a dynamic and smiling woman who knew how to live her times with an uncomplicated femininity, we were dazzled by the grace of genial virtues naturally exercised.

The demand for access to work done by men, that is, to alienated labor, is not without political consequences: just as the worker had to liberate himself from old relationships of domination to be able to sell his labor, so too does women's historical demand for work require liberation from old relationships of domination (for example, equality at work), and therefore has a revolutionary character.

But this situation is not without ambiguity; indeed, beyond the demand for equality, woman, wanting to defend her anthropological specificity, becomes prey to bourgeois ideology and, in the end, perpetuates the ideological model of femininity (cf. magazines promoting "women's liberation," alienating fashions, and exploitative advertising all at once). Woman-as-gadget maintained the illusion of sexual liberation through the eroticization of sexuality alienated in spectacular investment.

On the necessary alienating liberation of women.

Women's labor is the crux of a fundamental contradiction in the capitalist system; namely, between:

—technological rationality, which requires the deliberate and total exploitation of the available workforce (either as employees or as a reserve of unemployed workers) for the sake of profitability—but Marx demonstrated that this rational use of the workforce presented a revolutionary danger to the system, inasmuch as concentration was accompanied by a process of socialization;

—and institutional conservativism: institutions, especially the family, being guarantors of the permanence and perpetuation of the existing social order, presented as a natural order (women having a "natural" role within this order). This contradiction is only a special form of the contradiction between the need for growth and the fear of real change putting its very existence into question.

The attempt to achieve balance by associating these two poles leads to the overexploitation of women in relationships of domination comparable to those established in underdeveloped countries between workers and proprietors. This is, to the extent that the capitalist system uses archaic, institutional relationships to overexploit the workforce by placing *relationships of domination*—implicating the reciprocal rights and duties of *relationships of production*, which, originally, were established upon the rupture of old feudal relationships of domination, implying a *liberation* of the workforce, since relationships of domination adopt a unilateral character in capitalistic exploitation.

• As a social consensus, the permanence of capitalism involves an integration of Nature that follows an already accomplished appropriation of culture. The introduction of Nature permits an immutable order to be invoked regardless of visible changes, ensuring the permanence of a social structure rejuvenated by culture.

• Women who work constitute a reserve of labor of the colonial type (underqualified, unequal wages, etc.). This type of abundant and low-cost labor is necessary for the proper functioning of a competitive market economy.

• Women play an especially important role in the perpetuation of the species. This biological role is the main justification and instrument for the survival of the repressive patriarchal family, which is the optimal vector of the dominant ideology.

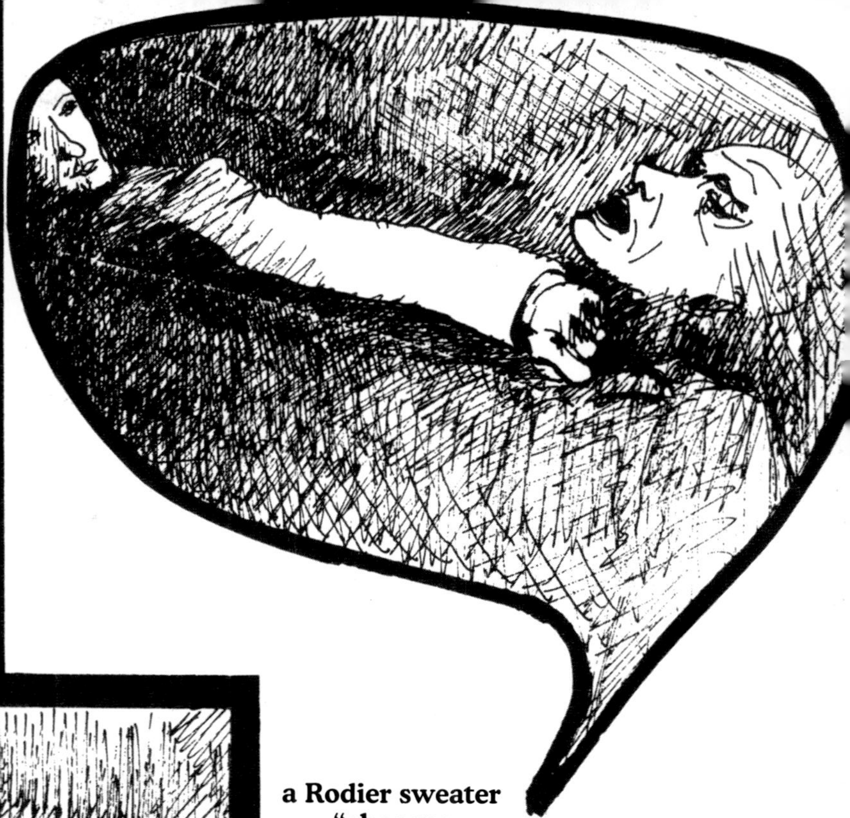

But the women who work leave the patriarchal order and enter the market economy. The contradiction between the logic of the capitalist economy and the necessity of perpetuating the social consensus that permits this economy to develop is masked by the introduction of femininity as a *natural*, and thus immutable, order for women in the cultural realm. That is, by establishing an absolute division of social functions between men and women, thus allowing the progressive demands of women who want to go beyond their biological role to be neutralized.

If male labor tends to be completely devaluated, to be an archaism that needs to be transcended (leisure, automation, status), the labor of women is always a means of achieving independence, but an independence that would be perfectly compatible with their institutional condition as depositaries of family responsibilities.

It is within this series of contradictions that the logic of the class strategy unmasks itself; work for men is the last sector in which class oppositions are clearly apparent and the place where workers are a constant threat to the order of the dominant class, while the work of women is the best means to delay women's escape from the patriarchal order. Burdened by double loads of work and contradictory obligations, but aware of participating both in the emancipation of women and in the transmission of the *fundamental values* of femininity, women are doubly incapable of calling the existing order in question and they perpetuate it in raising their children.

After having given a dark picture of women's labor, a recent inquiry by a women's weekly magazine concluded: "If they are good for men's work, men's work

is good for women. No doubt, they continue to suffer much inequality… But they have overturned many barriers in the last fifty years. And for the last twenty years their progress has accelerated, work is their future." And the whole paternalistic Left takes up the refrain of women's liberation through work, of the functional equality between men and women. More day-care centers and laundromats will absorb unwanted femininity!

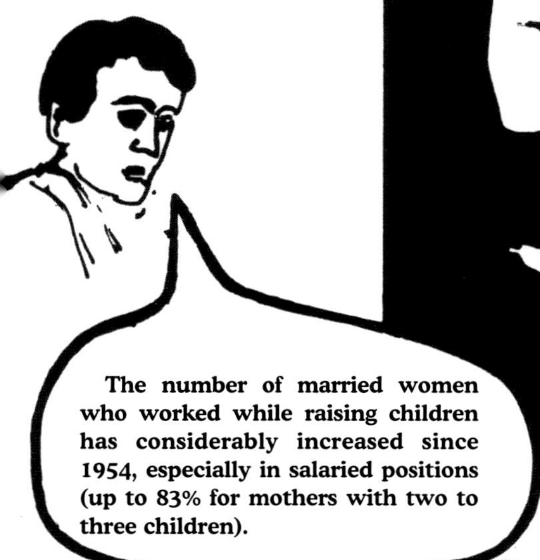

But what will have changed in the institutional condition of women, in her social and sexual alienation, which involves women's *naturalness* of women, that is, their reification? Will all of these working women eradicate the myth of mothers, wives and sisters?

It is equally unjustifiable to condemn women to be but a means of perpetuating the species and its governing ideology, as it is to condemn them to resolve some irreducible femininity through a functional equality with men; and equally contributes to hiding the fact that femininity is not necessarily synonymous with alienation.

WOMAN IN THE SOCIAL PROBLEMATIC.

"Thanks to the decisive role that it assigns to women... beyond the family circle in socially organized processes of production, big industry nonetheless creates the economic basis upon which a superior form of the family and relationship between the sexes will arise."

K. MARX
CAPITAL, BOOK I, VOL. II, P. 168

The critical study of women in capitalist society requires an institutional analysis; it has to refrain from reinvesting the ideological discourse with the phenomenological analysis of women's being-in-situation—the coming to consciousness, at a level that remains ideological, of the problematic of women in bourgeois society.

In order to avoid this obstacle, the process that led women to this result has to be analyzed (the term "women" will be understood to refer to the totality of women grouped around the same problematic, and not Woman, the hypostasized eternal feminine); this analysis is therefore based on the historical development of the economic and social role of women through the sexual division of labor, especially through a study of the decline of the institutional condition of women within the capitalist mode of production, the latter arising at the origin of "the problems of women" as a reality and coming to consciousness at an ideological level of this reality. The problematic of women becomes a structuring element *of the social problematic.*

Critique of Urban Ideology[*]

We will deal in particular with the phenomena of alienation, repression and integration. We will show, not the guilty urbanism of The Logic of Urbanism, *but the networks, systems of consumption and infrastructure that tend to normalize a life fragmented into activities (work, leisure, everyday life, sexuality), into a single project whose fulfillment, that is, coherence, is to take place in the new vision of the city and urban life reformed beyond class struggle.*

We will show the convergence of institutional and professional urbanism—"shameful labor," the level of "urbanist activity"—and the "spontaneous" urbanism of the "free market" obeying the laws of the circulation of commodities—the level of "urbanist practice"—which, within the present structures of capitalist production, tend to integrate "urban practice" and integrate itself into [urban practice]. By integrating urban practice, "urbanist practice" endeavors to normalize it to its models (derived from the world of commodities*), and on the other hand, by integrating itself to [urban practice], "urbanist practice" (and its induced and deduced phenomena) palms itself off as "natural," social and ineluctable. This creates an* urban logic *that includes "urbanism" formally and goes beyond it. This logic is based on an urban ideology (or many? remains to be seen) that is but the quintessence of a set of ideas implicitly and explicitly formulated by the class that still wants to dominate and by the groups that really dominate. It is taken up by the base and productive classes inasmuch as the logic of the ideology is relayed and transmitted by the media, whose present deployment would not be possible without urban agglomerations in their present forms. Although this urban logic and this ideology do not impose themselves, do not dominate directly and dictatorially (in their "name"), they nevertheless exercise a power that is all the more real for being insidious, subterranean; above all they convey a global project and work towards its completion; but not without aligning*

[*] This article briefly presents a number of themes and theses that will be developed in *Critique of Urban Ideology* (forthcoming).

urban life according to the models of industry, for the bourgeoisie does not and cannot transform its productive force, which it considers indispensable and to which it intends to submit the intellectual and labor forces of production and mode of consumption.

In order to maintain itself, power presents the current problematic as inevitable and establishes a supremacy of technique.

The Knowledge of Urbanism and the Urbanism of Power

1.

The question is not so much to explain the relationships that exist between what we call *urbanism*[1] and the society in which it develops, than it is to grasp why urbanism was created and by what kind of society. I will study its role and social status not in the abstract but implicated within a specific social structure; that is, within a specific mode of production. It will not be a matter of looking for *Urbanism-in-itself* but of finding out why such a society has an urbanism.

2.

Let us start by setting the limits and pinning down the mystifications that are rife in this area.

Let us place ourselves not in the perspective of the Science called Urbanism but in that of reality: the CITY. Let us forget the idea that assumes that the solution to the urban problematic

1. We will basically use the word URBANISM, which seems to refer to both the problematic of the city and the ideology of the discipline. Not only that, but its long career gives it a priority over other terms of more recent coinage: to mask the ideology, many terms are used to refer to a same idea, a manner that is aided and abetted by our habits of segmentation, of division of labor. Therefore, under the term of "urbanism" we include all the substitutes that refer to the same problematic, namely urban and industrial. Such as: the organization of space, urban development, urban planning, regional development (which structure their activity around centers, nuclei, poles of attraction, metropolises…), etc., the various urbanisms: organic, semiological, spatial, subterranean… Lastly, polistics, urbanology, ekistics, etc.

will be found when a scientific corpus, a scientific rigor and a complete knowledge called Urbanism will have been constituted. Forget it! Why, you ask? Let us ask the question. Is the urban problematic external to that of the overall society structured by the capitalist mode of production?

We have raised in an undisciplined way the problem of urbanism's knowledge. Is the social questioning raised by the "urban"[2] immanent or transcendent relative to a historical society's mode of production? Is the foundation of the great questioning with which we are dealing dependent on Civilization, a phenomenon of the Great Universal History, beyond individual societies and modes of production? Or does it depend directly—as I implied at the beginning of this introduction—on the social structures, that is, on a specific social practice that has one or several definite goals, integrated in the mode of production, and integrative of social relationships?

A crucial question. Either we define the city as a *space* that receives the social and consequently has to adapt to the present social structures—in which case we fully realize the importance of technology (of technique) and the minimal role of politics, which in this perspective is only a temporary effect in the broad development of Civilization—or we define the city as a *practice*,[3] in which case it is an entirely different matter. Politics is no longer an effect but fundamental to the understanding of the social strategy of power. We are no longer confronted with a homogeneous totality, civilization, but with modes of production, institutions, and ideologies. According to one definition, we are at the level of the Universality of the city, of its historical development, attested by the bureaucratic identities of East and

2. [27] Concerning the concept of "the urban," see: H. Lefebvre, *Le droit à la ville*, éd. Anthropos, 1968, especially p. 56 passim; *La vie quotidienne dans le monde moderne*, éd. Gallimard, coll. Idées, 1968, pp. 234–5 passim; and also *Court essai réflexe sur les fragments d'un urbanisme*, UTOPIE no. 1, éd. Anthropos, May 1967, p. 64 et seq.; *Preface to Introduction à l'urbanisme*, M. Poëte, éd. Anthropos, 1967, p. XXII, by the author.

3. The word practice ("pratique") as used here means the following: "By practice in general, we mean all the processes of transformation of a given and determinate raw material into a determinate product, whose transformation is effected by means of determinate human labor using determinate means (of 'production')." But with the stipulation that "in all practice considered in this way the determinant moment (or element) is neither the raw material, nor the product, but practice in the strict sense: the moment of the work of transformation itself, which implements in a specific structure the men, the means and a technical method of the utilization of the means." In *Pour Marx*, Louis Althusser, éd. Maspéro, 1966, p. 167.

West. We would refer to a unitive planetary cosmology; there would be a divine, peaceful totality based on World History. Beyond petty conflicts, the humanist task would be to save Man's major work—the CITY—from the destructive ravages of machine society. According to the other definition, we would be within the field of the objective conditions for the becoming of *a* society, implying *ipso facto* the plane of class struggle, of hierarchy, (of Authority) and social difference. We would feel the concrete structures of production. Although it is a work ("oeuvre"), the city is no longer a functional object regulated by technology, but part of the mode and process of production.

3.

Here we have a series of questions that must be parsed quickly. It is a matter of engaging in a radical critique of the knowledge called "urbanism." For nearly thirty years, the latter has been running into insurmountable questions, for it rests on a purely idealistic base that renders it sterile in practice, turning it constantly against itself. Its conscious failures demonstrate its theoretical ineptness, its knowledge incapable of analysing them with its idealistic instruments. Lacking a theoretical foundation, basing itself directly on pragmatic urban reality as regards its apparent and immediately perceptible contradictions and the development of its role and status, "urbanism" (as knowledge or as practice) is on the decline, desperately grasping at the branches of humanist ideology. Its theoretical insufficiency saps all the institutions, the profession—in a word, the practice—by stuffing all of its products into a rough pragmatism: radical critique must not spare the practice, because it has an influence on knowledge.

Here, again, the epistemological analysis remains to be done and will be possible only if we break the urbanist idealism, the philosophy of Civilization, the ideology of happiness, of the fulfillment of Man, etc. It is not a matter of mere chance, nor of the crass mediocrity of man, if the theoretical practice of the city does not exist; it is a concerted attitude of power, it is part of the strategy of the established power in our society.

Understanding this kind of phenomenon requires the elaboration of a theory, hence the importance I grant to theory in "urbanism," if only to show that this urbanism is in fact only a part of the global ideology of power, to attest to the uselessness of such a realm, or to found it on an analysis, a theoretical understanding of the problematic in view of building a *practice*. No theory would be worthy of this name if it did not call into question limits and established categories when the moment for theoretical practice has come; it is futile to want to elaborate a theory without formulating the problem at the epistemological level.

4

Several previous studies on global society have shown us a certain situation of the city and of the discipline that deals with it. Their results will form our basic hypotheses:

The city does not transcend the social problematic of our society.

The urban problematic is not innocent within the global strategy of class power, since our society—as far as we know—is a class society.

"Urbanism" is not a problem in itself outside of the class struggle.

The calling into question of "urbanism" emerges as part of the logic of the social conflicts between power and knowledge that are presently shaking France and the world.

The Social Practice of Urbanism

The history of the city is very significant; no system of conditioning will arrest it. Ideology endeavors to do so, and hinders the elaboration of a practice, a practice to be based on proper theoretical foundations, a true theoretical practice, such that it corresponds to a *real* object and not to an object that has been ideologically transformed and presupposed. It is therefore not a matter of applying existing formulas to a preexisting content.

If we want to elaborate a theory of the city and its problematic, we have to analyze urban practice in conjunction with "urbanism": to start with the *base*, which is the only possible and viable referent. But what is this "mass" (in and of the city) today, after thirty years of manipulation due to the political institution of opposition? In order to realize this project we will proceed by analyzing both the concrete foundations of social reality and ideology, while knowing that we are not sheltered from ideology ourselves.

The City of Class Struggles

It will be a question here of the city at the moment of the confrontation, constitution, and establishment of class struggles and their historical result: the advent of the need for rationalization.

Repressive "urbanism" as an institution (discipline and agency) appears when industrialization is practically accomplished. It is also the period that sees the introduction of a science of the rationalization of industrial labor, ergonomics, in tandem with the establishment of social psychology in American business. It is the point of inception of a concerted policy of rationalization at all levels of society.

The city (a legacy of the previous period, of the feudal mode of production) presented undeniable advantages at various levels; as much in terms of the yield and control of the means of production, as in terms of the circulation of money and goods, as well as the accumulation of capital. The bourgeoisie has turned the city into the sovereign mistress. In this period, as before, the city is the preferential place that does not go beyond the preferential. It plays an important part in the formation of the Bourgeoisie, as well as in the formation of the classes and in the division of labor. Karl Marx noted: "The greatest division of material and intellectual labor is the separation of town and country," and added that "we may understand the separation of capital and land ownership as the beginning of an existence and development of capital independent of land ownership, as the beginning of property based solely on labor and exchange."[4] The breaking up of the union of Labor-Capital-Land of the corporatist economy entailed not only the fundamental town-country split, but also the separation of the haves (capital) and the have-nots—the proletariat (the workforce). The new mode of production that was taking shape was to profoundly transform social relationships; especially in the creation of the day labor required by new modes of production. The appearance, due to day labor, of

4. K. Marx, in *L'idéologie Allemande* (1845–46), I. Feuerbach, éd. Sociales, pp. 80–81.

the plebeians (of the cities) transformed the balance of forces that existed between the medieval city and its successor, the monarchic city. The class of have-nots that operated the instruments of production turned the city into a concentration of population, furthered the accumulation and establishment of capital, of leisure and of needs. As Marx wrote: "It is the most blatant expression of the subordination of the individual to the division of labor, of the subordination to a determined activity forced upon him" (*ibid.*).

Let us elucidate the current situation. The city continues to be what it was, the depot of the mode of production; of its instruments as much as of the circulation of commodities, of the systems that maintain commodities as much as of the peons that operate it. The very fact of the concentration of the means of production forces the State, as the protector of capital, to conduct strict and rational policies regarding cities. The wish for a rational apprehension of the urban, a spatial and temporal sectioning into differentiated and compartmentalized activities, together with an impoverished reconstitution of the "original" urban practice, contributes to the constitution of a repressive structure entirely subject to the project of the class society, leading "naturally" to segregration and to collaboration in the maintainance of the class struggle. Power tries to turn the city into the product and the means of capitalistic domination.

what is a complex

From being a place for the accumulation and protection of capital, the city has also become—without losing any of its past prerogatives—the place for the deployment of commodities. It is

What do we mean by packaging complex?

It is a material composed of several elements, intended to keep out atmospheric agents, as well as others such as water, oil, gas etc. ... To wrap and protect all parts, staples, and materials is the very purpose of the packaging complex.

"Water resistance," the essential quality in this domain, is obtained by welding the complex onto itself.

- This operation is very simple

It's what we call the thermosealable complex

Capital's potential. In order to fulfill this potential, structures are put into place that force us to scrutinize as closely as possible the generic scope of the term "urbanism," in order to disclose the operative concepts covered up by this word; concepts that will also permit us to better define the game of the class struggle. We have distilled three concepts that circumscribe three levels of action or operationality. *Urbanist activity* refers to the Institution (administration, legislation…) and to the profession. *Urbanist practice* encompasses the work done on and in the city by all the networks and systems referring *directly* to the socioeconomic structure (commerce, the police, associations, etc.) and which acts structurally and perceptibly. The third level, *urban practice*, contains on the one hand the first two levels and on the other hand urbanity, everyday life, philosophy and non-philosophy, the dramas, the joys, in a word, the *praxis*, the force of liberation, and especially a sum of "have-nots" of the class society who until then have been more or less subject to alienation, to integration in "social norms," to the falsification of the System, but who make history.

In reality, we observe that the haves and the have-nots now have a place for their struggle. Outside of the city there was no class struggle in advanced industrial society. It is played out "in the city," where our three levels come in. As the institution that tries to rationalize urban space, exchanges, and the flow of commodities, urbanist activity acts, plans, organizes and is relayed in this task by urbanist practice, which refines or transforms the final purpose—actions that basically perpetuate the system. What does urban practice do, apart from the two previous actions? History will tell. Remember the Commune of 1871 and of May–June 1968; these were examples. The city is both the place of consolidation and of explosion.

"Urbanism" which has the city as its object is implicated in one way or another in the class struggles that have not ceased.

Repressive City!

Within the international campaign for the economic self-regulation of the social, the rational and rationalized city is produced as an ontological need, as the essence of *industrial happiness*, counterbalanced by its opposite, nature (everyday leisure, escape). It is also an ideal object, ideated and idealized by

The city is at once a commodity resulting from the mode of production, the place where commodities are deployed, and the means for producing social relations as a commodity.

LE CHAMPO

power. A few irreducible, immediate contradictions remain. Rationalization presents itself in a reassuring light, as liberation from every inhibition, anxiety and suppression—but also as conservative. You can find everything in it. Today's city has a very complex place in what may be called *the trial of social work*. The city is both a commodity resulting from the mode of production and a means to produce commodities. What would consumption be, what would production become, what would become of the product, and of the objects without this fundamental ambiguity? This is the destructive plurality of the urban specificity; its lack of identity among identities. The city is a constant question. It pops up as a problematic at the very moment that bourgeois society is called into question. Remember Baron Haussmann, the pauperism under Louis-Napoleon, look at the novels of Hugo and Balzac… It not only contains the dramas, but channels them, exhibits them, exposes them in a thousand different ways. Even the easily perceptible materiality of the city is neither a space, neither neutral, smooth, nor free; but already history, a fully-occupied territory. The territority's imbroglio is not chaos; it determines its reason, from which those who try to appropriate it suffer. Man's own creation, and he mystifies and reduces the city at the same time. Mystifies it by turning it into everything, all of life. Reduces it by considering it as a mediation between work and leisure, between daily life and the exceptional in life. It is both Les Halles and the Rue des Marronniers.

Politics is also streets and sewers. In them, organization (bureaucracy) is the pendant of agitation (revolution). Organization counters and suppresses agitation by maintaining it in scattered expressions. The subtle game unfolding at that point is the very play of contradictions. The exceptional rubs elbows with the everyday, without the one rubbing off on the other; their mere friction sometimes suffices for the spontaneous explosion of contradictory forces. Rubbing elbows with the other in no way implies that the unitary exists, or that there is homogenization; on the contrary, the proximity accentuates the fragmentation of the social totality. The city *completes* and *fixes* man within the narrow bounds of his present being. In this, he finds the fulfillment of his alienation. There, he is entirely subject to objects and their new system of distribution; he finds his place in it as object-producer of these objects. Here the "commodity" produced by the city is considered as the means for producing determined and finished products.

All of these elements are found—dreamlike—in the "street," at all ends of the space of everyday time, in the spaces of habit turning into spaces of lassitude, which nonetheless provide joys here and there: the future happy memory. A vulgar place too often trod underfoot, too often rebuffed, too worn out by countless minor habitual fatigues, countless minor troubles. The great boredom, so meagre, eclipsed by the organized joy of leisure. Everyday life. That which apparently remains untouched by the totalitarian will of the State, by its machines, but still subject to alienating rationality: what is left of it? After the mystified life, conditioned by aestheticism, modernism? Nothing escapes the Holy Light of control, except the nooks and crannies: the residue of everyday life.

Everydayness does not flaunt itself in the plowed fields: Flaubert and Baudelaire were not fooled. Where do Bouvard and Pécuchet drag their boredom? Where did they meet? On a bench on the Boulevard Bourdon. What are they? Employees? No, they are the dullness of life in the city. They are experiencing the new city as a new life. They make the great passage, creating the city and the life planted and tamed by the bourgeoisie in power. Would it be a travesty to set these two chaps up in some new town?

The city is the proper place for a revolt, a revolution, for it is there that the banality and triviality of everyday life run their course. A possibility that arises from a resistance due to the class struggles and consciousness found in the residue of the conditioning operation of everydayness. The city exposes itself as the public dump of social conflicts and dramas. The great ambiguity is lifted: by veiling its strategy with the city and the idea of the city, power unwittingly discloses its global project, which we have already outlined. Rational argument battles the truth of everyday life. Positivism suffers from a distortion between rational organization and this place of principle and interest which deploys its irrationalism, its utopia again. The functionalist philosophy of Le Corbusier is killed by urban practice. The vacant lot is still filled with old moles and history does not dig itself in. The dump is not useless, nor is utopia, and contradiction even less so. The tragedy of Capital plays itself out in the urban forum.

Coherent Repressive Rationality

The appropriation of the city by those holding the instruments of production implies an integration of the contradictions of competitive capitalism, or of neo-capitalism, into urban practice. According to this perspective, the city has a privileged position in the project of the class in power and in control of production, inasmuch as its essential "substance"—capital—finds its place there. The city, the space of Capital, is far from being an aesthetic object.

We cannot limit our analysis to the economics of bourgeois society; by its essence it has a project for society: what are its principal articulations?

This project does not contradict class exploitation, the deprivation of knowledge, or the scattering of labor. The purpose of the project is not entirely contained within this rule; it would be limiting the pretensions of the bourgeoisie to think that its culmination would lie in pure miserly enjoyment of its capital—if this were so, wouldn't the latter crumble into dust? Behind it is a conception of the world, of which the capitalist economic system is the foundation; a will to create a new social practice, whose structure is precisely that of alienated labor. Advertising, in this sense, is—altogether—nothing but the propagandist philosophy of the new happiness and its mode of propagation.

The "new existence" is based on profit, the social and technical division of labor, and thus on fragmentation: the separation of functions from one another, of forms from one another, of forms from functions. It is also based on the hierarchy passing itself off as a natural play of social structures, on the opposition of private and public life, on the dislocation of everyday life (everydayness), of work, of leisure (of play), etc; to cite only Hegel's *Civil Society*, Balzac's *Human Comedy*, Lefebvre's *Critique of Everyday Life* and *La conscience mystifiée*, etc. The edifice is built upon a highly rational and rationalized class structure. We tend to make society fit this scheme by looking for its coherence in production and consumption; how could it be otherwise, since social relations are induced by relationships of production.

Whereas separation infiltrates everywhere, the edifice is covered by a monolithic Totality, one and indivisible: the State. A homogeneous and universal state, for it is everything: the masses, the classes (which democratically elect their representatives—even of the proletariat—who constitute the State) and power (capital). It is the coherence of coherences, an army of bureaucratic, military and informational systems. The State: infallible master of History. The "cogito, ergo sum" of the Nation. The State rests upon "human sand," to use Nietzsche's metaphor. Each grain is isolated and isolatable (the symbol of private consciousness, of individualism, and gregarious interests, the distinctive sign of the petty bourgeois, the middle class and of the bourgeoisie), but the whole comprises a mass—the heaviest mass of all.

State reason decides on the rationalization of social practice. Planning (development, regulation, organization...) is the principal mode that keeps advanced industrial societies from succumbing to their own contradictions. Rationality is deployed to maintain the commodity system (of money). It concerns specific places. The everyday life of the city (from sexuality to play) is organized, then rationalized. Production is rationalized in relation to consumption. The rationale of the industrialist tends to close the production/consumption circle. Our analysis shows that the city is situated at the buckling point of the production/consumption circle, and the basic relationships between base and superstructure—as we currently know them—are strongly shaken since, depending on the level of reality that we are examining, the city, while it is often taken to be only the superstructure, is both at once. The urban problematic is a bastion of the class struggle.

As mentioned before, despite or beyond all the separations, there is a coherence between the productive purpose and the social purpose (even if they appear detached). The first is achieved through technical refinement and the second by political domination. Thus it is very difficult to differentiate between techniques of industrialization and political techniques. Herbert Marcuse goes so far as to say that the techniques of industrialization are political techniques. Is there a closing off [*clôture*] of society in that case? The existing order would transcend itself into a total Order. Actions undertaken towards the formation of a closed society, towards constructing the System, bear upon social practice, or, more exactly, on particular practices (political, ideological, theoretical, technical, urban) that constitute praxis. The goal is to bend them to the logic of commodities, to include them within the system of objects. We know this conflict from philosophy, it is the conflict between Subject and Object. As Lukacs shows, the reification of the subject—its transformation into an object—fosters the implantation of the capitalist system, itself facilitated by the eradication of class consciousness, each is an individuality, a "grain of sand." The object, in the nonphilosophical sense, is the result of a production, it is a *product*, and in the economic system, a commodity. The operation of objectality is favorable to the process of industrial production, to its systems of control, to quantification, to distribution, to modernity. Social relationships considered as objects can be rationally organized and integrated into the logic of commodities. Have we come to such a homogeneity? Some think so, while others are still finding "holes" and cracks. We are tending toward enclosure [*clôture*], but does that mean that the closing off [*clôture*] has already happened?

This leads some theoreticians susceptible to the terrorism of structure, of the System, to observe a unification of the aspirations of various social classes, of national interests, and of Big Business (Capital). This unification goes so far as to absorb the historical forces of liberation. The homogenization of society is part of the bourgeois class's project for Society. All that the theoreticians (R. Aron, J.K. Galbraith) are doing is to shout from the rooftops that social classes no longer exist, and so neither does the class struggle, nor ideologies, nor ideology itself, which is only the "opium of the intellectuals." Why? Because everything is organized and planned. Homogenous cities for a homogenous society. This would be the triumph of man over nature and the return to natural laws of balance and ecology. And so dissent and criticism are likened to nature's struggle to eliminate the weaker elements, to remedy the deviations caused by the event: violence reminds power of the way of "history" and is at the same time the stabilizer. Over-rationalization appears as naturalness tamed and used for social balance. After periods of violence, power can shamelessly admit—without any trace of false consciousness—to the necessity of introducing revisions in the distribution of *the* powers, even renovations or reforms that are contradictory to its practice before the violence. It integrates the force of protest by approving it on the one hand and, on the other, gives the appearance of respecting its message. The supremacy of the ideology of technics plays its political role, for to each problematic there is a technical solution.

—Is there an urban problematic? Oh, I see, "urbanism"... well then, get on with it!

No! That's precisely where the whole thing explodes, where the mirage of speculative philosophy evaporates. Reflection—methodology, technology—cannot do everything. The solution—the surpassing—of the urban problematic is not in the city. The transformation of the conceptual apparatus of philosophy and its approach, with an eye to solving one or more partial lines of questioning—included in a totality without compromising its coherence—as technical instruments or a methodology of fragmentary disciplines formulates an extrapolation that presents the pseudo-guarantees of rigor and the appearances of theory. Philosophical reason and philosophy elaborate a project and its realization belongs to us. This realization will be possible only by surpassing the speculative limits of the philosophical. *Metaphilosophy* does not suppose a continuation of the speculative falsifications of the philosophers: speculations into which many theoreticians of "urbanism" like to jump. Through dialectical reason, which assumes a double critique of philosophy and social reality, metaphilosophy strives to elaborate a strategy with the purpose of, on the one hand, abolishing the capitalist process of production and all its induced and deduced phenomena and, on the other, implementing the project contained within philosophy. A project that can be accomplished only by a revolutionary praxis. If the city and "urbanism" have a central place in metaphilosophy it is because it is in this site and in this discipline that contradictory forces come into play, forces that must be either resisted or strengthened.

Utopia and the Failure of the Enclosure

Coherence and cohesion, rationality and Reason are the foundations of advanced Industrialization. In order to carry out its project, society does not shrink from creating unproductive institutions (bureaucracy, technocracy), to check the forces of history and supervise the establishment of a "dispatching" agency suitable to its rationale and its purposes. Industrial practice combined with the ideological practice of the bourgeoisie sweeps away all the social practices that have not yet capitulated to the commercial rationale. It structures the institutions, turning them into instruments of control and repression. Efficiency is the sermon of the day. The organization and colonization of everyday life is the nectar of the ideology of capitalist consumption. The guidelines of structure organize our existence.

The enclosure of society seems to underlie the project. Has it been completely achieved? It would seem not. Marx used to say: "Now we have to fulfill philosophy by surpassing it." His wish has almost been granted. The system created by speculative philosophy has been concretely constructed by bourgeois society, except that no surpassing occurred and philosophy continues to theorize for bourgeois society, as P. Nizan showed in *Les Chiens de garde.*[5] Bourgeois society and its project were established on the foundations of the Civil Society of the great bourgeois philosopher L.G.W Hegel; imperfectly, as it should be, with a differential between Philosophy and life. The homogenization, the closing off [*clôture*] makes it seem as if "everything, including the convulsions of the world, points to the end of history," as the Hegelian philosopher Alexandre Kojève put it. This would mean that history set up a universal and homogenous state; a way of life devoid of negativity. Thus the bourgeoisie and bourgeois thinking that had no place in history, that seemed but an "interlude," a transition on the way to the great industry that alone permits socialism, will have found a space in the parking lot of history, all the while being its crowning achievement! No, Mister Hegel, we are not at the end of history, and if we may grant you, *a posteriori*, that the bourgeois State is the *Sunday of history*, don't, dear philosopher, forget the *Monday*. We are discovering the complicity between *knowledge* and *power* in the strategy of the integration and falsification of the World. Let us answer with J.L. Borges that, "in the dream of the dreaming man, the dream woke up."

The Operationalism of Urbanism and the Operationality of the Urban Practice

The man of everyday life is the purest protector of the patterns of subjection in everyday life. Henri Lefebvre somewhere said that proletarians do not have the status of humans and that they will acquire it only by surpassing their proletarian lives. Insofar as this constitutes a definition of the proletarian and the proletariat—to which we can add the deprivation of creation, of its product—then it applies to all those who, by means of their practice, are subject to everyday life as defined by the author. The proletariat that furnish the city, that live in it and fashion it, is omitted. No participatory structure, however fine, will allow the proletariat to reappropriate the city, for doing so would imply calling the social structures as a whole into question. This is where the break between urbanistic discourse—which moves ever further away from the discourse of the city—

5. Editions Maspéro.

and everyday urban practice lies. Participation is a comanagement that leaves power in place. Comanagement renovates class society. To put an end to our exploitation, the best solution is to not share with those exploiting us. It is only a last resort of "repressive satisfaction" (H. Marcuse). "Urbanism," following the movement, catches up quickly to reality wearing glasses of ideology.

The theoreticians and ideologists of power project an ideal man onto the city, a man who finds his exact place within the splendid machinery of capitalist society and who is so well imaged by the advertising that constitutes the basic psychology of modernity: it's Madame "express"; or the "pleasure of smoking Astor that begins as soon as you open the pack"; or the one who has a "gentle way of leading women by the nose—with the Eau de Toilette from Dana"; and he is also the one who can say "Jet pilots wear a Rolex GMT Master"; it's "Hom, the underwear that make the virile man"; "MAILCOTT, a man's reality"; "Ahhh! another man, a real one... who smokes CLAN"; "a style... a hit... a young and relaxed way of life, Drug'style Bata"; and not least, "with Ritual, night erases the days; let sleep and Ritual do their work. Abandon yourself to this sacred ritual. At last, time no longer matters... or only a little."

And so the models and laws of urban life, of the new urbanity, are forged. The models become a part of social practice, of urban reality. Supported and transmitted by the media this happens smoothly, or rather with the reformist clashing required by every modernism worthy of being called *modern*; hence the game of criticizing the media supported by power. This dissent leaves what we call objectivity free; a certain objectivity that permits a certain dissent. Concerning us, for example, pertinent critiques of the "villes nouvelles" may sometimes be found in LE FIGARO; but then, imperceptibly, the justifications creep out. "In the end, it is not so bad." After all, social practice completes things, history asserts and roots itself in these new creations, little by little the planning is checked, the split between work and habitat fades, a social life is created in this body without a soul, and man and his humanity assert themselves, etc. For those who know how to read between the lines, this satisfaction (self-satisfaction) is an implicit critique of the existing order and its ideology. To straighten things out, we invoke social practice and history—which everywhere else is fought—it shows that there is something other than the State and that it bends backwards in the face of social demands. Its reality does not always correspond to its overall project. The social practice of the

Z.U.P. points out the falsification of the bourgeois order. Of course, it is not complete disalienation. Organization does not let itself be defeated so easily. But pockets of real and active protest do exist. A concrete analysis of the city shows that it is still a bit hasty to conclude that classes and history have come to an end.

Some will think that we have gone astray. Not at all. Advanced industrial capitalism has indeed appropriated the city. The city is experienced in an industrial mode, along the lines of industrial practice. We have situated and defined urbanism within the logic of integration that leads toward the enclosure of Society. Where else than "in the city" is the rationality more perceptible or tangible? Where else is the falsification of our society written in so many words? This question is not without an answer.

"Urbanism" holds a special place in the overall project cooked up by the class in power.

Thus it is very understandable that the operational urbanists bump into all the "raw" sectors of everyday life and the city's real history, which, although considerably encroached upon and dulled, still remains present. I have already stressed that what we call "urbanism" is restricted neither to a precise body, nor to a specific, isolated action in society. Urbanists are therefore only one of the links in the chain of "urbanism" and are associated with the tasks involving the ordering and the "concrete" organization of existence; that is, the integration into models from culture and from advertising. Even when assisted, the professional, the pluri-, multi- or interdisciplinary team runs into many difficulties: these are constantly exacerbated by the base's growing awareness of the dispersive tactics of the repressive structures—as well as by the lessons leaked by advertising, news and the press. These flows are also intercepted by urbanistic activity, but often quite late, because it is equipped with a heavy—and inevitable—bureaucratic apparatus. This means that urbanistic activity is sometimes delayed. Urbanistic practice is powerful, and it often subtly and indirectly guides urbanistic activity. Shopkeepers, landlords (of all stripes), public entertainers and the police are at the heart of urban ideology; their malignant acuteness leaves the institution that deals with the city behind. It is important, however, not to move too quickly and to distinguish between the game of power and the power of play in the dissenting daily life of the city.

The representation made of "urbanism" is only the tranquilizing aspect of the complete takeover of both the urban "phenomenon" and urban life in order to control the flow of production, to ensure the protection and maintenance of the proprietary classes, and therefore the circulation of money and the perpetuation of a political-economic system: capitalism. The city has to submit to treatment by a sort of liberal nationalization, and by the path of democracy the Master takes care of the slave.

In light of this state of affairs—which remains uncriticized—the theoreticians elaborated sets or fragments of systems that were supposed to be coherent in the face of incoherence. In the process they even wanted to render the incoherence of the world coherent, but without calling its foundations into question—a godsend for power. Given this, we could define "urbanism" as the philosophy of happiness. Thus by means of fragmentary observations and in the absence of a radical critique, we built a domain without a territory, or rather of all territories, an inadequate pragmatic-theoretical apparatus. Meanwhile, the urban problematic grew, the takeover of the city by industrial practice. The "urban man" of urbanism was born a stranger to the man in the street; he will go to live at one pole, a vacant extremity that is either the rock bottom of his triviality driving him a little more into the corner of his alienation, or a Golden dream that makes him forget his triviality without surpassing it. Stuck in industrial rationality, urban man is included within the spectacle of his life and within the life of the social spectacle. The city is a great stage for the play of what life should be.

Even in a moment of revolutionary euphoria—a moment of complete desacralization in celebration—institutional urbanism, in addressing its criticism to the State and to itself has not transgressed its underlying ideologies; there was only an apparent shift from the technical to the political without benefit of a theoretical explanation.[6] This at a time when the products and the results of the urbanistic activity and practice were trod underfoot, when functionality was crushed, when limits and meanings were transcended, the urbanistic syntheses sublimating the division of labor in this realm were dismantled, rationality was derationalized and bourgeois urbanity was scoffed at. Urbanism was torn up like paving stones and urban practice established.

In order for the project of the total bourgeois Society to be achieved, there must be a super-rationalization, and this can be

6. Cf. the STCAU motion: *Le partage des pouvoirs, essai sur la participation: autonomie et solidarités, partage des décisions*, special issue no. 9 of *Revue 2000*, May–June 1968, especially the appendix: "L'Urbanisme en question: la Revue de l'ADELS," *Correspondance municipale*, June–July 1968, etc.

done only through technology. But technics must be freed of the ideological impurities that differ from the ideology of power. The progress of technics is confounded with history, the becoming of technology with politics. The "need" for profitability and efficiency in the urban sector correlates with the planning will of the capitalist economy. The balance between production and consumption can be maintained only by a certain type of planning. Here, not only a technique of the plan comes into the picture but all the techniques of maintenance or renewal; which in no way permit contradictions to be surpassed, but only that form be given to things. The act and art of rationalization are executed by a specialized and "technologized" knowledge. "Urbanism" is no different from the other repressive structures derived from the same system.

The need, the "desire" for a rationalization of the city is sublimated only by the integration, if not the "forcing" of elements external to urban practice that only increases the difference between producers and consumers. Urban rationalization combined with the ideology of Nature and of escape contains the *formal* disappearance of the city and the retention of its social contradictions—not the surpassing of the city and its contradictions. There has always been a confusion between the abolition of the city-form and the disappearance of the town/country opposition, of segregation, of the division of labor, and it is believed that by breaking up and scattering the city out and creating green spaces all of these problems will cease.

"Urbanism" is a structure for direct integration to the extent that it imperceptibly and materially touches on everyday life. Its mission is the ordering of urban existence and, given the theoretical weakness that characterizes "urbanism," it is difficult to see its critical ability; its apparatus for refusing the desiderata of power, or its possibilities for protest (instruments, fields of reception, or the site of its critical speech). Upon what analysis would its dissent be based? This is an important question, and a negative answer can be given. Its analysis would be worthless if it rested solely on the city without being connected to an overall social project, for the city in itself has nothing to do with this: what is at stake is society as a whole. And this clearly raises the question of the foundation and frame of reference for this dissent. If it refutes the *social commission* forced upon it, "urbanism" has to accept the *social demand* that emanates directly from the base. Thus this "discipline" would take a political option, would reinstate its political mission. More questions appear. In whose name and for whom would it fight? Can it really fight while remaining an instituted body, a partial and specialized discipline? I doubt it, for how can one avoid the interference of power when one is power? And yet, don't we know to whom the *product* of urbanism is addressed? We are calling into question the one who commissions the product and the product itself. Could there be a sort of implacable determinism here that would reduce "urbanism" to an accomplice of power? We are describing an institution whose doors are being closed, if they are not closed already. We are defining the strange ambiguity of "urbanism," a specialized and partial discipline and field that is struggling with its own contradictions and those of society as a whole. We are bringing to light the internal convulsions of a science of synthesis which, in a society wholly subject to the social and technical division of labor, attempts to totalize separations established by the ontology of bourgeois society. These attempts at coalescence are doomed in advance if they are done without economic-political might. To formulate the problem in political terms and situate it on the level of class struggles assumes a radical calling into question of the policies conducted by power regarding the city and "urbanism." If we refuse to raise the political problem, then there is only one route left. It is the route of global society, the route of technics. We are bringing convulsions to light, those of bureaucratic societies. There are of course technical problems, but they are never *purely* technical, independent of all ideology; at the very least of the ideology of handling and the game of technics. Technics as shelter, the civilization-mission and civilizing mission that "urbanism" assigns itself with the tacit approval of power are the fantasies of an "urbanism" that does not show its real face.

"Urbanism," a concept that indicates a closed and empty totality, that marks and details an absence of theory, and all the new terms, like *urbanology*, *polistics*… only accentuate the theoretical void without filling it, only brandish sophisms. The theoretical void involves the persistence of the contradictions willfully pushed aside by reflection. The research, the essays in doctrine or theory are nothing but empty discussions among nominalists. The term and its full meaning predominate. Everything is a question of language, of definition! But what do the definitions matter! "What is to be done?" is the only question worth pausing for in the city. The search for a technological "urbanism" tending toward the homogenization of social contradictions excludes it from urban reality, from a conflicted reality.

"Urbanism" arranges existing conditions, distributes scarcity—the old and the new—and creates scarcity; it is implicated in and respects the constraints of laws, determinisms, rationality, and Culture. The technique of "urbanism" believes that it is resolving—with money linked to technology—all the contradictions that crop up "in the city," while it only accelerates the urban problematic with its partial and specialized answers. Now, it is not a matter of reducing or absorbing the questioning, but of surpassing it by and for urban social practice: it is in the manner of solving this task that we see a diversion [*détournement*] for the sake of the class project. Nevertheless, considering the problems, since nothing exists in the absolute, the answers are both correct and antinomous. It is not a matter of separately solving problems as dispersed aggregates or regrouped pieces, but of transforming society such that these problems no longer exist. Each answer given by technics has the appearance of a political answer to a social question, only pushing the problem away to let it resurface at another level. It is the opposite of surpassing the contradictions or oppositions by forces capable of fighting them, which is how the dialectics of social forces work. The action of technics—the almighty policy—only causes a displacement of the problematic.

What needs to be called into question is indeed knowledge rather than the problematic; "urbanism," rather than the urban problematic. Urban practice has tracked institutional "urbanism" down and forced it to make its self-criticism, which is only at its beginnings; it has been insufficient up until now, and only pushes it into its own duplicity. Analysis in itself has never been enough; class struggle is its theoretical foundation and the appropriation of the means of production by the producers remains the condition sine qua non of the reappropriation of the city by the workers.

The reasoning does not finish there; its end can only be in praxis. I have closed the circle neither through reasoning, nor through writing, for the world is not closed yet. Establishing a critique of "urbanism" does not mean tautologizing, as some might think, or mystifying the knowledge of "urbanism" and setting up a critical critique of it. Society is not free yet; it is up to us to liberate it. The path that goes through theoretical practice is the one that leads to freedom. May it be ours.

H.T.
July 1968

The skillful formation of the established order, or the great dialogue with the invisible.

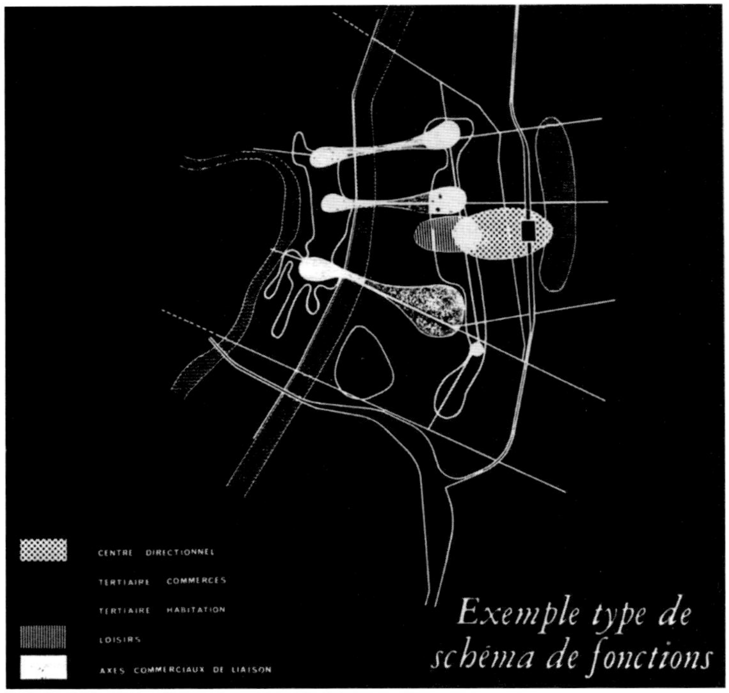

Tübingen, 9, 1, 68

Dear friend,

Thank you for this repressive Logic of urbanism. There is an internationality of cities like there is one of chains for social life. You wrote that partial urbanism would be an ideology "destined, like all ideologies, to mask the real problems, to offer false solutions." Considering the most oppressive urban manifestations, I don't know if ideology is still a problem of true or false. Urban life, I believe, does not express an ideology, it is a fully accomplished ideology. Is it still a problem of partial or universal urban plans? Instead, the ideology of urbanism seems to me completely materialized, the fulfillment of the dominant thinking. Like you, I see very little chance for non-repressive urban plans: the administration of finances (thus of execution) and of social life exists through an introversion of its exploitative and class character. What we need is a negative urbanism: in the process of the emancipation of the repressive structures of social life, which raises the problem of an active, socialist anti-politics; this question must show us that the city is becoming too tight. The best planning in the programmed society can only be a springboard to destroy the structures of the repressive society. This classic city—capitalist—and this is what the progressive planners absolutely must see, this city can succumb under capitalism, in the form of a totalitarian planning by the planners of social property. Is not the alternative to this idea-ideology of total planning—which is totalitarian—in a non-emancipated society, the "incoherent, unruly, gigantic, noisy, dirty and vicious" city? But full of room for a rebellious imagination! Can progressive urban planning build more than hygiene for modern zoos? I think one would do better to observe and study these workers' cities, the slums, the factories built in 1850, in the midst of filth, chance and sadness; yet chance could still manifest a solidarity of action against the repression of the ruling class. These fresh, new, sterile cities with lawns like clean carpets, with too open streets and large windows; not for light, again, but to be able to control private life. The achievement of a non-repressive city, light, free and progressive, would only be the place of an absolute introversion of any revolt against programming; this achievement will be the best perfected control of the individual, and not a means to liberate man. Over and against total planning, I would prefer the capitalist city—based on private property—with all the chance involved in private property. But this is no longer an alternative.

Cordially,
Hans-Dieter Barh

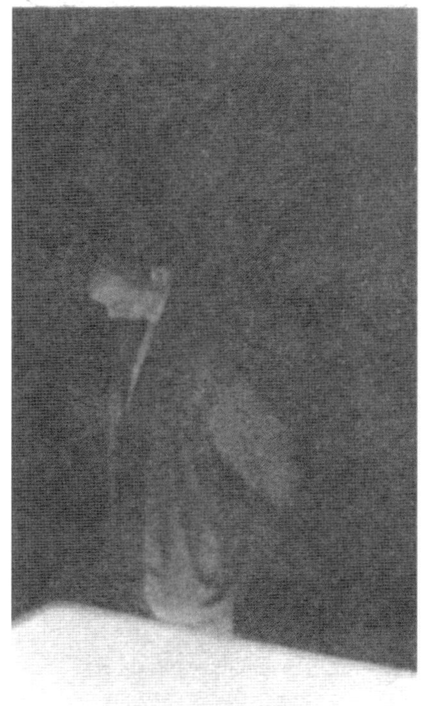

From Urban Science to Urban Strategy

I. The Urban Phenomenon

a) To characterize the reality and tendencies of the society being created in the modern world, the theoretical hypothesis we propose here is that it can be given the name "urban society," and that we have a right to prefer this denomination to all others (such as industrial society, technical society, consumer or leisure society, etc.). Agricultural production has lost its autonomy in most of the great modern countries; it is nothing more than a sector of industrial production, subordinate to its imperatives and constraints. The effects of economic growth and industrialization are extended throughout the national and regional territory. Being absorbed into ever greater units, the traditional grouping of farm life (the village) is integrated into industry and to the consumption of this industry's products. The concentration of the population parallels the concentration of the means of production. Small and medium agglomerations find themselves caught up in the urban fabric, with the exception of stagnant or decaying areas that raise distinct and specific problems of their own. With the disappearance of the village, agricultural producers—the "peasants"—are faced with the prospect of an "agrocity." As a result, a hypothesis and a possibility impose themselves as the destination of acquired knowledge, and as the starting point for new research and a new project: one hundred percent urbanization. By means of, or rather, at the heart of the bureaucratic society of directed consumption, urban society is in the making. This hypothesis should not make us forget either the existence of urbanization's different modalities according to certain characteristics of the society in question (neo-capitalist or socialist, still developing or already highly industrialized), nor the difference between quantitative economic growth on the one hand and qualitative social development on the other. On the contrary, these features come into the foreground in the analysis of the overall process.

b) The expansion of urban fabric and urban concentration have exploded the City of preindustrial and precapitalist times. To replace it with what? This question immediately and fully raises the concrete problematic: that of the *urban phenomenon*, and the knowledge of this urban phenomenon; terms preferable to "city," which seems to designate a definite and definitive *object*, whereas theoretical reasoning calls for a critique of this "object."

II. The Complexity of the Urban Phenomenon

a) It astonishes us today because of its enormity, which surpasses the means of knowledge and practical action. It stems from descriptive methods (ecological, phenomenological, empirical), which highlight certain aspects of the urban phenomenon, in particular its complexity. Do they allow us to know it? Beyond a certain point, description, no matter how detailed or refined, no longer suffices. The limits of morphology have been reached. To persist in the same direction would be to elude the problematic, by avoiding certain questions (such as that of the urban center or of centrality, and in the process, ratifying the trend towards the disappearance or deterioration of certain centers) means substituting description with an ideology—without warning. We must pass from phenomenology to analysis. The urban phenomenon presents itself as an overall (or, if one prefers, *total*) reality that calls into question social life as a whole, both theoretically and practically. This globality cannot be grasped immediately; it is better to proceed analytically, moving towards it. A difficult approach. Risks must be taken at each step to avoid pitfalls and obstacles. All the more so as with each step forward, with each tentative probe, an ideological interpretation suddenly appears, which immediately transforms itself into a *reductive and partial practice*. Presentations of economic space and development that deny specific urban space by absorbing social development within industrial growth, subordinating urban reality to general planning, provide a good example of ideologies that correspond to mutilating practices.

b) Each specialized discipline cuts out of the overall phenomenon, a certain "field" or "domain"—its own—elucidating it in its own fashion. For now at least, there is no need to choose between the thesis of cutting up or of elucidating. Moreover, each particular science is fragmented into secondary specialized disciplines. Sociology contains political sociology, economic sociology, rural and urban sociology, religious sociology, etc. Particularized and specialized disciplines thus operate *analytically*; they result from and perform analyses. Concerning the urban phenomenon as a whole, geography, demography, history, psychology, and of course, sociology: all contribute results of analytic procedures. Not without some injustice, we leave aside the contributions of the biologist, the physician and the psychiatrist, not to mention those of the novelist and the poet. Geography studies in particular the site of the conurbation and its situation within a regional, national and continental territory. Along with the geographer, climatologists, geologists, and the specialists of the fauna and flora bring their indispensable information. The demographer studies population, its origins, the "sex ratio," birth rates, growth curves, etc. What does the economist study—either as a specialist of urban reality, or when interested in general phenomena of growth? He does not lack objects: production and consumption within the urban framework, distribution of incomes, strata and classes, types of growth, population structure (active or passive, "secondary" or "tertiary"), etc. The historian is concerned with the genesis of a particular conurbation, the events and the institutions that have marked it. And so on. Without analysis' progressive and regressive approach (in time and space), it is impossible to conceive of *the science of the urban phenomenon.*

c) Each discovery in these fragmented disciplines permits a new analysis of the total phenomenon. It is not impossible that on the basis of the theory of hierarchized interactions (homeostases) that we may define certain urban realities and replace the old organicism and its naive finalism with rational concepts. On the basis of the formalized theory of graphs and computer programs, models of urban space could be elaborated (cf. the work of Christopher Alexander, "Architecture, mouvement, continuité," 1967, no. 1). Linguistics has recently made great leaps, which have allowed for the extraction of an idea, that of systems of *signs* (and of signification). Nothing prevents us from considering the urban phenomenon through this method and in light of it. That the city and the urban phenomenon are rich (or poor) in signs, significations and meanings is not devoid of interest, of course. That the city and the urban phenomenon constitute a *system* (definable by signs, comprehensible via linguistic models such as those of Jakobson, Hjemslev or Chomsky), is a dogmatic thesis. On the one hand, the concept of sign system does not cover the urban phenomenon completely. If there is a language of the city (or language in the city), if there is urban speech and "writing," and so the possibility of semiological study, the city and the urban phenomenon cannot be reduced to a language, a form of writing, or a semiology. *Urban practice* goes beyond these partial concepts. On the other hand, in the city and the urban phenomenon presently, there is probably not one system of signs and significations, but *several*, and at several *levels*: that of the modalities of everyday life (signs and significations of *habitation* and habitat, of daily behavior and gestures)—that of the urban society as a whole (semiology of power, of authority, of culture considered as a whole or in fragments)—that of the particularized urban space (semiology of the features particular to any one city, its landscape, its specificity). The notions of *isotopia* and of *heterotopia*, which may be useful in the analysis of urban space, come from linguistics (u-topia and the topical come from philosophy). In any case it is impossible for knowledge to keep the levels and dimensions external to one another, as juxtaposed or superimposed. Whatever the limits may be in applying semiotics to urban reality, it is nonetheless remarkable when the progress of a discipline reveals new aspects of this reality.

III. Myths and the Necessity of Cooperation Between Fragmentary Disciplines

a) Complexity renders an "interdisciplinary" cooperation indispensable. The full extent of the urban phenomenon does not belong to any specialized discipline. Even if we posit the methodological principle that no discipline should renounce itself, and that, on the contrary, each specialization should use its resources to the fullest in order to reach the overall phenomenon, none of these disciplines can claim to exhaust it. Nor to govern it. Once this has been acknowledged or established, the trouble begins. Who, among those concerned, can ignore the disappointments and fiascos of so-called "inter-" or "pluri-disciplinary" meetings? The illusions of this kind of research and its mythology have been experienced and denounced. They are dialogues of the deaf, pseudo-meetings, devoid of common ground, whose first problem is terminology. In other words, language. Rarely do the participants agree on the words and terms of their discourse, and even more rarely on concepts. As for theses and theories, they are usually found to be incompatible. Confrontations and face-offs are considered successes. The discussions that usually take place are just short of controversies. Assuming that we have managed to define "objects," it almost never happens that we follow the well-known rule, substitute the definition for the defined, without logical failure. The methodological and theoretical difficulty grows when we notice, in the course of these discussions, that each one is searching for synthesis and wants to be "a man of synthesis." It is obvious that the urban phenomenon, as a *global reality*, urgently calls upon fragmented knowledge. The specialists conceive of this synthesis only on their own territory, using their data, their terminology, their concepts and theses. And so we regularly witness the return of scientific imperialism; the imperialism of economics, of history, of sociology, of demography, etc. Each takes the other "disciplines" to be its auxiliaries, its vassals, its servants. We oscillate between particularism and scientific parochialism, on the one hand, and confusion or "Babelism," on the other. During so-called interdisciplinary meetings, it quickly becomes impossible to maintain specificities without separation, or unity without amorphous mixtures. By dint of fatigue, we conclude with mediocre compromises, because we have to stop and because the time for colloquia and seminars is limited—as are the funds. Convergence, as it is called, recedes from view. It is an ideology that intervenes in "synthesis," filling the gaps between the fragments of knowledge.

b) The urban phenomenon (just as much or even more than "industry," social work, or "society" as a whole) manifests its *universality*. This would be enough to justify the creation of a *university* for its analytical study. Let us note from the beginning, that it is not a matter of claiming for this study an absolute priority over other, already institutionalized disciplines and fields of study and disciplines: the arts and letters, or the various sciences. It would suffice to design a faculty gathering all existing disciplines around the analysis of the urban phenomenon, from mathematics (statistics, but also information theory and cybernetics) to history and linguistics, in relation to psychology and sociology. This concept requires a modification of accepted ideas about teaching, so that a faculty might be instituted, not on the basis of established knowledge (so-called), but around a *problematic*.

On the other hand, the status of such an institution cannot be so clearly defined. The project may be seductive, but this seduction does not succeed in hiding certain obstacles. We risk reproducing, in institutional form, what takes place in our occasional encounters. How to ensure that specialists overcome their terminology, their lexicons, their own special syntax, their way of thinking, their jargon and professional deformations, their tendency to esoterism and their arrogance as proprietors of a field? Imperialism remains the rule. Today we see this with linguistics and ethnology—as it was yesterday with political economy! How to keep the specialists from wanting to get the command positions for their specialty, for themselves? We know only too well that whoever fails to manoeuver with skill will be passed over, reduced to silence and subjection! The plan for a Faculty of Urbanism (or "Urbanology," or "Politology," horrible neologisms) is not an injunction to yield to the myths of interdisciplinarity. Research of this kind does not produce miracles. It is not enough to institute it in order to have an exhaustive analysis of the urban phenomenon. Can there be an exhaustive analysis of this phenomenon at all? Or of any reality whatsoever?

IV. The Urban Problematic

a) Might we not say of each particular discipline that the farther it takes its analysis, the more it brings to light a *residue*? This residue eludes its grasp. It turns out to be fundamental; it is the province of other methods. Thus the economist finds himself faced with "certain things" that escape him; the residual, in his case. Yet these things are the province of psychology, history, etc. More generally, numbers and numbering, bring dramas to light that do not belong to them. Neither psychology, sociology, nor history, which focus on these dramas, can exhaust or reduce them to a defined and definitive knowledge, to known and classified concepts. This would already apply to social work, to the productive activity of industry, and to political rationality and irrationality. It would be even more true of the urban phenomenon—numbers and drama.

Yet if each "discipline" reveals a residue, it soon proclaims itself irreducible to the others. Difference will coincide with irreducibility. Which calls the convergence into question. Or, the irreducibility of the urban phenomenon will be claimed vis-à-vis all of the fragmentary disciplines, including those of "man" or of "society." This is not devoid of risks. Either man (in general), society (in general), or the urban phenomenon will be identified with the residual set. This is interesting, theoretically, but has its dangers as well: irrationality, etc. The problem remains: "How to pass from fragmentary sciences to total knowledge? How to define this demand for *totality?*"

b) We may also suppose that the complexity of the urban phenomenon is not that of an "object." Does this notion of the object (of a science) withstand close scrutiny? We might ask ourselves this. Although apparently more precise and rigorous than "domain" or "field," it involves daunting complications. The object presents itself or is given as being *real*, facing analysis and study. We might say: no science without an object, and no object without a science. But can we say that political economy explores or possesses an identifiable object; or, for that matter, sociology or history? Can we say that urban economy has its object, like urban sociology, and the history of the city? Is it possible to conceive that knowledge of the urban phenomenon—or of urban space—consists of a sum or collection of objects: those of economy, sociology, specialized history, not to mention demography, psychology, and the natural sciences like geology, etc.? The simple and practical notion of a scientific object does not go without the intention to simplify, which may hide another intention or will. Even if it is conceived of as a system of relations, and if its relations with other systems are subsequently restored, an object is isolated. Could it not be the will-to-system that hides behind the apparently "objective" concept of scientific object? The searched after system constitutes its object as it constitutes itself. After which the constituted object legitimates the system. This attitude is all the more disquieting as the system under consideration might want to become a *practice*. Such that partial knowledge and its resulting action function as *reducers* of reality and possibility. The concept of *city* does not correspond to a social object; and so it is a pseudo-concept, sociologically speaking. Meanwhile, the city has a historical existence that cannot be ignored. The image or representation of a city can be expanded, outlive its conditions, inspire an ideology and urbanistic projects. In other words, the sociological object is here the image and the ideology.

Urban reality today appears more like chaos and disorder—which doubtless contain an order yet to be discovered—than like an *object*. What is the range and what is the role of what we call *urbanism*? There are urbanists, often drawn from the ranks of the architects. If they already know urban order, then they do not need a discipline. Their urbanism already contains this knowledge; it apprehends the object, enclosing it within its system of action. If they do not know the urban order—hidden or in the making—then they need a new discipline based on the cooperation of all disciplines. But what is urbanism, then? An ideology? An uncertain and partial practice that intends to be global? A system involving technical elements and which counts on authority to impose itself? There is reason to ask. Might the various aspects of urbanism today (ideology, limited rationality pretending to be definite and definitive, applied practices), be but a *superstructure* of the industrial period, prior to the urban problematic and urban practices?

c) Could the reality of the urban phenomenon be instead of a given object, that of a *virtual object?* If there is a specifically sociological concept, then it is surely that of "urban society." And yet it is not the province of sociology alone. A paradoxical situation: which urbanist, which urbanism elaborated this idea? Urban society, with its specific forms of order and disorder, is taking shape. This reality encompasses a series of problems: the urban problematic. Where is this phenomenon headed? Towards what is the process of urbanization leading social life? Which new social practice, or which new practices does it imply? How do you take this process in hand and direct it? Towards what? These are the questions: the ones that urbanists sometimes ask of specialists, who can answer only through an abuse of language.

d) In order to become global and overcome its incoherence, social practice already demands—"hic et nunc"—*synthesis*. Indeed, *industrial practice* has achieved a high degree of coherence and efficiency: planning, programming. Urbanist practice wants to follow suit. Yet interdisciplinary research, proceeding analytically, should forbid itself recklessness and excess on the path to synthesis. More exactly: extrapolations. We (who? theoreticians and practitioners, conceptualizers and users) are clamoring for a man of synthesis. No opportunity should be overlooked to repeat that this synthesis can be the work neither of the sociologist, nor of the economist, nor of any other specialist. True, the architect and the urbanist, in pretending to escape as practitioners from the imperialism of a specialty, claim this title and role for themselves. Why? Because they design, because they execute plans and projects. An abusive pretension.

In fact, they fall back into the situation mentioned previously. The imperialism of drawing and of draftsmen is no better than that of the economist or of the demographer, not to mention the sociologists. As for the pretension of drawing a synthesis out of such and such a technique or partial practice (automobile traffic, for example, or the circulation of merchandise or of information), simply formulating this technocratic ambition suffices for it to fall apart—in theory and in practice.

e) Are we going to feed *all* of a problem's data into computers? Why not! However, the machine uses only data provided by questions answered by "yes" or "no." And it answers our questions only with "yes" or "no." Who dares to pretend that *all* of the facts have been collected or are known? Who will legitimize this use of *totality?* Who will prove that the language of the city—if there is one—coincides with machine languages—algol, syntol, fortran—and that this translation is not a betrayal? Furthermore, is the machine not in danger of becoming an instrument in the hands of certain pressure groups or policies? Is it not already a weapon for people in power and for servants of politics?

We could entrust the synthesis to *prospective* research. However, prospecting extrapolates on the basis of facts, tendencies: a known order. Yet the urban phenomenon today is characterized by a *critical situation* in which neither definite tendencies, nor an order, are clearly detectable. Upon what should the prospecting—this series of investigations involving the future—be based after having extracted the elements of the forecast? What would this type of research contribute to the previously formulated hypothesis: the eventual possibility of complete urbanism, a hypothesis that refers precisely to the critical point of the situation we are entering? What would *prospecting* say more precisely and more concretely than the *perspective* that would show the convergence at the horizon of the lines drawn from the fragmented disciplines?

f) Of these fragmentary (specialized) knowledges, we know that they tend toward globality, claiming this abusively, and that they issue partial practices, which also pretend to globality (for example, the urbanism of traffic). This fragmentary knowledge, however, results from the *division of labor*. The division of labor in the theoretical (scientific and ideological) realm has the same functions and levels as in society. A difference stands out between the *technical division* of labor, rationally justified by instruments and tooling, by the organization of productive activity, and *social division*, which derives unequal functions, privileges, and hierarchies from this organization—divisions not unconnected with the class structure in the relations of production and ownership, of institutions and ideologies.

The technical division of labor in knowledge transforms itself into a social division, that is, into *institutions* (scientific, cultural) with their structures and devices, their values, norms and corresponding hierarchies. These institutions perpetuate compartmentalization and confusion. Thus knowledge is the province of distinct institutes and an entity: Culture. Born of/within the social division of labor, these institutions become part of it in serving it, adopting or adapting it, as the case may be. They literally work for and within the social division of intellectual labor, which they conceal beneath the "objective" demands of technical division, transforming the "technical" relations of sectors and domains, of procedures and methods, of concepts and theories, into a hierarchy of prestige and income, into functions of management and governance. This vast operation founds itself on the separations which it accentuates by consecrating them. Under such conditions how to attain, or even aim for totality? To be sure, the functioning of these scientific and cultural institutions goes beyond the satisfaction of the market's immediate needs and of its demand (for technicians, specialists, etc.). But their "creativity" can hardly quit the realm of the *ideologies* linked to this market, whether ratifying it, or sometimes contesting it. What are ideologies? Like institutions, they are superstructures elaborated or constructed during a given period, which is to say, industrialization within equally given social frameworks. Not so long ago, competitive capitalism tried to adapt the superstructures of rural life marked by the long-standing predominance of agricultural production. More recently and presently, neo-capitalism continues this task, which goes beyond the urbanization of society. It comes to pass that, in pushing illusions and appearances to the extreme, a certain institution tries to take charge of the totality, ratifying separations, and reuniting them only in a Babel-like confusion. Classical philosophy and traditional humanism had this ambition, keeping themselves just short of the (technical and social) division of labor, of fragmentation into particular sciences, as well as of the problems inherent in this theoretical situation. As for the University, for many centuries it offered to adopt universality together with classical philosophy and traditional humanism.

Precisely to the extent that it institutionalizes the social division of labor by preparing it, developing it, and inserting itself into it, it can no longer hold this "function." Which threatens it with explosion. Is not this the "function" reserved for the University today: to adapt the specialized production of intellectuals to the social division of labor, and the technical and social division of knowledge to the demands of the market? Science (like urban reality) becomes a means of production. As for the philosophy born in the time of the separation of material and intellectual labor, and later consolidated *against* this division, can it still claim to be, and conceive of itself as, total?

A difficult situation. Abstract thought seemed to have gone through more difficult trials and come out for the better; it appeared to be resurrected in the sciences after the speculative Good Friday and the death of the Logos incarnated in classical philosophy. All the more surprising, then, come Pentecost, to admire the specialized intelligentsia speaking in tongues, as linguistics takes on the role of science of sciences abandoned by philosophy, which itself believed it had supplanted religion. It is at this moment and under this cover that a certain industrial practice imposes its constraints.

V. The Role of the Philosopher

From Philosophy to Metaphilosophy

a) It is worth pointing out that *positivism* opposed itself to classical philosophy, to its speculative extensions. The positivist subscribes firmly to the facts that belong to his discipline and to his methodology. He sticks to the facts and picks his way carefully through the concepts; he is wary of theories. There is a physical positivism, but also biological, economic and sociological positivisms; in other words, a physicalism, a biologism, a historicism, an economism, a sociologism, etc. Positivist thinking does not ask whether the facts it collects result from a cutting up or from an elucidation, whether it has an "object" before it or not. There are *facts*, classified and specified as belonging to such and such a discipline. Yet the positivist tendency never forbade the leap of empiricism to mysticism, and of precise language to (more or less esoteric) jargon. Moreover, the tendency according to which philosophy no longer has, or never had, a meaning, is not incompatible with a staunch imperialism. The specialist claims the exclusive validity of his discipline; he edges the other disciplines out or reduces them to his own. Thus, logico-mathematic empiricism wants to impose mathematical models on all the sciences, rejecting the concepts specific to these sciences. Economism excludes all levels of reality other than that which involves political economy, growth models, calculations, forecasts. For some time we have been experiencing a vogue of linguistic models, as if there were only one model definitively acquired by this discipline, as if this model could be transported outside of its original place in order to confer a rigorous epistemological status on other "disciplines," like psychology or sociology. As if the science of words were supreme since everything is said and written in words!

b) In fact and by right, an interpretation of this kind stands on a territory prepared by philosophy. It is already, or is still philosophy, although not in the sense of classical philosophy. When the positivist wants to extend his property (his proper domain) and his operative activity, when he threatens or invades other territories, he shifts from science to philosophy. Knowingly or not, he uses the concept of *totality*. He leaves behind the fragmentary, the particularized; in short, the analytical. As soon as one clamors for synthesis and totality, one expands classical philosophy by detaching its concepts (totality, synthesis) from the philosophical architecture and contexts in which they were born and formed. The same goes for the concepts of system, of order and disorder, of reality and possibility (virtuality), of object and subject, freedom and determinism. Not to mention structure and function, form and content. In being transformed by scientific knowledge, can these notions be completely divorced from their philosophical elaboration?

c) Philosophy has always aimed at totality. When the philosopher tried to attain or realize totality by his own efforts, he missed the mark. He failed and lost himself in speculative abstractions. And yet, it is the philosopher who brings this aim and this vision. It is from the philosopher that others borrow this concept when they extrapolate on the basis of more or less aquired knowledge, which they believe to be definitive and from which they want to derive a rule for all of knowledge. The philosopher and philosophy can do nothing by themselves; but what can we do without them? Would it not be fitting to start with all of philosophy, while taking all of scientific knowledge into account, in questioning the urban phenomenon? And in so doing, be able to examine its process, its trajectory, its horizon, especially where the "being of man" is concerned, his achievement or failure in the coming urban society? It is not impossible that philosophy itself and its history appear differently along this trajectory, as a project (whose? the "human being's"). Has philosophy not already appeared in this way, exposed in a new light by industry and industrial practice in formation? This meditation does not take place on this side of philosophy, nor in philosophy, but beyond philosophy, as a specialized, constituted, and instituted. This is what defines *metaphilosophy*.

d) The objective is not to reconstruct the old humanism, which has been compromised ever since Marx and Nietzsche submitted it to the harshest critiques. The question is to find out whether urban society permits the elaboration of a new humanism, since so-called industrial society—capitalist or not—has denied the former one. It should not be ruled out that the investigation conducted by metaphilosophical meditation on the basis of philosophy may lead to the acknowledgement of a new failure. The urban problematic cannot reject this possibility in advance without falling back into the categories of faith and challenge, that is, into extrapolation.

e) What does the spirit of philosophy contribute? First of all, a radical critique of the fragmentary disciplines as such. This spirit refutes all dogmatism, from the ventures of the fragmentary disciplines and their respective pretentions to grasp *the whole*, to each one's withdrawal into an "object," a "sector," a "domain," or a "system" considered to be private property. Radical critique thus defines a methodological and theoretical *relativism*, an *epistemological pluralism*. The "objects," (including the corpus constituted for and by a particular field of study) are subject to the same relativism. The models are always provisional. No method guarantees an absolute "scientificity," whether theoretical or practical. Notably in sociology (urban or not). Neither mathematics, nor linguistics guarantee a perfectly and definitively rigorous approach. There are models, but none is complete, nor completely satsifactory; none can be generalized, transported, exported, or imported outside of the "sector" in which it was constructed without taking the greatest precautions. The methodology of the models takes up and may refine those of the concepts. There are specific concepts, specific to each partial discipline; none determines an "object" entirely by circumscribing it, tracing its contours, approaching or grasping it. The effective elaboration of such an "object" is fraught with danger; even if analysis constructs "objects," they are provisional and the product of reduction. And so there is a variety of models and concepts, and they do not form a coherent and complete series. Science, or rather the sciences, progress as roads are built or as land is reclaimed from the sea. How could there be a definitively established scientific "corpus" (corpus scientiarum)? or even unchanging nuclei? This would be to confuse experimental and theoretical research, empirical and conceptual research using *hypotheses* (verifiable, and therefore falsifiable: cf. R. Boudon "À quoi sert la notion de structure," pp. 191 et seq.—and thus revisable, containing a portion of ideology) with formulation and axiomatization. Yet what seemed to have been fixed by demonstration changes, appears, and will appear otherwise; including the axioms and even the forms that reflection distills in all their purity. Sooner or later, radical critique detects an ideology in each model, and maybe in "scientificity" itself!

The spirit of philosophy today permits *finalism* to be destroyed. Traditional finalism, a product of philosophy, and more specifically of metaphysics, is collapsing under the blows of the critique that reveals philosophy's contribution. As far as historical development and action are concerned, there is no predefined, prefabricated goal reached in advance, so to speak, by some god or in his name, by some absolute idea or spirit. No *objective* presented as an *object* (already real or realizable). Conversely, no goal, or "objective," proclaimed as the meaning of action and becoming, is impossible. No synthesis achieved in advance. No original and final totality in relation to which every relative situation, action, and moment could be alienated and alienating. Conversely, nothing which denies the demand, the will, and the conception of totality, which blocks the horizon, except the alienated-alienating attitude that decrees the theoretical and practical existence of a thing. From whom and from what could the totality come into being? From a strategy and a plan that extend the ancient philosophy to a new level. Thus the philosopher (or rather "metaphilosopher") no longer pretends to bring the purpose, the synthesis, the totality. He rejects the philosophy of history and of society to the same degree as classical metaphysics and ontology. He intervenes to remind us of the demand for totality, the impossibility of accepting fragmentation and division. He radically criticizes finalism in general, and also particular finalisms: economism, sociologism, historicism.

Philosophy turned into metaphilosophy no longer displays a reality that is already finished or that has gone astray—for instance, "man." It designates an *orientation*. While it provides some conceptual tools to blaze a trail toward this horizon, it is no longer the ground on which time progresses. It shows the scope of the problematic and its immanent contradictions, the first of which is the relationship between *rationality* that asserts, develops and transforms itself, and *purpose*, which falls apart. Yet rationality seemed to imply finalism, and did indeed imply it in the speculative conceptions of the universe. If rationality is to advance from speculation to global rational practice, from political rationality to social rationality, from industrial rationality to urban rationality, then it will be by resolving this immanent contradiction. The goal? The end? They are conceivable; they declare themselves and will carry the day only if they allow for the most comprehensive strategy. They are not separated from the constitution of a *praxis* (social practice), and this assumes practical interventions; namely of social and political forces. Consequently, other forces can intervene, stop the process and, for example, immediately decree that the only things that matter are the organization of industry, business, and industrial production.

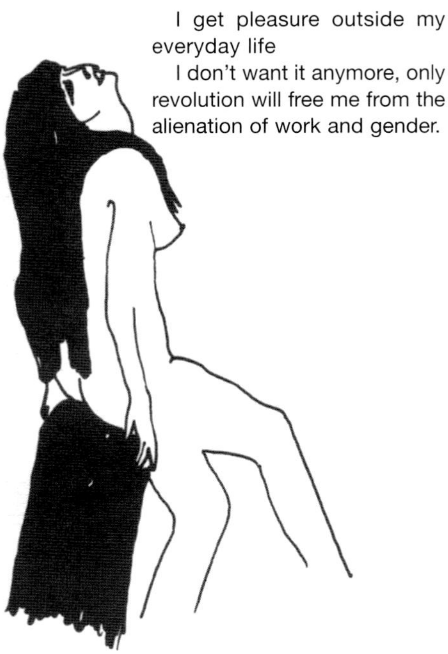

f) The discussions regarding man, humanity, and humanism take up Marx and Nietzsche's arguments against classical philosophy and its implications in debatable terms. The criterion advanced during these controversies, that of coherence, a substitute for harmony and "human scale," surely corresponds to a necessity. This does not mean its sufficiency has been demonstrated. The path that opens leads to the reconstruction of a humanism in, by and for urban society. Theory paves the way toward this "human being" in the making, as fact and as value. This "being" has needs, already observable or debatable. An analytic of need and desire is required. Which is not to say that a philosophy of need based in Marxism, sociology, psychology, industrial rationalism, can be elaborated. On the contrary. The so-called theory of needs is only an ideology of need, consecrating the constraints of a definite and limited period: that of industrial praxis. Rather than being a "positive" study of needs in view of their establishment and classification, such as they are, as objects, this field of knowledge could be constituted through an analysis of the errors and inadequacies of architectural practice and urbanistic ideology. Would an indirect and negative method not be more pertinent than sociological positivism? If there are needs that can be functionalized, there is also desire, as well as desires, just short of and beyond the needs inscribed in things. The functionalism of need completes the functionalist ideology only too well. Needs are classified only in terms of economic imperatives and social norms. Classification and denomination have a contingent nature. Specifically, the representations of functionalized (institutionalized) habitat and habitation, those that involve individual and social needs, cannot be considered necessary and absolute. Within needs, anthropologically speaking, there is the "drive" (*Trieb*): general and confused, instinct, outburst, vital energy, impulse, or whatever. Outside of them function the social filters and controls: language, norms and values, repression. Why not formulate these different levels in terms of "id," "ego," and social "superego"? However, we run the risk of falling back into the philosophy of need and the ontology of desire.

In terms close to everyday experience and speech, we observe that human beings are first children, then adolescents, then aging adults. This prematurity and immaturity tend toward maturity, and then it's over. It ends there. Maturity arrests and is a death sentence. A vision of this kind (finally) rejects philosophical finalism, that of human ascension without gaping contradictions, that of preestablished harmony, a finalism that survives today in a few comfortable visions: official Marxism, the Teilhardian doctrine, humanist theology. We already know that the slow maturation of the human being, which makes him dependent on his family, on habitat, and habitation, on his surroundings and the urban phenomenon, implies teachability and leads to an ever surprising plasticity. There are within this growing and unevenly developing "being" urgent needs and needs that are deferred. His wretchedness is his grandeur; his disharmonies and dysfunctions prod him on. He is never free of ambiguity. The dramatic and antagonistic nature of needs and desires have, therefore, an *anthropological* significance. This still uncertain discipline can only constitute itself dialectically. Human beings need to accumulate and forget. They need, simultaneously or successively: security and adventure, sociability and solitude, satisfactions and dissatisfactions, balance and imbalance, discovery and creation, work and play. The house, abode, lodgings and apartment, neighborhood, district, city and conurbation have corresponded, correspond, or no longer correspond to these or those fundamental needs. The theory of the family "environment," the work "environment," the "functional framework" or "spatial framework" tendered to these needs are nothing but dogmatic monstrosities, and might well create monsters out of the human larvae we entrust to them.

The present reality (social and urban) reveals some fundamental needs; not directly, but *through* that which repressively controls them, filters them, oppresses or deflects them. They reveal themselves retrospectively and are found in the past that is known through the present, rather than in the present known through the past. Which gives a legitimate place to history, to a historicity without historicism. A dialectical anthropology is to be elaborated on the basis of the urban problematic. In turn, this knowledge contributes its findings to the problematic. It cannot claim either to formulate or to resolve all problems by itself. It enters into the disciplines taken into consideration, with no other privilege than that of being born at the same time as the problematic concerned.

An anthropology of this kind includes elements or aspects tied to the old philosophy. What does it teach? That there is a sort of "human material," not without laws (biological, physiological), but without *preexisting form* at the level of reality that we call social or human. Its prerogative is an amazing plasticity, a remarkable adaptability and ability to learn. Forms appear, conceived and deliberate, capable of modeling this material according to its various possibilities. These forms act on different levels. Does urban society not propose—in fact or within the realm of possibility—a form?

The specialists most determined to proclaim themselves scientists in their own right do not shrink from appealing to

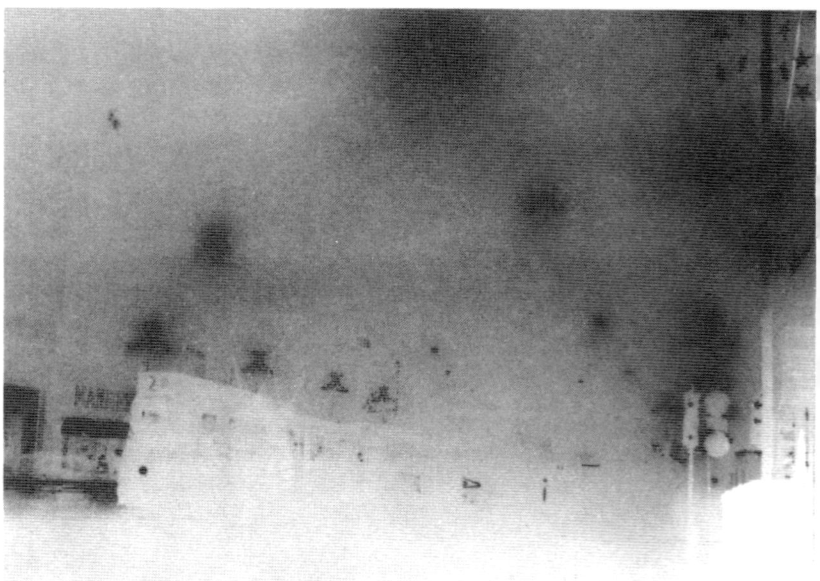

rationality. Have they forgotten that this general notion is inconceivable without philosophy, even—and especially—if philosophical reason is but one moment or element of rationality? Proclaiming rationality in the absence of any context, in the absolute, only pins it down and mutilates it. To buttress the controversies on this decisive point, here are the successive forms of reason. The *logical reason* formulated by Greek thought (Aristotle) was followed by *analytical reason* (Descartes and European philosophy) and then by *dialectical reason* (from Hegel and Marx to contemporary thought). Each form criticizes the previous ones without destroying them, yet not without problems either. Similarly, *philosophical reason* elaborated by the entire Western philosophical tradition was followed by a practical *industrial reason* (Saint-Simon, Marx, etc.), which is being surpassed in our day by the *urban rationality* that is in the making. On the social and the no longer solely mental level, the rationality of *opinion* has given way to the rationality of *organization*, which

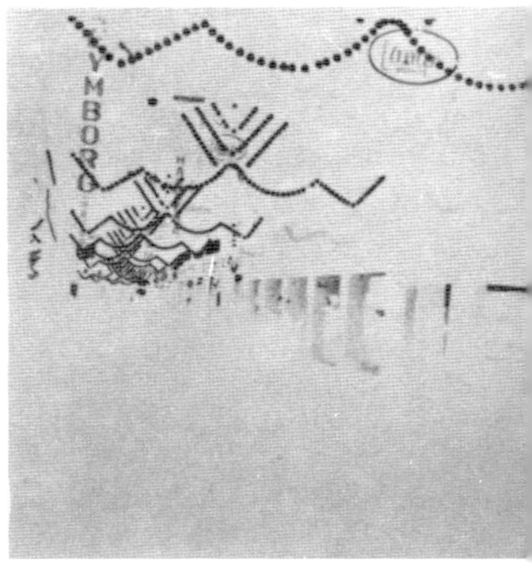

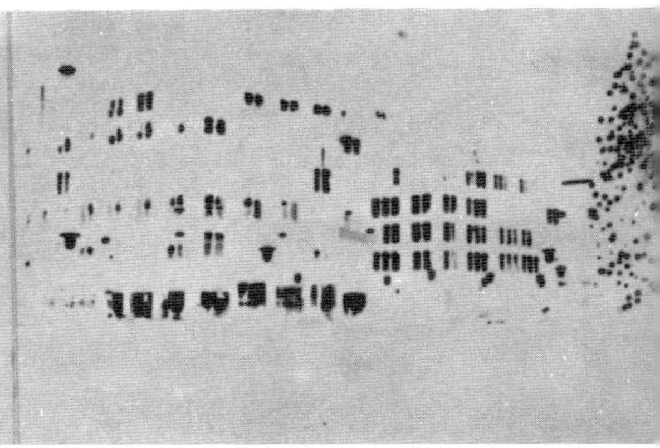

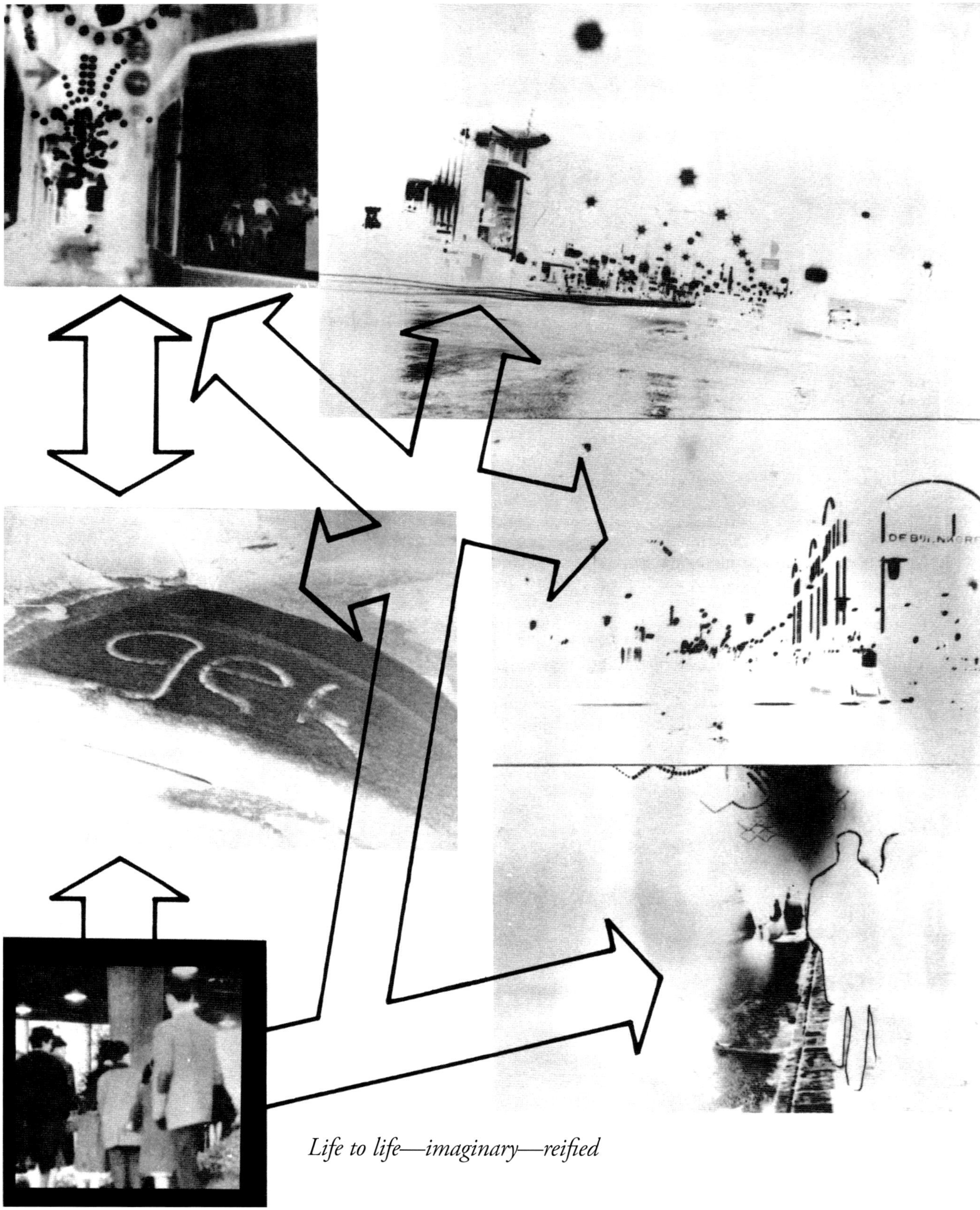

Life to life—imaginary—reified

cannot do without raising questions about the purpose and meaning associated with the rationality of *accomplishment*. At this level, that of purpose, an *abstract humanism* (liberal and classical) has been able to maintain itself as an ideology only by going through the test of *critical humanism*, which in turn gives rise to a humanism that is concrete, practical, *developed* (thus aiming for the totality). The image of the human being—his abstract project presented and represented by philosophers—corresponds to the first stage of humanism. The second stage corresponds to the fundamental calling into question of the goal, the meaning. Elaborated at the third stage are the concept and the will to plenitude (finite, relative, but "total").

Reason and Rationality

logical	→	philosophical	→	opinion
↓		|		↓
analytical	→	industrial	→	organization
↓		|		↓
dialectical	→	urban	→	accomplishment

Humanism

abstract humanism	→	image and project
critical humanism	→	contestation
developed humanism	→	finality

It is certainly not *space* (social, urban, economic, epistemological, or devil knows what) which can bring form, meaning, purpose. However, this theory breaks through from all sides: space as a rule, norm, and superior form, around which a scientific consensus, if not a "corpus" of sciences, might be reached. Yet space is only a *medium*, a milieu, a means, instrument and intermediary. More or less suitable, that is, either favorable or pathogenic. It never has an existence *in itself*, but refers to something else. To what? To time, both existential and essential, and going beyond these philosophical determinations, both subjective and objective, fact and value. It is the supreme "good" of those who live, well or ill. It is the end as well as the means. But it is no longer the time of philosophers. Nor that of the scientists—physicists, biologists, historians, sociologists. The "space-time" articulation—or, if we prefer, the inscription of "time in space"—becomes an *object* for knowledge. But, is it an object in the usual sense, isolatable, with well-defined contours? Surely not. Could it be a sociological object? Perhaps, but first in a negative sense, as a factor of inadequacy. The relation between time and space, by giving absolute priority to space, reveals itself as a social relation inherent to a society dominated by a certain form of rationality. Thus, ideology and science get muddled. This relationship is part of an upside-down world. It, too, needs to be "put back on its feet."

g) Let us return to the relations between fragmentary sciences. How are they to be conceived? Several hypotheses are possible:

i) *Convergence*. But where? At what point? Nearby? This is the hope and the myth of interdisciplinary encounters. One believes that convergence is to be defined on a nearby plot, like a junction. But this junction is badly defined and never reached. If there is a convergence, it is at the horizon, in perspective, if not in a projection to infinity. This "putting into perspective" is still to be determined. Here and now, for example, we are turning not toward traditional "man," but toward the reconsidered and reconstructed "human being" of the urban society in formation.

ii) *Integration* (of fragments defined by fragmented disciplines). But into what? Into the one which has been promoted to dominance? Unacceptable. Into a praxis? But in this sense, the idea of praxis falls under the blows of radical critique. It is a way out, a delayed due date. A probable fiasco. Notably in light of this unfortunate precedent: the failure of *economism*, an ideology and a practice based on a fragmentary concept.

iii) *Pragmatism*. That is, the use of information given here and there by so-and-so (sociologist or other). This is what often happens. Scientism turns into its opposite: the lack of rigorous criteria.

iv) *Operationalism*. A variation of pragmatism veiled by an ideology, that of technocracy—along with its already denounced myths. Only operative concepts are desired. The validity of the concepts is no longer to be demonstrated. We restrict ourselves to demanding of them simply an ability to classify.

v) *Hierarchization.* Yes, but in the name of what particular criteria? Who would decree that a sociologist has more value than a geographer or a demographer? The norms will be those of institutions and their rivalries, the last traces of competition. The scientists will entrust to the politicians the key to the city of Science. The latter will decide: at their will and discretion they declare what is normal and its opposite, the anomic (abnormal, pathological). This thesis argues from the standpoint of the (methodological) notion of *level.* But if each expert occupies one level in a hierarchy, then issues of priority and precedence become critical. At the very least this seems a hindrance.

vi) *Experimentalism.* Interaction of partial fields or sectors? An "inter-sectorial" concept of ideological and scientific exchanges? The analyst provisionally selects abstract "objects," studies them with the help of various disciplines, confronts them with experiments in the field? Maybe, but by abandoning totality, he also abandons the objective, the meaning and the purpose, and doubtless coherence itself. We will oscillate between an abstract utopia and an immediate realism, between utilitarianism and irrationality.

None of these options can be considered satisfactory, rationally speaking. Only one thing is certain: the impossibility of gathering specialists around a table on which an "object" or collection of objects has been set; the impossibility of adding up special knowledge, formulated in different vocabularies, starting out from particularized and limited "points of view."

VI. For an Urban Strategy

a) The theoretical situation today is comparable to some extent to the one experienced by Marx. Radical critique was already paving the way for both thought and action. Marx, as we all know, began with German philosophy, English political economy, and French thought on revolutionary action and its objectives (socialism). The critique of Hegelianism, of economic science, and the reflection on history and its meaning enabled him to conceive of capitalist society both as a *totality* and as a moment in a total transformation. Out of the negativity of critique a new positivity emerged. For Marx, the negativity of the radical critique coincided, theoretically and practically, with that of the revolutionary proletariat. It paved the way to a new practice, that of industry, with its demands and rationality. The theory elaborated and conditioned a practice, with thought moving from the practice in formation to theory. The envisioned and predicted totality was, for Marx, nothing but the *praxis* of industry and its demands: information, planning, and rationality on the scale of society as a whole. To this he subordinated the fragmented knowledge, partial activities, and the resolution of the contradictions of bourgeois society. The differences between this situation and that of the second half of the twentieth century are readily apparent. To the critique of philosophy, political economy, and ideology (religion is covered by philosophy, since, according to Marx, philosophy implies the critique of religion, and so the critique of philosophy affects religion twice over) today we should add the radical critique of specialized disciplines. Only such a critique will bring out the contribution of each to the totality in formation, to urban society and rationality; the road to totality must go this way, and not through the addition or juxtaposition of the "positive" results of these disciplines. Taken separately, each loses itself in fragmentation or confusion, in dogmatism or nihilism. On all sides, we run into the problem of ideology and its relationship to the practice towards which we must find our way: urban practice.

The critique of the specialized disciplines cannot do without a critique of the specialized policies, agencies and their ideologies. Each political group and especially each agency justifies itself by an ideology it upholds: nationalism or patriotism, economism or State rationalism, philosophism, liberal humanism (classical). One inconvenience of this is that it masks some basic problems: those of urban society and of the mutation in this direction (or the transformation, or revolution, as the case may be). These ideological and institutional superstructures stem from the period of industrialization and industrial rationalism, as well as from the division of intellectual labor within this framework. It is up to social and political forces—and not the politicians and political ideologies—to act in order to create urban practice. By introducing (without abusing it) the methodological notion of level, so as to distinguish tactics from strategy, we can formulate several propositions:

1. At the level of projects and planning, there is always a distance between elaboration and execution. Along the way, we run into demands and opposition, which are all too often confused with one another. Opposition manifests the ideologies of the groups and classes that intervene, including the ideology or ideologies of those who contributed to the elaboration of the projects: *ideological urbanism*. The possibility of opposition brings these ideologies to light and permits their confrontation, and measures the degree of urban democracy. Only by such means can concrete *urban practice*, (that of groups and classes—their way of life, the available morphologies, which they tend to modify) confront urbanistic ideology.

2. The question of knowledge, whether established or not, poses itself at the level that may be called epistemology. This definition of the problematic does not seem to permit the constitution of a "body" of established knowledge. The problematic dominates scientism. In other words, ideology and knowledge are muddled, and telling them apart is a never-ending task. However, a discipline can be considered to have a stake in the knowledge of the urban phenomenon only on two conditions: that it contribute specific concepts and that it renounce imperialism, a requirement that implies permanent criticism and self-criticism.

As far as sociology is concerned, it undeniably contributes a set of specific concepts: among others, that of *ideology*, with its implications, and those of *institution* and *anomie*, with their critical relevance. This list is not exhaustive; it is only the critical exemplarity of these concepts that gives them pride of place. It would take an in-depth discussion to determine whether certain concepts elaborated by Georges Gurvitch (for example, those of *effervescent behavior* or *plurality of time*) can be adopted and used for the analysis of the urban phenomenon. This can be evaluated. On the other hand, neither the notions nor the representations of centrality, urban fabric, and space appear to belong to sociology alone.

3. At the highest theoretical level, we have to imagine the mutation (or transformation, or revolution) by which so-called industrial society changes itself into urban society. This mutation

determines the problematic; that is, the problematic character of the real. Can we say that the phenomena linked to industrialization within a certain overall framework (institutional, ideological) have given way to urban phenomena? That the latter subordinate the former? No. Today's society sits in the *transition*. But the phenomena and implications of industry are declining. At this level, we may note that "socialist" countries were the first to change their institutions to respond to the demands of industrial production: modified rationalism, planning, programming. "Capitalist" countries have caught up with them to a certain extent in this respect. The urban problematic is global; the approach depends on the economic, social and political structures of countries, as well as on their ideological superstructures.

Knowledge of the urban phenomenon can be constituted as science only within and through the constitution of an overall urban *praxis*, supplanting at a greater or lesser rate the existing industrial praxis, with its own particular rationality. The scientific, ideological and institutional results of this period (industrialization) no longer suffice. Doubtless, they are starting to deteriorate. It is in the midst of this complex process that analysis cuts out "objects" or builds "models," all of which are provisional, subject to revision, and criticism. All of which supposes, in the first instance, the above-mentioned confrontation between urbanistic ideology and the urban practice of social groups and classes; secondly, the intervention of social and political forces; and thirdly, the liberation of the potential for invention, without excluding the utopianism that comes closest to the "pure" imaginary.

This is a good opportunity to point out the overthrow and reversal of habitual perspectives. Urbanization is generally thought of only as a consequence of industrialization, the dominant phenomenon: the city and conurbation (megalopolis) are brought into the examination of the industrialization process, and urban space into the space of general development. The reversal consists in considering industrialization as a stage of urbanization, a moment, an intermediary, an instrument. In the double process (industrialization-urbanization), the second term tends to come to the fore after a period dominated by the first. It can no longer be a question of "city thinking" limited to deploring human alienation in contemporary society (via atomizing individualism or super-organization), or longing for a return to the ancient city-states of Greece or the Middle Ages. These so-called models of critical knowledge are nothing but variations of the urbanistic ideology, to be rejected simultaneously.

The *critique of everyday life* takes on a role, in this perspective, that may appear surprising. It cannot be considered a minor aspect of sociology. What it studies in a critical fashion is not some "object," or some "subject"; it does not have a definite domain. It uses economy and economic analyses as much as sociology, psychology, or linguistics. Conversely, it cannot be assimilated with any of these classifications. To be sure, it does not cover the entire praxis of the industrial period, but keeps certain of its essential results in mind. This reasoning includes the critique of objects and subjects, of sectors and domains. In showing how people live, the critique of everyday life formulates the indictment of the strategies that lead to this result. Critical reflection transgresses the boundaries between the specialized sciences of human reality. It elucidates the practical use of these disciplines. It indicates the emergence and urgency of a new social practice that will no longer be that of "industrial society" but that of urban society. In this capacity and in this sense, the critique of everyday life (a perpetual, never-ending critique, at times spontaneous self-criticism, at times conceptually formulated) takes over the greater part of what is known as "sociological" research in industrial countries. Confronting the real and the possible (which is also a "reality"), it draws conclusions, without requiring a set "object" or "subject," a fixed "system" or "domain." Seen in this way, we could even imagine urban sociology being given a definable status someday: through the critique of the existing "needs," "structures," ideologies, and practices.

Urbanism, as an ideology, hides its strategies. The critique of urbanism has two sides: a critique of urbanistic ideologies and a critique of urbanistic practices (as partial practices and class strategies). This critique reveals *what really happens* in urban practice: awkward or enlightened efforts at formulating and solving certain problems of urban society.

b) Reflection on the urban phenomenon, extending philosophy to a new plane, and making use of all sciences by means of radical critique, can define a *strategy*. This putting into perspective rationally defines the horizon and the point of convergence for apparently separate lines.

This strategy is twofold, although this disjunction does not succeed in hiding a fundamental unity, because knowledge—integral and unitary—becomes *political* in the fullest sense of the word: a science of (urban) political reality. Relatively speaking, the strategy breaks down into a cognitive strategy and a political strategy. Its coherence combines theory and practice. Incidentally, this is neither in an existing system ("real"), nor in the theory of such a system. If there ever was a system of the city and of urban reality, this can only have been at some particular historical period: perhaps in the Orient, with the Asian mode of production, or maybe during the European Middle Ages. As we know, this system exploded. Instead of a system, reflection stands before a vast process with variable degrees of cohesion. The goals and the verifications, the input of the contents and the formulation are spread out in time and not in some schematic space represented as contemporary.

c) Should the science of the urban phenomenon address pragmatic demands or immediate requirements? Planners, programmers and users demand recipes. What for? To make people happy. To command them to be happy. A strange conception of happiness. The science of the city and of the urban phenomenon cannot reply without taking the risk of consenting to constraints from elsewhere: from ideology and power. It constitutes itself slowly, through hypotheses and experiments as much as concepts and theories. It cannot do without imagination, which is to say, utopia. It has to take many kinds of situations into account along the way. Here, demography dominates reality, and therefore knowledge. This does not lead to the dominance of the demographer, but permits him to speak for a while, yet without giving him the right or the authority to pin down the future. There, economics dominates, which includes the intervention of the planner, but quickly exposes him to radical critique, which may be a nuisance to him, but very useful—and only productive. Elsewhere, sociology and the sociologist have their say. Besides, nothing prevents research on the city and the urban phenomenon from permitting the construction of "models" at the macro-sociological level. It may be that, in the course of this (strategically oriented) process, sociology in general and urban sociology in particular, forced to reconsider their concepts and categories, will establish themselves as scientific "disciplines." Whatever happens, nowhere and in no case should the means replace the end, the partial the overall, the tactics the strategy. The tactic of any particular specialty will be severely criticized as soon as it tries to become a strategy at the global level, that is, imperialistic.

d) The strategy of knowledge cannot be isolated. It aims at practice; above all a continuous confrontation with experience, and secondarily the constitution of a global, coherent practice, that of urban society (the practice of *appropriating* time and space for the human being, a higher modality of *freedom*).

In the meantime, until there is a new order, social practice belongs to politicians. Or rather, they seize it by means of institutions and devices. More exactly, specialized policies block the constitution of a higher rationality, that of urban democracy, which would correspond to the practice in such a society. They exist precisely within the institutional and ideological frameworks that need to be surpassed. Which makes the situation that much more difficult. The strategy of knowledge finds itself faced with a double obligation. It cannot keep from taking political strategies into consideration. It needs to know them. How could it keep these "objects" and "subjects," these systems and this domain separate from knowledge? The political sociology of public agencies and bureaucracy has a lot to say on the matter, as long as they do not consider themselves to be "positive" and purely "positive," which serves the interests of the people in question, of the pressure groups and the systems. Among the strategic actions, therefore, belong *propositions* to the politicians, statesmen, factions, and parties. Which does not mean that critical knowledge devotes itself to specialized policies. On the contrary. How do you present projects and programs to them without renouncing the critical analyses of the ideologies and results? How do you persuade or oblige them by responding to their pressure with your own pressure? It isn't easy, of course. But it would be fatal to knowledge to abandon its right to criticize the decisions and institutions. After the abdication, an almost irreversible process would begin.

e) The strategy includes an important item: the optimal and maximum use of technologies (of *all* technical means) for the solution of urban problems and in the service of everyday life in urban society. This creates the possibility of transforming everyday life such as we know it through the rational use of machines and technologies. An important item. A series of contemporary experiments shows that the economical forecasts and state powers rarely consider this optimal use of technical resources and means contributed by the sciences. They use them only when they are pushed and forced to do so by opinion, by urgency, by criticism (when it can be exercised). Why? For budgetary and financial reasons; that is, for "economical" reasons. It is easy to save money in this area. The motives hide deeper reasons. The authorities have their strategy and the apparatuses have their interests, which all too often relegate these questions to the background.

The recourse to philosophy in no way implies nostalgia for the past. On the contrary. This is where the distinction between philosophy and metaphilosophy takes on its full meaning and significance. Philosophical meditation can be called upon in order to view the full extent of the present "problematic"—that is, the present as problematic—and to open up perspectives. It must be specified that we are shifting, then, from classical philosophy to metaphilosophy.

f) Totality? Dialectically speaking, it is there, here, and now. And it is not. In every action, and perhaps even beginning with "nature," *all* the moments are there: work and play, knowledge and rest, effort and enjoyment, joy and pain. But these moments require an "objectification" in reality and in society; they also await being put into a form that elucidates and proposes them. Totality in this sense is near, and equally far: lived immediacy and horizon. Urban society transcends the gap dug between nature and culture by the ideology of the industrial epoch.

H.L.

Technics as Social Practice

Every technical practice is a social practice, every technical practice is soaked in social determination. But it doesn't present itself as such: it claims autonomy, innocence, a technical rationality founded on science. This rationality subtends the ideology of faith, which imposes itself on our society as morality, wherein technical practices, separated from social reason, become a technique of the *social*, and more precisely of social manipulation, and therefore a technics of power.

The practical efficiency of technics changes in social efficacy. But this is too general a statement.

It would be interesting to see how, in different epochs, technical assets were seized by the logic of privilege. In the fifteenth and sixteenth centuries, the wealthy reserved avant-garde techniques: they served their festivals. Through the ages, but in a far more evident way during the twentieth century, the leading technical practices have been military, an exclusive domain of power. The directing classes only let those filter down that were strictly for the reproduction of productive forces—sometimes even organizing stagnation or a deliberate technical deficit. In any era, technical knowledge and its use has divided the social body into distinct airs, categories, zones of privilege. Technical discrimination is a given throughout history.

Nevertheless, it is only when technical knowledge definitively emerges from religious, ritual, playful, or corporate constraints, as in the Industrial Revolution, that it becomes a "free" productive force, while at the same time it establishes itself in the totalitarian myth of modern societies. But this, here again, is too simple; it is not the effect of a global authority called technics on a global society that must be analyzed, it is how society stratifies itself as a function of technical knowledge, what relationship diverse groups and classes maintain, each with the others, across technics as practice and as myth—and what type of relationship exists between social discrimination in the order of a system of values called technical knowledge and the social discrimination according to other systems of values—cultural, for example.

Contrary to the myth that demands—in the inverse of culture, the place of a hereditary inequality—that technics should be a "democratic" dimension:

— the myth according to which individuals of every social origin would be more naturally, more spontaneously equal before technics than they are in regard to culture and art (with even an inverse privilege for non-privileged classes, closer, as one would like to say, to the empire and to the mechanical arts);
— the myth according to which technics would be a more rational domain, and therefore more democratic, since virtually accessible to everyone through academics training and practice—in contrast to the subtle paths that bring one into culture and political science;
— the myth according to which technics would be an innocent domain, distinct from politics, innocent because linked to the mastery of nature while culture, economics, and politics would be more directly implicated in social organization and mastery.

In fact, technics is only in the first place, but an instrument in mastering nature and liberating productive forces. It is therefore simultaneously an instrument for restructuring social relations and for elaborating a social rationale. Once it has gone beyond a certain level of mastery of natural forces (and we crossed this threshold a long time ago), technics becomes, despite itself, an instrument of mastery and social control.

This happens in two ways: directly as an auxiliary of politics, indirectly as a mechanism of acculturation.

1. Politically. Every social imperative was subordinated to that of faith and therefore to the directed exercise of technics, to the mastery of technical research conditions and the exclusive control of advanced technological operations (military research in particular) creating, to the profit of power, a radical privilege, on the basis of which the political game unfolded. Every investment and economic rhythm depends on this monopoly. The confinement of sacred devices and secret rituals was never, in any era, in any society, as exclusive as the secret, technological manipulation of the state in our modern societies.

The structures of this monopoly must of course be explored, defining the techno-political decision-making groups in opposition to the pure technicians and traditional politicians—defining the technical ideology proper to these groups in opposition to the technocratic myths available to everyone, etc.

2. Culturally. Technics, far from homogenizing society through knowledge, affects, from level to level, a discrimination as precise, is not as traditional and hereditary, as cultural initiation. This system of differentiation functions, just as the other does, through:

— consecrated authorities (Research Institutes, the Academy of Sciences, the Centre nationale de recherche scientifique, Atomic and Space administrations) which sanction technics as a model and universal value at a higher level. At this level, technics sublimates itself in research and science;

— a scholarly system of technical teaching as a subordinate vocation (in our Western societies certainly, but we can ask if the celebration of technical values in the East is not fundamentally linked to economic objectives), which is always ambiguous in its double, shameful relationship with cultural education and education in scientific theory.

The remarkable inequalities that this apparatus institutes in the real participation in technics and that tend to mask the diffuse mythology of technology, this hierarchy, official or officious, is the object of a very strong social code. From theoretical practice to vulgar practice, from a noble technical knowledge to applied knowledge or, lower still, to the application of simply technical recipes in manipulation and construction—from access to the treatises on nuclear physics to reading "Science and Life" or the "Manual of Domestic Techniques," it is all a sliding scale of status that we go through. Each of these indices signals a social condition and a relation to others for assigning each group its respective rank.

This is clearly a question of status and not of knowledge. It is not about concrete differences in knowledge, which, logically, have nothing to do with the social hierarchy of people. It is a question of social *distinction*, of class distinction founded on the *quality* of knowledge taken as an index of *value*—therefore of a *properly cultural system*, of a code of social designation not through literary or artistic habitus, for example, but across a

> If, for years, Daimler-Benz has spent tens of millions of Deutsche Mark to participate in all the competitions in the world, from Carrera Mexicana to the Grand Prix in Monza, it was not just to amuse the crowd. This presence in competitions had to be profitable on two levels: advertising and technology. One of the results, after the victory of Mercedes at Carrera Mexicana, for example, was the cancellation of contracts for the purchase of Italian typewriters in favor of German typewriters.

ANALYSIS OF VALUE APPLIED TO PACKAGING

CONSEQUENCES AND IMPLICATIONS OF THE PRODUCT: "Product" (commodities or work) as a mediator of ideology and of the image of technology, *At a first level, this mediation takes place through "products." Indeed, the social imaginary, a collectively alienated consciousness, organizes its alienation through systems of signs linked to objects that enable one to "live" technology in a symbolic mode, retarding consciousness. Because such systems tend to fix an ideology tied to a particular state of technology, representations that simply present an appearance of technology without implementing its potentials, they* more or less elevated level of *initiation* into the technical order.

In the social logic of culture, this system of technical order comes into play in relation to the system founded on "humanist" values, as a parallel *system of acculturation*, relaying the other and supplementing it through mechanisms analogous to the failings of traditional cultural integration.

Technics effectively constitutes one of the most powerful themes of "mass culture." Large strata of the population, at bottom hardly touched by the properly cultural models, integrated only through dreams, impulses, fragmentary understandings that are dispersed to them in the domain of technics.

The vast phenomenon of autodidacticism, the process of cultural education characteristic of the social emergence of the middle classes, nourishes itself in large part through technics. All the givens accounted for in scientific or cultural training are welcomed in one way or the other in technics. Not that that is their natural propensity: it's the logic of the global cultural system that assigns them to this subculture that lives, in unconscious resignation, off of the prestige of science.

To the direct power that it confers through political efficacy, technics connects the parallel power and ideology that it draws from functioning like a pseudo-culture, a second culture more particularly destined to the "uncultivated" classes—but a systematized culture nonetheless, in its equipment, its legitimating authorities, its mechanisms of diffusion, its models and norms—in brief, functioning like a total cultural system coming to reinforce the other to clinch the social hierarchy of powers. Thus one can only grasp the ambiguity of technics by analyzing the position that is assigned to it in the order of a global system of values: made sacred as an absolute spring for power over the international economic chessboard, technics remains a shameful academic and cultural value. One must also analyze how our societies fail to make technical values autonomous as full and transcendent values, this failure (or its rationalization) in a universalist myth of technics.[1]

But fundamentally, if our societies fail to rationalize their social practice of technics (and not only their technical practice), this lapse is not at all innocent: to rationalize technical practice equals failing to establish a social strategy on the *mystery* of technics.

1. Socialist countries have elevated the power of technical culture. However, it seems that at the end of a period, the scale of traditional values, in a hurried moment, tends to reconstitute itself, benefiting cultural values. In any case, the profound changes in cultural habitus can only appear over the long term.

reduce the practice of technology to a pseudo-technical practice.

This appearance of technology seems nonetheless to achieve a superficial, but ideologically effective satisfaction, of social demand, and in this way enables the forgetting the real potentials, objects of a deeper satisfaction. In effect, social practice develops not only in terms of the objective possibilities of its practice, but equally in terms of a relativized vision of possibilities, referring to a Weltanschauung (overall vision) that is itself more or less dominated by an ideology of technology conveyed by the mass media and "gadgetized" objects, who broadcast, within everyday life, a representation of technology, a distorted and distorting intrusion of technological rationality in every dimension of lived experience.

Sometimes, however, new relationships are formed out of the blue. For example, household objects—modernist extensions of existing utensils—tend to promote the establishment of a new, concrete sexual division of labor. But these facts are not in themselves detached from the ideological context. The ideological reference being in this case the liberation of women for the sake of profitable economic activity, the new objects—ideological signifiers inscribing themselves in preestablished systems of signification (and representation)—do not generate new combinatorial rules, the latter only being created by (or on the basis of) new experiences that induce new situations, by means of a PRAXIS. The analysis, on this point, of the social imaginary is not located at the level of technical knowledge, but on the level of the relationships between this knowledge and social practice, for it is precisely at this level that the social imaginary is structured and that the ideological filter intervenes. The relations effectively establish technical knowledges, duly hierarchized, -a truly dichotomized "technological culture"—upon which the social imaginary plays.

In a hierarchical society, technics must, like other things, no longer have a function, but a mystery of functionality. And this mystery, that weighs on each technical product, on each technical articulation of the social body, is a social mystery.

The Mythic Organization of Technics

Technics opens directly onto the social level, which is to say, when one leaves the abstract and rational level of pure technology, as a divided system, as the systematic opposition of two terms where each is the functional alibi of the other: a metatechnics and an everyday practice. A transcendent technics, hypostasized in fiction, and a banal technics, reified in consumption.

This distortion of technics is often formulated in terms of effects: everyday life, maintained (for strategic reasons) in a state of technical infantilism, would meanwhile benefit from high-tech "effects." This presumes the thesis of the unequal development of different sectors of social reality, and, behind that, the hypothesis of a theoretical homogeneity, of a technical transparency, the diffusion of which would be opposed only by social structures.

In fact, there is no other technics than that elaborated by men in such a social context, nor another sense of technics than that which it assumes in social logic. This social logic immediately imposes technics as an ideological system with two poles. Not that social organization comes simply to divide unitary technics in principle; it and it alone institutes technics and institutes it as divided, disassociated, and fundamentally, in its status as social signifier, in the logical distance between these two poles. Sublime technics, banal technics. Fiction, everyday. Between the two, neither a split nor "effects," but a logical distance and a contradictory implication.

In this, technics is homologous with culture—both of them obeying the same social logic. There is no longer an educated culture from which mass culture would be "fallout" (according to the model/series schema); there is a direct cultural system founded on the logical distance between educated culture and mass culture—one defining itself as a function of the other, one implicating the other, one exclusive of the other—to the evident benefit of educated culture, which maintains absolute models.

In the same way, one can admit that advanced technics is founded, *in its advancement*, only on the principle of the technical segregation of everyday life and of the forced assignment of everyday life to consumer stereotypes. It is therefore not a social accident if everyday life is in a chronic state of technical underdevelopment. It is not a dysfunction: it is a *logical* function of the system, entirely like the flight from scarcity and poverty is a functional element of the "welfare state."

The imagination plays on this tactical division. Advanced technics, cut from everyday technical practice and confusedly identified with science, comes to be able to serve the imaginary of the banal technics of "consumption"—exactly as how educated culture fundamentally serves as an imaginary model for mass culture. The spatial, nuclear, futuristic heroization of technics, that entire demiurge, that science fiction comes into play and is revealed in domestic gadgets: that would thus not at all be experienced as effects, but transfigured as signs and as the promise of a total technological revolution, whose model is already here, suggested everywhere in the exalted and euphoric discourse on technics (which always doubles as a moral, pessimistic discourse, complicit with the first, and which only reinforces the "dizzying" effect). Across the washing machine's control panel, the average person thinks of himself as a distinct citizen of the technological revolution, though this control panel, precisely in its caricature of power is linked to an archaic world of functions, only sends him back to the absence of a total, innovative, structuring technics—and makes him consume it as an absence. The smallest of everyday objects underscores a myth of the absolute functionality of a completely technological world, beyond social contradictions and history. This is the other aspect of the social mystery which we mentioned above.

This technics completes itself in grand mythic oppositions, like that of spatial fusion and the automobile. In fact, the opposition between a prestigious technology and an obsolete technology is only apparent: the concrete dictatorship of the automobile, which has swallowed an entire civilization, and the abstract fascination of spatial adventures are the two poles of a systematic implication in which technics and everyday life are both enclosed and alienated.

A consequence of this division of the system, where one term can imagine the other: is that technical objects do not intervene directly in everyday life, as mediators of structures and new social functions, but on the contrary as *already mediated by the idea of technology* and by a metaphysics of rationality.

Concretely, this signifies that the objects or new technologies are not experienced as practical and social innovations but as erratic novelties, drawing their fascination from their complicity with myth, with the future, with the imaginary, and not at all from their possibility of changing the present. This is how they are received as *objects*, which is to say, fixed and idealized as *avant-garde* signs, peopling an unreal everyday world. This is how they fall into *consumption*. And, according to this paradox, the more they are technologically new, the more they are perceived as aesthetic and desired for privileged consumption.

Thus technology, submerged in everyday life, realizes itself as science fiction, nourishing all of its powers in the prestige of consumption. What happened to cinema happens a little to every object or technological group. Edgar Morin has clearly demonstrated how, from the immense possibilities for information, communication and social change that cinema initially opened as a scientific technology of the image, it has almost entirely and, it seems, irremediably—teetering in the imaginary—become cinema-spectacle, a cinema of consumption.

Conclusion: "ALL TECHNICS IN THE SERVICE OF EVERYDAY LIFE?"

If one admits that technics presents itself directly, in the social logic of class, as the system of opposition that we have come to describe, and thereby as a system for the mythic transfiguration of real contradictions (those of everyday life and of social structures),[2] then what happened to the revolutionary slogan: "All technics in the service of everyday life" (Henri Lefebvre).

Effectively, so that there could be a technical revolution of everyday life, there would already have to be a revolution of the entire system to make technics something other than what it is.

This hope is founded on the postulate of the fundamental rationality of the technical order, that it would be sufficient to

2. This does not exclude the *real* changes that technology engenders every day in social relations and in everyday life. These are incontestable and considerable. Simply put, these changes operate *within the system* whose precise function is to control evolution and make sure that the changes never initiate open contradictions.

liberate and articulate it within in social reality for the world to be overturned. But this isn't so easy. This rational level of technics really exists: it's technology. But as private individuals or social subjects, we have no other business with technology other than with technics as a system of value and ideology. Can we hope that if technics is the product, in its most effective substance, of a social order that sanctions failure and contradiction, masking them in its prodigious flight and thereby clearing away the chances of resolving them—how can we hope to place it in the service of a social revolution?

Maintaining every proportion, this would be the same illusion as demanding that "the police enter into service for the collectivity"—though it is by definition social, in the service of private interests and of power. One could say the same thing about culture.

In short, one must be careful when considering the dereliction of the technics of everyday life as an accident along the way, such that it would suffice to shift technics onto the right path, to liberate its virtualities to change life. One must see that it is our society itself, in its most fundamental organization, that reinvents technics at every moment as a dimension of salvation, and not of knowledge, as a mythic system and strategy of power, and not as a rational instrument and revolutionary social practice.

In any case, a revolutionary "outbreak" of technology wouldn't take place in a concrete society. For technical innovation to inaugurate real structural changes, it would first be necessary to initiate a *technical culture*, which is to say, the slow and difficult substitution of another system of values for traditional culture, and this through *a radically different educational system*, not so much in its contents as in its educational *techniques*. Finally, one must separate technics from the technical spectacle and from the myth that encloses it, so as to recognize it in its principle, which is that of "capability and rational exercise,"[3] and bring this principle to the root of social training, if one wants to put an end to magical manipulation.

J. B.
March 1968

3. Speaking rigorously, this principle has nothing to do with science or constituted technics. One must separate "the" technic from its absolute use, so as to reveal its concrete efficacy, wherein it is always the technique for something: training and rational exercise.

The 1914–1918 war improved things for women. They were needed in the factories.

- Women workers: 85% out of necessity; 15% by inclination. (I.N.S.E. survey.)
- Women civil servants: 92.5% for financial reasons. (C.N.R.S. survey.)
- Women readers of ELLE: 40.5% for financial reasons; 20% because work is fulfilling; 15% out of love for a specific job. The rest (25%) out of fear of being downgraded after a break; out of fear of being bored at home. (An ELLE survey.)

An irresistible historic movement

The Technical Production of the Imaginary

By means of art, as with speech and techniques, man gives concrete shape to a universe whose dimensions correspond to his nature and to the limits of his temporary ability to intervene, as manifested by actions determined by representations. Every action, every feigned image creates reality. A society does not apply truths, but establishes them.

Pierre Francastel
La figure et le lieu

Preliminary:

1. The precondition for the *total implementation* of the possibilities of a given state of technique in a given society is the clarification of the system of relationships and connections between various (actually or apparently) entangled or separated spheres of knowledge and practice. This requires, on the one hand, a recognition of the existence of the relationships that specific functions of social practice maintain and, on the other, an illumination of the fact that relationships are established according to the mode proper to a specific social practice. Contrary to appearances, in our so-called society of abundance and consumption this implementation is far from having been carried out.

2. The social practice of technique normally results from a technical practice and the continuous process of technique modifies society's system of representations. This system is the expression both of the ideology in which a society recognizes itself and the possibilities of transforming practice and ideology. Technique implements the (immediately apprehensible) means of organizing a given and temporary reality, which

THE IDEOLOGICAL IMPACT OF TECHNICAL CULTURE.[3] *The second level on which the ideological screen unfolds is that of culture; again, we have taken up position in the "in-between" zone, on the middle ground between the dialectics of knowledge and technical practice, at the center of the opposition between metatechnique and everyday life—where the fundamental dialectic of the relationships of production (of knowledge) comes to the surface. Ideology "founds" (gives a foundation to) the dichotomy based on the process of production; this leads to an institutionalization of the separation between the classes, of the distinction between technique-as-research and everyday life through the institution of so-called mass culture. The transparency techniques offer onto a possible opening of possibilities is instead rendered opaque by the social structure. The purported social homogenization in the wake of technique, as well as the*

3. Cf. "Technics as Social Practice," pp. 209–216.

Covers (figures on the right) and back covers (figures on the left) of two journals: spectacular technique and disgraceful technique.

exactly corresponds either to technological reality and the possibilities that flow from it, or to a social deprivation of these possibilities pursuant to a class project.

3. There is not, on the one hand, technique and concrete realizations (which presuppose a technical practice), made tangible through the means they offer (in a practice of technique) and, on the other, social and ideological practice in keeping with a society's vision of the world. Social practice is lived, to a large extent, in the possibilities of a practice of the given technique specific to a given society.

4. The control of technique's process and its applications—that is, of technical practice and the practice of technique—is indispensable to the realization of a class project. Technique is directly dependent on economico-political reality. The social imaginary that invests reality determined in this way sometimes modifies its tidy organization by transforming society's established code of the signs, and thereby permits social demand to manifest itself.

The implication of technique in everyday life certainly contributes to the transformation of consciousness, but it would be too simplistic to see in it a mere causal relationship. The transformation of consciousness depends on a structural modification of the relationships between men who live and work—in other words, a structural modification of economico-political relations—whereas technique can only induce new formal relationships between men and the products of technique, new formal relationships that present themselves as structural modifications of the relationships between men. While it cannot be denied that products of technique interfere with social practice, they cannot run *a contrario* of the ruling ideology. It is politics that uses technique and inflects its process in order to realize its project, and not the process of technique that conducts politics. In order to show that the mere transformation of things does not flow from new relationships between people, it must be shown how the new possibilities of technique enter into overall social practice only after having cleared the hurdle of class opposition. It is essentially society's mode of apprehending the world which is in question here.

The virtualities of technique can be taken into consideration differently according to social groups, but the process of

POUR 50 FRS PAR MOIS SEULEMENT
...Découvrez les merveilles du ciel et des horizons terrestres
The continents move
SCIENCE IS PREPARING "UNDERWATER" CITIES FOR US
You will soon be able to break the sound barrier yourself
is it a new washing "machine"?
Non ! pas une machine, mais un petit "machin" extraordinaire dont vous me donnerez des nouvelles !
1 ELECTRONICS ENGINEER
FINALLY!!!
a new plane
100% French
airframe, jet engine, equipment

Every apostle of order founded on technological ideals should know that this doctrine only preaches the submission and adaptation to social relationships instituted by the bourgeois order, and that they themselves are constitutive of this order.

"My visits to Cape Kennedy made a profound impression on me. It is a veritable sanctuary of research and modern technology, which the imagination can compare to those that the high priests of Egypt or Babylon devoted to astronomical observation. This complex is a powerful pole of activity and it has already become a *major economic driver* in the United States. However, the impact of the space sector is rich in meanings not only on the quantitative level but also on the qualitative level. As Von Braun (the maker of the V2) and Dryden, the directors of Cape Kennedy, point out: "Probably the greatest economical treasure is the technological progress required for the increasing complexity of the space missions. This new technology is progressing at an incredible rate and it is benefiting the entire industrial and economic system." Apart from the space missions themselves and the implications of the interdependence between the spatial and military powers, there are many instances of a *penetration of the new techniques into the economic life of the nation*...

"What we basically need are a few clear and comprehensible goals at the cutting edge of technology—so as to be stimulating—and with an eye to useful results, but also able to elicit the enthusiasm of those who will have to support this effort. This will be more effective than any debates about the rationale of an action or the optimal forms of an organization to which we deign to attach precise and immediate tasks...

"Economies must be periodically renewed by the development of new sectors whose scope might seem very limited at first, but which contain a potential for growth. "Space can be one of these sectors to the same degree and, probably with an even greater effect of economic stimulation than nuclear energy and computers..."

J. Delorme, "Les techniques de l'espace au service de l'économie" in *Revue politique et parlementaire* no. 793, 1968

"Before analysing the indirect economic advantages that may result from a program of space research, a preliminary remark is necessary: however significant these indirect advantages might be, they cannot represent by themselves the entire motivation to undertake a program of space research. The decision to undertake (or associate oneself with) a program of space research must correspond to precise objectives of a nation's scientific and economic policies....

"It is essentially through its potential for technological innovation, through its driving power and promotion of a new spirit that a program of space research and application can provide a favorable economic impact of a high order, given the expenditures that need to be made…

"Space research programs indeed benefit from these advantages, and experience has shown that the *theme of space* is particularly exalting and *exerts a driving power of its own on the scientific and industrial sectors.* A space research program therefore constitutes a primary element in the scientific and technical research policies of a nation. It brings with it a sense of urgency and an interdisciplinary impetus that furthers initiatives made in various scientific disciplines.

"Lastly, with the exception of rocket technology, space is a topic of research that can easily be separated from military and strategic implications, thus permitting productive international cooperation free of political constraints. It gives scientists and engineers opportunities for intellectual and technical enrichment through encounters, visits, and training programs that can be very profitable to a developing country.

"In his 1965 report to the National Planning Association, Mr. Summer Myers wrote: '*People are influenced by and tend to accept the goals and values adopted by their reference groups as if they were their own wishes. Space scientists and engineers are a reference group for industry personnel.*'

"This new technical 'philosophy' that integrates ideas of optimization, reliability, life span, technical precision and minimal costs should permit man to better use the techniques and resources at his disposal. It is certainly the most productive and lasting indirect contribution of space research to economic and social progress."

M.J. Claverie, "Les 'retombées' techniques et industrielles d'un programme de recherches spatiales," in *La recherche spatiale,* CNES, Sept. 1968

To the basic question: "Is the technical milieu specifically tied to the production relationships that structure capitalist society?" G. Friedman replied (in Sept études sur l'homme et la technique*): "We note that the technical milieu… does not characterize Western society alone, it can also be seen in a structured society like the U.S.S.R. of today." When asked "to what degree does the transformation of the relationships of production in a planned and collectivist society modify the effect of such a milieu on the individual?" the same author replied: "Are fifty hours a week on the assembly line of a tractor or automobile factory more 'attractive'* per se *in Gorky than in Detroit?"*

Détournement of technique and the technique of détournement.

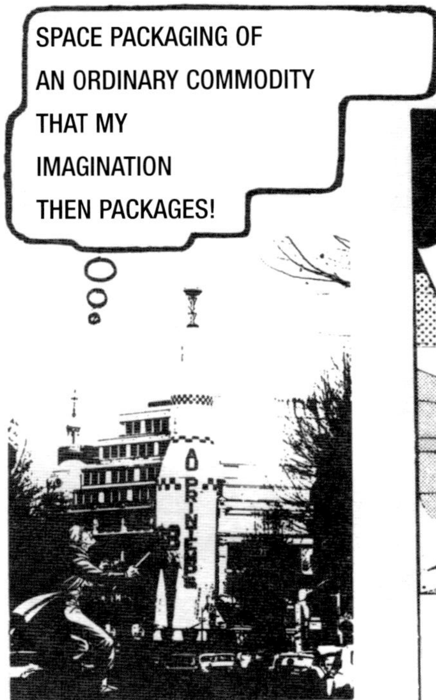

" AVENTURES-FICTION "

Les récits que nous publions sous ce titre sont imaginaires, faut-il le dire ? Cependant, ils n'ont pas la prétention comme la fiction littéraire de présenter des faits actuellement vraisemblables. Ils ouvrent la porte à l'imaginaire pur... sans autre soutien que la perpétuité des sentiments humains. Si l'on veut bien se souvenir que les passions des hommes sont demeurées les mêmes à travers les divers décors que leur ont prêtés les âges, on comprendra que la jeunesse ait adopté avec enthousiasme ces fables qui avouent honnêtement l'artifice de leur figuration, mais gardent leur pathétique.

« Il était une fois »... a peut-être menti...

« Il sera peut-être une fois... » pourra être vrai !...

Réclamez

" AVENTURES-FICTION " N° 1

5 récits complets INÉDITS par numéro...

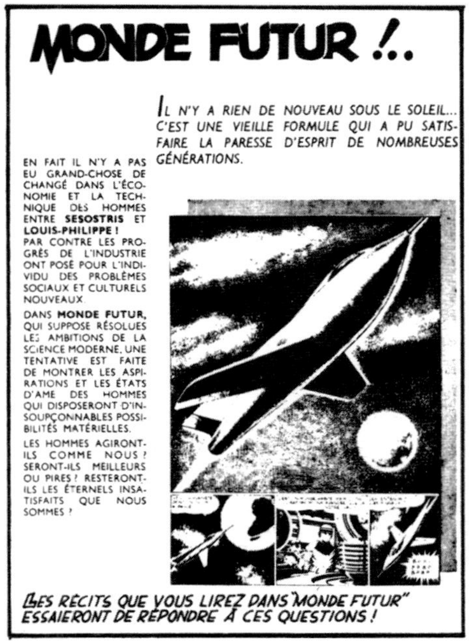

"innocent" advertising for comic strips or official and prevailing thought through fable.

technique itself is not independent of the political choices of the society in which it develops. These virtualities either fit into practice, biased toward a reinforcement of the social group wielding political power—which generally seems to require making restrictive choices coherent with the logic of a class project—or they are fully used in order to contribute, with other forms of knowledge, to the transformation of social practice. What permits this transformation is not the introduction of the virtualities of technique into social practice but the ideological basis: they are means, not causes.

Technical practice is the implementation of a state of technique's possibilities within the continuing developmental process of technical means. The practice of technique is the social use (or nonuse) of these virtualities in keeping with the order of society. In a way, technical practice comprises the substrate necessary for any practice of technique, but it is the latter that highlights technique as a means and it is particularly at this second level that the modes of integrating technique into society operate. We can say that, if the first level (technical practice) is almost (but not completely) solely dependent on its own process, the second level (the practice of technique) is never innocent in the social logic. But the appropriation of the possibilities of technique, brought close to hand by technical practice, necessarily requires a practice of technique.

It is not enough to highlight the fact that concrete connections exist between the various systems of expression[1] comprising the knowledge of a society, we must also analyze those connections, which are the direct result of economico-political relationships in society. We will restrict ourselves here to an analysis of the relationships between technical practice, the practice of technique, the products of technical practice and the works that materialize the value system of a society.

Technique is the foremost means of permitting one of the formative relationships of the group (of society): the opposition to Nature, the emergence from a natural order that serves as the constant frame of reference—at once a point of reference, a starting point, and an antagonistic power, always considered to be an immobile, absolute Nature. Technique situates the group within the synchronic order of nature and gives it the means to extricate itself from it. Technique as a means must be closely subordinated to the group project. It is the continuing process

1. System of expression: here, the term covers all the practices through which the overall knowledge and particular knowledge of a society expresses itself, and so with technical practice and the practice of technique.

of technique that gives the group ever renewed means for maintaining its own cohesion. However, this continuous process should not elude the control of the group, which strives to direct its course through choices made from the range of possibilities, controlling the universe available at a given stage of knowledge and of the technique applying this knowledge. And so, even at the highest level, there is no technical process completely independent of the social logic. The practice of technique, knowledge, and the system of values are mutually interdependent. But it is in everyday life that the possibilities of concrete experience can be modified. A new technical practice does or does not permit a new practice of technique; thus new behaviors and new modes of perception are elaborated and are materialized and institutionalized in sign systems that transmit the representation of a consensus, and tend toward a consolidation of the existing order. On the one hand, this existing order selects the possibilities of technique and orients a practice of technique, sometimes even enacting restrictions necessary for its preservation; on the other hand, this order permits a certain inevitable development, channeling it into a system of representations that it has made completely docile.

It is, at the same time, these systems of signs that carry the social imaginary: in the forms of plastic and aesthetic objects, the forms of useful or unusual objects, in the forms of experience and the forms of everyday life. To the extent that the transformation of experience actually occurs, that is, if an idea of technique does not obliterate the actual practice of technique, it modifies the everyday practice of objects and offers new objects to this practice. The hierarchy of concrete, spatial, and temporal relationships through which the value system of a society expresses itself essentially depends upon it. We may imagine that concrete relations to things, to balances of power, to a consciousness of the possibility of changing the order of the world "within the limits of one's momentary ability to intervene," one way or another—either through the explosive coincidence of isolated events, or through a quantitative accumulation intervening in the qualitative order—these relations manage to establish themselves in order to create a new consensus. This is a dynamic, a possibility of transformation that leaves the most closed system open and makes the most fateful intent uncertain. This *social dynamic*—which ultimately foils the class project of the ruling class (which does not take the other classes into consideration)—we see, to a large extent, in the social imaginary.

idea of a neutral technique, is an illusion. The social logic immediately institutes a bipolar technical system, and the cultural system is based from the start on this logical distance—a distinction complementary to the social imaginary. The latter (an ersatz utopia) rests on technique (an ersatz of culture) of which the media—radio, television, magazines…—are also principal disseminators (of the ideology of technique). As it is, the social imaginary (symbolized by magazines that marry do-it-yourself with high tech, feeding on the ideology of technique) will play on this dichotomy again, drawing on the spectacle of metatechnique to fuel and elucidate obscure everyday practice. Advanced technique assimilated with science (the magazine Science et Vie*) acts as an imaginary for ordinary technique, as the inaccessible often does; the "gadgetized" objects become a sign and a promise of technical revolution, of social revolution by means of technical revolution. In a way, the social imaginary acts as a reified social revolution, whose area of deployment would be everyday life. Thus, ideology, derived from the process of production, intervenes in a feedback loop in the process of production to reinforce it, all the while spreading the belief in a transition to a technically and socially new era.*

[continued p. 230]

The social imaginary seems to partake of the relationship that establishes itself between the process of production, for which there is necessarily a technique, and the process of assimilation of products by society. It represents the dynamic phase of this relationship, which exists only in the constant interdependence and interaction between the technical means actually at society's disposal and the system of values and representations organizing the practice of this technique. The static phase, represented by ideology, is, on the contrary, constituted when the relationship is established only in one direction: that of the system of representations organizing the practice of technique according to a representation (an idea) it has of it, without the particular practice of a technique intervening in the elaboration of this representation. The social imaginary and ideology comprise the two antagonistic but inseparable phases of the relationship between product and social practice; a fundamental dynamic that permits the diachrony of social practice: the *instituting phase* and the *instituted phase*. The term "social imaginary" may be misleading: it is not a sum of *individual imaginaries*. The individual imaginary means *experience* in the imaginary mode. It permits a kind of escape from reality through private fantasies, which in pathological cases, may completely hinder communication between the individual and the outside world. The individual imaginary is actively solicited by advertising. The consumption that proceeds from advertising occurs in the imaginary mode: the packaging, aura, and social status of the object are consumed more than the object itself. Nor is the *social imaginary* to be assimilated with the *collective imaginary*. This is humanity's common fund of symbols, a legacy that interferes both with the formalization of individual fantasies and the organization of the social imaginary's upsurges. It is a substrate, not a dynamic resulting from the dialectical relationship between the social repression necessary for the survival of the group and a continual process destructuring the existing order.

The social imaginary is the expression of the spontaneous consensus that is established in this way. It contains in fact the creative potential of a society, and in that sense we can say that all individual creations proceed from it to the extent that the creator "crystallizes" social virtualities, as yet unthought and free of social constraints, according to his own mode. An example would be the flowering of tracts and texts written on walls in Paris in May, and in Prague in August, which expressed a different vision of the world, one liberated by a situation. A village name plaque replaced with a sign in Russian, that read "It's our business!," etc. Out of the social imaginary come new combinations of objects and situations that inflect social logic or disrupt it.

It is obvious that the classes in power and those that are assimilated to them in sharing their ideological system, tend to reduce as much as possible the margin of uncertainty that constitutes the social imaginary, but they are stuck with the contradiction of not being able to stop the technical process without also weakening themselves. The logic of their development demands more and more activities, more and more consumption of raw materials, more and more social connections, more and more precision in the techniques of social manipulation, etc. This indispensable progress is not arrested, but directed so as not to induce possibilities of transforming the existing order. The systems of signs that represent and diffuse ideology are continuously refined for the sake of an ever more complete hold on social reality. Indeed, it is not in the implementation of actual relationships in social practice but through representations of practice, through signs, that the class project consolidates itself; and it is for this reason that it is always vulnerable in concrete situations. This project is expressed particularly in the realm of objects and representations that "colonize" everyday life in the so-called consumer society.

As soon as they are put into use, the products of technical practice partake of the *system of objects*,[2] that is, they are implicated, as objects, in social practice as mediations of specific relationships between man and matter, and according to a given order constituted by ideological practice. For each product there is a level at which the product is raw, so to speak, and a level at which the product is integrated into social practice through its participation in the ideology. Thus we may say that the level at which the product is only a product, the result of a transformation, is preliminary to practice and that each *product* necessarily becomes an *object*; hence a sign within practice and a sign of practice in the system of meanings pervading this practice.

But the degree of participation in ideology varies according to the object, and depends on the object's value as a sign in the system of meanings that represents and disseminates this ideology. Some objects have no sign value in a given system, so to speak,

An incredible amount of ingenuity is spent in perfecting small devices and household appliances for use in *cleaning*, peeling, grinding, *washing*, etc. at prices that even the most modest budgets can afford, and this is starting to revolutionize household tasks well beyond the confines of the middle class.

G. Friedmann, *Sept études sur l'homme et la technique*

Give

buccamatic

to the smiles you love

Buccamatic: a revolution in brushing teeth. An electric toothbrush with case, wall fixture, four interchangeable heads. Well-being, white teeth, a stimulating massage for the gums, perfect safety and hygiene for the teeth and mouth. Price 98F, sold in pharmacies.

...the female consumer pays five times the real price of the detergent that she buys. This is due to promotional and advertising costs. When she buys a several-kilo box of laundry detergent for her washing machine, she pays 25F. The box generally contains 5F's worth of product; the rest of the price reimburses the packaging (the bigger and brighter it is, the better it sells), and the advertising... and guarantees a profit.

Jacqueline Dana, "Ceux qui font mousser la lessive," in *Le Nouvel Observateur*, 11/4/1968

2. Jean Baudrillard, *The System of Objects*.

The techniques of aesthetic production, although usually presented as being completely free of ideology—in the name of the "purity of Art" (whether architecture or "design")—are not essentially different from other techniques, inasmuch as they are immanent in the mode of production. But for them, too, the deck is already stacked: their content depends closely on their mode of production and their means of distribution; whether "gadget" or work of art, they lead to the production of a "pseudo-aesthetic" object, a commodity. This means that its aesthetic characterization (its use value) is pressed into the service of its exchange value. These techniques are therefore also at the service of power to the extent that their near exclusive role is to perpetuate and reinforce the values of bourgeois domination. Thus it is important to show how such an appropriative strategy at the service of power applies not only to the explicit level—that of the plain practice (in the sense of use) of technique—but also to the implicit level of the ideology of Technique and ideological practice, which creates ideology and techniques.

Thus the strategy of Power is played out through techniques that are supposed to be free of all ideology, but are in fact directly at the service of ideology through the mediation of the reduction of the "technically possible" to the "socially probable" in a specific socioeconomic structure.

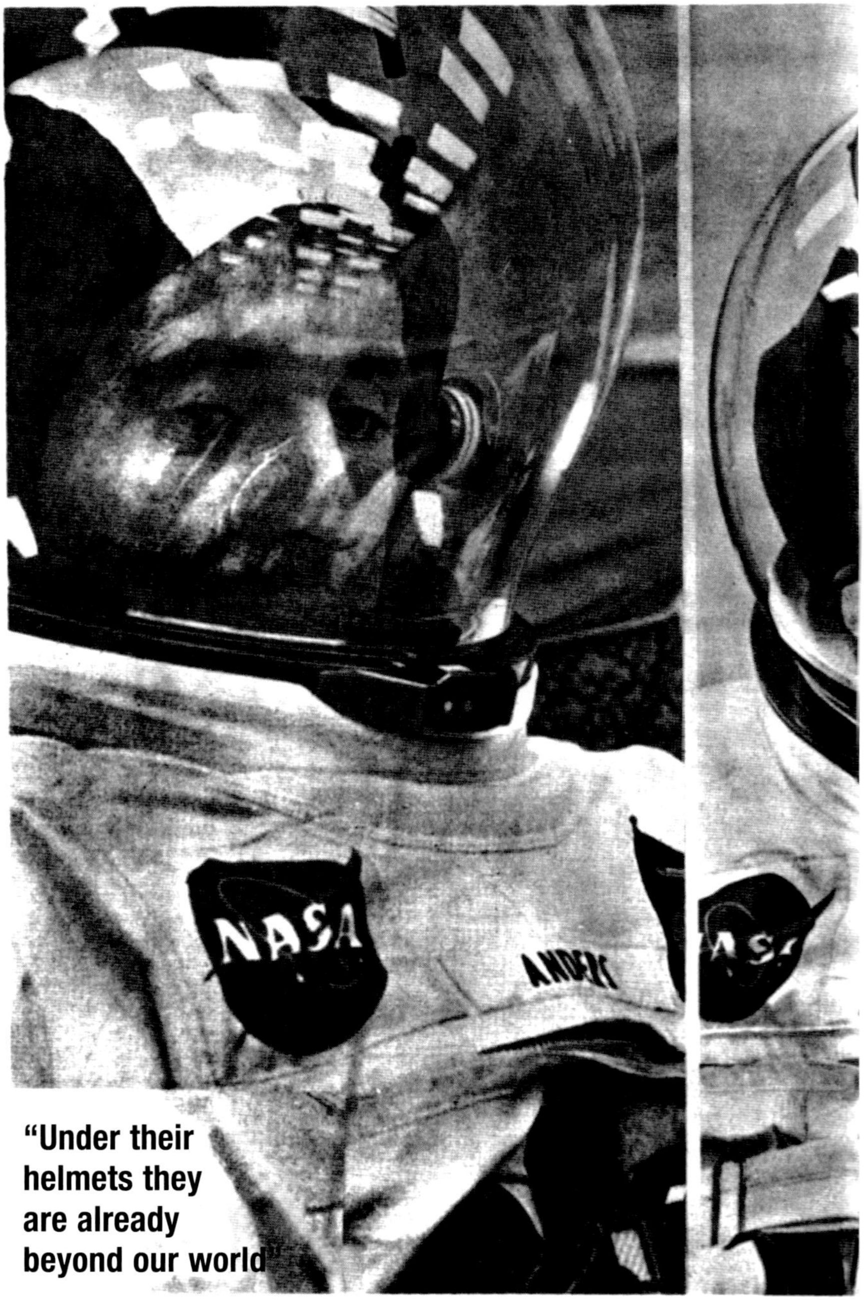

"Under their helmets they are already beyond our world"

and are only the means for a particular immediate experience. Tools, for example, represent this category of objects perfectly, as long as they are not picked as signs representing a category of actions within a system of meanings. Such a choice, along with the convergence of meanings on a single object, surpasses by far

Choisis parmi 35 éléments Scholtès réels pour incorporer ici à une cuisine imaginaire (de gauche à droite) poste de cuisson RE 164, réfrigérateur 230 l, hotte anti-odeurs 6580 OZ, four électrique F 68 E, table de cuisson mixte T 65 GEE et un lave-vaisselle standard 9

the object's signification as taken from concrete experience; it conceals technological reality and may obliterate the perception of values elaborated by experience (instituting perceptions) in favor of the perception of a preexisting order (instituted perception) that is accepted by society rather than being elaborated by it. But it is also through the spontaneous and momentary fixation of a sign value to an object representative of both the state of technology and the state of sensibilities at a particular moment, that the social imaginary constructs and manifests itself.

The ideological veil that intervenes between products and social practice is the means by which they partake of this practice. It manifests itself in the imaginary representations relating

"TECHNIQUE COMPLETELY AT THE SERVICE OF EVERYDAY LIFE" *means the opening of possibilities and is opposed to the closure of needs in a hierarchic repertory of the kind promoted by economic analyses using double-entry columns (input-output). In such analyses, the previously ideologically and socially limited need is surreptitiously replaced by the capitalized, alienated economic need. After reducing the social demand to a social command (this development is not genetic; it has validity only at the level of analysis), and desire to a need, this command is transformed for our dear economists into a new form of alienated demand, via a meaningful falsification: solvent demand is coupled with an offer that stands in a stimulus-response type of relation to demand (a relation of mere causality). This is:*

"TECHNIQUE COMPLETELY AT THE SERVICE OF POWER," *that is: all technique at the service of the preservation of the structures, at the service of resistance to change.*

CH.G., J.P.J., A.S.

the products within a system of signs. But the specific delay of consciousness links technical practice, and above all the practice of technique, to systems of representation that are inadequate to the temporary state of technique. Objects are elements of this system of representations and meanings in which there is not necessarily a correspondence between technical practice and ideological practice. Furthermore, the constant process of elaboration of a system of signs in and through everyday life is constantly foiled by the fact that each sign system institutionalizes modes of perception and organization of a specific sensibility corresponding to a specific state of the means of production, of technical practice, and so tends to definitively set the practice of technique, the temporary representations and ideologies of a society. Sign systems require constant reevaluation, an adjustment to the conditions of technical practice. If this reevaluation is not made, that is, if the instituted phase of society's relationship with things predominates over the instituting phase, these representations will have the appearance of technique, but the supporting objects will not really have the capacity to implement the possibilities of technique; they thus will not contribute in any way to modifying action on the world. Any real modification of the relationships of action invariably transforms the system of relationships between objects and the system of relationships to objects. If it does not automatically institute a system of signs, it proposes new *potential* combinations of signs.

The form of the object is the support for its meaning. It is the means by which society apprehends and appropriates products. It is, in a certain sense, the appearance of the product, its representation, which becomes part of a network of signs and represents more or less faithfully its ability to intervene in practice. The object (the product and its appearance) intervenes in social practice through the social imaginary and by means of a constant readjustment of the imaginary system to the possible uses of the product. Ideology, however, sets a specific status for the object in a value system that tends toward finality, this status of the object being made explicit by its form. And so we end up attributing too much importance to the form as a support for signification, assimilating form with signification, and, in the end purport to intervene in social practice through the manipulation of forms.

The perception of the signification of a form elaborates itself from the synthetic organization of parts of this form in relation to a system of references. The perception of signification constitutes the decisive element of the process of a form's integration into a system of relationships and imaginary significations sustained by and elaborated within a practice. The form in itself has no capacity to transform social relationships: it is a sign of the virtualities of products. As a sign, it intervenes only according to a definite (predefined) order within a given ideology, and only to the extent to which this ideology is sufficiently shared. Ultimately, it represents a technological change, without being able to effect this change.

Two levels of signification invest form. One is perceived in the practice of the object and is directly linked to the form's probable meaning, such as it is proposed by the practice proper to the object, yet not necessarily integrated into a particular social practice. It is a level of *explicit* signification, or, rather, a signification largely innocent of the set of representations and ideologies that manipulate the object, and pretend, in so doing, to manipulate social relationships. The other level, the *implicit level*, appears only in reference to the context of the ruling ideology defining a society; it is the level apprehended by social practice and is instituted by the social imaginary. It may happen that in certain cases the levels of explicit meaning and implicit meaning are inseparable; that is, that the probable signification is the object's social signification, as in the product of a specific practice whose use is determined by this practice without participating in the ideology. For most objects, however, the two levels do not coincide. The explicit signification of the object does not contain its full signification.

The apprehension of the product and the possibility of its being put into circulation as an object in society involve the signification given to its form in reference to a technical and ideological practice constitutive of the social imaginary, and also to a status established within such and such an ideology. This social existence of products seems to be organized according to three modulations that may be broadly defined as follows:

1.— The referential function completely obliterates the object's level of explicit signification. The form does not define a usage, but illustrates the implicit meaning, the ideological frame of reference; this is the case with advertising objects and works of art (or not).

2.— The ideological referential function makes the implicit level appear to be explicit. For example, the appearance of the object presents itself as the qualitative technical modification of concrete experience, and thus possibly of the individual's overall behavior vis-à-vis this object, while the explicit meaning accounts only for a quantitative modification of experience. This is the case, for example, with electrical household appliances which are often only improvements on traditional objects: they permit no new use, or new relationships with the objects, all while sporting a modernism of use and even of the social relationships induced by the presence of the new object. Consequently, they offer no possible transformation of practice, and even inhibit these possibilities by satisfying social demand through the appearance of technique. This shows very clearly an exclusive function of ideology. Nonetheless, we can imagine that in the long run and cumulatively these objects could bring about certain irreversible modifications in practice. This separation between the functional practice of the object (the level of explicit meaning) and the social practice of the object (the level of implicit meaning) has become so ingrained in contemporary mores that it provides a perfect argument for advertising. A recent advertisement for Simca cynically played on this antinomy, banking on the efficacy of the representation and the social implications of the representation: "The SIMQUATRE is the only four horsepower automobile that produces four horsepower without looking like four horsepower… does an economy car have to look cheap?"

3.— The level of explicit meaning and the level of implicit meaning complete each other and are associated: the best example of the tendentious rhetoric through which objects are apprehended. On the one hand, the explicit level represents a technical practice and modernity justified by actual technical application; on the other hand, the level of implicit meaning also underscores the exceptional character of this use of technique, the necessary social privation, its reservation for very limited and specific uses. Obviously, the choice of these points of application is determined by the ideological premises shared by society, or presented as being shared by society. The consequences of this choice intervene more particularly through social practice, which determines a practice of technique and the relationships to the object; they intervene in the representation that a society gives itself of technique by means of the spectacular. This is the case, for example, with nuclear tests and progress in aeronautics.

It is a system of imaginary representations dependant on concrete experience, but also and first of all, it is the ideological precondition for this experience that makes it possible to draw out signification.

Work becomes the most contingent part of life; there is no place for it in the imaginary system. But one of the irreducible contradictions lies in the fact that widespread abundance is completely incompatible with the unequal distribution of resources, the division of labor, and the social hierarchy that comprise the basis for the so-called society of abundance. It is from a plethora of imagery that the necessary shortage of reality will be defined, for shortage will be even greater if the possibilities on offer—we saw this in the realm of technique—respond insufficiently to the demand inspired by the imaginary system of the society of abundance. We participate in the "society of abundance" through the ritual of consumption. Consumption, as promoted and lived, is at the disposition of the ruled classes; it tends to make each consumer into a virtual owner, a candidate for a modest place in the bosom of the class in power. The "society of consumption" exists in direct proportion to the unequal distribution of resources and possibilities. This *de facto* situation is justified by an imaginary system within

SOME FACTS
Packaging has a direct effect on sales:

For products of general consumption,
in 95% of the cases in the U.S.A.
in 75% of the cases in Europe
for industrial wares,
(especially protection)
in 60% of the cases in the U.S.A.
in 30% of the cases in Europe.
Surveys 1966–1967: Bureau of Census—American Management Association—American Foundation for Management Research—OCDE Arthur D. Little—IFEC.

which a minority has ready access to models (which they have not necessarily produced—since models are products of the social imaginary—but which belong to them by law), most of whom, since they own, never really appear to really consume, while a majority strives to attain the same lifestyle, to models—

through the consumption of mass-produced objects that are but images. The consumption of images will never lead to possession.

What the class in power tries to conceal as carefully as possible is the fact that it is at the mercy of the imaginary system that it has set up for the sake of its own protection. Giving the appearance of social and technical progress as society's only road—since there is no *reasonable* alternative proposition to progress—demands a formal modification of the manifestations of power, which may bring about some disturbance without actually modifying it: these are only formal revolutions whose subsequent successes and failures conceal all the better the constancy of the fundamental principles. However, these formal modifications leave power in such a precarious balance that any flagrant incoherence between its project and the forms in which it is dressed might quickly endanger its very existence at any moment.

What we have tried to show is the elaboration of images that constitute the imaginary system assuring the dissemination of a society's models, as well as the functional relationship that exists between image and ideology, and how under certain conditions, images elude the grasp of accepted ideology and contribute to the elaboration of another ideology. This relationship is constituted whenever the social consensus is sufficiently broad. Every social cohesion is *de facto* repressive and self-repressive. In our advanced capitalist-industrial society, or "society of abundance," self-repression is due both to the ruled classes sharing a consensus based on an ideology—this consensus, which masks their condition as a ruled class, is perpetuated by self-repression—and to the class in power. Indeed, the ruling class, which instills and uses this consensus to spread its ideology, is also a captive of the narrow confines of the ideal situation it has given to itself in society. In fact, everything happens as if on one side there were ruled classes, and on the other, ruling classes, classes with divergent interests (a situation favorable to class struggle), and as if, for the preservation of the class in power, this situation had to be masked by the appearance of a homogenous, classless society, or at least one in which there existed a community of interests between classes, and general acceptance of a purpose common to all classes: the building of the "society of abundance." We live the "society" of abundance in the imaginary mode.

The system of significations covers all of reality and even "covers" reality in the journalistic sense of the term, that is, describes it, translates it, and transmits an image of concrete experience in which contradictions are erased or relativized.

It is a coherent ensemble, which can serve as a referent for the experience it orients or explains. The fruits of concrete experience [*épars*], hard to interpret, no longer exist as a sufficient referent.

The system of reference which we have brought to light appears as a society of abundance. The whole experience refers to a theoretical abundance in which all objects would seem to essentially participate. Equality and fraternity in abundance hide the fact that it is in the relations of work that the real relations of force between the dominated classes and the classes in power define themselves.

The society of abundance exactly opposes the general availablity of the means proposed by an appearance of technique. But the very function of this appearance of technique is also present as inevitable the notion of progress which freezes an existing order, and perhaps to oppose the elaboration and foundation, upon specific bases, of the truth proper to our society.

I.A.
March–August 1968

UTOPIA IS NOT WRITTEN IN THE FUTURE TENSE

Poster-pamphlet distributed on the occasion
of the Congress "UTOPIA E/O RIVOLUZIONE"
in Turin April 25, 26, 27, 1969.

The alternative: utopia and revolution, utopia or revolution is a petty bourgeois question. Leave the utopians in want of humanism, the revolutionizing congress-goers searching for justifications for their integrated and integrating practice in the visionary illusion of the revolution!

THE ILLUSION OF ENCLOSURE

The refinement of the means of control and of self-control implemented by the capitalist system in order to realize its liberalist project raises doubts as to the possibility of its being overrun by the play of its own contradictions.

The system tends toward closure, thus realizing Hegel's philosophical project of the "Civil Society."

In the light of Marxist analysis, the ruling class strives to mask the erasure of everything that justifies the protest of the exploited class, everything that gives power back to the class struggle. In order to dismiss the proletariat's struggle as unreal, it strives to perpetuate a world in which the experience of the unreasonable is reasonable and, as such, determines the rational, in which repression is the condition for freedom, and stability the safeguard against contradictions.

This class, the bourgeoisie—a coalition of production, finance and political power—paves the way for the future with peaceful means. It piles up administrative and institutional reforms, but refrains from mentioning that it maintains the same conditions of production. It establishes a *conservative, or bourgeois socialism.* The State—that is, class power—wishes to be neither bourgeois, nor capitalist; it lets its ideologists and theoreticians declare that searching for *another* freedom means fooling those who have honestly worked to acquire the life they now have; a life incomparably better than the one that workers had not so long ago. "The socialism of the bourgeoisie consists in saying that the bourgeois are bourgeois… in the interests of the working class" (*The Communist Manifesto*).

Given this context, the decline of the bourgeois State that gives way to a classless and nonrepressive society seems to melt into the haze of utopia. Contrary to the dialectical analysis of objective reality, bourgeois common sense holds that all societies are necessarily repressive, hierarchic and alienating; but the present one rather less than others.

For the bourgeoisie, utopia is whatever lies beyond its field of possibilities, whatever puts the system in jeopardy. Marxism, which critiques social relationships and provides means to realize them, is a direct threat to the bourgeois order: Marxism, a utopia?

But the bourgoisie, apart from exposing the contradictions of its order, also gives the name utopia to imaginary revisions of that which, far from rattling order, consolidate it. The collusion between these two acceptations of utopia is another defense against the irruption of overwhelming criticism; it is within the falsifying logic of the system.

Formalized futuristic projections are also always within the order of the system, even when they adopt the theses of historic materialism. Even if it likes to think of itself as outside of the existing order, utopia understood in this way presents itself merely as the logical negation of this order, and so is entirely defined by the bourgeois world, whose preoccupations it only perpetuates. It is its inverted perspective. The alibi of geographic or historical isolation is of no help, since utopia—the alienated dream of the metamorphosis of the real—does not give itself the historical means for the transformation of reality.

THE FETISHISM OF UTOPIA

From the utopists of the early nineteenth century,
precursors of radical critique, to speculative utopias

The utopian socialists may be considered as the precursors of socialist theory as it was elaborated by Marx and Engels. Yet they were dependent on the historical situation in which they found themselves: their formalizations, perfectly in line with the contemporary productions of the imaginary and the state of scientific knowledge and technics, represented fairly well the criticism they leveled at the industrial society of their time. They believed that they were giving themselves the means to "liberate humanity" but their critique remained incomplete; above all, it remained subject to the development of productive forces, to the class situation, to the maturity of the capitalist mode of production. While pointing the way that led elsewhere, they remained bound to the existing order.

But now there is talk of the "End of utopia." Some claim that the liberating pseudo-power of technics and of technology, activated by who knows what trigger of consciousness, will suffice to realize the utopia of a socialist society. In this way, a "something," a mutation that suddenly establishes a new principle of output, one not antagonistic to the pleasure principle, would make utopia useless from now on by opening up possibilities—presented as being independent of the modes of production—for the end of shortage. For we know and believe that everything is possible in this world where technology can accomplish everything. In this statement we grasp the double meaning of utopia, the double signification referring back to those of philosophy. The idea being defended plays on two registers: on the one hand, the formal utopia (from Fourier to Fuller via the World of the "A"s and the "Non-A"s...), a spitting image of bourgeois speculative philosophy, and, on the other, the utopia-desire, in which undesirable and undesired instincts and needs shamefully take refuge.

Which means in fact letting oneself be fooled by the very ideology of the class society, the ideology that makes us believe that, for the first time in history, the end of shortage is at hand. Utopia is also—in each one of us—the mode of preservation and acceptance of the models of the existing order. Indeed, we can only speak of *shortage* and the *end of shortage* in relation to the overall state of development of the global population at a given moment, particularly in relation to the quantity of products considered necessary for physiological and psychological survival within a given society, as well as of the distribution of these products.

A significant contradiction of the system resides in the fact that the development of productive forces linked to technological progress normally leads to an increasing liberation of workers, through the decrease, and even disappearance, of work time. This technological liberation inspires most of today's utopian formalizations, yet the achievement of automation is impossible in the bourgeois world, for only the exploitation of man's labor permits the reproduction of surplus value, the foundation of the system.

Only the spectacle, offered by the technologically advanced sectors supporting our society's imaginary, permits the illusion of the coming end of shortage. And so shortage, an invention achieved and implemented by bourgeois society, has been exorcised in the science-fiction utopias.

The aphorism, "*today's utopias are tomorrow's realities*," instills the cohesion of the fragmented society. The possibility of realizing utopia, presented as the privilege of power, always deferred, invalidates critical thought. It is not the end of utopia—rendered useless by the realization of a nonrepressive society—but the apparition of the visionary formalization of utopias, a subtle cog in the class society in the advanced industrial period. Utopia has become the emasculated expression of the tensions that reveal a conflictual reality.

Utopias abound, they have simply changed names. Without modifying the established order, the many superb philosophical, technical, architectural, urbanistic and galactic utopias festoon the economists's prospectivist grids. They are the utopian-realities-of-tomorrow, varying assemblages of new materials—or presented as such—that create the illusion of change. In this way, some believe and make us believe that the development of techniques alone, and of the science of the environment resulting from it, will modify the backward and alienated state of the populations subordinated to Capital; that class conflicts will dissolve in the society of abundance. They believe it and make others believe, but they are working only to prolong class oppression. Mobile cities, walking cities, soft software, the end of shortage, omnipotent technology, the playfulness of gadgets, city lights, the technology of the Concorde, the technology of Gemini, the soft revolution… And in the meantime, in everyday life, nothing of this: work, weekends, work, and more work! The mirage by which the daily repression of the dominated class becomes blurred, vanishes when the latter thinks it is about to touch it, only to reappear a little further away, secreted by the oppressive power.

Between the quest for utopia and the utopians offering their panaceas, their wares, there is no exit, for transformation is not desired, only the maintenance of the status quo, of decent surplus value from the lives of producers. The sleight of hand that tries to evade the radical critique of the mode of production is achieved in a subtle dialectic between possibilities that will never be and a false utopian consciousness that surrounds itself with marvels.

What do you think of the fetishism of utopia? Utopia is a luxuriant merchandise, of sparkling dazzle. What will the utopias and demonstrations about utopia financed by industrial sponsorship change? This money is the surplus value gained from the proletariat. The congress-goers of "Utopia and/or revolution" who lay out their blissful positivism are the idols of utopia.

The mode of production, given as *natural* and ineluctable, besieges consciousness in order to prevent it from calling it into question. In offering workers only the alienated dream of the metamorphosis of reality, the ideologists of the mode of production try to break the class consciousness of the workers at the present stage of capitalism, as well as their ability to change the existing world.

Utopia is the decoy showing ideology, skirting class struggle and fragmentation, the reality of the street, the reality of work, of sexual repression and urban repression. This phantasmatic phenomenon in bourgeois society exerts the redeeming power of *imagining* something else. The imaging function of transcendence is filled by the imaginary which, sublimating its unsatisfied desires, replaces them with reductive representations of practice. To survive, the bourgeoisie also has to invest the world outside of work and alienate everyday life, as it has alienated labor. This superstructural deployment aims to veil the system's infrastructural contradictions. Yet this falsification, which tries to thwart all actions against its foundations, has caught the bourgeoisie in its own trap, subjecting it to its superstructural hypertrophy, leaving as the only alternative, refuge in the imposed dream or the field of class struggle.

This is why UTOPIE will propose no "utopia" nor will it acquiesce, to any. The only "utopia" is the complete emancipation of the proletariat: a *utopia for the bourgeoisie but not for itself*. We have rummaged through the unconscious of the bourgeoisie and have brought out the unacceptable. We provoke. The only task is the realization of the utopia of philosophy, the project of Marx-Engels, and of Marxism.

THE WORLD OF CLASS STRUGGLE

At the same time as it posits the bourgeois world as reality and rationality, bourgeois discourse defines it, and stakes out its reassuring limits. For the bourgeois world, the presence of a contradiction in the system can only be absurd, for it does not fit into the legal discourse of the capitalist system. But the assurance of the bourgeois future diminishes as the mode of production and the mode of consumption tend toward a minimum profitability. It matters little that the poles of decision are protected, for at every instant the logic of exploitation reaches its breaking point and can reinstate class struggle with all its force. The only response being formulated by modern capitalism is formal. Marxism has rightly shown that man was substance before being form, that a form of freedom will not give freedom, and that, even if alienation is less visible, if the proletariat is no longer dressed in rags, this does not mean it is no longer being exploited.

Could it be that the world is closed? Society coherent? That which is structured not destructurable?

An obvious separation, one which determines all the others, is that of the classes: an active separation, perceptible in the places and conditions of labor, there where the falsifying superstructure gives way to infrastructure, veritable organizer of the relationships of production, and therefore of social relationships. It is there, in the practice of alienated labor, that the class situation shapes the consciousness of the working class. And it is at this level that the necessity of class struggle reveals itself, the necessity of a radical transformation of the conditions of production in order to transform social relationships.

The coherence, the unity of the world that derives from the superstructural and that camouflages the contradictions of the economy, of production, and of the monetary system, has been exposed by Marxist analysis. Consequently, it has shown the possibility of a dialectical transcendence of class society to build a free society of producers in and through praxis. We place ourselves in the lineage of Marx and Engels, as well as that of Fourier. Both showed the possibility of establishing new social relationships, but one only had an intuitive grasp of it, and the other applied the scientific analysis of the present forces and of the conflicting relationships between classes as a means of transforming social relationships. They showed that the lived relationships—at the historical moment in which they were experienced—were not *natural*. Our goal is the same, but the historical conditions are different. Our project, like Marx's, is utopian in the eyes of bourgeois common sense: we accept this epithet.

It is not the forms that we retain from Owen and Fourier, as so many contemporary visionaries have done, but the "seeds of great ideas breaking through everywhere" (Engels). Fourier's dialectic precedes Marx's. But, unlike the utopian socialist, and especially their successors—who only reproduced social and spatial forms of organization, while neglecting the implicit critique contained in these forms at the time that they were proposed—Marx showed the relationship between labor and the development of productive forces. He also showed how theories aiming at the transformation of the world should rest both on an analysis of the mode of production and on a recognition of the class whose exploitation in labor makes the perpetuation of this mode of production possible, and which alone can annihilate it.

It is the end of philosophy, of the explanation of the world, and the beginning of its transformation. It is also the end of utopia as a means of coming to an awareness of the possible transformation of the capitalist mode of production. Marx established radical critique as a mode of demonstrating the exploitation of man by man, and discovered the role of class consciousness within the process of history. All those (utopians, visionaries, professionals of futurism) who borrow from their nineteenth-century precursors their manner of formulating ideas confirm the bourgeois order, for they negate *de facto* the history of productive forces; history as the history of class struggle. They will never arrive at a politic, a praxis. The proletariat doesn't give a damn about their proposals; it can take its existence into its own hands by appropriating the means of production, and so produce its own life and the *forms* it will take.

We deny any kinship with these visionary formalists. Our position is theoretical and strategic. It is not a matter of nursing a new imaginary, a new revolutionary hope. To hell with revolutionary Messianism!

We believe that the negation of the bourgeois world brings into praxis the foundations of new social relationships. It is not a question of nihilism, but rather of recognizing reality with the aim of transforming it, such that the appropriation of life will no longer be impeded by class domination. The confusion orchestrated by bourgeois thinking, which consists in taking the negation of the capitalist world for the negation of all freedom, all pleasure, has merged with the confusion between negativity and nihilism. This is what led the political opposition of international socialism to the positivism diverting class struggle away from its violent terrain. But negation is the motor for the capture of objective reality; more exactly, historically determined negation is a political negation. Critical negativity is the socialist positive in bourgeois society, while being the negation of the latter.

Critique can only be radical. We refuse to be institutional critics of the system, partaking of the ideology of positivity and of the negative apology of the concrete. We refuse to propose concrete "critical" solutions that would only solidify the existing order.

"It is no longer a question of explaining the world, but of transforming it." Nor is it a question of formalizing it. The Marxist project is to realize both philosophy and utopia. This realization can only come about through theoretical and practical work within the field of class struggle.

Revolutionary struggle is possible only through the unity of critique and action, that is, on the basis of dialectical materialism. Only the proletariat can realize the revolution, for only the exploited class can establish this unity between critical theory and practical action, in praxis. For us, the task is to pursue the struggle against alienation through nonalienated forms of struggle.

UTOPIE
Paris–Turin, April 1969

Address
to the First Week of International Encounters
construction and humanism

THE MONEY OF URBANISM

Urbanizing does not mean *spending money.*
Urbanizing means making money.

Le Corbusier

In light of the recent violent manifestations of class conflict and last November's financial crisis, these Encounters take on a particularly sharp profile amid the economic, political and cultural vicissitudes of a country like France.

1. FIRST, THE OPENING TITLE: CONSTRUCTION AND HUMANISM

This label covers two distinct realms.

The term CONSTRUCTION was not chosen by chance. There are broader and nobler terms, like architecture, living environment, urbanism, planning, etc. But only "construction" refers to the direct intervention of private and public Enterprise; it alone means that monopolistic (Saint-Gobain, ELF-ERAP, RENAULT, etc.) and high-finance capital take the future in hand in a realm into which they had ventured but little before. In the field of construction, economic production asserts itself and tightens its hold, while playing on the obvious ambiguity between increasing its own profits and satisfying a social demand that it manipulates at will all the while. The only outcome of this pseudo-alternative is greater social discrimination disguised as a beneficial expansion of the economy, or of industrialization—which amounts to the same thing. In this way, the capitalist mode of production and, consequently, bourgeois democracy ensure their continued existence.

The choice of the second term, HUMANISM—which was not a matter of chance either—slid into place through the insidious effects of the pressure of the dominant ideology. The philosophy of the watchdogs—which we suppose to be far removed from the concerns of construction and urbanism—is the theory of Humanism. Bourgeois humanism determines the relations of oppression as if they were natural. It explains that the future of men of good will and integrity depends on conscientiousness at work and the care one takes to balance out a life made of prudence and a fear of history. The key to bourgeois humanism is that each is where he belongs, that it would be madness to aspire to anything else; that it would be out of place to complain, since things are as they are supposed to be and men cannot change their logic. This is the mean life of living from day to day, an existence made of pennies and little else, radiant with past splendors, but as hard as gold. This featureless world taps into a "magical, bewitched, and inverted world, in which Mister Capital and Mistress Earth—social beings and things simultaneously—dance their spectral dance. Political economy gets the credit for having dispersed these mists and mirages: the transformation of the social elements of wealth into independent and stable entities, the personification of things and the reification of relationships—that religion of everyday life" (Marx). This humanism—which we have described in its most everyday aspect, as it is actually experienced, and which has never been applied to anything else than daily bourgeois life—has taken such a beating that it threatens to collapse.

The clerks of capitalism are surely aware of the fact that if bourgeois culture and knowledge collapse, the social determination of oppression will also end, for they know that *social existence is what determines men's consciousness*. They are taking a mortal risk. It is in the cities that men's social existence determines itself according to the order of advanced industrial society. The primary role of the city delineates itself and outlines the role of urbanism. The clerks of Mister Capital have to take measures if they want to avoid seeing their class being backed up to the abyss of history, if they do not want to lose their dominance of the entire social structure. But it's already a lost cause. The motivations that uphold the bourgeois order and bludgeon the proletariat are weakening their hold. The highly praised capitalist monolith is a joke and radical criticism will reveal the true face of bourgeois democracy. It will show itself to be cowardly and sadly bloated with profit. Exposed in broad daylight, the abuse of life and men by the bourgeoisie will sign its own death sentence.

The humanism of liberal urbanism, trapped in this game and rich in raw material, takes the mission of man's well being and happiness upon itself. And how it equips and organizes to do so! What does it mean to manage rarity and shortage, if not to make rarity even more rare and shortage even more necessary? Stop proclaiming that abundance is at our doorstep! Anyone who has exercised "practical, operational urbanism" knows the extent of the rarity and shortage. Amid the confusion between map and territory looms an emasculated vision of social reality.

With its abstraction, the map offers the hope of planning and establishes the metaphysics of Organization, which—intentionally or not—remains the place where the alienated consciousness reifies itself via technocratic organization (the reification of relationships and the personification of things). This is the philosophical announcement of the basis of reifying Urbanism.

The workers of the highly industrialized nations must destroy this logic. The internationale of the oppressed classes is the only road to emancipation, to total liberation in the face of reification.

The battle between those who have and those who have nothing to lose but their assembly line will be nothing if not a violent class struggle to be pursued in the cities. All history is a story of class struggle, of conflicts between exploiting and exploited classes, the rulers and the ruled; regardless of how much social development the one or the other may have attained.

While the specialists of urbanism convene, the proletariat organizes for the struggle.

This is a first explanation of the happy wedding of two words carried aloft by gusts of ideology under the aegis of large-scale capital and Gaullist power. It is, by the same token, a first explanation of the role of urbanism.

2. URBANIZING THE CLASS STRUGGLE

No speeches are necessary to understand that the city is the site par excellence for popular uprisings, just as it is the most profitable place for the distribution of the product of capitalist industry: merchandise.

In light of this, the global bourgeoisie is currently elaborating a theory of the appropriation of the city in order to develop itself rationally and strangle the proletarian struggle. If there is a bourgeois internationalism, there is also a proletarian internationalism; the identity of the bourgeois viewpoint corresponds to the identity of the struggles of the working class.

What presuppositions does the introduction of URBANISM AND PARTICIPATION imply?

Here is the complete text:

URBANISM AND PARTICIPATION

"How can the man of tomorrow participate in the interplay of technical, economic and cultural forces that determine his existence? The only solution is to establish communication.

"This communication can be established on two levels: first, the communication connecting all the professions participating in construction. Today, compartmentalization, differential training, distinct objectives and disparate languages create obstacles and hinder cooperation. The channels that will convey reciprocal information, the knowledge of the successive imperatives and the definition of a coherent program must all be defined. To foster a common language everyone must meet face-to-face, rethink their own professional circumstance and participation in the harmonious concert of skills. And so the whole series of operations, from the conception to the realization, will be established in the necessary order, and no longer through the antagonism of functions.

"However, beyond this encounter, this putting into order of urbanism, another dialogue must be arranged so that the public no longer has to endure urbanism as some remote function; the *public* must be consulted, so that it will adhere to and change urbanism according to its own needs. Once the basics have been taught, then continued information about the technical developments must be made available, along with the options regarding possible programs and the aims and plans of all the operations. This information must be prepared by professionals and transmitted to the public in a language to be defined by social communications experts.

"Lastly, if consultation is to be more than mere information, the forms and modalities of the public's participation in these areas have to be defined. What opportunities will they have to change objectives or constraints? This is a political problem that each country will have to solve according to its own institutions, by defining the degrees of this participation."

What man of good will would not further such a noble idea? How could technicians, artists and scientists not rally to this new flag of human progress?

The class in power says more in this text than it bargained for. At the heart of it, the ideological implosion bursts the ideological sack.

The philosophy of Participation effects the reductions necessary for its establishment. The most flagrant one being: the public. The language is not innocent of politics; it conveys ideology. Its actions and realization betray its class content. The use of the word "public" thus reveals the moral intentions of the existing order.

Those who are to be consulted and involved are already the spectators, the audience of the spectacle of life, and the public is the merchandise of the spectacle of the city. The spectacle is of a cultural nature. But the urbanism that deploys itself there does not find its fulfillment in it, for its works are all guided by political economy; its basis serves the unquestionable mistress who manages the capital controlled by the State.

The philosophy of participation goes even further. It tries to elaborate a homogenous problematic of the city—one that supposedly reflects the social cohesiveness put into practice by the dialogue with and consultation of the "public"—and tries to demonstrate the foolishness of the class struggle. Urbanism is supposed to be about that. No more will there be exploiters or exploited, directors or directed. Everyone will work together. But one problem will remain: communication! Since it formulates no criticism of the intellectual and manual division of labor—which is only one of the facets of the social division of labor—urbanism can only accentuate the lack of cohesiveness of social space and the "antagonism of functions" that expresses the very logic of capitalist society.

Power poses the problem in terms of communication and language difficulties; evidently, since this is the channel through which the vox ideologica expresses itself. It takes precautions by pointing out the need for communications experts. Some critics of capitalism have observed that communications experts, far from being mere translators, act as censors, as ideological filters, since the translation has to propose minimal formative models of the body of language accepted by a larger "public." The basis for these models is nothing other than the moral norms of bourgeois culture. Otherwise the discourse produced, by not referring to known references would be an abstract language, devoid of reality. In the same way that the bourgeoisie finds the proletariat's idea of a life without class exploitation and the struggle for its realization abstract, so too would a discourse not based on the categories of alienated life be completely abstract.

By announcing their intention to have the "public" participate in the work of urbanism, the institutions of the State are duping the working class. For, in the same breath, they take pains to make it understood that property and real-estate capital are only superficial hindrances—and not the basis of the system. In the end, it wants to eradicate the class oppositions that are so blatantly manifested in and through the city. Their general aim remains to destroy the consciousness of the proletarian class, for it impedes bourgeois social progress. Masking class struggle amounts to contributing to the increase of capital gain and profit.

The trick of participation resides in the fact that it gives the appearance—but only the appearance—of effective influence on economic and political decision making. As far as the modalities of intervention are concerned, there is no reason not to give the "public" all the guarantees of formal democracy. But by subtly slanting participation toward the problems of the city, power replaces the proletariat with a purely abstract notion, one unrelated to the process of production, that of the *inhabitant*; a notion that does its best to supplant the frustration experienced by workers in their economic and political lives. Thus, by disappearing as a class, the proletariat interiorizes the aims of the ruling class and perpetuates them.

"*Vouloir l'urbanisme*" (Let's have urbanism)! A gamble. Whose urbanism? Why urbanism? Urbanism in a class society will never overcome class determination. Urbanism can only be that of class power, and so we can translate the call of the technocracy as: let's have the urbanism of the ruling class, of capital.

No! to the urbanism of the Holy Trinity (Capital, Land, Labor)!

The exploited of the cities—and not only in the cities, of course—have only one recourse: the violence that expresses class struggle.

Power is aware of the danger represented by the noncontrol of a population mass still imbued with freedoms and franchises, of

popular masses put under conditions favorable for communication and exchange. A mass of this kind is virtually revolutionary to the extent that its conditions of existence permit no more than survival. The bourgeoisie skirts this danger by using technology and technocracy in urbanism. The mirror of the ideology of technique never fails to dazzle. Technical rationalism camouflages the social problematic. The vapors of the magic potion will not make us forget the workers' exploitation and precarious survival. Technique and technology in a class society are pirated and pressed into the service of profit and the accumulation of capital. Technique as a saving grace is a mystification.

Finally, the supposedly basic question is raised in these terms: "What possibility would the public have of changing objectives and constraints?" The option is obvious. Here is the answer: "This is a political problem that each country will have to solve according to its own institutions, by defining the degrees of this participation." Those are plain words. The idea at stake is not the transformation of social relationships in order for real democracy to exist among men, but rather a modernization of the present society in order to make a new start. The presupposition is that all existing structures are *de facto* accepted as being valid.

If the city and urbanism have not been taken seriously until now it is because, on the one hand, capital had not yet reached its present stage of development and, on the other, because it was no longer faced with the violence of the proletariat. The Holy Trinity shone brightly and the alienated basked in its rays. The tranquility of boredom was a daily holiday.

Given this, the first week of International Encounters takes place *de facto* on the level of class conflict and, by participating in the capitalist undertaking, takes position against the proletariat.

3. THE CITY AS OUTLET FOR MERCHANDISE

One of the means used by the ruling class to neutralize the workers' inclination towards dissent is the expansion of the merchandise system.

The land in which the divine flower of merchandise could take root is missing. The city is this Promised Land.

Taking the distribution of merchandise in the city into consideration permits it to be placed within the production/consumption cycle. There, the capitalist "urban society" can be read. The goal of production is the establishment of a mode of consumption favorable to the accumulation of capital. Urbanism acts within this limited framework. Merchandise is a complex thing, "full of metaphysical subtleties and theological hair-splitting." It hides a

The analysis of the city as a site for class struggle and the unmasking of urbanism as an instrument of class domination can only lead to a praxis that tends toward the social liberation of men alienated by conditioning and repression. Only violent struggle will destroy the instruments of domination; and urbanism is on the list. The fetishism of the city—the reification of social relations—will be abolished when daily city life is liberated.

secret and secretes a fetishism disproportionately cultivating itself in and through the city. The capitalist city flaunts the mystical nature of merchandise in the ascetic spectacle of shopping. The mercantile spectacle is in full swing in the city. Merchandise with a capital M—as social relationships, encounters or products—transcends itself without ever going beyond itself. It takes on a seemingly autonomous growth and coats everything. It justifies the monumental magnificence that it secretes by the increase in profits that it provides to the entrepreneurs. The celebration of merchandise helps sell merchandise.

This International Encounter is nothing but the global show and display of the Merchandise known as urbanism. Its blatant uselessness has no other utility than reinforcing urban ideology.

As it is, these Encounters close with the apotheosis of the only urbanism that calls itself by name: the urbanism of commerce. Deliberately or not (it matters little which), the discussion moderated by the Vice-President of the *Association Internationale URBANISME ET COMMERCE*—

who is also executive manager of the *Société Delhaize Frères & Co. "Le Lion"* and president of the *Association Belge des entreprises d'alimentation à succursales* (of supermarket chains)—is the introduction to the 2nd International Congress of URBANISM AND COMMERCE, whose topic is: *does the city center have a future?* It will be held in Sweden in May. If the world bourgeoisie permits this particular urbanism to show its ass, it is in order to make us believe that there exists a less mercantile and more human (all too human) urbanism that sublimates the corporatist particularities of specialized urbanism. An urbanism owned by the State that guarantees Order, Morality and Urbanity. And the urbanists consider themselves as so many Vidocqs serving the science of the State.

4. THE URBANISM OF MONEY

This meeting has a significance, as we have said and shown. The bourgeoisie and capitalism are waking up. Revolutionary confrontation forces them to invent and develop ever more refined means of doing battle. Urbanism is one of these means.

Our purpose here is not to improve a discipline that legislates the details of the old world. Nor to found a critique of urbanism. Critical urbanism is merely the flip side of class urbanism. Critical urbanism is the scientification of ideology. We mark out for destruction the system that builds itself around the urban problematic in order to mystify it, absorb it and make it disappear.

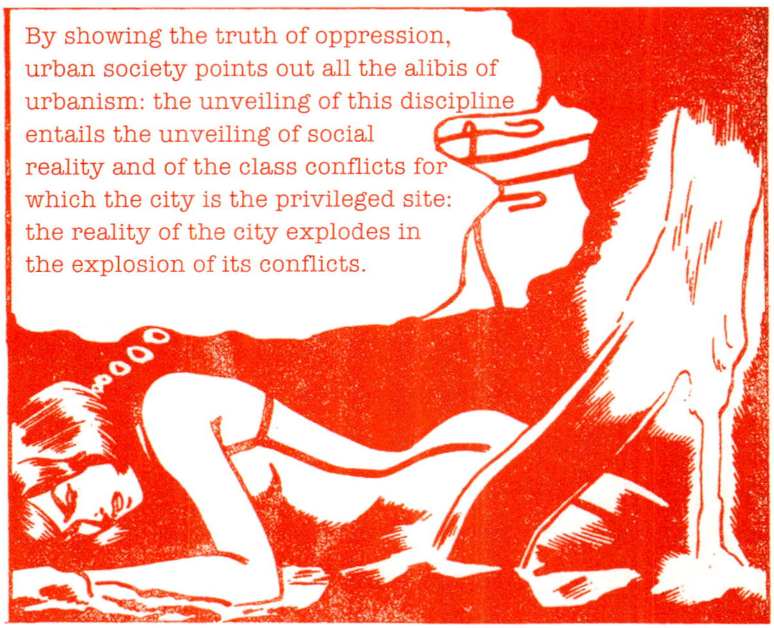

At the present stage of capitalist development, urbanism is no longer a guilty or partial urbanism, as we demonstrated in *The Logic of "Urbanism,"* but an urbanism directly based on the interests of capital. An urbanism that finds its raison d'être in the mode of production as well as in the mode of consumption, in the infrastructure as well as in the nexus of alienation. That is to say, an urbanism that fulfills the normalization of life by fragmenting it into activities (work/leisure/daily life/sexuality, etc.), whose accomplishment—cohesiveness—would realize itself in the new vision of the city and its reformed urban life.

Urbanistic logic shows the convergence of institutional and professional urbanism and the "spontaneous urbanism of free trade," an urbanism that exactly obeys the laws of the circulation of merchandise that, in the structures of capitalist production, tends to integrate urban practices and to merge into those practices in turn. By integrating urban practices, the urbanism of free exchange tries to make it conform to its models; that is, to turn urban practices into a merchandise to take its place as such within the fetishistic world of merchandise. Within this framework, Urbanism is the scientific and practical process of the commodification of the city.

The fabrication of an urban logic that converges with the logic of the ruling class, this logic formally includes urbanism by going beyond it. Urbanism will never be more than partial and the plaything of Master Capital. This logic is nothing but the quintessence of a set of ideas explicitly or implicitly formulated by the class in power. It endeavors to fundamentally inculcate the lesson that the bourgeois order is the most perfect accomplishment in history.

Without resorting to violent imposition or dictatorial domination, this logic and urban ideology exercise a no less real power, a power all the more real as it is insidious and subterranean.

This new form of domination must be destroyed. Together with production, the urbanized city will fulfill the ambition of the bourgeoisie, which seeks to establish its apogee there—emulating the great civilizations of the past that also reached their highest level of development in the city. It also sees this as a good opportunity to increase its profits—two birds, one stone…

UTOPIE
Cannes, March 10, 1969

The group Utopie
considers itself to be represented sufficiently by this text,
and so will not attend the Encounters. All mail can be sent to:
UTOPIE, P.O. Box 69, 92—Antony

The French group, which has been invited to this conference, has decided not to bring a positive contribution. The group believes that too many matters, and essential ones, have not been voiced here as regards the social and political status of Design, as regards the ideological functions and the mythology of environment. In these circumstances, any participation could not but reinforce the ambiguity and the complicity of silence which hangs over this meeting. So we prefer to present you a text expressing our positions.

The burning question of Design and Environment has neither suddenly fallen from the heavens nor spontaneously risen from the collective consciousness: It has its own history. Professor Banham has clearly shown the moral and technical limits and the illusions of Design and Environment practice. He didn't approach the social and political definition of this practice. It is not by accident that all the Western governments have now launched (in France in particular for the last six months) this new crusade, and try to mobilize people's conscience by shouting apocalypse.

In France, the environment issue is a fallout of May 1968, more precisely a fallout of the failure of the May revolution. Ideology, which the political power tries to divert onto rivers and national parks, could happen in the street. In the United States, it is not a coincidence that this new mystique, this new frontier has been developed during and parallel to the Vietnam war. There is in France and in the States a potential crisis situation. Both here and there the governments restructured their fundamental ideology in order to face this crisis and surmount it. We see that ultimately the real issue is not the survival of the human species but the survival of political power. In this sense, environment, design, the fight against pollution, and so on, pick up the torch in the history of ideology from the great crusade of human relations which followed the great 1929 crisis. At that time, the capitalist system succeeded in reviving production and in restructuring itself by means of an immense injection of publicity, of services, of public relations into consumerism, enterprises, and social life.

Today, when new and larger contradictions affect the internal structures of the overdeveloped countries and force them, all together, on a world scale, into opposition with the underdeveloped countries, the system comes up with a worldwide ideology that could remake the holy union of mankind, beyond class discrimination, beyond wars, beyond neo-imperialistic conflicts. Once again, this holy union created in the name of environment is nothing but the holy union of the ruling classes of the rich nations.

In the mystique of human relations, it was a question of recycling, readapting, and reconciling both individuals and groups to the social context given as norm and as ideal. In the mystique of environment, it is a matter of recycling, readapting, and reintegrating the individual in the context of nature given as an ideal. Compared with the preceding ideology, this one is even more regressive, more simplistic, but for that reason even more efficient. Social relations with their conflicts and history are completely rejected in favor of nature, with a diversion of all energies to a Boy Scout idealism, with a naive euphoria in a hygienic nature.

The theory of environment pretends to be based on actual and evident problems. But pollution, nuisances, dysfunctions are technical problems related to a social type of production. Environment is quite another problem, crystallizing the conscience on a Utopian model, on a collective enemy and, moreover, giving a guilty feeling to the collective consciousness. (We have met the enemy and he is us.) The crusade of environment goes from technical problems and technical solutions to simple and pure social manipulation.

War and natural catastrophes have always been used to unify a disintegrating society. Today, it is "la mise-en-scène" of a natural catastrophe or of a permanent apocalypse which plays the same role.

In the mystique of environment, this blackmail toward apocalypse and toward a mythic enemy who is in us and all around tends to create a false interdependence among individuals. Nothing better than a touch of ecology and catastrophe to unite the social classes, except perhaps a witch hunt (the mystique of antipollution being nothing but a variation of it).

Problems of design and environment only look like objective ones. In fact, they are ideological problems. This crusade, which puts again, but on another level, the themes of Kennedy's New Frontier, as well as the fighting against poverty as the theme of the Great Society (in France, the New Society), constitutes a complete ideological structure, a social drug, a new "opium of the people."

In one sense, it would be too easy to compare napalm bombing in Vietnam with the loving care with which people here protect flora and fauna—one could make a fabulous list of all the evident contradictions in which this new idealism is sinking. But there is here a misunderstanding, and the opposition between chlorophyll and napalm exists only in appearance. In fact, it is the same thing. In Vietnam, the fight is against communist pollution. Here the fight is against water pollution. To lock Indians and black people (in France, Algerians and Portuguese) in reservations and ghettos, that is also a fight against pollution. It is the same logic that organizes all these aspects, the ideological process consisting in disguising in humanistic values some practices (such as the fight against pollution) to oppose them formally to other practices (such as war in Vietnam), which are then considered only as a deplorable reality and an accident. We must clearly see that there is a same policy, a same system of values fundamentally operating here, and that everywhere the established power has always fought against pollution, evidently against the pollution of the establishment itself. This enemy that each of us is invited to hunt and destroy is all that pollutes social order and production order.

It is not true that society is ill, that nature is ill. The therapeutic mythology which tries to convince us that, if things are going wrong, it is due to microbes, to virus, or to some biological dysfunctions, this therapeutic mythology hides the political fact, the historical fact that it is a question of social structures and social contradictions, not a question of illness or deficient metabolism, which could easily be cured. All the designers, the architects, the sociologists who are acting like medicine men toward this ill society are accomplices in this interpretation of the question in terms of illness, which is another form of hoax.

In conclusion, we say that this new environmental and naturistic ideology is the most sophisticated and pseudoscientific form of a naturistic mythology, which has always consisted in transferring the ugly reality of social relations to an idealized model of marvelous nature, to an idealized relationship between man and nature.

Aspen is the Disneyland of environment and design. We are speaking here about universal therapy, about apocalypse in a magic ambiance. But the real problem is far beyond Aspen—it is the entire theory of design and environment itself, which constitutes a generalized Utopia, a Utopia produced by a capitalist system that assumes the appearance of a second *nature* in order to survive and perpetuate itself under the pretext of *nature*.

REQUIEM FOR THE MEDIA

INTROIT

There is no revolutionary theory of the media. The "revolution of the media" has to date remained empirical and mystical, as much in Marshall McLuhan as among those who stand so willfully apart from him (the intelligentsia of the Left in particular). McLuhan himself has said, with his Texo-Canadian brutality, that with the appearance of the telegraph, Marx's theory, a contemporary of the steam engine and the railroad, was already obsolete during his lifetime. In his candid fashion, he is saying that Marx, in his materialist analysis of production, has almost circumscribed a privileged domain of productive forces from which language, signs and communication have been excluded. To tell the truth, Marx does not even have a theory of the railroad as a "medium," as a mode of communication: it isn't considered. All technical evolution in general is only considered under the heading of production—primary, material, infrastructural—the sole determinant of social relationships. Dedicated to an intermediary ideality and a blind social practice, the "mode of communication" has been at leisure for a century to "make its revolution" without changing anything in the theory of production.

From here, and on the condition (which is already a revolution in relation to orthodox Marxism) that the exchange of signs is not considered as a marginal, superstructural dimension among beings that the single true theory (materialist) defines irrevocably as "producers of their real life" (of goods destined to satisfy their needs), we can envision two perspectives:

1. We retain the general form of Marxist analysis (dialectical contradiction between forces of production and relations of production), but we admit that the "classical" definition of productive forces is a restricted definition, and we enlarge our analysis in terms of productive forces to the entire field thus far blind to signification and communication. This implies setting loose in all their originality the contradictions freed from this theoretical and practical extension

of the field of political economy. This hypothesis is the point of departure for Enzensberger in his article in *New Left Review* ("Constituents of a Theory of the Media"): "Monopoly capitalism develops the consciousness shaping industry more quickly and more extensively than other sectors of production; it must at the same time fetter it. A socialist media theory has to work at this contradiction." But this hypothesis accomplishes little more (and, in this sense, it is also late) than to virtually extend the commodity form to every domain of social life. And in fact there already is a "classical" theory of communication, a "bourgeois" political economy of signs and their production, as there came to be one of material production since the eighteenth century. It is a class-bound theoretical discipline.[1] Until now, no fundamental critique, no logical extension of Marx's critique, has responded to it. The critique of the political economy of the sign has been rendered impossible by the relegation of this entire domain to the superstructure. Thus, at best, Enzensberger's hypothesis could only make up for the tremendous delay in classical Marxist theory.

2. This hypothesis is only radical in the eyes of orthodox Marxism, which, completely immersed in the dominant models, and for its own survival, forbids itself even this much. But the radical alternative is elsewhere. In place of reinterpreting the crucial problem posed to revolutionary theory by the production of meanings, messages, and signs in terms of classical productive forces—which is to say of generalizing a Marxist analysis considered to be definitive and sealed with the approval of the "spokesmen of the revolution"—the alternative is to disrupt these terms in light of the irruption of this problem in the theoretical field (which no Marxist who "respects himself" would do, even as a hypothesis).

In other words, maybe the Marxist theory of production is itself irremediably partial, and cannot be generalized. Again: the theory of production (the dialectical continuity of contradictions linked to the development of productive forces) is strictly homogeneous with its object, *material* production, and cannot be transferred, as a postulate or theoretical framework, to contents that it was never given.[2]

1. This political economy of the sign is structural linguistics (along with semiology and all its derivatives, of which communication theory will be discussed below). We know that, in the general ideological framework, structural linguistics is today's master discipline, informing anthropology, the human sciences, etc., just as political economy did in its time; its postulates profoundly informed all of psychology, sociology, and the "moral and political" sciences.

2. In this sense, the expression "consciousness industry" which Enzensberger uses to characterize the present media, is nothing but a dangerous metaphor. It supports his entire analytic hypothesis, which is to extend to the media the Marxist analysis of the capitalist mode of production, to the point of rediscovering a structural analogy in these relations:

dominant class	/	dominated class
producer-entrepreneur	/	consumer
transmitter	/	receiver

The dialectical form is adequate to certain contents, those of material production: it exhausts its meaning, but does not exceed, as an archetype, the definition of this object. The dialectic is in ashes because it offered itself as a system of interpretation for the *separated* order of material production.

This hypothesis is, all in all, logical. It attributes Marxist analysis with a global coherence, an internal homogeneity which forbids it from retaining such and such an element and from excluding such and such an other, according to a technique of *bricolage* of which the Althusserians are the most subtle pyrotechnicians. Conversely, we will give Marxist theory credit for a maximum of coherence, and it is for this same reason that we will say that this coherence should be broken, because it is without response before a social process which far exceeds that of (material) production.[3]

ENZENSBERGER: A "SOCIALIST" STRATEGY

Lacking a theory and an offensive strategy, Enzensberger claims, the "left" remains disarmed. It contents itself with denouncing mass media culture as ideological manipulation. It dreams of taking control of the media, sometimes as a *means* of aiding the masses' assumption of a revolutionary consciousness, sometimes as a *consequence* of a radical change in social structures. A contradictory impulse, which simply reflects the impossibility of integrating the media into a theory of infra- and superstructure. Lacking a conception of the media as new and gigantic, potentially productive forces (Enzensberger), the media (and one should add the entire domain of signs and of communication) remains a social mystery for the "Left": it is split between fascination and panic before this wizardry, which it cannot escape, but which it morally and intellectually reproves (this of course is the "Leftist intellectual" speaking through Enzensberger's self-criticism). This ambivalence reflects only the ambivalence of the media, without surpassing or reducing it. As a good

3. In fact, Marxist analysis can be questioned on two very different levels of radicality: insofar as it is a system of interpretation for the separated order of material production and insofar as it is a system of interpretation for the separated order of production (in general).

In the first case, the hypothesis of the non-pertinence of the dialectic outside the field of its "origin" should logically be extended: if the "dialectical" contradictions between productive forces and relations of production largely efface themselves in the field of language, signs and ideology—*maybe they have never truly been at work in the field of material production either*, since a certain capitalist development of productive forces was able to absorb them, not every conflict, of course, but the revolutionary antagonisms at the level of social relations. What is, therefore, the validity of these concepts, if not a purely conceptual coherence?

In the second case, it is at the root itself (and not in its diverse contents) that the concept of production should be questioned, with the separated form that it institutes, with the schema of representation and of rationalization that it imposes. It is undoubtedly there, at the extreme, that one must go.

Marxist sociologist, Enzensberger imputes the "phobia" of the Leftist intellectuals and movements to their bourgeois or petit-bourgeois origins: they defend themselves instinctively against mass culture because it shatters their cultural privilege.[4] True or false, maybe it would be better to ask what responsibility the intelligentsia of the Left have in this fascinated contempt, this tactical disarray, and this refusal of investment before the media. Precisely what responsibility Marxist prejudice, its nostalgic idealism of the infrastructure, its theoretical allegiance to everything that is not "material" production and "productive labor." "Revolutionary" doctrine has never accounted for the exchange of signs other than in functional use: information, diffusion, propaganda. And the current, new look in public relations material, the entire modernist subculture of Leftist parties is not made to break this tendency: it shows well enough how bourgeois ideology can pass elsewhere only through "social origin."

All this results, following Enzensberger, in the political schizophrenia of the Left. On one side, an entire revolutionary (subversive) faction launches itself in the apolitical exploration of the new media (subculture, underground). On another side, the "militant" political groups still live essentially with archaic modes of communication, refusing to "play the game," to exploit the gigantic virtualities of electronic media. They reproach the students of May '68 for having had recourse to traditional artist's means (Beaux-Arts) for the diffusion of their slogans, and for having occupied the Odéon, a cultural capital, rather than the ORTF. [ORTF: French radio and television headquarters. *Trans.*]

Enzensberger's thought attempts to be optimistic and offensive. The media are currently under the monopoly of the dominant classes, which turn them toward their profit. But their *structure* remains "fundamentally egalitarian" and it falls to revolutionary practice to release the virtuality inscribed in them but perverted by the capitalist order—saying the word: to liberate them, to return them to their social *vocation* of open communication and unlimited democratic exchange, to their true socialist destination.

It is clear that this is a question of the extension of the same schema forever allotted, from Marx to Marcuse, to productive forces and technology. They are the promise of human accomplishment, but capitalism blocks and confiscates them. They are liberators, but we must liberate them.[5] The media, one sees, do not escape the fantastic

4. One finds this type of reductive determinism in Bourdieu and in the phraseology of the Communist Party. It is without theoretical value. It makes of the *mechanism* of democratization a revolutionary *value* in itself. That the intellectuals repudiate mass culture does not suffice to make a revolutionary alternative. The aristocrats frown on bourgeois culture in the same way: this never sufficed to make the latter anything but a class culture.

5. Thus the institutions of power and of the state according to whether they are in the grip of capital or if the people have taken them over, empty themselves or are filled with revolutionary content, without their form ever being interrogated.

logic of the filigreed inscription of the revolution in things. To hand the media over to the logic of productive forces is thus no longer a critical act: it more firmly encloses them in revolutionary metaphysics.

As usual, this position is lost in contradictions. On one side, though their own (capitalist) development even assures a more and more extended socialization—even though it should be technically thinkable, there is no closed circuit television for the happy few, "because this would go against the grain of the structure" of the medium. "For the first time in history, the media make possible the participation of the masses in a collective process that is social and socialized, participation in which the practical means are in the hands of the masses themselves." But the "socialist movements must fight and will fight for their own wavelengths." Why fight (in particular for wavelengths), if the media realize socialism on their own? If this is their structural vocation?

Enzensberger claims, following Brecht (*The Radio as an Apparatus of Communication*, 1932), that the present order reduces the media to a simple "medium of distribution." We need to make the media a veritable medium of communication (the same dream always haunts the Marxist imagination: to tear objects from exchange value and return them to their use value), and this transformation, he adds, "is not technically a problem." But:

1. It is false that the media in the current order are "purely and simply a means of distribution." Here again, this makes them the relay of an ideology which would find its determination elsewhere (in the material mode of production). In other words, the media as marketing and merchandising of the dominant ideology—in which there is the assimilation of the employer-employee relationship with that of the producer-transmitter of the media—to irresponsible receptive masses. This is not as a vehicle of contents, it is in their form and their operation even that the media induce a social relationship, and this relationship is not exploitative, it is one of abstraction, of separation, of the abolition of exchange. The media are not coefficients but conductors of ideology. Not only are they not revolutionary in destination, they are not even, elsewhere or virtually, neutral or nonideological (the phantasms of their "technical" status or of their social "use value"). Reciprocally, ideology no longer exists somewhere else as a discourse of the dominant class before being invested in the media. It is the same in the sphere of commodities: nowhere do they possess some other status as reality (the "use value of the product") other than the form they assume in the operation of the system of exchange value. And ideology is no longer some imaginary floating in the wake of exchange value, it is itself the operation of exchange value. After the Requiem for the Dialectic, we should sound the Requiem for the Infra- and for the Superstructure.

2. It follows that when Brecht and Enzensberger affirm that the transformation of the media into a veritable medium of communication is not technically a problem ("it is" Brecht claims, "but the natural consequence of their development"), one must understand in effect (but conversely and without playing on words) that it is not exactly a technical problem, since the ideology of the media is on the level of form, of the separation that they institute, and which is a social division.

SPEECH WITHOUT RESPONSE

The mass media are characterized by being intransitive, anti-mediators, manufacturing noncommunication—if one accepts the definition of communication as an *exchange*, as the reciprocal space of speech and response, and therefore of a *responsibility*; not a psychological and moral responsibility, but a personal correlation from one to another in exchange. In other words, if one defines communication as something other than the simple transmission-reception of information which could be reversed in feedback. The entirety of contemporary media architecture is founded on this definition: *the media forbid response forever*; they make every process of exchange impossible (excepting in the form of the *simulation* of a response, itself integrated into the process of transmission, which doesn't change the unilaterality of the communication in any way). This is their true abstraction. And the system of social control and power is based on this abstraction.

To clearly understand the term *response*, one must understand it in the strong sense, and for this one must refer to its equivalent in "primitive" societies: power belongs to the one who can give and *to whom one cannot respond*. To give, and to do it in such a way that one cannot respond, is to disrupt the exchange to one's profit and to institute a monopoly. The social process becomes unbalanced. Response, on the contrary, disrupts this power relationship and institutes (or restores), on the basis of an antagonistic reciprocity, the circuit of symbolic exchange. The sphere of the media is the same: it speaks and *no response can be made*. This is why the only revolution in this domain—and everywhere besides, the revolution as such—is in the restitution of the possibility of response. This simple possibility presupposes the overturning of the current structure of the media in its entirety.

No other theory or strategy is possible. Every impulse to democratize its contents, to subvert it, to restore the "transparency of the code," to control the process of information, to manage a reversibility of the circuits, or to assume power over the media, is hopeless if the monopoly of speech is not broken; and this not to offer it individually to each of us but so that it can be exchanged, given and responded to,[6] as one would a look and a smile now and then, and without ever being able to be stopped, clogged, stockpiled and redistributed to some place in the social trial.[7]

For the moment, we live in nonresponse, in irresponsibility. "Minimal autonomous activity on the part of the spectator and voter," says Enzensberger. The first and most beautiful of the mass media is in effect the electoral system: its crowning achievement is the referendum, in which the response is implied in the question, as in polls. It is a speech which responds to itself through the simulated detour of a response, and there again, the absolutization of the speech beneath the formal mask of exchange is the definition of power. Roland Barthes points to the same nonreciprocity in literature: "Our literature is characterized by the pitiless divorce which the literary institution maintains between the producer of the text and its user, between its owner and customer, between its author and reader. This reader is thereby plunged into a kind of idleness—he is intransitive; he is, in short, *serious*: instead of functioning, instead of gaining access to the magic of the signifier, to the pleasure of writing, he is left with no more than the poor freedom either to accept or reject the text: reading is nothing more than a *referendum*" (Roland Barthes, *S/Z*). Today, the status of *consumer* defines this relegation, and the general order of consumption is nothing other than that wherein it is no longer permitted to give, to respond or exchange, but only to take and to use (appropriation, individualized use value). In this sense, "consumer" goods are also a mass medium. They answer to the general form we have described. Their specific function is of little importance: the consumption of products and messages is the abstract social relation that they establish, the taboo cast on every form of response and reciprocity.

Thus it is not true, as Enzensberger affirms, that "for the first time in history, the media make possible a mass participation in a production social process," nor that "the practical means of this participation are in the hands of the masses themselves." As if owning a television or a camera inaugurated a new possibility of relation and exchange! Strictly speaking, no more than owning a refrigerator or a toaster does. There is no response to a functional object: its function is there, integrated speech to which it has already responded, and which leaves no place for play, for a reciprocal gesture (except for its destruction or

6. This is not a question of "dialogue," which is never anything but the functional adjustment of two abstract speeches without response, wherein the two "interlocutors" are never present one to the other, but only their stylized speech.

7. We can see that taking the ORTF in May '68 would have changed nothing in itself, other than to scuttle the ORTF as such: the entire technical and functional structure of it reflects the monopolistic use of speech.

for turning it away from its function).[8] The functional object, like all messages made functional by the media, like the operation of the referendum, therefore controls rupture, the emergence of meaning, and censorship. At the limit, if the authorities are not also obsessed with contents and convinced by the media's force of ideological persuasion, and therefore of the necessity of controlling messages, they would offer each citizen a television without concern for its programs. It is effectively useless to fantasize about the police appropriating television for the authorities (Orwell *1984*): Television is, in its mere presence, a social contract at home. It is unnecessary to conceive of it as a spyglass of the regime into our private lives, because it is better than that: it is *the certainty that the people will no longer speak*, that they are definitively isolated before a speech without response.

Such is the structure of television as a mass medium. And, in this sense, McLuhan, whom Enzensberger contemptuously characterizes as a ventriloquist, is much closer to a theory when he says that "the medium is the message" (except that, totally blind to the social form we are discussing, he exalts the media and their planetary message with a delirious tribal optimism). "The medium is the message" is not a critical proposition, but, in its paradoxical form, it has analytical value. Enzensberger's ingenuity on the "structural nature of the media" (!),[9] such that "no power can permit the liberation of their potentiality," on the other hand and although it wants to be revolutionary, is only mysticism: the mystique of the socialist predestination of the media, inverse but complementary to the Orwellian myth of their terroristic manipulation by the authorities. Even God would approve of socialism: the Christians say so.

SUBVERSIVE STRATEGY AND "SYMBOLIC ACTION"

One might object that the mass media played a role in May '68 by spontaneously amplifying the revolutionary movement. At one moment at least during the action, they were (involuntarily) turned against the authorities. The subversive strategy of the American Yippies (Hoffman, Rubin) is based on this necessity and this possible redirection. In worldwide revolutionary movements, a theory of "symbolic action" has been elaborated from it.

8. Multifunctionality evidently changes nothing here. Multifunctionality, pluridisciplinarity, polyvalence in all its forms are the responses of the system to its own obsession with centrality and uni-equivalence. They are reactions of the system to its own pathology, but they leave its logic untouched.

9. Enzensberger interprets it in this way: "'Medium is the message' is a *bourgeois* proposition. It signifies that the bourgeoisie has nothing left to say. Having no further message to transmit, it plays the card of medium for medium's sake. If the bourgeoisie has nothing left to say, 'socialism' would do better to keep quiet."

Redirect the media through their ability to chain react. Use their power to generalize information instantaneously. The assumption here is that the impact of the media is reversible, that it is a variable in the class struggle that one must know how to integrate to one's profit. This must be questioned; it might be only a large strategic illusion.

May '68 can serve as an example. Everything would lead us to believe in the subversive impact of the media during that period. Suburban radio stations and newspapers echoed the student actions everywhere. If the actions were the detonator, the media were the resonator. The authorities accused them directly of "playing the revolutionary game." But this evidence was based on an absence of analysis. I would say on the contrary that the media never played their role so well and that they were, in their function of *habitual* social control, on top of the events. This was because they maintained their *form* (amid the disruption of their contents) and that this form, no matter the context, makes them inexorably in solidarity with the power structure. By diffusing the event in the *abstract universality* of public opinion, they *imposed* a sudden and inordinate development on it and, through this forced and anticipated extension, they deprived the original movement of its rhythm and its meaning—in a word: they short-circuited it.

In the traditional field of politics (Left and Right),[10] where sanctified models of canonical speech are exchanged, the media transmit without altering the meaning. They are as homogeneous to this speech as they are to the circulation of commodities. But transgression and subversion don't pass over the waves while being subtly denied as such: transformed into *models*, neutralized as *signs*, they are emptied of their meaning.[11] There is no model, prototype, or series of transgression. It is therefore still the best way to reduce them. Fatal publicity is still the best way to lessen the impact of transgression. Earlier, this operation might have led us to believe in "spectacular" results. In fact, it is equal to dismantling the movement by removing its primary impulse. The act of rupture is

10. This distinction has no meaning in relation to the media. We can give them credit for having largely contributed to its effacement. The distinction is linked with an order characterized by the *transcendence* of politics, and it has nothing to do with what is announced in many forms as the *transversality* of politics. But we should not be fooled: the media only contribute to the liquidation of the transcendence of politics so as to substitute their own transcendence, that abstraction of the form of the mass media that is definitively integrated and offers nothing more than the structure of conflict (Left/Right). Transcendence in the mass media is therefore a reduction of the traditional transcendence of politics, but it is still much more than the new transversality of politics.

11. This form of "exposure" or "propagation" is also to be found in the fields of science and art. Generalized reproducibility obliterates the process of work and of meaning so as to deliver contents as a model of itself (cf. *Diogène* nº 68 [1969]; Raoul Ergmann, *Le miroir en miettes*; Baudouin Jurdant, *La vulgarisation scientifique*).

changed into a distant bureaucratic model—and this is what the media does.[12]

All of this is readable in the derivation, the distortion of the term "symbolic." The action of March 22nd at Nanterre was symbolic and transgressive because, at that moment in that place, it invented a radical rupture or, returning to the analysis proposed above, invented a *response* there, where the administrative and pedagogical power of the institution held forth and kept others from speaking. The broadcast and contagion of the mass media did not make this action symbolic. Today, however, it is more and more this last sense (the impact of exposure) which suffices to define symbolic action. At the limit, the subversive act is no longer produced *save as a function of its reproducability.*[13] It is no longer created, it is produced directly as a model, like a gesture. The symbolic has slipped from the order of the production of meaning even (political or otherwise) to the order of its reproduction, which is always that of power. The symbolic becomes *coefficient*, pure and simple; transgression becomes exchange value.

The entirety of rationalist critical thought (Benjamin, Brecht, Enzensberger) sees decisive progress in this. The media does nothing but actualize and reinforce the "demonstrative nature of any given political act" (Enzensberger). This evidently agrees with the *didactic* conception of the revolution, and, moreover, with the "dialectic of consciousness rising," etc. This rationalist thought has not renounced the bourgeois thought of the Enlightenment, it inherits all of its conceptions of the democratic virtue (here revolutionary) of the diffusion of knowledge. In its pedogogic illusion, this thought forgets that—the political act deliberately targeting the media and expecting power from it—the media itself is deliberately targeting the political act to depoliticize it. An interesting fact might be cited here as support: the contemporary eruption of news in the political

12. We should note that this labor always doubles a work of selection and of reinterpretation at the level of group adherence (Lazarfeld's *two-step flow of communication*). Hence the highly relative pregnancy of the contents of the media and the multiple resistances that it provokes. (We should ask ourselves, however, if these resistances intend, even more than the contents, toward the abstraction of the media itself: in this sense, Lazarfeld's double articulation would, since the second articulation is a network of *personal* relations, be opposed to the generality of the media's messages.) Significantly, we have this "second" reading, wherein group membership opposes its own code to that of the transmitters (cf. Umberto Eco's thesis, discussed below), not to neutralize it, to "reduce" its dominant ideological contents in the same way as critical or subversive contents. To the extent that the first (cultural models, systems of imposed values without alternative or response, bureaucratic contents) are homogeneous with the general mass mediated form (nonreciprocal, irresponsibility) and integrate themselves therein through redoubling, there is as an effect of overdetermination and therefore a pregnancy greater than the dominant ideological contents. This "passes" better than the subversive *contents*. But it is not essential. It must be recognized that the form of transgression does not pass "more or less"; it is radically denied by the form of the mass media.

13. For Walter Benjamin, in "The Work of Art in the Age of Mechanical Reproduction," the reproduced work becomes increasingly "designed for reproduction." For Benjamin, therefore, the work passes from ritual to "politics." The "exhibition value" revolutionizes the work of art and its functions.

sphere (which converges with Benjamin's idea of the passage of the work of art from the political stage through its reproducability). A tidal wave in Pakistan, a black boxing match in the United States, a bistro owner shoots a youth, etc. These kinds of events, once minor and apolitical, find themselves invested with a power of diffusion which gives them social and "historic" scope. Undoubtedly the new sense that they assume, the confrontation of incidents that never before made the news, and in which the new forms of politics are crystallized, is to a large extent created by the media. These news items are unplanned "symbolic actions," which return through the same process of political signification. Doubtless, their reception can only be ambiguous, and if, thanks to the media, politics returns under the heading of minor news items, thanks to the same media, minor news items invade politics. Elsewhere the status of the news has changed with the extension of the mass media: from parallel category (related to almanacs and popular histories) it has become a social system of mythological interpretation, a tight network of models of signification from which no event escapes. This is mass mediatization. It is not a group of technologies for the diffusion of messages, it is the imposition of models. Here again is McLuhan's formula: "Medium is the message" performs a transfer of meaning in the medium itself as a technological structure. This is still technological idealism. In fact, the great *Medium* is the Model. That which is mediated is not that which passes through the press, the TV, the radio: it is that which is fulfilled by the form-sign, articulated in models, regulated by the code. Similarly, commodities are not produced industrially, they are mediated by the exchange value system of abstraction. One sees that at best what functions under the sign of the media is the formal surpassing of the categories of news and politics and of their traditional separation, so as to more easily assign them together to the same general code. It is strange that we never wanted to measure the strategic impact of this forced socialization as a system of social control. Once more, the electoral system is the first great historical example of this. And it has never lacked revolutionaries (once among the greatest, today the least significant) who believed themselves capable of "playing the game." The general strike itself, an insurrectional myth for so many generations, has become a reductive schema. That of May '68, to which the media contributed largely by exporting the strike to every corner of France, while apparently the culminating point of the crisis, was in fact the moment of its decompression, of its asphyxiation through extension, of its defeat. Of course, thousands of workers went on strike. But they didn't know what to do with this "mediatized" strike, transmitted and received as a model of action (by both the media or the unions). Abstract in a sense, it neutralized local, transversal, and spontaneous forms of action (not entirely). The Grenelle accords didn't betray it.

They sanctioned the passage to the generality of political action, which brought an end to the singularity of revolutionary action. Today, it has become (in the form of the calculated extension of the strike) the final weapon of the unions against wildcat strikes.

The electoral system and the general strike are thus also media of a certain kind. Playing with extensive, formal socialization, they are the subtlest and most assured institutions for filtration, dismantling, and censorship. There is no exception nor miracle.

Walls and words, silk-screen posters, and hand-printed flyers were the true revolutionary media in May, the streets where speech started and was exchanged: everything that is an *immediate* inscription, given and returned, speech and response, moving in the same time and in the same place, reciprocal and antagonistic. The street in this sense is the alternative and subversive form of all the mass media because it is not, like them, an objectified support for messages without response, a distant transit network. It is the cleared space of the symbolic exchange of ephemeral and mortal speech, speech that is not reflected on the Platonic screen of the media. Institutionalized by reproduction, spectacularized by the media, it burst.

It is therefore a strategic illusion to believe in a critical reversal [*détournement*] of the media. Today such speech passes through the *destruction* of the media such as they are, through their deconstruction as systems of noncommunication. This does not imply liquidation any more than the radical critique of discourse implies the negation of language as signifying material. But this certainly implies the liquidation of their present functional and technical structure as a whole, of their operational form, if I can put it that way, which reflects their social form throughout. At the limit, of course, even the concept of the medium disappears, and should disappear: exchanged speech, reciprocal and symbolic exchange denies the notion and the function of the medium, of the intermediary. It can imply a technical apparatus (sound, image, waves, energy, etc.) as well as a corporeal apparatus (gestures, language, sexuality), but this no longer acts as a medium, as an autonomous system regulated by a code. Reciprocity passes through the destruction of the medium as such. “People meet their neighbors for the first time while watching their apartment houses burn down.” (Jerry Rubin, *Do It.*)

THE THEORETICAL MODEL OF COMMUNICATION

To summarize these diverse hypotheses:

1. McLuhan (remember): the media create, they are the revolution, independently from their contents, from their singular technological structure. After the phonetic alphabet and

books, radio and cinema. After radio, television. Here and now we live in the era of instantaneous, global communication.

2. The media are controlled by power. We must tear them away from it, either by taking power ourselves, or by reversing them by raising the spectacular stakes through subversive content. Here the media are viewed only as a message. There is no question of their form (any more than there is, of course, in McLuhan, who views the medium only as a medium).

3. Enzensberger: the present form of the media induces a certain type of social relationship (assimilated into that of the capitalist mode of production). But through their structure and their development, the media possess the virtuality of a socialist and democratic mode of communication, of a rationality and a universality of information. Liberating their potential will suffice.

From the perspective of a revolutionary strategy, only Enzensberger's (Enlightened—Marxist) hypothesis and that of the radical American left (spectacular—Leftist) interests us (we are not talking about the practice of the official Left, Marxist or not, which is confused with that of the bourgeoisie). We have analyzed these positions as strategic illusions, the cause being that both of them share with the dominant ideology implicit reference to the same *theory of communication*, a theory admitted everywhere, on the strength of received evidence and a highly "scientific" formalization by a discipline, the semio-linguistics of communication, applied to structural linguistics on one side and infomatics on the other, endorsed by the universities and mass culture (mass media professionals are its connoisseurs). The entire conceptual infrastructure of this theory is ideologically in solidarity with the dominant practice, as it was and still is to classical political economy. It *is* the equivalent of that bourgeois political economy in the field of communication. And I think that if revolutionary practices remain bound to the strategic illusion of the media, it is because they have never made anything more than a superficial critical analysis of it, without carrying out a radical critique of the ideological matrix of its theory of communication.

Formalized most specifically by Jakobson, its basic unity is provided by the sequence:

transmitter — message — receiver
(encoder — message — decoder)

The message itself being structured by the code and determined by the context. To each of these "concepts" corresponds a specific function: referential, poetic, phatic, etc. Each communicative process is thus vectorized in a single sense, from the transmitter to the receiver. The receiver can become a transmitter in turn, the same schema repeats itself. Communication can always be reduced to this simple unity where the two polar terms are never exchanged. This structure is offered as objective and scientific, since it follows the rules of the method: it breaks its object down into parts. In fact, it contents itself with formalizing an empirical given, abstracting the evidence and lived reality. This is to say that the ideological categories through which a certain kind of social relationship speak, precisely that wherein one speaks and the other does not, wherein one chooses the code and the other has the sole freedom to submit or abstain. This structure is based on the same arbitrariness as signification: two terms are artificially isolated and artificially reunited by an objectivized content called a message. There is no reciprocal relation nor presence of one to the other of these terms,[14] since both are determined in isolation in their relationship to the message and the code, an "intermedium" which maintains both of them in a respective situation (the code holds both of them in "respect"), distanced from one another, a distance which comes to fulfill the full and automated "value" of the message (in fact: its exchange value). This "scientific" construction institutes a *model of simulation* of communication from which reciprocity, the antagonism of the partners, or the ambivalence of their exchange is immediately excluded. What effectively circulates is information, content in the supposedly readable and univocal sense. The authority of the code guarantees this univocality, and thereby even the respective positions of the encoder and the decoder. So far so good: the formula has a formal coherence which assures it is the only *possible* schema of communication. But if one suggests an ambivalent relation, it all falls apart. Because there is no code for ambivalence. Without a code, no encoder or decoder: the extras flee the stage. No message either, since the message is defined as "sent" and "received." The entire formalization is only there to avoid this catastrophe. Therein lies its "scientificity." In fact, it establishes the terrorism of the code. In this directive schema, the code becomes the sole authority which speaks, which exchanges itself and reproduces itself through the dissociation of the two terms and the univocality (or the equivocality, or the multivocality, it hardly matters: through the nonambivalence) of the message. (Similarly, in the economic process of exchange, people no longer exchange, the system of exchange value reproduces itself through people.) This formula at the basis of communication succeeds in offering, as a reduced model, a perfect shortcut for social exchange *as it is*, as in every case the abstraction of the code, forced rationalism, and the terrorism of separation regulate it. Such is the objectivity of science.

14. The two terms are so minimally present, one to the other, that it is necessary to create the category of "contact" to theoretically reconstitute the group!

Separation and closure: it is already the same schema active at the level of the sign in linguistic theory. Each sign is divided into a signifier and a signified, assigned to one or the other, but in a "respective" position, and each sign on the basis of its arbitrary isolation "communicates" with all the others through a code called language. There too, the scientific taboo is cast on the terms' potentiality for symbolic exchange, beyond the signifier-signified distinction, in poetic language for example. In poetic language, as in symbolic exchange, the terms *respond* to one another beyond the code. We have indicated this response throughout this text as deconstructive to every code, every control, every power, which, inversely, is always based on the separation of terms and their abstract articulation.

Thus the theory of signification serves as a nuclear model for the theory of communication, and the arbitrariness of the sign (this theoretical schema for the repression of meaning) assumes all its political and ideological scope in the arbitrariness of the theoretical schema of communication and information.[15] Which, as we have seen, echoes not only in the dominant social practice (characterized by the virtual monopoly of the pole of the transmitter and the irresponsibility of the pole of the receiver, the discrimination between the terms of the exchange and the *diktat* of the code) but also, unconsciously, through all the velleities of a revolutionary media practice. It is clear, for example, that everyone who aims to subvert media contents can only reinforce, in its autonomy, the separated notion of the message and therefore the abstract bipolarity of the terms of communication.

THE CYBERNETIC ILLUSION

Sensitive to the nonreciprocity of the current process, Enzensberger believes this can be helped by demanding that the same revolution intervene at the level of the media as that which disrupted the exact sciences and the subject/object relation of understanding, which has been engaged in a continual "dialectical" inter-reaction ever since. The media would have to take into account all the consequences of the inter-reaction, whose effect is to break the monopoly and to permit everyone's integration into an open process. "The programs of the consciousness industry

15. The developed form of this opens logically onto analysis in terms of classical political economy. In *La communciation de masse* (S.G.P.P, 1971), Burgelin discusses mass communication as a "*market* of messages," repeating all the schemas of liberal economy: competition, offer and demand, equilibrium, needs and consumer "choice," etc. This is the *unchanged* extension of bourgeois political economy, just as Enzensberger extends *unchanged* the critique of that political economy.

must subsume into themselves their own results, the reactions and corrections that they call forth… they are therefore to be thought of not as means of consumption but as means of their own production." This seductive perspective:

1. leaves the separated authority of the code and the message intact;

2. attempts, on the other hand, to break the discrimination of the two poles of communication, toward a more supple structure of the exchange of roles and feedback ("reversibility of circuits"). "In its present form, equipment like television or film does not serve communication but prevents it. It allows no reciprocal action between transmitter and receiver; technically speaking it reduces feedback to the lowest point compatible with the system." There again, we fail to surpass the categories of "transmitter" and "receiver," despite the effort to mobilize them through "switching." *Reversibility* has nothing to do with reciprocity. Undoubtedly, for this profound reason, today cybernetic systems understand very well how to put this complex regulation, this feedback, to work without changing anything about the abstraction of the process as a whole, or allowing any real "responsibility" into the exchange. This is even the systems' best defense, since it thereby integrates in advance the possibility of such a response.

One can no longer effectively conceive, as Enzensberger shows in his critique of the Orwellian myth, a mega-system of centralized control (a control system for the current telephone system would have to surpass it *n* times in complexity, and is therefore excluded practically). But it is a little naïve to think that censorship should be eliminated though the extension of the media. Even in the long term, the impossibility of police mega-structures simply signifies that the current systems integrate within themselves, through feedback and self-regulation, these henceforth useless mega-systems of control. They know how to introduce that which denies them *as a supplementary variable*. There is censorship in their operation itself; they don't need a mega-structure. They never cease from being totalitarian: they realize in some way the ideal of what we can call a decentralized totalitarianism.

At a more practical level, the media also know very well how to put in place a formal "reversibility" of circuits (letters from readers, listener call-ins, polls, etc.), without leaving room for any response, without changing the discrimination of the roles.[16] This is the social and political form of feedback. Enzensberger is therefore always, in his "dialecticalization" of communication so strangely proximate to

16. Here again, Enzensberger, who analyzes and denounces this integration of control circuits, meanwhile connects with this incorrigible idealism: "Naturally [!] such tendencies go against the grain of the structure, and the new productive forces not only permit, but indeed demand [!] their reversal"(108). Feedback and interaction are the *logic* of cybernetics, and there is the same illusion in underestimating the possibilities of the system for integrating these "revolutionary" innovations as in underestimating the capacity of capitalism to develop the forces of production.

cybernetic regulation, a victim, though in a more subtle way, of the ideological model we are discussing.

From the same perspective, breaking the unilaterality of communication, which translates itself at once into the monopoly of specialists and professionals and that of the class enemy over the media, Enzensberger proposes as a revolutionary solution that *each of us become a manipulator*, in the sense of an active operator, an editor, etc., in short, pass from the status of receiver to that of producer-transmitter. Therein is a kind of critical reversal [*détournement*] of the ideological concept of manipulation. But here again, because this "revolution" retains as its basis the category of "transmitter," it is content to generalize as separated, making each of us his or her own transmitter; it fails to check the mass media. If each of us possessed his or her own walkie-talkie or Kodak, and made his or her own films, we know what would result: personalized amateurism, the equivalent of Sunday *bricolage* on the periphery of the system.[17]

This is evidently not what Enzensberger wants. He is thinking of a newspaper edited, distributed, created by its own readers (as *Underground* was in part), of video networks for the use of political groups, etc.

This would be the sole means to unfreeze a blocked situation: "In the socialist movements, the dialectic of discipline and spontaneity, centralism and decentralization, authoritarian leadership and anti-authoritarian disintegration long ago reached a deadlock. Network-like communications models built on the principle of reversibility of circuits might give new indications of how to overcome the situation." This is a question of restoring a dialectical practice. But can the problem continue to be posed in dialectical terms? Is the dialectic itself dead at this point? The examples he gives are interesting in that they surpass a "dialectic" of transmitter and receiver. One finds in effect a process of immediate communication, not filtered by bureaucratic models; an original form of exchange, in fact, because there are *not transmitters and receivers*, but people who *respond*. The problem of spontaneity and of organization is not surpassed dialectically here; its terms are *transgressed*.

That is the essential difference. The other hypotheses leave the separated categories to subsist. In the first case (the private demultiplication of the media), transmitter and receiver are simply reunited in a single person: manipulation is in some way "internalized."[18] In

17. Enzensberger draws his argument from the fact that Xerox retains its monopoly on photocopying (the possibility of general "free press") and only rents at exorbitant rates. But having our own Xerox or short wave-length is inessential. The true monopoly is never that of technical means but that of speech.

18. This is why the *individual* amateur cameraman remains in the separated abstraction of mass communication. Through this internal dissociation between the two authorities, the entire code and all of the dominant models engulf and seize his practice.

the other case (the "dialectic of circuits"), transmitter and receiver are simultaneously the two sides: manipulation becomes reciprocal (hermaphroditic combination). The system can act on its two tableaux at the same time as on the classical bureaucratic model, and in every possible combination of the two categories. What is essential is that these ideological categories should be saved, and with them the fundamental structure of the political economy of communication.

Once again, in the relationship of symbolic exchange, there is a simultaneous response, there is neither transmitter nor receiver for one part and another of a message, nor is there any longer a "message," a *corpus* of information to decipher in a univocal way under the auspices of the code. The symbolic consists precisely in breaking the univocality of the "message," or restoring the ambivalence of meaning, and eliminating in the same blow the authority of the code.

This can help us evaluate Umberto Eco's hypothesis. Briefly stated: changing the contents of the message changes nothing, one must modify the reading codes, impose other reading codes. The receiver (who in fact is not one) intervenes here essentially, he opposes his own code on that of the transmitter, he invents a veritable response escaping the trap of directed communication. But in what way is this reader "subversive"? Is this still reading, in the sense of deciphering, the recovery of an univocal meaning? And what is the code that he opposes? Is it a singular mini-code (ideological, but without interest) or another schema directing reading? In which case it is only a question of textual variation. An example might illustrate Eco's perspective: the reversal [*détournement*] of advertising with graffiti after May '68. It's transgressive not because it substitutes another content, another discourse, but because it responds, there, in place, and breaks the fundamental rule of all media, nonresponse. Does it oppose a code with another code? I don't think so: it simply breaks the code. It does not offer itself as a text to be deciphered alongside the advertising discourse. It lets itself be seen as transgression. Hence the slogan, the transgressive reversal of discourse, does not act by means of another code, as a code, it acts by means of the instantaneous deconstruction of the dominant discursive code. It volatilizes the category of the code and that of the message.

Therein lies the key to the problem: wanting to conserve (even by "dialectically surpassing") *any of the separated instances of the structural communication grid*, one forbids oneself from changing anything fundamentally, and condemns oneself to fragile manipulatory practices, that it would be dangerous to mistake for a "revolutionary strategy." In this sense, only that which radically checks the dominant form is strategic.

† REQUIESÇANT MEDIA IN PACE

J. B.

CODICIL

When the necrophagic practices of revolutionaries parasite so effectively the great principles of bourgeois order, we have to wonder whether they draw their whole determination from it. What, then, is the death of a revolutionary? The fact recently abstracted from the gigantic construction of an event is clear about this.

"They" were the ones who killed; that is the scandal, while we, revolutionaries, jump into the deadly fray and know it, an executive in danger dares to legitimately gun down a revolutionary in action. It is not a question of accepting this as a sort of normality, but of asserting that there is nothing to be surprised about, which implies acknowledging the fact that revolutionary action also leads to the destruction of the body. But it is the fact that this surprises us that is surprising, although we are only manipulating death. It is not a matter of grieving over the body or pointing fingers at the terrible torturers, but of knowing what the inclusion of sudden death implies in the political context, and what revolution does with death in general

For deaths appear every day in *France-Soir*: brutal, but not tragic; maids stabbed for cheating on their lovers, unemployed fathers kill their children *in front of* their wives and then cut their throats, children are burned by or in stoves, men die after having downed twenty-four cognacs in a beer glass on a bet, burglars shot in cold blood by miserly shopkeepers. It is precisely with cold deaths such as these, rejected from social practice, and therefore surprising, that the dailies fatten their headlines.

It was not Overney's political tenor that made such a good corpse of him, but the way in which he was killed: an incongruous shot in a place where one usually died only by degrees, and the unexpected eruption of the uncontrollable on the terrain of politics. The radical violence of so public a death disrupts the traditional framework of politics; to reduce it to a political event simply replaces the decor.

The spirit of the times stepped into the picture, destiny worked overtime; destiny always manifests itself when a life is considered guilty—in fact, a life that was already condemned became culpable as a result. All of these guilty lives are incarnated one day in a death. A day, a bar, or a fine political event at La Courneuve; forgotten as soon as the parade has passed. On another day there is a nice corpse on the Ile Seguin. The dead are daily fare.

Everything seems to depend on the treatment of death. This one was manifested as a political will to coalition, and it succeeded where all the great political issues had failed miserably—which is already a

judgment on the organizations. Is it its proximity? A death in front of our very eyes! But it is obvious that "we" don't care any more for the dead than the bourgeoisie does for the faraway soldiers who shed their blood for its sake. Of course, there is no kingdom of God anymore! Nowadays, we die for nothing afterwards; death is the end of life. Once cold and lain to rest, we put the matter into a coffin and then into the ground, no matter how it died. Death no longer has any life.

While death is completely suppressed in bourgeois Christian consciousness, revolutionaries wallow in this basic taboo with the exhilaration of vampires who need the dead for their survival. The cult of the dead inscribes death into a communal practice of the living, ensuring them of the concreteness of their lives. It protects them from their mortality by definitively separating the dead from the living. This cautious procedure may not keep anyone from dying—yet death is always a contingency of life in this sense—but it does give the life that expresses itself a claim to permanence. To honor the dead means in a way to ensure the survival of honor and its hideous procession of moral values. All established governments, all declining heads of State on the decline make it a favorite practice.

The magnificence of funerals consecrates the exceptionality of the Event, marking the total separation of death from life. It is through the rational subterfuge of kinship that eternity is guaranteed, the unbroken chain of generations, hand in hand, reduces the course of time, of destiny, of all that is uncontrollable, into an economy of the future.

As for the past, it is in the wrong; the absent are always in the wrong. The ceremony that accompanies the manner in which we get rid of the dead in bourgeois society clearly shows that it is a matter of warding off a curse: the principle of evil that led the deceased to abandon the world of the living. And when it is a case of violent death, the horror is such that only the weight of a collective process can suppress the eruption of the evil forces of destruction. Shut in a box, surrounded by propitiatory rites, put in memory's reserve, there can only be one place for the dead in the social game: that of death. Death can only be dead for a bourgeois society, where whatever is flawed enough to perish loses the value that justified its existence, or takes on the value of death. The times are long gone when one could be submitted to the Question, drawn and quartered, left to die on the stake, and then still be hanged; so that a sentence could be executed in full, as if in death one were present, recognized, and still active. There is a world of difference between this and our heroes fallen on the field of honor and immediately excluded, embalmed, reified, abstracted like so many signs of revolutionary martyrdom. Also long gone is the time of the nocturnal stroll of the corpses by common people of 1848, who, come morning, would perish so that what we call the revolution of forty-eight could be born. By playing the game of the absolute separation of death from life, the revolutionaries settle into the masochistically comfortable role of victims of all the separations and into the fantasy of the *post mortem* abolition of all separations, that is, after the great night. In the meantime they justify their existence as heroes through the suffering of their torments and institute the consciousness of suffering as the general mode of the realization of the reunification of separations. Suffering, abstracted like death from life in general, fuels the very precise economy of the political discourse.

The death of a revolutionary who works towards the death of society makes his project so present that the scandal is promptly reeled back into less terrifying interpretations. For the anxiety of making a hole in the concrete is modeled on the emptiness left by the dead in a social practice that exiles the dead to the graveyard, and revolutionary discourse constantly tries to ward off this image of the void in planning its future. That the anxiety of personal death, in projecting itself on the project of the death of the system, encounters profound resistance, resistances that perpetuate it in revolutionary manifestations, does not surprise us very much, for revolution in the capitalist process transforms, but does not subvert.

The revolutionaries who give their dead popular funerals celebrate their funerals and nothing more. Those who claim ownership of the dead of the Commune, the dead of the Kronstadt, the dead of '36, the dead of '68, may they keep them well and may they isolate them above all from the dead of work accidents, the dead in traffic, the dead of old age, for they are much more dead than the others; they have become signs, not symbols of the system's death, but positive signs of revolutionary action fully playing the cultural pattern's game, according to which death is the basic taboo of the bourgeois mode.

Undertakers, you too will die in your beds after the great night! A violent death momentarily disrupts the order of the political economy, associates the dead with the movement that destructures the order in a radical compatibility between death and life.

We should have danced with his corpse in the streets.

THE MIRROR OF PRODUCTION

A specter haunts the revolutionary imagination: the phantasm of production. It sustains an unbridled romanticism of productivity. The critical thought of the *mode* of production doesn't touch the *principle* of production. All of the concepts that it articulates describe only the dialectical and historical genealogy of the *contents* of production; they leave its *form* intact. The form itself reemerges, idealized, behind the critique of the capitalist mode of production. This critique does nothing, in effect, but strengthen the revolutionary discourse, through a curious contagion, in terms of productivity: from the liberation of productive forces in *Tel Quel*'s unlimited "textual productivity" to the factory-machine productivity of the unconscious in Deleuze (and already, the "work" of the unconscious), no revolution can place itself under any other sign than this one. Productive Eros is the watchword. Social wealth or language, meaning or value, sign or phantasm, there is nothing that isn't "produced" according to some "labor." If this is the truth of capital and of political economy, it is entirely replicated by the revolution: we are going to subvert the capitalist mode of production in the name of an authentic and radical productivity. We are going to abolish the capitalist law of value in the name of a de-alienated hyper-productivity, of a productive hyperspace. Capital develops productive forces, but it slows them as well: they must be liberated. The exchange of signifieds has always hidden the "labor" of the signifiers: liberate the signifier! the textual production of meaning! The unconscious is surrounded by social, linguistic, Oedipal structures: return it to its brute energy, restore it as a productive machine! Everywhere the productivist discourse reigns, and whether this productivity has objective ends or is deployed for itself, in either case, productivity is the form of value. Leitmotif of the system, leitmotif of its radical contestation: a terminological consensus like this is suspect. Perhaps the discourse of production is only a revolutionary metaphor—the reversal and return of a concept, which essentially emanates from political economy and obeys the reality principle of that economy. But this metaphor is dangerous if it is meant to designate a radical alternative. Perhaps the alternative isn't radical and contamination by the productivist discourse signifies more than a metaphoric infection—it signifies a real impossibility of thinking beyond or outside the general schema of production, which is to say in counter-dependence on the dominant schema.[1]

But isn't this dominant schema, metaphorizing all azimuths, itself a metaphor? Is the reality principle that it imposes anything other than a code, a cipher, a system of interpretation? Marx shattered the fiction of *homo economicus*, the myth that summarizes the entire process of the naturalization of the system of exchange value, of the market, of surplus value and its forms. But he did it in the name of the emergence into action of labor power, of man's own power to make the value of his labor visible (*pro-du-cere*), and we can ask if there is not an equal fiction, an equal naturalization, which is to say an equally arbitrary convention, a model of simulation destined to *code* all human material, every eventuality of desire and of exchange in terms of value, finality and production. Production in this case would be nothing other than a code, imposing a kind of deciphering, imposing decipherment where there is properly neither finality, cipher, or value. It is a question of a gigantic secondary elaboration which hallucinates in rational terms the predestination of man for the transformation of the world (or for the "production" of himself, a humanist theme generalized today: it is no longer a question of "being" oneself but of "producing" oneself, from conscious activity to the wild "productions" of desire). Everywhere man has learned to reflect himself, to assume himself, to *direct* himself according to this schema of production, which is assigned to him as the final dimension of value and meaning. At the level of the entirety of political economy, there is something of what Jacques Lacan described in the mirror stage: across this schema of production, this *mirror* of production, the human species comes to consciousness *in the imaginary*. Production, work, value, everything through which an objective world appears and in which man recognizes himself objectively—all of this is the imaginary wherein man has embarked on the incessant decipherment of himself through his works, finalized by his shadow (his own end), reflected by this

1. Marx evidently played an essential role in rooting this productivist metaphor. Marx radicalized and definitively rationalized the concept of production, he "made it" dialectical, and gave it its title of revolutionary nobility. It is in large part through unconditional reference to Marx that this concept pursues its prodigious career.

operational mirror, this kind of ideal of the productivist ego—not only in the materialized form of economic obsession with output, determined by the *system* of exchange value, but more profoundly in this *overdetermination by the code*, by the mirror of political economy, in this identity that man dons in his own eyes, when he can no longer think of himself other than as something to produce, to transform, to make visible as a value. This remarkable phantasm is confused with that of representation, in which man becomes—for himself—his own *signified*, enjoys himself as *contents* of value and meaning, in a process of self-expression and self-accumulation whose form escapes him.

It is clear (despite the exegetical prowess of structuralist Marxists) that the analysis of form/representation (the status of the sign, of the language which directs all western thought)—the critical reduction of this form in its collusion with the order of production and of political economy—escaped Marx. Nothing is served by making a radical critique of the order of representation in the name of production and its revolutionary watchword. The two orders are inseparable and, as paradoxical as this seems, Marx didn't submit form/production to radical analysis any more than he did form/representation. These two great, unanalyzed forms imposed their limits on him, the limits of the imaginary of political economy. We understand this to mean that the discourse of production and the discourse of representation are the mirror wherein the system of political economy comes to be reflected in the imaginary and to reproduce itself as determinant authority.

In order to grasp the radicality of political economy, it does not suffice to unmask what is hidden behind the concept of consumption: the anthropology of needs and use value. We must also unmask everything that hides behind the concept of production, of the mode of production, of productive forces, of relationships of production, etc. All the concepts fundamental to Marxist analysis need to be questioned starting even from its demand for radical critique and for the transcendence of political economy. What is axiomatic about productive forces, about the dialectical genesis of modes of production from which revolutionary theory springs? What is axiomatic about the generic wealth of man—labor power, about the motor of history, about history itself, which is only "the production by men of their material life"? "The first historical act is thus the production of the means to satisfy these needs, the production of material life itself. And indeed this is an historical act, a fundamental condition of all history, which today, as thousands of years ago, must daily and hourly be fulfilled merely in order to sustain human life" (Karl Marx, *The German Ideology*).

The liberation of productive forces is confused with the liberation of man: is this a revolutionary watchword or one for political economy? Almost no one has doubted this final evidence, certainly not Marx, for whom men "begin to distinguish themselves from animals as soon as they begin to *produce* their means of subsistence" (why must man's vocation always be to distinguish himself from animals? Humanism is an *idée fixe* that comes to us—it too—from political economy—but let's leave that aside). But is existence itself an end for man, an end for which he must find the means? These little innocent phrases are already theoretical ultimatums; the separation of ends and means already constitutes the most ferocious and most naïve postulate about the human species. Man has needs. Does he have needs? Is he sworn to satisfy them? Is he a labor power (through which he separates himself, as means, from his own ends)? Prodigious metaphors of the system that dominates us; a fable of political economy still recounted to generations of revolutionaries, infected even in their political radicality by the conceptual virus of this same political economy.

CRITIQUE OF USE VALUE AND LABOR POWER

In the distinction between exchange value and use value, Marxism assumes its greatest force but also its weakness. The presupposition of use value, the hypothesis, beyond the abstraction of exchange value, of a concrete value, of a human finality of commodities in the moment of their direct relationship of use for a subject: we have seen that this value is only an effect of the system of exchange value, a concept produced by the system, in which the system completes itself.[2] Far from designating a beyond for political economy, use value is but the horizon of exchange value. A radical questioning of the concept of consumption begins on the level of needs and products. *But this critique assumes its full scope in its extension to that other commodity, labor power.* The concept of production then falls under radical critique.

Don't forget that according to Marx himself the revolutionary originality of his theory consists in unleashing the concept of

2. See Jean Baudrillard, *For a Critique of the Political Economy of the Sign* [1972] trans. Charles Levin (St. Louis, MO: Telos Press, 1981).

labor power from its status as an exceptional commodity, the insertion of which, in the cycle of production *under the name of use value* carries the X element, the differential extra-value which generates surplus value and the whole process of capital. (Bourgeois economics speculates on simple "labor" as one factor of production among others in the economic process).

The history of the use value of labor power in Marx is complex. Adam Smith attacked the Physiocrats and the Exchangists with the concept of labor. Marx in turn deconstructed abstract social labor (exchange value) and concrete labor (use value) in the double concept of labor power/commodity. And he insisted on the necessity of maintaining in all their force the two aspects, the articulation of which alone can aid in objectively deciphering the process of capitalist labor. To A. Wagner, who reproached him for having neglected use value, he responds: "… the *vir obscurus* overlooks the fact that even in the analysis of the commodity I do not stop at the double manner in which it is represented, but immediately go on to say that in this double being of the commodity is represented the *twofold character of the labor* whose product it is: *useful labor* i.e., the concrete modes of the labors which create use values, and *abstract labor, labor as expenditure of labor power*, irrespective of whatever 'useful' way it is expended… that in the development of the *value form of the commodity*, in the last instance of its money form and hence of *money*, the *value* of a commodity is represented in the *use value* of the other, i.e., in the natural form of the other commodity; that surplus value itself is derived from *a 'specific' use value of labor power* exclusively pertaining to the latter, etc. etc., thus for me use value plays a far more important part than it has in economics hitherto; however, that is only ever taken into account where it springs from the analysis of a given economic constellation, not from arguing backwards and forwards about the concepts of words 'use value' and 'value'" ("Notes on Wagner").

It is clear that in this text the use value of labor, losing its "naturality," recovers a "specific" value that is much greater in the *structural* functioning of exchange value. Also, that in maintaining a kind of dialectical equilibrium between qualitative concrete labor and quantitative abstract labor, Marx—while granting logical priority to exchange value (the given economic formation), retaining, even in that structure, a kind of concrete precedence, a concrete positivity of use value—still retains something *of the apparent movement of political economy*. He does not radicalize the schema to the point of reversing this appearance and revealing use value *as produced by the play of exchange value*. We have shown this for the products of consumption, and it is the same for labor power. The fact of defining objects as useful, and responding to needs, is the most complete, the most internalized expression of abstract economic exchange: its subjective closure. The fact of defining labor power as the source of "concrete" social wealth is the complete expression of the abstract manipulation of labor power: the truth of capital culminates in this "evidence" of man as producer of value. Such is the twist by which exchange value retrospectively originates and logically closes itself off in use value. In other words, here the signified "use value" is still an *effect of the code*, the final precipitate of the law of value. It does not suffice to analyze the operation of the quantitative abstraction of exchange value *starting from* use value, one must still make visible the conditions for the possibility of this operation: to understand the production of even the concept of the use value of labor power, of a specific rationality of productive man. Without this generic definition, no political economy. Therein, in the last instance, lies the foundation of political economy. It is therein as well that one must disrupt it, by unmasking this quantitative-qualitative "dialectic," behind which the definitive structural institution of the field of value is hidden.

WHAT IS CONCRETE ABOUT LABOR: THE QUANTITATIVE-QUALITATIVE "DIALECTIC"

"The quantitative consideration of labor could only come about once it had been universalized during the eighteenth century in Europe… Until then, different forms of activity were not comparable in their breadth… At first, all tasks presented themselves as diverse qualities" (Pierre Naville, *Le nouveau léviathan*, page 371). Qualitative labor, differentiated in relation to its process, its product, and the destination of its product. Historical epoch of the artisanal mode of production. Succeeded, in the capitalist mode of production, by the double aspect under which labor is analyzed: "While labor which creates exchange values is *abstract*, *universal*, and *homogeneous*, labor which produces use value is concrete and special and is made up of an endless variety of kinds of labor according to the way in which and the material to which it is applied" (Karl Marx, *Contribution to a Critique of Political Economy*). Here we rediscover the moment of use value: concrete, differentiated, incomparable. In opposition to the quantitative measure of labor power, labor use value remains a qualitative potentiality. Neither more nor less. It is specified by its own end, the material that it works, or simply because it is the energetic expenditure of a particular individual at a particular moment. The use value of labor power is the moment of its actualization, of the relation of man to the useful expenditure that he possesses—it is basically an act of (productive) *consumption*—and this moment retains, in the general process, all of its singularity. At this level, labor power is incommensurable.

There is a profound enigma in the articulation of Marx's theory: how is surplus labor born? How does the actualization of labor power, by definition qualitative, come to be "more" or "less," if not by supposing that the "dialectical" opposition of the quantitative and the qualitative only expresses an apparent movement.

In fact, this is again a question, with the *effect* of quality and of incomparability, of the *apparent* movement of political economy. What the universalization of labor in the eighteenth century, and its reproduction thereafter, produced, was not the reduction of concrete qualitative labor into abstract quantitative labor, but, from the outset, the structural articulation of both terms. On the basis of this "fork," labor is truly universalized, not only as market value but as human value. Ideology always proceeds in this way through a binary structural division (or by redoubling in a qualitative structural effect, which is an effect of the *code*), investing the entire field of possibility. Henceforth, there can only be labor—qualitative or quantitative. The quantitative still only signifies the comparability of all forms of labor in abstract value. The qualitative, under the banner of incomparability, goes much further: it signifies *the comparability of every human practice in terms of production and labor*. Or again: the abstract and formal universality of the labor power commodity underlines the "concrete" universality of qualitative labor.

But the word "concrete" here is an abuse of sense. It seems to oppose abstraction to the interior of the fork; in fact it is the fork itself which grounds abstraction. In the play of one and the other—of abstract and concrete, of qualitative and quantitative, of exchange value and use value—the autonomization of labor is sealed. The fetishism of labor and of productivity comes to be crystallized in this structured play of signifiers.[3]

What is concrete about labor? Marx: "The indifference as to the particular kind of labor implies the existence of a highly developed aggregate of different species of concrete labor, none of which is any longer the predominant one. So do the most general

3. Another great disjunction on which the critique of political economy articulates itself: the technical and social divisions of labor—subjected to the same analysis. Transfiguring the technical division as both sides of the social division, it preserves with the same blow the fiction of an ideal distribution of labor, of a "non-alienated" concrete productivity, and it universalizes the technical mode and technical rationale. Thus the dialectic of productive forces and relations of productivity: everywhere the "dialectical" contradiction ends in a Möbius strip, though in the meantime it has had the time to circumscribe the field of production and to universalize it.

abstractions commonly arise only where there is the highest concrete development, where one feature appears to be jointly possessed by many, and to be common to all" (Karl Marx, *Contribution to the Critique...*). But if no type of labor dominates all the others, it is because labor itself dominates all the other regimes, that it substitutes itself for all other forms of wealth and exchange. Indifference in regard to determinate labor corresponds to a much more complete determination of social wealth by labor. And what is this social wealth, placed entirely under the sign of labor, if not use value? The "richest concrete development" is the qualitative and quantitative multiplication of use values. "The greater the extent to which historic needs—needs created by production itself, social needs—needs which are themselves the offspring of social production and intercourse, are posited as *necessary*, the higher the level to which real wealth has become developed. Regarded *materially*, wealth consists only in the manifold variety of needs." (Karl Marx, *Grundrisse*). Is this not the program of an advanced capitalist society? Because it does not conceive of a mode of social wealth other than that founded on labor and production, Marxism no longer furnishes, long term, a real alternative to capitalism. Adopting the generic schema of production and needs, there is an astounding simplification of social exchange by the law of value. A fantastic proposition, if conceived correctly; arbitrary and fantastic in regard to the status of man in society; belied by the analysis of all primitive or archaic organizations, and by the feudal symbolic order, and even by that of our societies. It is clear that all of the perspectives opened up by the contradictions of the mode of production drive us into political economy.

The dialectic of production only redoubles the abstraction, the separation of political economy. And this leads to the radical interrogation of the Marxist theoretical discourse. Since the dialectic abstract-concrete relationship is in the final instance defined by Marx as the relationship between "scientific representation and real movement" (what Althusser will analyze precisely as the *production* of a theoretical object), it appears that this theoretical production, itself caught in the abstraction of representation can only redouble its object, in this case the logic and movement of political economy. Between the theory and the object (this goes not only for Marxism) there is effectively a dialectical relation, in the fatal sense wherein it encloses them both in an unsurpassable specularity.[4] Thought beyond the production form, beyond the representation form becomes unthinkable.

4. We will come back to this reciprocal neutralization of the theory and the object in relation to the rapports between Marxist theory and the workers' movement.

In fact, the use value of labor power is no more real than the use value of products, no more real than the autonomy of the signified and the referent. The same fiction reigns in the orders of production, consumption, and signification. Exchange value makes the use value of products appear as its anthropological horizon. The exchange value of labor power makes use value visible as the originality and concrete finality of the act of labor, as its "generic" alibi. The logic of signifiers produces "evidence" of the "reality" of the signified and of the referent. Throughout, exchange value makes concrete production, concrete consumption, and concrete signification appear as a kind of abstraction, as an abstract distortion. Exchange value foments this concreteness as its ideological ectoplasm, as its originary phantasm and its surpassing. In this sense, needs, use value, the referent "don't exist": they are only concepts produced and projected in a generic dimension by the same development of the system of exchange value.[5]

In the same way, the double potentiality of man, that of needs and labor power, that "generic" double face of universal man is only that of man as he is produced by the system of political economy. And productivity is not there at first as a generic dimension, as the human and social seed of all wealth, that one must extract from the dross of capitalist relations of production (the eternal empiricist illusion); one must reverse all of this, and see that it is the development of abstract and generalized productivity (the developed form of political economy) that makes the *concept of production* itself visible as movement and generic end of man (or again the concept of man as producer).

In other words, the system of political economy produces not only the individual as labor power sold and exchanged, it produces the concept of labor power as the fundamental human potentiality. More profoundly than in the fiction of the individual freely selling his labor power in the market, the system takes root to the extent that the individual identifies with his labor power and his act of "transforming nature toward human ends." In a word, there is not only the quantitative exploitation of man as productive force by the *system* of capitalist political economy, but the metaphysical overdetermination of man as producer by the *code* of political economy.[6] In the final instance, that is how

5. This is not to say that they have *never existed*: another paradox to which we will have to return.

6. The same for nature: not only the exploitation of nature as productive force, but the overdetermination of nature as referent, as "objective" reality, by the code of political economy.

the system rationalizes its power. *And in this Marxism aids the capitalist deceit by persuading men that they are alienated by the sale of their labor power, censuring the much more radical hypothesis that they could be alienated as labor power, as the "inalienable" power of creating value through labor.*

If Marx affiliates himself with the ulterior fate of labor power objectivized in the process of production, as abstract social labor, under the aspect of its exchange value—the existence of this human (energetic, physical, intellectual) capacity of production, this productive potentiality which is that of all men, in every society, "to transform their surroundings toward ends useful for the individual and society," this *Arbeitsvermögen* is never questioned by Marxist theory. Its critique and history halt strangely before this anthropological postulate. Curious fate for a Marxist concept.

The concept of need in its present operation (the consumption of use value) appears in the same light. It offers the same marks of singularity, of differentiation, of incomparability, in short, of the "qualitative" as the concrete capacity of labor. If one can be defined as a "particular type of action producing its own work," the other can also be defined as a "particular type of tendency (or other psychological motivation, of course, because all of this is only bad psychology) searching for its own satisfaction." Need also "decomposes matter and form…in infinitely diverse types of consumption." One is that by which man offers a useful objective end to nature, another is that by which he offers a useful subjective end to products. Needs, labor: double potentiality, double generic quality of man, same anthropological sphere which defines the concept of production as the "fundamental movement of human existence," as defining a rationality and a society proper to man. Moreover, one finds them logically reunited in a kind of final perspective: "In a superior phase of communist society…when labor will not only be a means of living, but will itself become the primary vital need" (Karl Marx, *Manuscripts of 1844*).

Marxist theory, radical in its *logical* analysis of capital, sustains itself with an *anthropological* consensus with Western rationalist options, in the definitive form that it assumed in the bourgeois thought of the eighteenth century. Science, technology, progress, history: an entire civilization understands itself as the producer of its own development and draws its dialectical momentum toward completing humanity, designated in terms of totality and happiness. Genesis, development, finality: Marx invented none of this, nor did he change anything essential, nothing of the *idea* of man *producing* himself in his infinite determination and continually surpassing himself toward his own end.

Marx translated this concept into the logic of material production and into the historical dialectic of modes of production. But to differentiate the modes of production is to render unsurpassable evidence of production as determinant instance. It is to generalize the rational mode of economics over the entire stretch of human history, as a generic mode of human becoming. It is to circumscribe the entire history of man in what is undoubtedly only a gigantic model of simulation. It is in a way to turn against the order of capital by using as an instrument of analysis the most subtle ideological phantasm that capitalism itself has elaborated. "Dialectical" reversal? Is it not the system that is leading its own dialectic here, that of its universal reduction? If one advances the hypothesis *that there never has been and that there never will be more than a single mode of production, regulated by the capitalist political economy*, this concept only makes sense in relation to the economic formation which produces it (observe the theory that analyzes this economic formation). Thus the generalization of this concept, even if it be "dialectical," is but the *ideological* universalization of the system's postulates.

ETHIC OF LABOR; AESTHETICS OF PLAY

This logic of material production, this dialectic of modes of production always returns, beyond history, to a generic definition of man as a dialectical being, understandable based on the sole process of the objectification of nature. This is heavy with consequences to the extent that, even through the fortunes of his history, man (whose history is also a "product") will be ruled by this clear and definitive reason, by this dialectical schema which acts like implicit philosophy. Marx developed it in the *Manuscripts of 1844*, Marcuse revives it in his critique of the economic concept of labor: "Labor is an ontological concept of human existence as such." He cites Lorenz von Stein: "Labor is...in every way the actualization of one's infinite determinations through the self-positing of the individual personality [in which the personality itself] makes the content of the external world its own and in this way forces the world to become a part of its own internal world" (Herbert Marcuse, "On the Concept of Labor"). Marx: "Labor is *man's coming-to-be for himself* within the *externalization* or as *externalized* man...[that is] the *self-creation* and self-objectification [of man]." And even in *Capital*: "So far, therefore, as labor is a creator of use-value, is useful labor, it is a necessary condition, independent of all forms of society, for the existence of the human race; it is an external nature-imposed necessity, without which there can be no material exchanges between man and nature, and therefore no life" (Karl Marx, *Capital vol. 1*). "Labor is, in the first place, a process in which both man and nature participate, and in which man of his own accord starts, regulates, and controls the material reactions between himself and nature. He opposes himself to nature as one of her own forces setting arms and legs, head and hands, the natural forces of his body in motion in order to appropriate nature's productions in a form adapted to his own wants." The dialectical culmination of all this is the concept of nature as "the inorganic body of man": the naturalization of man and the humanization of nature.[7]

On this dialectical basis, Marxist philosophy unfolds in two directions: an ethics of labor, an aesthetics of non-labor. The first across the entirety of bourgeois and socialist ideology—the exaltation of labor as value, as an end in itself, as a categorical imperative. Labor loses its negativity here and stands as an absolute value. But is the "materialist" thesis of the generic productivity of man far from this "idealist" sanctification of labor? It is in any case dangerously vulnerable here. Marcuse: "Insofar as they take the concept of 'needs' and its satisfaction in the world of goods as the starting point, all economic theories fail to recognize the full factual content of labor… The essential factual content of labor is not grounded in the scarcity of goods, nor in a discontinuity between the world of disposable and utilizable goods and human needs, but, on the contrary, in an essential excess of human existence beyond every possible situation in which it finds itself and the world." In the name of which he separates play as a secondary activity: "In the structural sense, within the totality of human existence, labor is necessarily and eternally 'earlier' than play." Labor alone founds the world as objective and man as historical, only labor founds a real dialectic of transcendence and completion. It even justifies metaphysically the burdensome nature of labor. "In the final analysis, the burdensome character of labor expresses nothing other than a negativity rooted in the very essence of human existence: man can achieve his own self only by passing through otherness: by passing through 'externalization' and 'alienation'." I have only cited this long passage to show how the Marxist dialectic can lead to the purest Christian ethic (and inversely of course: today we see a large contamination of these two points of view on the basis of this transcendence of alienation and this intraworldly asceticism of effort and of the overcoming that Weber located as the radical germ of the capitalist spirit). And also because since the

7. Engels, always a naturalist, goes on to praise the role played by labor in the transition from ape to man.

beginning, this aberrant sanctification of labor found itself to be the secret vice of Marxist political and economic strategy. Walter Benjamin stigmatized it violently: "Nothing has corrupted the German working class so much as the notion that it was moving with the current. It regarded technological developments as the fall of the stream with which it thought it was moving. From there it was but a step to the illusion that the factory work which was supposed to tend toward technological progress constituted a political achievement. The old Protestant ethics of work were resurrected among German workers in secularized form. The Gotha Program already bears traces of this confusion, defining labor as the 'source of all wealth and all culture.' Smelling a rat, Marx countered that '... man who possesses no other property than his labor power' must of necessity become 'the slave of other men who have made themselves owners...' However, the confusion spread, soon thereafter Josef Dietzgen proclaimed, 'the savior of modern times is called work. The... improvement... of labor constitutes the wealth which is now able to accomplish what no redeemer has ever been able to do'" (Walter Benjamin, *Illuminations.*) Is this a question of a "vulgar" Marxism, as Benjamin suggests? No less "vulgar" in the case of the "strange delusion" Paul Lafargue denounced in *The Right to be Lazy*: "A strange delusion possesses the working classes of the nations where capitalist civilization holds its sway." Apparently orthodox Marxism preaches the liberation of productive forces under the auspices of the *negativity* of labor. But is this not a question, faced with the gospel of labor, of an "aristocratic" idealism? The other is positivist, and Marxism wants to be "dialectical," but they have the hypothesis of man's productive vocation in common. If one admits that it raises the purest metaphysics,[8] then the difference between "vulgar" Marxism and the "other" would be that of a mass religion and a philosophical theory—which, as we know, is not much.

Confronted with the *absolute* idealism of labor, dialectical materialism is perhaps only a *dialectical* idealism of productive forces. We will return to this to see if the dialectic of means and ends which is at the heart of the principle of the transformation of nature does not already virtually imply the autonomization of means (the autonomization of science, of technology, and of labor, the autonomization of production as generic activity, the autonomization of the dialectic itself as general scheme of development).[9]

8. Insofar as it conceives of man as the union of a soul and a body—which took place, as we know, in an extraordinary "dialectical" flowering during the Christian Middles Ages.

9. This autonomization is the key which turns Marxism toward social democracy, the key to its present revisionism, and to its total positivist degradation (which also includes bureaucratic Stalinism as well as Social Democractic liberalism).

In the fine print of Marxist thought and against this labor ethic, the regressive character of which evidently maintains what it represses—Marx's capital discovery about the double aspect of labor (his discovery of an abstract and measurable social labor)—there is an aesthetics of play, of non-work, which is based on the dialectic of the quantitative and the qualitative. This is the perspective, beyond the capitalist mode of production and the qualitative measure of labor, of a definitive qualitative mutation in communist society: the end of alienated labor, the free objectification of man's own powers. "In fact, the realm of freedom actually begins only where labor, which is determined by necessity, and mundane considerations ceases; thus in the very nature of things it lies beyond the sphere of actual material production... Freedom in this field can only consist in socialized man, the associated producers, rationally regulating their interchange with Nature, bringing it under their common control, instead of being ruled by it as by the blind forces of Nature; and achieving this with the least expenditure of energy and under conditions most favorable to, and worthy of, their human nature. But it nonetheless still remains a realm of necessity. Beyond it begins that development of human energy which is an end in itself, the true realm of freedom which, however, can blossom forth, only with this realm of necessity as its basis" (Marx, *Capital, III*). Or again, Marcuse, returning to less puritanical (less Hegelian) conceptions, though undoubtedly entirely philosophical (Schiller's aesthetic philosophy): "Play and display, as principles of civilization, imply not the transformation of labor but its complete subordination to the freely evolving potentialities of man and nature. The ideas of play and display now reveal their full distance from the values of productiveness and performance. Play is *unproductive* and *useless* precisely because it cancels the repressive and exploitative traits of labor and leisure" (Marcuse, *Eros and Civilization*).

This *beyond* of political economy called play, non-work, or non-alienated labor, is defined as the reign of finality without end. It is in this sense that it is and remains, in the very Kantian sense of the term, an *aesthetic*, with all the bourgeois ideological connotations that this implies. And it is true that the thought of Marx, if it settled its accounts with bourgeois morality, remains defenseless against bourgeois aesthetics, the ambiguity of which is more subtle, but whose complicity with the general system of political economy is also profound. Once again, it is at the heart of its strategy, in the analytic distinction that it makes between the quantitative and the qualitative, that Marxist thought inherits from the aesthetic and humanist virus of bourgeois thought—the concept of the qualitative is burdened with all these finalities, whether the concrete finality of use value or the endless idealist and transcendental finalities. This is the defect of every notion of play, of liberty, of transparency, of disalienation, the defect of the *revolutionary imagination*—insofar as in the ideal type of play, of the free play of human faculties, we are still in the process of repressive desublimation. This sphere of play effectively defines itself as the fulfillment of human rationality, as the dialectical culmination of man's activity, of his incessant objectification of nature and the control of his exchanges with it. It presupposes the full development of productive forces, it remains "mixed up with" the reality principle and the transformation of nature. It can only flourish, Marx says clearly, when based on the reign of necessity. This is to say that, wishing itself beyond labor, but in its *prolongation*, the sphere of play is never only the aesthetic sublimation of its constraints. We are still well within the typically bourgeois problematic of necessity and freedom, the double ideological expression of which has always been, since coming into existence, the institution of a reality principle (repression and sublimation: principle of labor) and its formal surpassing in an ideal transcendence.

Work and non-work. "Revolutionary" theme. Therein lies the most subtle form of the previously mentioned binary structural opposition. The end of the end of the exploitation by labor is truly this inverse fascination with non-labor, this inverse mirage of free time (obligated time—free time, full time—empty time: another paradigm that seals the hegemony of the order of time, which is always merely that of production). Non-work is still only the repressive desublimation of labor power—the antithesis that acts as an alternative. The sphere of non-work, even if one does not confuse it immediately with that of leisure and its present bureaucratic organization, wherein the desire for death and for mortification and its management by social institutions is as powerful as in the sphere of work. Even if one envisions it in a radical way that *represents it* as other than the model of a "total availability," of a "liberty" for the individual to "produce" himself as a value, to "express" himself, to "liberate" himself as authentic *content* (conscious or unconscious), in short the ideality of time and of the individual as an empty form, to be filled in the end by his freedom. The finality of value is always there. It no longer inscribes itself, as in the sphere of productive activity, in *determined* contents. It is there henceforth as *pure form*, but no less determining. Exactly as the pure institutional form of painting, of art and theater shines, emptied of its contents, in anti-painting, anti-art, anti-theater—non-work shines with the pure form of labor. The concept can therefore be fantasized as the abolition of political economy, it is bound to fall back into the sphere of political economy, as a sign—and only a sign—of its abolition. It already escapes the revolutionaries to enter into the programmatic field of the "new society."

MARX AND THE HIEROGLYPH OF VALUE

In *Semeiotike*, Julia Kristeva writes: "From the viewpoint of social distribution and consumption (of communication), labor is always a value of use or a value of exchange... Value is measured by the quantity of time socially necessary for production. But Marx clearly outlined another possibility: *work could be apprehended outside value*, on the side of the commodity produced and circulating in the chain of communication. Here labor no longer represents any value, meaning, or signification. It is a question only of a *body* and a *discharge*..."

Marx: "The use values, coat, linen, etc., i.e., the bodies of commodities, are combinations of two elements—matter and labor... We see, then, that labor is not the only source of material wealth, of use values produced by labor, as William Petty puts it, labor is its father and the earth its mother... Productive activity, if we leave out of sight its special form, viz. the useful character of labor, is nothing but the expenditure of human labor-power" (Marx, *Capital, I*, 43–44).

Is there a conception of labor in Marx different from the *production* of useful ends (canonical definition of labor as value in the framework of political economy and the anthropological definition of labor as human finality)? According to Kristeva, Marx's vision is radically different, centered on the body, expenditure, play, anti-value, non-utility, non-finality, etc. She would have him have read Bataille before writing, freely—forgetting it just as quickly: if there is something that Marx did not think, it is expenditure, loss, sacrifice, prodigality, play, the symbolic. Marx thought about production (already not bad) and he thought about it in terms of value.

There is no escape from this. Marxist labor is defined in the absolute framework of a natural necessity and of its dialectical overcoming as rational activity producing value. The social wealth that it produces is *material*. It has nothing to do with *symbolic* wealth which comes conversely from destruction, from the deconstruction of value, from transgression and expenditure, which mocks natural necessity. These two notions of wealth are irreconcilable, perhaps even exclusive of one another, and it is useless to attempt acrobatic transfers. According to Bataille, "sacrificial economy" or symbolic exchange is excluded from political economy (and from its critique, which is only its completed form). It is just to return to political economy what belongs to it: the concept of labor is consubstantial with it. For this reason, it cannot be turned to any other field of analysis, and it certainly cannot become once again the object of a science that claims to overturn political economy. The "labor of the sign," "intertextual productive space," etc. are ambiguous metaphors. There is a choice to be made between value and non-value. Labor definitively elevates the sphere of value. This is why the concept of labor in Marx (like his concepts of production and of productive force) must be submitted to a radical critique as an *ideological* concept. With all of its ambiguities, this is not the moment to generalize labor as a *revolutionary* concept.

The citations from Marx to which Kristeva refers do not in any way carry the sense she gives them. The genesis of wealth through genital combination of labor-father and earth-mother repeats well enough a "normal" productive-reproductive schema: we make love to have children, not for pleasure. The metaphor is that of reproductive genital sexuality, not at all that of an expenditure of the ecstatic body. But this is only a detail. The "expenditure" of human power that Marx speaks of is not an expenditure of pure loss, in Bataille's sense, a symbolic (pulsionary, libidinal) expenditure; it is still a productive, finalized, economic expenditure because it engenders only through coupling with this other productive force called earth (or matter). It is a useful expenditure, an investment, and not at all a festive and free volatilization of the power of the body, a game with death, the action of a desire. Moreover, this "expenditure of the body" does not have, as in play (sexual or otherwise), its response in other bodies, its echo in a nature that would play or expend itself in exchange. It is not based on symbolic exchange. What man offers of his body in labor is never *given* or *lost*, nor *rendered* by nature in a reciprocal mode. Labor intends only to "render the yield" of nature. Expenditure in this sense is therefore only an investment of value, a *making valuable*, opposed to every symbolic *play*, whether in a gift or an expenditure.

Kristeva poses the problem of redefining labor beyond value. In fact, for Marx, as Jean-Joseph Goux has shown, the line demarcating value passes between use value and exchange value. "If we proceed further, and compare the process of producing value with the labor-process, pure and simple, we find that the latter consists of the useful labor, the work, that produces use values. Here we contemplate the labor as producing a particular article; we view it under its qualitative aspect alone. Here it is a question merely of the time occupied by the laborer in doing the work—of the period during which the labor power is usefully expended" (Marx, *Capital*, *I*, 195). Thus the abstraction of value begins only that of the second stage, that of exchange value. This amounts to removing use value from the sphere of the production of value, or again: the sphere of use value is confused with that which is beyond value (this is Goux's point, in extending this proposition to the use value of the sign). Here, as we have seen, there is a very serious idealization of the process of concrete, qualitative labor and, in the end, a compromise with political economy—to the extent that the entire theoretical investment and strategy crystallizes on this line of demarcation within the sphere of value, the line "external" to the closure of this sphere of political economy is left in the shadows. By positing use value beyond exchange value, we enclose all transcendence within this single internal alternative to the field of value. Qualitative production is already the reign of a rational, positive finality—the transformation of nature is already the place of its objectification as productive power, under the sign of utility (this is simultaneously true of human labor). Labor and production—before even the stage of exchange value and of the temporal equivalence of abstract social labor—already constitute an abstraction, a reduction and an unsurpassed rationalization in relation to the wealth of symbolic exchange. This "concrete" labor, with all of its values of repression, of sublimation, of objective finality, of "conformity to a goal," of the rational domestication of sexuality and of nature, this *productive eros* already represents, in relation to symbolic exchange, the real cut that Marx himself displaces and situates between abstract quantitative labor and concrete qualitative labor. The process of "valorization" begins with the process of the useful transformation of nature, with the instauration of labor as generic finality, with the stage of use value. And this real cut is not between "abstract" labor and "concrete" labor, but between symbolic exchange and labor (production, economics). The abstract social form of labor and of exchange is only the completed form, overdetermined by capitalist political economy, of a scheme of rational valorization and production inaugurated long ago, breaking with every symbolic organization of exchange.[10]

10. For example, this passage from Marx on the social hieroglyph: "Value, therefore, does not stalk about with a label describing what it is. It is value, rather, that converts every product into a social hieroglyphic. Later on, we try to decipher the hieroglyphic, to get behind the secret of our own social products; for to stamp an object of utility as a value is just as much a social product as language" (*Capital*, *op. cit.*, I, 74). The entirety of this analysis of the mystery of value remains fundamental. But far from only being valuable for the distributed and exchanged product of labor, it already works for the product of labor (and for labor itself) understood as a "useful object." The utility (that of labor as well) is already this socially produced and socially determined hieroglyphic abstraction. The entire anthropology of "primitive" exchange forces us to shatter the natural evidence of utility and recreate the historical and social genesis of use value as Marx did exchange value. Only then will the hieroglyph be totally deciphered and the spell of value be radically exorcised.

Kristeva would like to escape value, but not labor or Marx. You have to choose. Labor is defined (historically and anthropologically) as what disinvests all the ambivalent and symbolic potentialities of the body and of social exchange, reducing them to a rational, positive, and unilateral investment. Productive eros pushes all alternative potentialities of meaning and exchange, in symbolic exchange, toward the process of production, accumulation, and appropriation. If we want to question this process which places us in the hands of political economy, of the terrorism of value, if we want to rethink expenditure and symbolic exchange, the concepts of production and of labor developed by Marx (not to speak of classical economics) must be resolved, analyzed as ideological concepts in solidarity with the general system of value. And if we want to find a realm beyond value (which is in effect the only revolutionary perspective), then we must shatter the *mirror of production*, in which all of Western metaphysics is reflected. Should we abandon Marx?[11]

IN THE SHADOW OF MARXIST CONCEPTS

Historical materialism, dialectics, modes of production, labor power: all these concepts by which Marxist theory seeks to shatter the abstract universality of the concepts of bourgeois thought (Nature and Progress, Man and Reason, formal Logic, Labor, Exchange, etc.). Marxism in its turn is in the process of universalizing them according to a "critical" imperialism as ferocious as that of bourgeois thought.

The proposition according to which a concept is not only an interpretive hypothesis, but the translation of the movement of the universe, comes under pure metaphysics. Marxist concepts don't escape this lapse. Thus, by all logic, the concept of history must maintain itself as historical, turn on and clarify itself by abolishing the context that produces it. In place of this, it is trans-historisized, it is redoubled in itself and thereby universalized. Dialectics, in all their rigor, should dialectically surpass and annul itself. Production and modes of production: radicalizing the concept in a given moment, Marx made a breach in the social mystery of exchange value. Thereafter the concept took all of its strategic power from its irruption, by which it deposes political economy from its imaginary universality. But it lost its power, already in Marx's time, by offering itself as a principle of explication. It cancels

11. Why not?

its "difference" by universalizing itself, returning by the same blow to the form of the dominant code, universality, and to the strategy of political economy. It is not tautological that the concept of history should be historical, the concept of dialectics dialectical, the concept of production itself a product (which is to say judged by a kind of auto-analysis). This simply designates the present, explosive, mortal form of critical concepts. From the moment they assert themselves in the universal, they cease to be analytical: the religion of meaning commences. They become canonical and they enter into the general system's mode of theoretical reproduction. At this moment too—and this is not by chance—they assume their scientific cast (the canonization of Marxist concepts from Engels to Althusser). They set themselves up to express an "objective reality." They become signs: signifiers of a "real" signified. And if, in the best moments these concepts have been practiced as such, this is to say without taking themselves for reality, nevertheless they have fallen into the *imaginary of the sign*, which is to say into the *sphere of truth*, no longer in the sphere of interpretation, but in that of *repressive simulation.*

From here, they can only evoke one another, in an indefinite metonymic process: man is historical, history is dialectical, dialectics is the process of (material) production, production is the movement of human existence itself, history is that of modes of production, etc. Scientific and universalist, this discourse (this code) becomes immediately imperialist. All these possible societies are summoned to respond. Interrogate Marxist thought to see if societies "without history" are something other than "pre"-historic, other than a chrysalis and a larva. The dialectics of the world of production is not yet well developed, but you lose nothing by waiting—the Marxist egg is ready to hatch. The psychoanalytical egg, elsewhere, is also already ready, because everything that we have said of these Marxist concepts goes for the unconscious, repression, Oedipus, etc. This is even better: the Bororos are closer to the primary processes than we are.

All of this constitutes the most surprising—and the most reactionary—theoretical aberration. There is *neither mode of production nor production itself* in primitive societies. There is *no dialectic* in primitive societies. There is *no unconscious* in primitive societies. All of these concepts analyze only our societies, regulated by political economy. These concepts have only a kind of boomerang value. If psychoanalysis speaks of the unconscious in primitive societies, should we ask what psychoanalysis represses or what repression produced psychoanalysis itself? When Marxism speaks of the mode of production in primitive societies, should we ask to what extent this concept fails to account for even our historical societies—the reason we export it. And there where all of our ideologues seek to finalize, to rationalize primitive societies according to their own concepts, to encode the primitives, should we ask what obsession makes them perceive this finality, what makes this code blow up in their faces. In place of exporting Marxism and psychoanalysis (not to mention bourgeois ideology, though on this level there is no difference), bring all of the impact, the entire interrogation of primitive societies to bear on Marxism and psychoanalysis. Maybe then we can shatter this fascination, this auto-fetishism of Western thought; maybe then we could escape from a Marxism which has become more specialized in the impasses of capitalism than it has a road to revolution, from a psychoanalysis which has become more specialized in the impasses of libidinal economy than it has in the ways of desire.

THE CRITIQUE OF POLITICAL ECONOMY IS BASICALLY COMPLETED

Understanding itself as a rationality of production superior to that of bourgeois political economy, the weapons that Marx thought he seized, have turned against him and make his theory the dialectical apotheosis of political economy. At a much higher level, his critique falls to his objection to Feuerbach for making a radical critique of the *contents* of religion rather than making this critique of the religious *form*. Marx made a radical critique of political economy, but he still made it in the form of political economy. Such are the ruses of dialectics. Therein is undoubtedly the limit of every "critique," a concept born in the West at the same time as political economy, a concept which is perhaps, like the quintessence of Enlightenment rationality, only the subtle, long-term expression of the system's expanded reproduction. Dialectics does not escape the destiny of critique. We will perhaps see that the return of idealist dialectics in dialectical materialism was only a metamorphosis, that it is the logic itself of political economy, of capital and of the commodity which is dialectical and that, in the guise of having produced the internal and fatal contradiction, Marx basically only offered a descriptive theory. The logic of representation, which is to say of the redoubling of its object, haunts all rational discursivity. All critical theory is haunted by this surreptitious religion in which desire is indexed by the construction of its object, and negativity is subtly haunted by the form even of what it negates.

This is why, after Feuerbach, Marx said that the critique of religion is basically completed (*Critique of Hegel's Philosophy of Right*), and that in order to overturn this ambiguous limit beyond which it cannot go (the reinversion of religious form in critique itself), it is necessary to pass resolutely to another level—precisely to the critique of political economy, which alone is radical and which can, by making the true contradictions apparent, definitively resolve the problem of religion. *Today we are at exactly the same point as Marx was.* For us, the *critique of political economy is basically completed.* Dialectical materialism has exhausted its contents by reproducing its form. The situation at this level is consequently no longer critique, it is inextricable. And according to the same revolutionary movement as Marx's, we affirm that we must move to a radically different level which permits, beyond its critique, the definitive resolution of political economy. This level is that of symbolic exchange and its theory. And as Marx thought that he should, in order to open the way to the critique of political economy, begin with a critique of the philosophy of law, we think that the preamble to this radical shift in terrain is the critique of the metaphysics of the signifier and of the code, in the entirety of its present ideological breadth—which we call, for lack of something better, the critique of the political economy of the sign.

THERE'S NO MORE GOVERNMENT

In Belgium, there is confusion and chaos, in Denmark, too much politics, in Great Britain, it is fifty-fifty plus a little extra, in the Netherlands politics is there by mistake, in Germany, politics pretends but does not exist, in France, it is powerful, but no one knows why, while in Sweden a tie in the parliamentary elections was broken by flipping a coin, heads or tails. Politics in Europe is a funny thing, less sordid than in the U.S.A., and yet also less abstract than in the U.S.S.R.

This nonexistence has long been a threat, never has politics been so visible, never has it spoken in this way; have we forgotten our emotion at the Talleyrands and the Metternichs? Do we not read with tears in our eyes the cruel confessions of Machiavelli? Do we not look up to all of them for examples and advice? Power has not let go, but become of a piece with methods of government, just as the economy is not dead but is purifying itself. To return to our thesis: that is where socialism is to be found.

A European example from last year is worth thinking about: the Netherlands had almost no government for nine months, and everything went well, a few foreign policy difficulties as no one could speak in the name of the Dutch people, and so on. It must be said that Holland is doubtless the best example of "soft" bureaucracy that we possess in Europe; rational and functional, omnipresent but only slightly annoying, in the end one can peacefully pursue one's existence. Weary of politics, in scorn, a coalition was formed, of which we have heard little; there must be government, they have one, titillate it a bit to justify it—the people in the end are kind to their leaders—but with or without it, the class struggle continues, the economy takes care of itself according to historical exigencies. It has been said and repeated: the greatest danger is the absence of government (whether "in service" or not). Yet the people perceived that they did not "need" government. Politics is no longer there, if it ever was, just as the economy was never in business, but existed internally, in the class struggle, and externally, in war.

The Club of Rome has the same official leeway, self-nominating and self-regulating, in any case it meets and becomes more powerful than any government elected by the people; the same goes for the regulatory bodies for business, elected but without any right to capital: same illegality, same power. Symptomatic were the reactions to Kissinger's words regarding the illegality of European governments, an outcry of indignation, a democratic demonstration of a surplus legality, perhaps, yet Pinochet does not draw any similar outburst.

This wrong does not only affect states: unions are victims of it as well. History, faltering, ends its cycle.

REVOLUTIONARY EXOTICISM

untamed energy

A fist is raised, black with coal, black with coffee, black with toil, black with violence. Is it the black or the fist that first strikes you in the face? Beware, black is on the way.

Black power, black might, black sexual energy, phallic fist, rape!

Beware, the beast is in the arena: the black has been liberated, the black is free!

Nothing but fantasy! If there has been a liberation—the black is no longer a slave—it is his labor power that has been liberated, an alienating liberation. Thank God his sexual energy has found a place to invest itself: not in rape—let's not invert the relationship, for in the end it is he who continues to get shafted—but in profit.

Gone are advertising slogans like "Y'a bon Banania," you've become a prole, like the rest of us, with a "preferred" treatment which you find in the archaism of the inter-ethnic relations (where imperialism bites its tail). And so there you are, standing on this subway platform, with your broom in hand, wondering where this poster is inviting you, for this liberated energy of the filthy Negro must be good for something better than boxing in a ring, pushing a broom, planting coffee, or showing itself off.

A poster on the subway walls, coffee, a new flavor: for you the pleasure of consuming the product of his force of labor, the pleasure is yours … the use value.

Thanks to the coffee industry (information?), the subway walls have color, coffee in the morning, eyelids half open, puts you in shape, gives you energy… and it begins again: engulfing ourselves in the sweaty miasma of the subway; a nice little cup of coffee tightens the nerves, perks you up; enough sleep, it is time for the train, and the ball and chain.

By what miraculous alchemy does black energy become the power of caffeine and promotional packaging/impact?

This is something that the mirror of production has reflected sufficiently for us; it is no coincidence that in the story's course we find the labor force, alienation, imperialism and use value. In this area, everything has already been said: in the code of production, the producer is already there in his double guise as producer of commodities and producer of history. To say that the Western proletariat participates in imperialist exploitation, is this any different from saying that it participates in and of its own exploitation?

But let us omit the title for a moment, the explicitly commercial signature (but do we also thereby remove the referent, has it been reduced by advertising discourse, or is it not there, full and in its entirety?); then let us move this anonymous poster, not more anonymous however, than the society which produces it, and, far from the authorized places for posters—windows of consumption—let us look for an empty wall on which the political tentatively expresses itself, near the graffiti of expropriation, and: a metamorphosis! The poster has become "revolutionary"!

revolutionaries from elsewhere

Revolutionary exoticism inscribes itself completely within the space of this representation, with its touristic appeal: literature and travel, posters and trinkets, with all its paraphernalia and dead heroes. Through the struggles of national liberation, from the Vietnamese to the Palestinian, a new historical subject is born, a divine child, to work on history. Since the proletariat in our world is no longer (not) proletarian, here are our new proletarians, those who will feed our bad good consciences as revolutionaries in need of a revolution, with fruits all the more savory as they are far away; let them be near an inaccessible space to be filled up with our reverie—the mysterious Orient, is it any different on the revolutionary market than it is on the market of consumption?

Through these struggles—which we can hardly believe will bear anything other than the "development," (self-centering) of capitalism, leading to the establishment of equivalence in the concert of nations—it is not only the Revolution that we consume, but a represented Utopia, the palliative for the anxieties of our present non-death. By means of these struggles it is again our world and its figure that is set up elsewhere. In setting itself up, our world also sets up its conflictual functioning, its reactive figures, *its* revolution in societies that did not even know its name; this is something we want to ignore and, inverting the proposition, we are now told that these struggles from elsewhere (but already from here) would be the modality of dissolution of our locus as "center" of the imperialistic relationship. Now, by inverting the site of the figure, we would learn from *their* practice[1] (reflecting our own in the negative); and here is what the struggles imposed by the formation-deployment of capital made by our world in its appropriate forms would teach us: the patterns of revolutionary identification are inscribed within capital's process of identification, the better to deny difference.

And yet here is where "socialism" imposes itself as the modality of transition to a generalized productivism, the discipline of work imposing itself on the discipline of the struggles themselves. The raised fist is the sign of its triumph, the triumph of labor liberated:

—there, in its sites of emergence, the triumph in the struggle establishes it as a valid partner, as an equivalent;

—here, in the asymptotic engagement of the militant by means of these struggles, revolutionary space comes nearer, as in the case of revolution, when it approaches the infinite.

For them, Marx, Lenin and Stalin only had the western triviality of the West… Mao makes "us" participate in the myth, in our myth of the other it must be said, and not in Chinese mythology, which eludes us. How to ignore the space of this dream so completely fitting to the poster? Here, through the poster, the economy of the sign "liberates" itself; through (revolutionary?) struggle, this black, yellow, or red power will find a way over there of investing itself in the bleached shroud of State power.

The proletarian and the revolution erected into norms—just as was the bourgeois not so long ago—now seem to elude us. But there where the economy is establishing itself spectacularly, reactivating good old exploitation, and good old class struggle, the normativeness of economic categories and, through them, the labor paradigm, will find a place to reinvest itself. New historical subjects, new motors of history, agents of radical rupture, making us forget in this way that the Vietnamese commune—beyond our myth and its bureaucratization—hinges upon its past and not upon our future. We are enacting racism in reverse: the more foreign, the more alien one is, the more proletarian one is. The proletariat is all the more revolutionary as it is far away… as it is not, forgetting that nowadays it is the revolution that produces the proletarian.

Che Guevara and Franz Fanon are the positivist theoreticians of the alchemy of capital, through which "workers of the world…" becomes "underdeveloped of the world…"

And all the more revolutionary as he is involved in a struggle for national liberation which means what it says: to liberate the State as

1. Although we never had reason to cease inflecting it in the direction of the occidentality of capital and of its revolution.

a Nation-State, to produce a national bourgeois/proletariat system.

As a result, imperialism emerges with a new national virtue—represented at the other extreme by the armed forces that activate it, essentially, in this case, the U.S.—a many-headed hydra that we assimilate by fighting it only in its national form, forgetting that in its imperialist form, capital remains a social relationship. Capital, generally stateless and supranational, thus gains a new national "vocation" in a Manichean vision, where good capital is that which *benefits* the interior, and bad capital that which benefits the "exterior" (but of what?).

The defense of homeland for the fighters of these last-ditch struggles is indeed the defense of a specific social practice, a relationship to space as habitat, but in the struggle the homeland establishes itself as a "national" space, capital nationalizes it for itself as the State's space, which effectively realizes the destruction of this relationship. National liberation struggles, with their ambiguity, are everywhere the foundational struggles of the nation State as natural to capital, and it seems that everywhere, Marxian systematics are the best adapted for this transition.

on strategy

From the moment the economico-political rule of capital relative to a territory—but also to its *inhabitants* (in the full sense of the term)—is in question, the logic is that of capital and the strategy that of the nation. By naming the enemy as such, we force him to wage war (and so/and then politics) by the "same" means: we establish, in the same breath, the means of a political order. We force the other to establish himself as adversary, as enemy, to oppose himself in equivalent terms in political exchange, to signify himself politically in the conflict. From then on, the game has already been won, for this is the result inscribed within the very practice of capital: the victory for the order of signification is inscribed within the struggle itself.

In the various movements and struggles for national liberation, war, struggle, assign a site to the reactive figures, the reactional forms. If, at the end of the struggle (a process of formation), this site represents submission to the discipline of efficacy—the very mode of setting up the code—it is not in this discipline that struggle finds its dynamic and violence, the essence of its real-apparent victory, but precisely in the forms that elude the code itself, and which, inherited from elsewhere, act by transgressing the forms of struggle within the struggle itself. These necessarily transgressive forms activate the struggle, provoke it, and to a certain degree, are disciplined by it within the order of the code; transgression representing both the conditions of *its* victory (that of the code) and of *their* loss (that of the reactive-transgressive forms).

Palestinian violence and Vietnamese habitation are not "conceived of" within the same restricted, narrow framework of the discourse and the site that speak them, already the political site of their resumption in the form of capital, in the form of "information," (even if, *a fortiori* Marxist-Leninist) but within the symbolic space that carries their practice. It is in this that this practice is both transgressive (doubly so, i.e., both in relation to its site of emergence and in relation to its terminal place of assignment); not insofar as it establishes itself against, or opposes capital, but inasmuch as it establishes itself within other forms not yet codified.

It is precisely in the dynamic of the struggle that they are assigned to an oppositional equivalence, and it would be only too easy to assimilate this to some dialectical process of transcendence or integration. The process of the capitalist form, as a form of social relationship, has not come to an end. At stake here, is the entire dynamic of formation and returning the analysis of capital to the terms of nation, even when it is presented in a critical fashion, hardly manages to account for the reality of the struggles (insufficiency of the opposition between national capital and foreign/international capital, positivized by Samir Amin, but negative in *Invariances*).

Palestinians and Vietnamese are not fighting only with the weapons of capital (including its political discourse), but it is precisely in combat that their weapons (their difference) establish themselves as equivalent, that they acquire their efficacy, that they become no longer those of symbolic practice, of habitation, but those of the institutioning Institution, those of the establishment of a new social relationship (that of the adversary who consumes conflict, in whatever form exists at that price, the strength of capital being its ability to recognize/reproduce in its opposition only its own negative image, its equivalence; the emergence of which is expressed unequivocally by the liberation of the Nation.

We do not pretend to measure these various movements with the yardstick of a revolutionary pseudo-purity, but if these movements are to be taken into consideration, then it should be for what they are and not for what they can never be: the place of our unrequited dream.

NOTE: The danger in the notion of *liberation* is to make us believe that by dissolving the form we effect the liberation of a content that exists in itself, while in fact, in the new form, we liberate what proceeds from the process of capital's formation: the force of labor, the nation, etc.

Yet, in the same way that the liberation of the labor force is above all—from the epistemological point of view—a liberation of the concept of the "force of labor," of the category around which the whole social problematic will hinge, national liberation is above all the liberation of the concept and category of "nation."

Force of labor, nation: moments of a rupture and/or expanded reproduction that the structures of inequality of the imperialistic relationship tended to block and freeze: the liberation *from* the tutor (with all due ambiguity), from the schoolmaster of Capitalisms, is realized only when the pupil, having well learned-understood his lesson, rebels.

on the historical subject

Blue, green, red… the spinning of the ball recomposes the colors of the rainbow into an eternal white. Suddenly blocked, the ball comes to a halt. The child follows it with his gaze and, at the foot of the obstacle, raises his eyes, and makes out …

Assuming that our ball is not the subject of the story, but history itself, does the child become, in the end, a historical subject? If that is his wish, then he can run away, but the old petrified, stratified world will always be in front to block him.

As in the Zen art of Archery, the child must become the ball itself, so that the energy of the ball will be strong enough to ignore the statues and change them into a curtain with scarlet folds.

As for the decomposition of colors in the prism of Marxist Knowledge, what is its reality, what good is it in the face of energy and movement? What good is the question of the real reality, of the real realized?

Satellites and Ideograms

The suppression of ideograms and the conjunction of American and Soviet satellites: the extraordinary simultaneity of the two in a super event.

The suppression of ideograms is the equivalent of a satellization of language: a transcendent and simplified abstraction that puts an end to the irreducible differences and singularities of style. As if by chance, the Roman alphabet and roman inscription is chosen amongst 75 or 175 different projects. Globalization, universalization, homogenization of sign systems: more important even than those of the market and political economy.

It is a new cultural revolution that puts an end to ideograms, to better promote ideology (what will *Tel Quel* have to say about this operation, they who saw the origin of the Chinese dialectic in the simultaneous operation of history and of ideogrammatic textuality)? It is the greatest capitulation of the Chinese, by which the revolution inscribes itself definitively in the order of a terrorist hyper-rationality.

It is their participation in a system of peaceful coexistence, which inscribes itself at the same time in the meeting between the two super-satellites. In satellization, we don't believe the one who is satelized: it is the planet earth, it is the terrestrial reality principle which is satellized and which, from now on, will gravitate indefinitely around the hyperrealist lunar module. Satellization signifies the autonomization of an orbital authority of control, of which the earth has become the satellite. In this way, the suppression of ideograms signifies the "orbital" authorization of an abstract, imitative language, in the orbit of which, from now on, formerly singular forms of language and writing will now gravitate.

WAR SCENARIO

How did this war, so hard, so long, so fierce, vanish overnight as if by magic?

Why did the American defeat (the greatest setback in the history of the U.S.A.) not have any domestic repercussions? If it had really meant the failure of the planetary strategy of the United States, it would necessarily have disrupted the internal balance and the American political system. But none of this happened.

Something else must have happened. Deep down, this war will only have been a crucial episode in peaceful coexistence. It will have marked China's coming into peaceful coexistence. China's non-intervention (it had intervened in Korea, where it had failed to turn the tables, while it *apparently* led to the final victory here), obtained and concretized in the course of long years by China's apprenticeship of a global *modus vivendi*, the passage from a strategy of world revolution to that of a worldwide sharing of forces and empires, the transition from a radical, irreducible change to that of a plain political power integrated in a world system that is now regulated for the most part (the normalization of relations between Peking and Washington): that is—or was—what was at stake in the Vietnam war, and, in this sense, the U.S.A. withdrew from Vietnam, but won the war.

The war ended "spontaneously" when the objective had been reached. That is why it fell apart and was so easily dismantled.

The same strategic process can also be deciphered in the field, in Vietnam itself. The war lasted as long as the elements irreducible to a healthy politics and discipline of power—even Communist, if need be—had not been liquidated. In the end, the war was finally wrested from the partisans and passed into the hands of the regular troops of the North. At that moment, the war could end: it had reached its objective. At stake then was a power shift, a political relay. When the Vietnamese were able to prove that they were no longer the bearers of unpredictable subversion, but amenable to a proper supervision by the social order, it could be put into their hands. No matter that it is a Communist order: it has proved itself already, it can be trusted. It is even more effective than Capitalism for the liquidation of "wild" and archaic pre-capitalist structures.

Exactly the same scenario as in the Algerian War.

The other aspect of this war (probably the basic aspect of all modern wars) is this: behind the armed violence, the murderous antagonism of the adversaries—in which life and death *appear* to be at stake, which is *played* as if this were the case (otherwise we could never send people out to get killed for this sort of thing), behind this *simulacrum* of a battle to the death and of global stakes without pity,

the two adversaries are fundamentally allied against something else, something unnamed, never stated, but according to which the objective goal of the war, with the collusion of the two adversaries, is the complete liquidation of tribal, communitarian, pre-capitalist structures, all forms of exchange, language, symbolic organization, all forms prior to rational and terrorist socialization. That is what has to be abolished, that is what war is there for to kill. With all its spectacular machinery of death, war is never anything else than the cover-up for this process of the terrorist rationalization of the social—the murder *par excellence* upon which social order can be established; sociality, of whatever obedience, Communist or Capitalist. Absolute complicity, or division of labor between two adversaries (who are even ready to accept very high sacrifices) to the same end of rationalizing and domesticating social relations; neutralizing and binding energies; colonizing in the fullest sense of the word. War in this sense is always colonial—even the mainlands have to be colonized.

"The North Vietnamese have been advised to participate in a scenario of liquidating the American presence, in the course of which face must not be lost."

This scenario: the intensive bombings of Hanoi. Their unbearable nature should not hide the fact that they were only a simulacrum to permit the Vietnamese to appear amenable to a compromise and to let Nixon make the Americans swallow the withdrawal of their troops. Everything was worked out—the only thing objectively at stake were the ideological appearances. War is not less atrocious for being a simulacrum; on the contrary, it is only more so. But the moralists of war, the advocates of the great referential values of war should not despair: the flesh still suffers, and the dead and the veterans that these make-believe wars produce are worth just as much as those of other wars. In a sense, this objective is always fulfilled—in the same way as that of the domestication of a territory, of the imposition of a disciplinary sociality. What no longer exists is the adversity of the adversaries, the reality of antagonistic causes, the ideological seriousness of war. But also the unreality of victory and defeat. War is a process that always triumphs well beyond these appearances.

WE ARE ALL STUFFED, LIKE ANIMALS

In the staging of the death of Baader and his comrades, it was less a matter of disinformation than of simulation, which has become the system's ultimate weapon.

The death of the inmates in Stammheim is like the counterpoint to the non-death of the hostages in Mogadiscio. Only this permutation will have permitted power to recoup for an instant an apparent existence, even if it is done along the lines of adulteration, scenario, inflation, on a model of simulation, and so as trash-existence. Saving the hostages was not enough, death still had to prevail—that of the Baader-Meinhof group. Two birds with one stone, in two different directions, corresponding to two different orders, which, once joined, territorialized something new, a place without contours, but a place all the same, a place to be bypassed, a place-to-come, on which there is still room to transpose the war, a place in the hands of the system. What was missing was a deadline for death, there where no one expected it anymore, neither in Mogadiscio, at Stammheim, nor in Schleyer's hiding-place. Everything happened as if all of them had long been dead, emptied of all specific content, as if all that was left was a juxtaposition of mannequins of power, in which the occasion of the second death was not meant to endow them with the power they lacked—among others, the mythic dimension, for their sole dimension was that of a foregrounded simulacrum through which power tries to legitimize its existence at the first level, the elementary dimension—but was to serve as a mediator in the enterprise of *verifying* death. From this point of view, the staging of the "suicides" of the Baader gang is strangely akin to the death of actors (in the U.S.) who are paid to actually die for the camera.

Verification, for death deferred has replaced real death.

And if the rescue has been tarnished (in the same way as the hijacking of a Boeing by the Japanese Red Army) by the spectacularly reinforced killing of the Baader-Meinhof group, it is because power is prisoner of the very logic of the system, which pushes it to radicalize its means of inscription, to better lubricate its mediatic mode of functioning, as if this were a vital issue for it, as if it found itself irremediably in the midst of the greatest unreality, and was trying desperately to reintroduce reality by reintroducing death. But that is where it snags, for it can only provide the return of death as a simulacrum.

Indeed, to recoup an "aura of power" it has to fight against death, that of the others and its own, an indispensable death for it to appear as a gain, an acquisition, accumulation, in a word, victory. But by dint of expulsing death, of defeating it, it adorns itself with the likeness of immortality, masks real death, and ends up dying of this real death, which it can no longer catch in the mesh of its net, except as a simulacrum, skating across itself, dispossessed of its own death, haunted by the general indifference toward it. This indifference signs the shutdown of the system, as if it were only a disaster area, an "abandoned factory." And it is *against this obsession with abandonment* that it threatens, in turn, to kill itself, in order to be once more an object of love; it is against this that it erects the simulacrum of death.

This is not the game of war. The system moves the battle to a completely different terrain, to which it *deports* all the romantics of subversive practice, all terrorism, in order to reflect for them—like a mirror sending its image to others in a closed room—the image and the pattern of their lives and of their deaths. Especially of their deaths, for only it possesses the virtue of radicalizing the sign, of unveiling it in all its nakedness.

The permutation of the dead could only reproduce death as a form and simulacrum.

Ulrike Meinhof's suicide served as a lesson. It was out of the question for the fate of the Baaders to be marked with the significance of challenge. It was a matter of finally putting terrorism as a radical challenge to death, and the exclusion of the symbolic meaning by the media was the main lever for this undertaking.

This does not mean that everything was planned in Schmidt's little brain; it is not in this sense that there was manipulation. On the contrary, because of its unreality, power no longer controls the unfolding of events. It was not able to play the game of putting the Baaders to death like one preparing a move in chess. It is as much a "victim" of the manipulation of the indeterminism that characterizes the system, which puts itself under the law of reversibility. But it benefits from an advanced position within this new territory, built on the basis of the reciprocal permeability of the political and the symbolic—that is what is new—and of this territory, which oddly enough begins with a vacuum, with an absence of contours (the two or three hours that followed the deaths of the Baaders); it is the swiftest, most efficient manager. That, incidentally, is what aggresses us, spits in our faces, and is the source of our determination.

The terrorists found themselves cut off from their means of production. They were proletarized in a manner of speaking. Thus terrorism dies from the very death of the political. (And we will find no consolation in the resurrection of the political through the collective anxiety of the German CEOs. After all it is the system that wins from having digested through simulation the dissolving of the antagonistic orders that occupied the front of the stage).

Terrorism has but the choice between participating or not participating in the dramatization: to be or not to be actors, not only in the course of a life in the star-system, but also in dying and in the post-mortem; to be or not to be bearers of the trash that will be splattered in the press and on TV after their deaths, with the aim of reintroducing meaning into death, giving it a deadline again, reestablishing it as an object of blackmail, taking it out of its banality, giving it once more a stake, not in the attribution of a new reality, of a new concreteness, but, on the contrary, in an aesthetic dimension—*obscene aesthetization*—in which the pleasure principle joins Thanatos, in which it is no longer a matter of dying for a cause (political), or for nothing (symbolic), but for pleasure and simulation.

Imperturbably, the logic of the system will have led the Baader-Meinhof group to playing the scenario of their deaths. Whatever our place in the game of simulacra may be, we are all stuffed. This taxidermization takes place in broad daylight and we are fascinated by it.

It remains to be seen whether beyond death (real, symbolic or pleasant) we will find weapons that will radicalize indifference and be able to escape simulation.

Afterword

Utopie *at the Beginning and Beyond the End*

A step forward is better than a dozen programs. This quotation from Karl Marx served as an introduction to Hubert Tonka, Jean-Paul Jungmann and Jean Aubert's contribution to *L'Architecture d'aujourd'hui* in September 1968. *Utopie*, indeed, was to become known more for its critical, pamphleteering style than for its elaboration of programs. This is something that readers will have noticed in browsing through this anthology.

Utopie *is not written in the future tense* is the title of a poster that Utopie first published for the conference "Utopie e/o Rivoluzione" in Turin in 1969. If not in the future tense, then it was in a certain manner because hope for tomorrow had already been buried in *Utopie*. Jean Baudrillard was the first who preferred to think in terms of after tomorrow rather than tomorrow. Generalized obsolescence, beyond the end—key terms in *Utopie*. Does stepping beyond tomorrow mean an enhanced lucidity? A stepping beyond rather than a dialectical resolution of contradictions? Towards a beyond of the time barrier, to see things *after* the end, to see whether something is left of an event; whether the heterogeneous, the foreign body that called the rules of the game into question remained or whether it was digested once and for all. Jean Baudrillard, who began as a Germanist, had always been a great reader and admirer of German thought of the 1930s and '40s, the nascent Frankfurt School, Benjamin's secular and Marxizing messianism, Arendt, and especially Kracauer and Günther Anders. Apocalypse and millenarianism? Some of that, probably, even if *Utopie* was never a sect and regularly renewed itself. Parousia? Heretical thinking? Yes, at any rate, outside the circle of pragmatics. A radicalization of Utopia rather than a renewal of Utopia—that's all.

Utopie, a "Magazine of Urban Sociology" at the end of the 1960s in France. Utopie at its beginnings: individuals rather than disciplines. Three architects, a sociologist-translator, a landscape architect, a sociologist-architect, an urban sociologist; just men and women who were surfing on ideas, implied in rather than preoccupied by a problematic. The decisive influence on the journal at its beginnings? Henri Lefebvre, of course; knowing that a master remains beyond institutions and leaves no legacy—while the professor has his student as a successor and transmits to him his chair. Lefebvre gave a great deal to his students at the Institut de Sociologie Urbaine in Nanterre-Paris X, but did not leave much to his disciples at *Utopie*—except for the essentials: the initial inspiration.

After thirty-five years of uncertainty and crises in France, we have gotten used to a somewhat enchanted perception of this postwar period that Jean Fourastié called "les Trente Glorieuses" ("*The Thirty Glorious Years*"). Yet if we look at the main topics of the then (re)nascent sociology a little more closely, cracks already begin to appear: "the heirs," the "youth culture," the "new working class": these were three concepts that were supposed to describe the society that grew out of the great growth, to which were added the first questions aimed at the *grands ensembles* and the emergence of urban issues. We're still there. And we were already there with *Utopie*, part of one of the two major innovative construction sites of Marxist sociology: the first being urban sociology—and the other being education. René Lourau, one of the protagonists of the journal's beginnings, devoted almost all of his work to it after 1969 with the publication of *L'illusion pédagogique*.

At the beginning, Utopie handled word and image jointly. While sociologists theorized, the architects used to say: draw in order to understand. The latter worked with views à la Piranesi in their ateliers, simply because he was still there, in their old library at the École des Beaux-Arts. Amazed, they suddenly discovered *Archigram* in the mid-'60s. There, everything came together: Piranesi, Hollein, Fuller, Isozaki, Constant… The first issue of *Utopie* in 1967 still contains traces of this revelation. The architects began to leaf feverishly through the Anglo-Saxon underground press: the *free press* at the time offered the quintessence of a "counterculture," which has since then become the dominant culture. The environment? It is still thought of in terms of the "packaging complex" and not yet under the auspices of decline. Our relationship to objects still had to be transformed because one could already feel, five years before 1973, that "the crisis" was not far off.

A flexible plan, inhabitable circulation, and why not the inflatable? Air, breath, water, walking on water, envelope for a maximum surface area, all vibrations, harmony. The bubble: a minimum of wrapping for a maximal area, somewhere in between environmental control—the inflatable also involves rigorous calculations—and the critique of the "packaging complex." No obsolescence possible, but no patina either. *At home anywhere!* What a strange period; hesitating between throwaway plastic without any ulterior motives and the return of "exposed beams" in the living rooms of the readers of the *Nouvel observateur.*

After the departure of the architects, in the wake of number 2–3 published in May 1969, the reader will have understood the inflection at work, and perhaps also the journal's radicalization. The second phase of *Utopie* opted resolutely to venture into the realm of theory, leaving behind the subtle alliances that had accompanied its beginnings. It may be that such mixtures were no longer feasible at the beginning of the 1970s, at the time of our transition from vertical domination to net-like hegemony.

— Jean-Louis Violeau

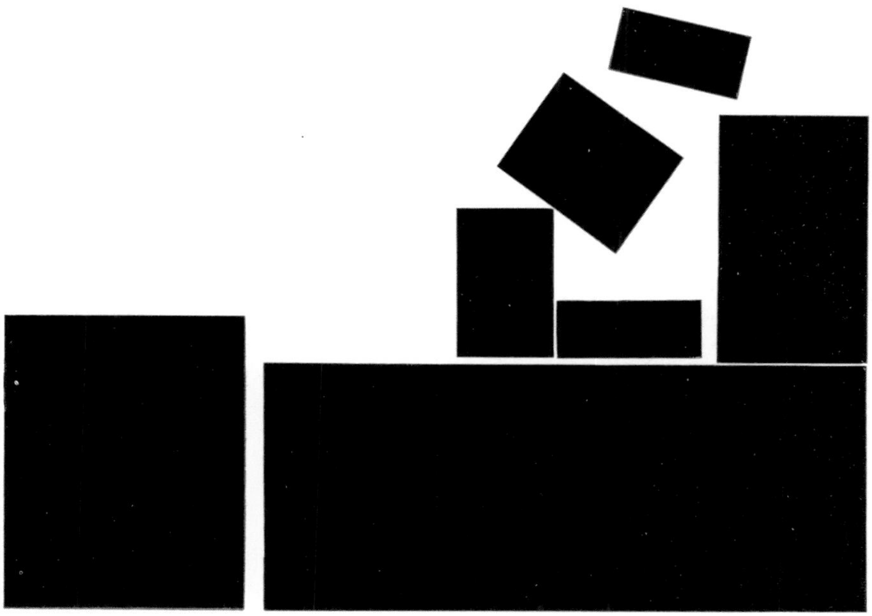

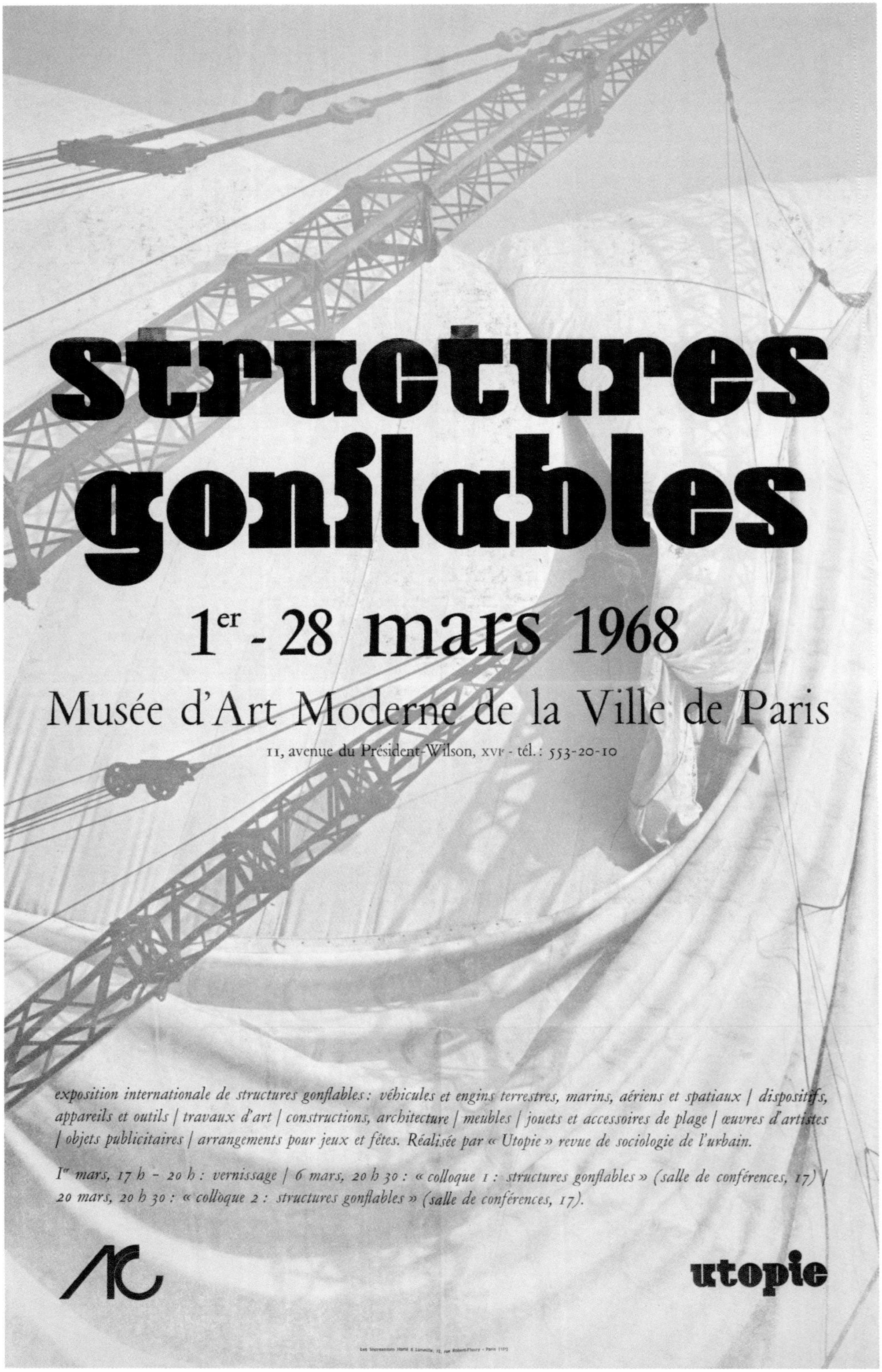
structures
gonflables
1er - 28 mars 1968
Musée d'Art Moderne de la Ville de Paris
11, avenue du Président-Wilson, XVIe - tél. : 553-20-10
exposition internationale de structures gonflables : véhicules et engins terrestres, marins, aériens et spatiaux / dispositifs, appareils et outils / travaux d'art / constructions, architecture / meubles / jouets et accessoires de plage / œuvres d'artistes / objets publicitaires / arrangements pour jeux et fêtes. Réalisée par « Utopie » revue de sociologie de l'urbain.
1er mars, 17 h - 20 h : vernissage / 6 mars, 20 h 30 : « colloque 1 : structures gonflables » (salle de conférences, 17) / 20 mars, 20 h 30 : « colloque 2 : structures gonflables » (salle de conférences, 17).
utopie

Bibliography of Articles, Issues, Pamphlets, Exhibition Catalogues, Books, and Posters issued by Utopie:

1967 "Voyage aux alentours d'utopie," Aubert, J. Jungmann, J.P., Stinco, A. Tonka, H. *L'Architecture d'aujourd'hui*. v. 37, n. 133.

Utopie: Sociologie de l'urbain, no.1 (May), Editions Anthropos, Paris. Editors: Jean Aubert, Isabelle Auricoste, Jean Baudrilllard, Catherine Cot, Jean-Paul Jungmann, René Lourau, Antoine Stinco, Hubert Tonka.

La Logique de l'urbanisme, November (Paris: Impressions Claude Harté). Pamphlet produced for World Urbanism Day.

1968 Utopie. ***Structures Gonflables***. (Paris: Musée d'Art Moderne de la ville de Paris, 1968).
Catalogue and poster for the exhibition *Structures Gonflables: International Exhibition of Inflatable Structures; vehicles, machines terrestrial, marine, aerial, and spatial, systems, tools, works of art ("travaux d'art"), constructions, architecture, furniture, toys, beach accessories, advertising objects, works by artists ("oeuvres d'artistes") and arrangements for games and parties*. March 1–30, 1968.

"Architecture as a Theoretical Problem," Aubert, J., Jungmann, J.P., Stinco A., Tonka, H., ***Architectural Design*** (June 1968), pp. 255.

"L'Architecture comme problème théorique," Aubert, J., Jungmann, J.P., Tonka, H., ***L'Architecture d'aujourd'hui***. 39: 139, (September 1968) p. 81–92.

1969 ***Des Raisons de l'architecture: L'architecture comme problème théorique dans la lutte des classes*** (Paris: Impressions Claude Harté).
Elaboration, and republication of texts and montages published in *Architectural Design* and *L'Architecture d'aujourd'hui*.

L'argent de l'urbanisme: adresse à la première semaine de recontres internationales construction et humanisme (Paris: Impressions Claude Harté). Pamphlet distributed during la première semaine de rencontres internationales construction et humanisme, Cannes 10 Mars, 1969.

Utopie ne s'écrit pas au futur. Poster published on the occasion of the conférence Utopie e/o Rivoluzione, April 26–29, Turin.

Utopie: Sociologie de l'urbain, no. 2/3 (May) Editions Anthropos. Editors: Jean Aubert, Isabelle Auricoste, Jean Baudrillard, Charles Goldblum, Jean-Paul Jungmann, René Lourau, Arnaud Suger [Antoine Stinco], Hubert Tonka.

"Relazione del gruppo Utopie," ***Marcatre: Rivista di Cultura Contemporanea***. No. 50–55, (1969), 86-95.

Utopie. ***La Logique de l'urbanisme***, November, 2nd edition (Paris: Impression Claude Harté).

Urbaniser la lutte de classe: December (Impressions Claude Harté). Brings together short texts published on other ocassions ("Utopie ne s'écrit pas au futur") and new ones such as "La Critique n'est pas une passion de la tête mais la tête de la passion," "La ville espace du capital est loin d'être un objet esthétique, ou la politique de M. A. Chalandon," "Parade de l'urbanisme."

1970 ***Urbaniser la lutte de classes, ou Remarques critiques sur la récente tentative de pacification des contradictions,*** September, 2nd Augmented Edition (Paris: Impressions Claude Harté).

La Logique de l'urbanisme, November, 3rd Edition (Paris: Impressions Claude Harté)

1971 ***Esthétique du recommencement*** (Paris: Impressions Claude Harté).

Utopie, no. 4, (October) Imprimerie Quotidienne. Editors: Isabelle Auricoste, Jean Baudrillard, Charles Goldblum, Hubert Tonka, Jean Varlet.

Que Fit la Mort ces Jours-Ci (supplement to *Utopie* 4).

1972 ***Utopie***, no. 5, ***Production, idéologie, dialectique*** (May) Imprimerie Quotidienne. Editors: Isabelle Auricoste, Jean Baudrillard, Michel Guillou, Hubert Tonka.

1973 ***Utopie***, no. 6, (February) Imprimerie Quotidienne. Editors: Isabelle Auricoste, Jean Baudrillard, Charles Goldblum, Michel Guillot, Hubert Tonka.

Utopie, no. 7, ***La Lutte de classe mise à nu*** (August) Imprimerie Quotidienne. Editors: Isabelle Auricoste, Jean Baudrillard, Charles Goldblum, Michel Guillot, Hubert Tonka.

1974 ***Utopie***, no. 8, ***Le Clou Bouclé*** (February) Imprimerie Quotidienne. Editors: Isabelle Auricoste, Frédéric Americo, Jean Baudrillard, Patrick Dansac, Charles Goldblum, Michel Guillou, Nicolas Politis, Françoise Tomeno, Hubert Tonka.

Utopie, no. 9, ***Radical Follies*** (April–May) Imprimerie Quotidienne. Editors: Isabelle Auricoste, Jean Baudrillard, Patrick Dansac, Charles Goldblum, Michel Guillou, Nicolas Politis, Françoise Tomeno, Hubert Tonka.

Utopie, no. 10, ***Devoirs de classe***, (June–July) Imprimerie Quotidienne. Editors: Isabelle Auricoste, Jean Baudrillard, Daniel Blanchard, Patrick Dansac, Charles Goldblum, Michel Guillou, Nicolas Politis, Hubert Tonka

Utopie, no. 11, ***Aujourd'hui*** (October–November) Imprimerie Quotidienne Editors: Isabelle Auricoste, Jean Baudrillard, Daniel Blanchard, Patrick Dansac, Charles Goldblum, Michel Guillou, Nicolas Politis, Hubert Tonka.

1975 *Utopie*, no. 12, ***Passions*** (December–January) Imprimerie Quotidienne. Editors: Isabelle Auricoste, Jean Baudrillard, Daniel Blanchard, Patrick Dansac, Charles Goldblum, Michel Guillou, Nicolas Politis, Hubert Tonka.

1976 *Utopie*, no. 13, (March–April) Imprimerie Quotidienne. Editors: Isabelle Auricoste, Jean Baudrillard, Daniel Blanchard, Gerard Boissard, Patrick Dansac, Charles Goldblum, Michel Guillou, Nicolas Politis, Hubert Tonka.

La cadavre en spirale, (May).

Utopie, no. 14, ***La vie en rose.*** (May–June) Imprimerie Quotidienne. Editors: Isabelle Auricoste, Jean Baudrillard, Daniel Blanchard, Patrick Dansac, Daniel Goldblum, Michel Guillou, Hubert Tonka.

1977 *Utopie*, no. 15, ***Utopie d'avril*** (April) Imprimerie Quotidienne. Editors: Isabelle Auricoste, Jean Baudrillard, Daniel Blanchard, Jean-Pierre Burgard, Hubert Tonka.

Utopie, no. 16, ***Utopie de juillet*** (July) Imprimerie Quotidienne. Editors: Isabelle Auricoste, Jean Baudrillard, Daniel Blanchard, Gérard Boisard, Jean-Pierre Burgart, Pierre Cvovcs, Gerard Huber, Annie Mignard, Hubert Tonka.

Cahiers d'Utopie no. 1: Hubert Tonka, ***Ombres exquises. Ballade sur l'échange symbolique et la mort.***

Cahiers d'Utopie no. 2: Hubert Tonka, ***Vague de sang. Lai.***

1978 *Utopie*, no. 17 (December–January) Imprimerie Quotidienne. Editors: Isabelle Auricoste, Jean Baudrillard, Daniel Blanchard, Boisard, Jean-Pierre Burgard, Dufo, Gerard Huber, Hubert Tonka.

Cahiers d'Utopie no. 3: Isabelle Auricoste, ***Les faiseuses d'anges. Pamphlet.***

Cahier d'Utopie no. 4: Jean Baudrillard, ***A l'ombre des majorités silencieuses ou la fin du social.***

Cahiers d'Utopie no. 5: Jean Baudrillard, ***Le P.C. ou les paradis artificiels du politique***.